'In Solitude, for Company'
W. H. Auden After 1940

AUDEN STUDIES 3

W. H. AUDEN

'In Solitude, for Company': W. H. Auden After 1940

UNPUBLISHED PROSE
AND RECENT CRITICISM

Auden Studies 3

EDITED BY KATHERINE BUCKNELL AND
NICHOLAS JENKINS

CLARENDON PRESS · OXFORD

1995

Oxford University Press, Walton Street, Oxford OX2 6DP

Oxford New York
Athens Auckland Bangkok Bombay
Calcutta Cape Town Dar es Salaam Delhi
Florence Hong Kong Istanbul Karachi
Kuala Lumpur Madras Madrid Melbourne
Mexico City Nairobi Paris Singapore
Taipei Tokyo Toronto
and associated companies in
Berlin Ibadan

Oxford is a trade mark of Oxford University Press

Published in the United States
by Oxford University Press Inc., New York

British Library Cataloguing in Publication Data
Data available

Library of Congress Cataloging in Publication Data
Auden, W. H. (Wystan Hugh), 1907–1973.
'In Solitude, for Company': W. H. Auden after 1940:
unpublished prose and recent criticism
edited by Katherine Bucknell and Nicholas Jenkins.
(Auden studies; 3)
Includes bibliographical references and index.
1. Auden, W. H. (Wystan Hugh), 1907–1973—Correspondence.
2. Auden, W. H. (Wystan Hugh), 1907–1973—Criticism and
interpretation. 3. Poets, English—20th century—Correspondence.
I. Bucknell, Katherine. II. Jenkins, Nicholas, 1961– .
III. Title. IV. Series.
PR6001.U4A6 1995b 811'.52—dc20 95–11105
ISBN 0–19–818294–5

1 3 5 7 9 10 8 6 4 2

Set by Hope Services (Abingdon) Ltd.
Printed in Great Britain
on acid-free paper by
Biddles Ltd,
Guildford and King's Lynn

PREFACE

THIS third volume of *Auden Studies* presents Auden in maturity—at the height of his powers as a poet, a lecturer, an essayist, a letter writer, and a model for younger poets. The four opening sections focus on original material by Auden which is published here for the first time. They begin with Auden's lecture, 'Vocation and Society', delivered during the war to a group of American undergraduates; the theme suggested by the title had obsessive personal and public importance to Auden in this period. The lecture is introduced and annotated by Nicholas Jenkins. After the lecture is a selection from Auden's energetic and revealing letters to his close friends from the 1930s onward, the late James Stern and Tania Stern. The letters are annotated by Nicholas Jenkins who also provides an introductory essay about the Sterns and their friendship with Auden, and about James Stern's career as a writer. The next item, 'The Fall of Rome', was originally prepared by Auden in 1966 for *Life Magazine* and is printed here for the first time with an introduction by the classicist, G. W. Bowersock. Following the essay on Rome is another lecture, 'Phantasy and Reality in Poetry', which offers probably Auden's fullest treatment of the relation between art and Freudian psychoanalysis. Katherine Bucknell introduces the lecture with an account of the career-long evolution of Auden's attitude to Freud and of the new light the lecture casts on Auden's work; she has annotated the lecture and in an appendix describes some of Auden's earliest reading material. Next, the Austrian writer Stella Musulin, who became a close friend of Auden during his final summers in Kirchstetten, offers a personal memoir with previously unpublished correspondence and with the English original of a short lecture that Auden delivered in a German translation she had prepared for him.

Following the sections containing original material by Auden, are a group of literary critical essays. The poet Alfred Corn offers a detailed analysis of Auden's Christmas oratorio 'For the Time Being'. Edward Upward, Michael Wood, Edna Longley, David Bromwich, and Lawrence Lipking join in a critical symposium about Auden's 1948 poem 'In Praise of Limestone'. And Ian Sansom looks at Auden's influence on the poet Randall Jarrell, author of some famous attacks on Auden's later poetry.

Finally, Edward Mendelson contributes an annotated list of

published letters by Auden. This is Mendelson's third supplement to the second edition of the Auden *Bibliography*; all three supplements have been published in *Auden Studies* and will eventually form part of the third edition of the *Bibliography*.

K.B. and N.J.

ACKNOWLEDGEMENTS

WE are grateful to the Estate of W. H. Auden and to Edward Mendelson, Auden's literary executor, for permission to print the unpublished material by Auden that appears in this volume. We are indebted to Swarthmore College for permission to print Auden's lecture 'Vocation and Society' and to quote from letters from Auden, Edith Philips, and John W. Nason about the lecture, and we are grateful to Michael J. Durkan, Swarthmore College Librarian, for his interpretations of ambiguities in the text of the lecture and for finding relevant material in the college's collections and publications. We wish to thank the Henry W. and Albert A. Berg Collection of the New York Public Library (Astor, Lenox and Tilden Foundations) for allowing us to print Auden's 1971 Freud Memorial lecture; a selection from Auden's letters to James and Tania Stern; a passage from Auden's 1929 journal; excerpts from two holograph notebooks (1941–2 and 1964–5); excerpts from Auden's letters to Orlan Fox, Wendell Stacy Johnson, Chester Kallman, Elizabeth Mayer, Caroline Newton, Hedwig Petzold; an excerpt from a letter from Kallman to Auden; a passage from Alan Ansen's unpublished notes on his conversations with Auden; and passages from the typescript draft of Charles Miller's memoir of Auden. Robert A. Wilson has kindly shared with us the text of Auden's essay on the fall of Rome. Other libraries have also allowed us to quote from Auden letters belonging to them: the Library of the American Philosophical Society, Philadelphia; Amherst College Library; the Department of Western Manuscripts, Bodleian Library, Oxford (MS. Eng. Lett. c. 464); the Rare Books and Manuscripts Collection, Butler Library, Columbia University; the Manuscript Division, Library of Congress, Washington, DC; the Harry Ransom Humanities Research Center, the University of Texas at Austin; the Lilly Library, Indiana University, Bloomington, Indiana; the University of Michigan Library, University of Michigan, Ann Arbor; and the Harvard University Archives. At the Library of Congress, we would like to thank Kathleen C. McDonough, Manuscript Reference Librarian, for locating material in the archives of *The American Scholar*. The Rhoda Weyr Agency has given us permission to reprint an excerpt from Randall Jarrell's 'The Old and New Masters'.

Sheilah and Rita Auden and Anita Money have once again allowed us to quote from materials among the papers of John Auden. Don

Bachardy has repeated his generous permission to quote from Auden's letters to Christopher Isherwood. We would also like to thank the late James Stern and Tania Stern for their help with research on their friendship and correspondence with Auden. Vicki Reeve, Robert Mark Ritter, Helen Gray, Lynn Childress, and Frances Whistler at the Oxford University Press have been extremely helpful, and we would especially like to thank Siri Huntoon, Bob Maguire, Sally Whitaker, and Debbie Daniel. Richard Davenport-Hines, John Fuller, and Lincoln Kirstein have contributed wise and well-informed advice; Edward Mendelson has once again given us his fierce and friendly support.

CONTENTS

ABBREVIATIONS

Works by Auden cited in this volume

ACW	*A Certain World: A Commonplace Book* (New York, 1970; London, 1971).
CP45	*The Collected Poetry of W. H. Auden* (New York, 1945).
CP91	*Collected Poems*, ed. Edward Mendelson, 2nd edn. (New York and London, 1991).
DBS	*The Dog Beneath the Skin or Where is Francis?*, with Christopher Isherwood (London and New York, 1935).
DH	*The Dyer's Hand* (New York, 1962; London, 1963).
DM	*The Double Man* (New York, 1941), American edn. of *NYL*.
EA	*The English Auden: Poems, Essays and Dramatic Writings 1927–1939*, ed. Edward Mendelson (London, 1977; New York, 1978).
EF	*The Enchafèd Flood, or The Romantic Iconography of the Sea* (Charlottesville, Va., 1950).
FA	*Forewords and Afterwords*, selected by Edward Mendelson (New York and London, 1973).
Juvenilia	*Juvenilia: Poems 1922–1928*, ed. Katherine Bucknell (London and Princeton, NJ, 1994).
LFI	*Letters from Iceland*, with Louis MacNeice (London and New York, 1937).
Libretti	*Libretti and Other Dramatic Writings 1939–1973*, with Chester Kallman, ed. Edward Mendelson (Princeton, NJ and London, 1993).
N	*Nones* (New York, 1951; London, 1952).
NYL	*New Year Letter* (London, 1941), British edn. of *DM*.
O	*The Orators: An English Study* (London, 1932).
PD	*The Prolific and the Devourer*, in *Antaeus*, 41 (Summer 1981), 4–65.
PDW	*Plays and Other Dramatic Writings 1928–1938*, with Christopher Isherwood, ed. Edward Mendelson (Princeton, NJ, 1988; London, 1989).
SP	*Selected Poems*, ed. Edward Mendelson (New York and London, 1979).
SW	*Secondary Worlds* (London, 1968; New York, 1969).

For works by Auden printed in *EA* and *CP91*, page references are given only to *EA*. For works appearing in *PDW* as well as in *EA* or *CP91*, references are given only to *PDW*.

Other abbreviations used in this volume

Ansen	Alan Ansen, *The Table Talk of W. H. Auden*, ed. Nicholas Jenkins (Princeton, NJ, 1990; London, 1991).
AS1	Katherine Bucknell and Nicholas Jenkins, eds., *W. H. Auden: 'The Map of All My Youth': Early Works, Friends, and Influences*, Auden Studies 1 (Oxford, 1990).
AS2	Katherine Bucknell and Nicholas Jenkins, eds., *W. H. Auden: 'The Language of Learning and the Language of Love': Uncollected Writings; New Interpretations*, Auden Studies 2 (Oxford, 1994).
ASN	*The W. H. Auden Society Newsletter.*
Bibliography	B. C. Bloomfield and Edward Mendelson, *W. H. Auden: A Bibliography 1924–1969*, 2nd edn. (Charlottesville, Va., 1972).
Carpenter	Humphrey Carpenter, *W. H. Auden: A Biography* (London and New York, 1981).
C&HK	Christopher Isherwood, *Christopher and His Kind 1929–1939* (London and New York, 1979).
Cunningham	Valentine Cunningham, *British Writers of the Thirties* (Oxford, 1988).
Early Auden	Edward Mendelson, *Early Auden* (New York and London, 1981).
Farnan	Dorothy J. Farnan, *Auden In Love* (New York and London, 1984).
Finney	Brian Finney, *Christopher Isherwood: A Critical Biography* (New York, 1979).
Hynes	Samuel Hynes, *The Auden Generation: Literature and Politics in England in the 1930s* (London, 1976; New York, 1977).
Lions	Christopher Isherwood, *Lions and Shadows: An Education in the Twenties* (London, 1938).
Miller	Charles H. Miller, *Auden: An American Friendship* (New York, 1983).
SE	Sigmund Freud, *The Standard Edition of the Complete Psychological Works of Sigmund Freud*, trans. and ed. James Strachey, in collaboration with Anna Freud, assisted by Alix Strachey, Alan Tyson, Angela Richards, 24 vols. (London, 1953–74).
Spears	Monroe K. Spears, *The Poetry of W. H. Auden: The Disenchanted Island* (New York, 1963).
Tribute	Stephen Spender, ed., *W. H. Auden: A Tribute* (London and New York, 1975).
WWW	Stephen Spender, *World Within World* (London and New York, 1951).

British and American editions are distinguished, where necessary, by the suffixes '(UK)' for books published in the United Kingdom and '(US)' for books published in the United States.

Descriptions of unpublished correspondence

ALI	Autograph Letter Initialled.
ALS	Autograph Letter Signed.
AN	Autograph Note.
APCS	Autograph Postcard Signed.
TL	Typed Letter.
TLS	Typed Letter Signed.
TN	Typed Note.
TPCS	Typed Postcard Signed.

Libraries and institutions

Berg	The Henry W. and Albert A. Berg Collection, New York Public Library (Astor, Lenox and Tilden Foundations).
Bodleian	The Department of Western Manuscripts, Bodleian Library, Oxford.
HRC	Harry Ransom Humanities Research Center, University of Texas at Austin.
Lilly	Lilly Library, Indiana University, Bloomington.

Except where otherwise indicated, all letters are in the possession of their recipients or the heirs of their recipients.

Vocation and Society (1943)

EDITED BY NICHOLAS JENKINS

Introduction

'VOCATION and Society', a rousing, polemical lecture on university teaching techniques and an exploration of the ways in which professors can inspire their pupils to discover a vocation, belongs to the most convulsive period in Auden's career, a time of crisis and reorientation occurring within the larger context of a world at war. The talk was delivered in the depths of an unusually harsh American winter, on the evening of 15 January 1943 at Swarthmore College, the small but prestigious, co-educational institution in Pennsylvania where Auden was then teaching. He spoke at a dinner for the Swarthmore chapter of the Phi Beta Kappa honour society to an audience of undergraduates—many of whom were facing conscription—and professors, some of them replacements for drafted colleagues, and some, like the German Gestalt psychologist Wolfgang Köhler whom Auden referred to in his talk, European exiles.[1]

The winter of 1942 to 1943 was the turning-point in the Second World War, the time when the allied armies began to go on to the offensive—the battle of Guadalcanal was raging in the Pacific, the battle of Stalingrad was grinding to its end in the Soviet Union—and when, despite enormous casualties, the eventual outcome of the conflict was becoming clearer. Although Auden only briefly mentioned Hitler and 'our enemies', global struggle was the lecture's inescapable background, and fascism's assertion, that, as Auden put it, 'war is the natural state of an industrialised society' was the historical challenge to which 'Vocation and Society' was, in part, intended as a response.

---

[1] An unsigned report of the lecture appeared as 'Auden Addresses Phi Beta Banquet on Self-Realization', *Phoenix*, Swarthmore College, 42.12 (19 Jan. 1943), 1. Phi Beta Kappa is the honour society for students who have distinguished academic records as undergraduates.

Auden was not, of course, the only writer rethinking basic issues during this bleak period. In early January 1943, for example, further up the frozen East Coast of the United States, Wallace Stevens was engaged in his own kind of metaphysical stock-taking. 'Bad is final in this light. | . . . It is deep January. The sky is hard,' he wrote. '. . . It is here, in this bad, that we reach | The last purity of the knowledge of good.'[2] In this socially rigid home-front atmosphere, at a moment when the United States had embarked on a society-wide drive for total mobilization in the war effort, Auden used his lecture to offer an alternative, far less communal perspective and to mount a fervent defence of the importance of individuality, solitude, and personal passion.

The mood of 'Vocation and Society' is, by the standards of Auden's earlier and later prose, remarkably sharp and self-suspicious; the lecture's language is relatively technical and its assertions (appropriately for the educational occasion) Socratically extreme. All these features make it a typical example of Auden's writing from the early Forties, a time when his poetry was moving away from the influence of the sensuous rhetoric of Yeats and towards the ascetic anti-rhetoric of Eliot, whose writing and personal example exercised a powerful sway over him throughout the war years. The Auden of this period was an artist turned back against himself, guiltily aware of what in 'New Year Letter' he had called his poetic 'crimes', and writing in opposition to his secular, collective, politically engaged outlook of the Thirties. The purged, rewritten, and alphabetically organized body of work he published as his *Collected Poetry* in 1945 is only the most explicit manifestation of his resistance to being defined in terms of 'Miss History', or the 'clever hopes' of the Thirties, or even his own chronological development as a poet.[3] By the beginning of 1943, when he spoke at Swarthmore, he had become a committed, existential Christian, had recently dismissed psychoanalysis, on which he had drawn so heavily throughout the Thirties, as merely one of the 'pagan *scientia*',[4] would soon scribble 'O God what rubbish!' next to 'A Communist to

[2] 'No Possum, No Sop, No Taters', *The Collected Poems of Wallace Stevens* (New York, 1954), 293–4.

[3] 'Miss History': 'The Rewards of Patience', *Partisan Review*, 9.4 (July–Aug. 1942), 338; 'clever hopes': 'September 1, 1939', *EA* 245. The *Collected Poetry* was published in 1945 but mainly compiled during 1942 and 1943. For a later comment by Auden on the arrangement of this book, see 'Eleven Letters from Auden to Stephen Spender', ed. Nicholas Jenkins, *AS1* 87.

[4] Didymus, 'Lecture Notes', *Commonweal*, 37.3 (6 Nov. 1942), 61.

Others',[5] and within a few months would be describing himself to Christopher Isherwood, with no hint of irony, as a 'last-ditch Protestant'.[6] This was the 'greatest revolutionary epoch since the Reformation', Auden had written a year or so before, and 'the external conflict of classes and nations and political systems is paralleled by an equally intense internal conflict in every individual.'[7]

Terms like 'sin', 'Grace', and 'suffering' are scattered throughout the talk. As such language indicates, 'Vocation and Society' was written at a time when Auden was passing through one of the most vehement phases of his rediscovered religiousness. In the early Forties he was preoccupied by issues that took on for him, as the Christian vision of a dying-to-self and a rebirth into a New Life would encourage, an almost cataclysmic quality. He was obsessed by the dark, radically individualistic theology of Søren Kierkegaard, and he wrote, as he declared approvingly that Kierkegaard had, from the point of view of 'a being in *need*, an *interested* being whose existence is at stake'.[8]

In 1936 Auden had written that 'left-wing friends' predicted he would 'linger on outcast | A selfish pink old Liberal to the last.'[9] This opinion about his future is displaced into other people's mouths, and neither exactly endorsed nor rejected by Auden. But by 1943 he had eradicated any hint of mid-stream, humanist muddling and had replaced his more or less mellow brand of English left-liberalism with a commitment to religious 'laws', 'commands', the Kierkegaardian 'Unconditional'. Even if all the social problems and external tribulations of humanity were to be abolished, Auden argued in his lecture on vocation, 'If we imagine or allow others to imagine . . . that there will no longer be a command before which a man must walk in fear and trembling, then we are middlebrows and the truth is not in us.' And in an essay analysing the high Victorian poets and their belief in an earlier form of the same liberal tradition he had once espoused himself, Auden wrote in terms that apply closely to his own evolving opinions in the early Forties: 'They were all of them uneasily aware of the possibility that the liberal creed might only hold for talented

---

[5] In the Swarthmore College copy of *On This Island*: quoted in Monroe K. Spears, 'W. H. Auden at Swarthmore', *Swarthmore College Bulletin*, 59.4 (Mar. 1962), 6, and Carpenter, 330.

[6] ALS to Christopher Isherwood, 18 July [1943].

[7] 'La Trahison d'un clerc', *Perspectives*, Ann Arbor, 5.2 (Jan. 1942), 12; supplement to *Michigan Daily*, 17 Jan. 1942.

[8] 'A Preface to Kierkegaard', *The New Republic*, 110.1537 (15 May 1944), 683.

[9] 'Letter to Lord Byron', *EA* 190.

and successful people like themselves, for men who might speculate upon the meaning of existence in general but never had to put the personal question "Why do I exist?" '[10]

By the start of the Forties, Auden was asking himself exactly this question. Instead of campaigning for social transformation, he began to work for a transformation of the self. 'Purely Subjective', an essay written around the same time as 'Vocation and Society', rises to a stark urgency in its description of the religious predicament:

I wake into my existence to find myself and the world that is not myself already there, and simultaneously feel responsible for my discovery. I can and must ask: 'Who am I? Do I want to be? Who do I want and who ought I to become?' I am, in fact, an anxious subject. . . . That is my immediate religious experience which allows me no rest until I believe I have understood it.[11]

In the midst of this 'intense internal conflict', the argument of 'Vocation and Society' seems almost deliberately to set out to contradict or deny the tenets of his Thirties liberal humanism in ways that, of all the people gathered at the Phi Beta Kappa meeting, only Auden himself could have been fully aware of. It is as if he were, for his own private benefit, counting up some of his mistakes. In 1934, for example, he had asserted in 'The Liberal Fascist', his essay about his schooldays at Holt, that one of the main things a teacher could do for a pupil is to 'remove as tactfully and unobtrusively as possible such obstacles to progress as he can'.[12] By 1943, though, just as Auden had abandoned his early theories about how a poet should forge an organic connection with his audience, he had also rejected the notion that the teacher should actively assist his pupils or indeed have any direct relation with them. Progressives, he argued in 'Vocation and Society', 'proceeded to assume that the way to help a child to discover its vocation was to remove every obstacle, to make its life as easy as possible[.] But passion is never aroused by ease, only by obstacles.'

In 1938, in an essay written for an American anthology, Auden had urged that: 'Education in a democracy must have two aims. It must give vocational guidance and training . . . and it must also provide a

---

[10] 'Introduction', *Poets of the English Language*, vol. 5: *Tennyson to Yeats*, eds., Auden and Norman Holmes Pearson (New York, 1950), p. xx.

[11] *Chimera*, 2.1 (Summer 1943), 3. See also n. 18 to the text of the lecture below.

[12] *EA* 326.

general education.'[13] Five or so years later at Swarthmore, Auden bluntly told his listeners: 'Vocational Guidance is a contradiction in terms.'

Swarthmore itself surely provided some of the stimulus for Auden's polemic. Before arriving there, he had written to his Ann Arbor friends Albert and Angelyn Stevens that the place sounded 'a little "Pi" '.[14] Shortly afterwards, he told his friend Elizabeth Mayer that 'Everyone is very nice but not very lively. . . . The place is a dump without either a bar or a movie house and the trains are so bad that going to Philadelphia is an excursion.'[15] He found the students at the college 'a little dull',[16] and he had doubts about the small town's spruce but staid atmosphere.[17]

In fact Auden was never completely reconciled to Swarthmore's temperate social climate. He once told James Stern: 'I am, after all, a crook, and need a more baroque and louche habitat to breathe in, than the Quaker's provide.'[18] And during the nearly three years he spent at the college from 1942 to 1945, Swarthmore, at least in his darker moods, came to represent for him a sort of American limbo, a passionless, conformist, liberal community, full, as he describes it in the poem 'A Healthy Spot', of 'nice . . . Kind and efficient' citizens, 'Happy marriages and unhappy people'.[19] It is an attack that restates, almost parasitically, the denunciations that Kierkegaard had launched a century earlier against stolid, bourgeois Copenhagen.

By early 1943, life in Swarthmore, like everywhere else in the United States, had been affected by the war effort. Coffee, sugar, rubber, gasoline, and heating oil had been rationed before the end of

[13] *EA* 376. The anthology was Clifton Fadiman, ed., *I Believe: The Personal Philosophies of Certain Eminent Men and Women of Our Time* (New York, 1939).
[14] ALS, [?19 Sept. 1942], (University of Michigan Library).
[15] ALS to Elizabeth Mayer, 2 Nov. 1942 (Berg).
[16] ALS to E. R. Dodds, 1 Feb. 1944 (Bodleian).
[17] The main printed sources for information about Auden at Swarthmore College itself are, besides Carpenter, Paul Seabury, 'Auden, Would-Be Mine Operator Favors Ungodly But Intelligent', *Phoenix*, 63.3 (14 Dec. 1943), 3; Monroe K. Spears, 'W. H. Auden at Swarthmore', *Swarthmore College Bulletin*, 59.4 (Mar. 1962), 1–6; [Unsigned], 'W. A. Auden dies; poet taught at Swarthmore', *Delaware County Daily Times*, 1 Oct. 1973, p. 12; Maurice Mandelbaum, 'Swarthmore', *Tribute*, 119–23.
[18] ALS, [5 July 1944], (Berg). See Letter 10 of 'Some Letters from Auden to James and Tania Stern', p. 87 of the present volume.
[19] *CP91* 328.

1942,[20] and Swarthmore's President John W. Nason recalled recently that 'College life was chaos'. During the war, nobody 'knew from one semester to the next how many students there were going to be' and about a quarter of the faculty had to be recruited each year.[21] In early January, Auden told the Stevenses that, although he was supposed to be teaching, and eventually did teach, a graduate seminar on Romanticism, he had been 'approached to see whether, if need be, I would be prepared to teach elementary chemistry'.[22]

A pragmatic, self-absorbed atmosphere in which people were preoccupied with immediate issues was obviously not a phenomenon confined to suburban Pennsylvania. All the elements of the cultural situation that in 1944 Auden described as a 'planned society, caesarism of thugs or bureaucracies, paideia, scientia, religious persecution. . . . Nor is there even lacking the possibility of a new Constantinism'[23] were already evident in 1943, the year that saw the election of the most conservative Congress since Roosevelt's presidency began in 1933. In 'Vocation and Society' Auden quoted with approval Charles Péguy's insistence that lives dedicated to a particular vocation must be 'a perpetual infidelity, for to remain faithful to the truth, they must make themselves continually unfaithful to all the continuous, successive, indefatigable, renascent errors'. These 'renascent errors' included a fresh round of controversy about the familiar questions of poetry, politics, and propaganda.

In America, as in Britain, writers were not exempted from political pressures during the Second World War, and the period of the conflict saw many of the old Thirties leftist arguments about literature and politics being replayed from the political centre and right. Even before the US entry into the war at the end of 1941, well-publicized arguments had been made about the duty of writers to abandon the detached élitism and autonomy of modernism and to rally to the democratic cause by propagandizing for the Allies.

Well into the summer of 1940, Auden was on friendly terms with the pro-interventionist Archibald MacLeish, Librarian of Congress, and a poet then at the zenith of his reputation—in Cleanth Brooks's

[20] See Allen M. Winkler, *Home Front U.S.A.: America During World War II* (Arlington Heights, Ill., 1986), 37; Paul Fussell, *Wartime: Understanding and Behavior in the Second World War* (New York, 1989), 190.

[21] Nason is quoted in 'War Years Reunion Draws Hundreds to Remember an Era', *Swarthmore College Bulletin*, 89.6 (Aug. 1992), 27.

[22] ALS, [?4 Jan. 1943], (University of Michigan Library).

[23] 'Augustus to Augustine', *FA* 39. The piece was written *ca.* mid to late May 1944.

Modern Poetry and the Tradition, published in August 1939, MacLeish was compared with Frost and Auden.[24] But on 19 April 1940, MacLeish had fired the first shot in the campaign to enlist writers in the struggle for the democratic way of life. On that day he gave the first in a series of speeches indicting the writers he called 'The Irresponsibles'—post-First World War authors like Dos Passos and Hemingway who had refused to defend explicitly the values of democracy in their work.[25] When Auden commented in a review in July 1940 that Rilke was a source of strength that would help artists 'to resist the treacherous temptations that approach us disguised as righteous duties', he was writing at a moment when poetry was again being challenged to assist in the 'struggle' for justice.[26]

A year or so later, in August 1941, as war tension in the States rose to a much higher pitch in the wake of the German invasion of Russia, MacLeish's attack was followed up by the literary historian of New England, Van Wyck Brooks. At a conference in New York, Brooks gave a speech called 'Primary Literature and Coterie Literature' in which he attacked by name most of the major first-generation modernists, including Joyce, Proust, James, and Eliot (the latter referred to as a 'dog in the manger') for 'defeatism' and 'coterie' writing.[27]

---

[24] (Chapel Hill, NC, 1939). See the chapter 'Frost, MacLeish and Auden', 110–35. Brooks calls the poets he discusses in the book: 'the clearest and most significant illustrations of our modern critical revolution' (p. ix). Auden's review of *Modern Poetry and the Tradition* (he does not mention MacLeish) is: 'Against Romanticism', *The New Republic*, 102.1314 (5 Feb. 1940), 187. MacLeish had helped Auden straighten out his US visa problems in October 1939 and in June 1940, during the Battle of Britain when a German invasion of Britain threatened, Auden, acting on a request from the Downs School, asked MacLeish about the possibility of expediting US visas for the boys and staff.

[25] For details of MacLeish's literary campaigning, see Scott Donaldson in collaboration with R. H. Winnick, *Archibald MacLeish: An American Life* (Boston, 1992), 334. The second of MacLeish's major speeches, in which he denounced Hemingway and Dos Passos by name, was 'Post-War Writers and Pre-War Readers', delivered on 23 May 1940.

[26] 'Poet in Wartime', *The New Republic*, 103.1336 (8 July 1940), 59. For more on Auden's rejection in the United States of an active, propagandizing role for poetry, see Stan Smith, 'Persuasions to Rejoice: Auden's Oedipal Dialogues with W. B. Yeats', *AS2* 155–63.

[27] See Raymond Nelson, *Van Wyck Brooks: A Writer's Life* (New York, 1981), 236–40; James Hoopes, *Van Wyck Brooks: In Search of American Culture* (Amherst, Mass., 1977), 233–6. Brooks, through his mouthpiece Oliver Allston, argued against 'coterie' writers, saying that they 'had broken their organic bonds with family life, the community, nature, and they wrote in a private language of personal friends'. Allston, Brooks says, using all the moralistic buzz-words of the period, aimed at 'the stiffening of American writers, promoting their maturity and health, giving them the sense of a group to which they are responsible' (*Opinions of Oliver Allston* (New York,

Brooks's ideas were immediately attacked by many New York intellectuals, most famously by the political essayist Dwight Macdonald, then a non-interventionist Trotskyite.[28] Auden, in Ann Arbor, contributed his own shaft of invective with a piece in one of the student newspapers. Apparently he based his charges against Brooks on Macdonald's piece and did not use any direct quotations from the 'Primary and Coterie Literature' speech itself. (He may not have read it.)[29]

In May 1942, as war-pressures increased, Auden admitted to the poet and critic Louise Bogan, another staunch defender of artistic independence in the face of political demands: 'The Lititoo situation is certainly not very cosy—Harvard professors calling Nietzsche a nazi and screaming for a BELIEF, no matter what, so long as we believe it all together, etc. As for Mr Van Wyck Brooks, if I ever meet him, I shall slap his face for his remarks about Eliot[.] Domestic servants must not forget their station.'[30] In an essay he wrote the same spring, Auden complained: 'the official critics are now talking like editorials in the New Masses' and added that the political authorities had now realized that they could use poetry as 'a useful means of persuading the masses to unity and order'.[31]

1941), 208, 227). The controversial speech 'Primary Literature and Coterie Literature' was released (without Brooks's consent) to the press in Sept. 1941 by the Conference on Science, Philosophy and Religion in Their Relation to the Democratic Way of Life (Nelson, *Van Wyck Brooks*, 237). It was then included in modified form in *Oliver Allston*.

[28] 'Kulturbolschewismus is Here', *Partisan Review*, 8 (Nov.–Dec. 1941), 446, 450–1. See also Michael Wreszin, *A Rebel in Defense of Tradition: The Life and Politics of Dwight Macdonald* (New York, 1994), 105–6.

[29] 'La Trahison d'un clerc', *Perspectives*, 12. In the first issue of *Partisan Review* in 1942, seven prominent intellectuals and writers criticized the 'Brooks–MacLeish Thesis' as it had become known: *Partisan Review*, 9.1 (Jan.–Feb. 1942), 38–47. Eliot himself replied, disdainfully, to Brooks in the following *Partisan* issue, implying a link between Brooks's views and fascist ideology: 'A Letter to the Editors', *Partisan Review*, 9.2 (Mar.–Apr. 1942), 115–16.

[30] ALS, [7 May 1942], (Louise Bogan Papers, Special Collections Dept., Amherst College Library). Auden's reference to attacks on Nietzsche probably alludes to *Nietzsche* (Cambridge, Mass., 1941), by Crane Brinton, McLean Professor of History at Harvard. See the chapter, 'Nietzsche and the Nazis', 200–31, which contains statements like: 'Point for point he [Nietzsche] preached, along with a good deal else which the Nazis choose to disremember, most of the cardinal articles of the professed Nazi creed' (231). The reference to professors 'screaming for a BELIEF' concerns the notorious Dr Pitirim A. Sorokin of the Harvard Sociology Department, who in books like *The Crisis of Our Age* (New York, 1941) advocated the replacement of the exhausted remnants of the old 'sensate' culture with what he termed a new 'ideational culture'.

[31] 'W. H. Auden Speaks of Poetry and Total War . . .', *Chicago Sun*, 14 Mar. 1942, p. 14.

By the time of 'Vocation and Society', MacLeish, Brooks, and their views had become less threatening than absurd, and Auden's attacks had dwindled into jokes. In *The Queen's Masque*, for instance, probably mostly written in December 1942, he sniped at 'Archie', and in a memo composed during July 1943 for the Harvard professor Theodore Spencer on 'The Teaching of English', he suggested as an example of the type of Ph.D. that is of 'no interest to *anyone else* . . . "the semi-colon in Archibald Macleish"'.[32] And in 'Vocation and Society', all that Auden, like E. M. Forster, was willing to grant to democracy was 'Two cheers'; he inserted into his talk a long passage from Nietzsche;[33] and he ended the lecture with an extract from Eliot's *Little Gidding*, calling its author 'the greatest poet now living'.

As Auden was thinking about his lecture in the days before he gave it, he told his friends the Stevenses that he was looking forward to 'a nice opportunity to say spiteful things about the Psychologists, who, had St Peter consulted them, would have said "The results of your Rohrshoch and Binet Tests show no religious aptitude. Try writing newspaper articles on Fishing["].'[34] But Auden's assault on

[32] *The Queen's Masque*, *Libretti*, 428; 'The Teaching of English', fo. 3 (Harvard University). Late in 1943 and in 1944 Auden was still occasionally on the attack against MacLeish and Brooks's arguments. In a review of Eliot's anthology of Kipling's verse, originally published in Oct. 1943, Auden argued: 'If today the war makes people discover that Kipling is good, it will be an excellent thing, but if at the same time they start saying that Eliot is "defeatist," it will prove that they have not discovered a poet, but only changed their drug to suit the new climate'; see 'The Poet of the Encirclement', *FA* 352. In an article for the Swarthmore college newspaper exhorting students to experiment and not to conform to authority, he jocularly called on his 'Fellow Irresponsibles' (MacLeish's term for the decadent modernists) amongst the student body to 'follow me. . . . let's go underground and make bombs', 'Student Government—or Bombs', *Phoenix*, 64.2 (21 Mar. 1944), 2.

[33] In 1940 Auden had praised Nietzsche in a poem as a 'masterly debunker of our liberal fallacies' (1940), *EA* 458. He continued to quote him and refer to him explicitly and implicitly throughout the war. In 'The Rewards of Patience', *Partisan Review*, 9.4 (July–Aug. 1942), for instance, he echoed Nietzsche's famous injunction in *The Gay Science* to 'live dangerously' when he wrote that 'one must go on or go under, live dangerously or not at all' (337). Two years later, in a review of Lewis Mumford's *The Condition of Man* (New York, 1944), he singled out for special scorn a piece of 'Colonel Blimp invective' in which Mumford attacked Nietzsche as a proto-Nazi: 'In Poor Shape', *Sewanee Review*, 52.4 (Autumn 1944), 597.

[34] ALS, [?4 Jan. 1943], (University of Michigan Library). He wrote to Elizabeth Mayer shortly afterwards in similar terms: 'Have to speak to the Phi Beta Kappa about Vocation—an opportunity to say a few sharp words about Psychiatrists etc'—ALS, 9 Jan. 1943 (Berg). This annoyance may in part reflect Auden's feelings about being turned down for service by an Army psychiatrist on 1 Sept. 1942. Auden was still referring to the decision five years later (see Ansen, 47, and pp. 55 of the present volume).

progressivist, war-time pieties went far beyond his scathing comments on positivistic psychology or his attacks on the calls for national unity and intellectual activism. He suggested to his Swarthmore audience that most educationalists were doing as much harm as good. His talk offered the idea that, in order to 'restrain our natural lust for power and approval', teachers should offer their pupils a 'careful indifference'—one that is genuine in the degree to which it is an 'obstacle' to the pupil, and a cause of 'suffering' to the teacher. 'To teach at all is hard,' Auden asserted, 'to teach well impossible.' (He went even further in a letter to Theodore Spencer, his Harvard friend, written shortly afterwards. He repeated his view of Vocational Guidance, calling it an 'absurdity' and added that 'our first duty' as educators is 'to refuse to help our pupils'.[35])

The morning after he had delivered 'Vocation and Society', Auden wrote to Elizabeth Mayer telling her that his 'speech . . . went off alright. It turned out to be mostly an exposition of the meaning of The Magic Flute.'[36] Swarthmore's President Nason had not been able to attend the dinner,[37] but he wrote to Auden shortly afterwards: 'You delighted many people, irritated a few, but stirred up everyone.'[38] With others he was franker; he told one correspondent admiringly that the lecture 'stirred up an immense amount of discussion. People reacted . . . violently for or against what he [Auden] had to say.'[39]

The reaction was so strong that Nason asked Auden for the text of his talk, and Auden apparently gave him the hand-written copy he had used at the meeting, asking Nason to throw it away after he had finished with it.[40] After reading Auden's script, Nason was even more impressed. On 8 February he wrote Auden a note, urging him to publish 'Vocation and Society' and suggesting that he send it to The American Scholar, the journal of the Phi Beta Kappa society. The American Scholar was at that time a venerable academic publication, thoroughly orthodox, 'non-political', and mainstream. Auden replied

[35] ALS, [20 Feb. 1943], (Harvard University Archives).

[36] ALS, [16 Jan. 1943], (Berg).

[37] See TLS from Nason to William A. Shimer, 12 Mar. 1943 (Archives of The American Scholar, Collections of the Manuscript Division, Library of Congress, Washington, DC).

[38] Carbon of TL, 18 Jan. 1943 (Swarthmore College Library).

[39] TLS from John W. Nason to William A. Shimer, 12 Mar. 1943 (Archives of The American Scholar, Library of Congress).

[40] Ibid. and carbon of TL from Nason to Auden, 8 Feb. 1943: 'You asked me to discard it' (Swarthmore College Library).

affirmatively to Nason the next day: 'Evidently I cant defend my honor any further without becoming a prude, so if the American Scholar wants it, they shall have it.' And he added a private swipe at the editor of *The Saturday Review of Literature*, an associate of Archibald MacLeish and an influential representative of the 'middle-brow' culture Auden had attacked in his lecture. 'It cant really have done any good', he remarked to Nason, 'because Henry Seidel Canby hasnt shot himself.'[41]

Auden insisted on typing up 'Vocation and Society' himself for submission to *The American Scholar*, and he appears to have begun the task around mid-February. But he procrastinated, and had not finished the chore by 8 March, when Nason wrote to him again, urging him to hurry because *The American Scholar*'s editorial board was due to meet soon.[42] Auden completed the job and around 12 March 1943 he gave the lecture to Nason who submitted it to the magazine at once.

William A. Shimer, the editor, mailed the typescript to three members of the editorial board. It went first to the literary scholar Marjorie Hope Nicolson of the Columbia Graduate School in New York, then to the President of Smith College, William A. Neilson, and finally to the Columbia philosopher and educationalist Irwin Edman. Where the reactions to Auden's talk at Swarthmore had been heated, *The American Scholar*'s responses were cool. When Nicolson replied, she called the talk 'very slight. Perhaps, because it is badly written . . . it gives an impression of having been scrambled together.'[43] Neilson answered that he was not very 'enthusiastic', saying he found Auden's work 'poor prose. It is needlessly difficult, and I should be surprised if the Swarthmore students knew what he was talking about half the time.'[44] And Edman, the last reader, wrote that

[41] ALS to Nason, 9 Feb. [1943], (Swarthmore College Library), Canby (1878–1961) was a popular essayist, educator, and editor. He had served during the first few months after America's entry into the war as a New York consultant to the Bureau of Publications of MacLeish's Office of War Information. He left that post in July 1942 to rejoin as editor *The Saturday Review of Literature*, the middle-brow magazine he had founded in 1926.

[42] Carbon of TL to Auden, 8 Mar. 1943 (Swarthmore College Library).

[43] TN from Marjorie Hope Nicolson to the Editorial Office of *The American Scholar*, [ca. 24 Mar. 1943], (Archives of *The American Scholar*, Library of Congress). Nicolson (1894–1981) wrote widely on 17th- and 18th-century English literature and its relations to the New Science.

[44] AN to the Editorial Office of *The American Scholar*, [ca. 5 Apr. 1943], (Archives of *The American Scholar*, Library of Congress). Neilson (1869–1946) was a scholar and historian of English literature, as well as the editor-in-chief of Webster's *New International*

the talk was 'irritatingly pretentious', adding disdainfully, 'I have always felt that in his prose writings (and sometimes in his poetry) Auden was living far beyond his intellectual income.'[45] Each voted not to accept the talk for publication and so Shimer's secretary wrote back to President Nason on 15 April 1943 declining 'Vocation and Society'.[46]

Nason was evidently disappointed by the decision and he seems to have talked about further possibilities with Swarthmore faculty members. Edith Philips, the chair of the Romance Languages Department, who had heard Auden give the lecture at the Phi Beta Kappa dinner in January, told Nason in a letter that she still thought it was a 'brilliant and provocative speech and a point of view which ought to shake all of us "educators" out of our smugness', and she suggested that Auden might submit the talk to John Crowe Ransom's *Kenyon Review*, which was 'less strictly academically minded' than *The American Scholar* and more interested in modern writers.[47] But Auden had not envisaged publishing 'Vocation and Society' in the first place, and, after learning of *The American Scholar*'s decision, he apparently decided not to try anything further, though he did later quarry a couple of passages from it for essays that he printed elsewhere.[48]

A Note on the Text

Auden read his speech on 'Vocation and Society' from a hand-written text which he later passed to Swarthmore's President Nason. Nason told him that he had read it with 'great interest and great difficult[y]'.[49] The manuscript is now lost, but 'Vocation and Society'

Dictionary. The general editor of the dictionary was Thomas A. Knott, whose house at 1504 Brooklyn Avenue, Ann Arbor, Michigan, Auden had occupied from February–May 1942. After Auden vacated, Knott had sued him for damage to the house and had recently won; see Farnan, 79–80; Miller, 69.

[45] TLS to William A. Shimer, 14 Apr. 1943 (Archives of *The American Scholar*, Library of Congress). Edman (1896–1954) had published a volume of *Poems* (1925) as well as many books on philosophy. He was a follower of John Dewey and George Santayana. At Edman's invitation, Auden had read the Phi Beta Kappa poem (probably a section from 'New Year Letter') at Columbia on 3 June 1940 (reported in an unnumbered clipping from the *Columbia Daily Spectator*, 4 June 1940).

[46] Carbon of TL (Archives of *The American Scholar*, Library of Congress).

[47] TLS from Philips to Nason, 18 Apr. 1943 (Swarthmore College Archives).

[48] 'Purely Subjective', *Chimera*, 2.1 (Summer 1943), 3–22; 'Mozart and the Middlebrow', *Harper's Bazaar*, 80.3 (Mar. 1946), 153, 252. See nn. 23 and 49 to the talk. Auden subsequently published only one item in *The American Scholar*, the 1947 Columbia Phi Beta Kappa poem 'Music Is International'.

[49] TL from Nason to Auden, 8 Feb. 1943 (carbon in Swarthmore College Archives).

survives as a double-spaced typescript, made by Auden on the rectos of twelve folios of 8½ by 11 inch paper, after Nason had persuaded him to submit the talk to *The American Scholar*. This typescript is now in the Swarthmore College Library.

It shows that Auden made a number of small revisions of verbal details as he was typing up the talk, so in all likelihood, the present text does not record exactly what Auden had said at the Phi Beta Kappa dinner on 15 January 1943. There is, however, no reason to think it differs in any important respect from the talk as it was delivered then. Besides typed corrections, there are a number of minor manuscript corrections to the typed text, some of which are in Auden's hand, and some of which have been made by an unidentified hand or hands. For the most part, my transcription silently incorporates changes which are probably or certainly Auden's while ignoring all those probably or certainly not by him. When Auden agreed to type up the talk, he told Nason: 'I shall have to take off its party frock and put on it a proper academic dress, footnotes and all.'[50] Ultimately, he created only one footnote (on pp. 21–2), which, as in his original, is marked here by an asterisk.

I have corrected a few misspellings (details of any more significant emendations are given in footnotes) and I have regularized the spacing and layout of the displayed quotations. 'Vocation and Society' draws extensively on Auden's thinking and reading from the period leading up to the lecture and foreshadows much in his writing during the years immediately following. It also makes heavy use of a terminology (amounting almost to a private dialect) which Auden used during this period, and in which such apparently everyday words as 'passion', 'serious', 'aesthetic' are endowed with precise theological meanings. Therefore, my footnotes supply some cross-references intended to illuminate important concepts, phrases, and ideas that appear elsewhere in Auden's work from *ca.* 1939 to 1947. In particular, some key Kierkegaardian terms are glossed, because their meanings are not always identical with those of vernacular usage. I have used as a reference-source the definitions given in Appendix 7 of volume 2 of Walter Lowrie, DD, *Kierkegaard*, 2 vols. (New York and London, 1938). This was the first major English-language exposition of Kierkegaard's life and work, and is roughly contemporaneous with Auden's text. Passages from Lowrie in the notes that follow simply

---

[50] ALS, 9 Feb. [1943], (Swarthmore College Library).

give a page number as a reference. Though he mentioned neither explicitly, two books were particularly important sources for some of Auden's ideas in the lecture: Kierkegaard's *The Present Age* and Denis de Rougemont's *Love in the Western World*. I have provided some references in the footnotes for passages in which Auden drew closely on these works and I have also reprinted some of his comments on *The Magic Flute* from the 1955 preface he wrote for his and Kallman's translation of the opera (*Libretti*, 129–33).

In most cases, I have also noted the translations used by Auden in his talk. His citations are often, strictly speaking, inaccurate. I have not of course corrected these, but a '†' preceding the text of a footnote registers the fact that Auden's wording is idiosyncratic.

Vocation and Society

W. H. AUDEN

Soon after the opening of the Second Act of *The Magic Flute*, Tamino and Papageno find themselves alone in a ruined temple in the middle of the night during a thunderstorm. Two priests enter, and the following conversation ensues.

First Pr.	—What urges you to penetrate within our walls?
Tam.	—Friendship and love.
First Pr.	—Are you ready to risk your life for them?
Tam.	—I am.
First Pr.	—Even though death should be your Fate?
Tam.	—Yes.
Second Pr.	—(to Papageno) Will you also fight for the love of acquiring wisdom?
Pap.	—Fighting is not my business; what's more, I've no longing for wisdom. I'm an ordinary sort of chap, satisfied if I can eat, drink and sleep—and, of course, if I could some day put my hand on a pretty little sweetheart—
Second Pr.	—She shall never be yours unless you submit to our trials.
Pap.	—What are these trials?
Second Pr.	—You must submit to all our commands and show no fear, not even of death.
Pap.	—I'll stay single.
Second Pr.	—Even if you should win a pretty and virtuous sweetheart?
Pap.	—I'll stay single.[1]

———————

Tamino, as a hero very properly should, braves the trials of fire and water, attains wisdom, and wins the hand of the Princess Pamina.[2] Of

---

[1] I have not been able to identify the source of this rather stiff translation. For Auden and Kallman's version of this passage in their 1955 translation of *The Magic Flute*, see *Libretti*, 156–8.

[2] This refers to *The Magic Flute*, Act 2, Scene 5, where Tamino and Pamina brave the Caves of Fire and Water together in order to reach the Temple of Wisdom (*Libretti*,

course, in that foreshortening which is at once the charm and the danger of Art,[3] the trials are over in the twinkling of an eye, whereas in life, not only do they last for ever, but also they are, not antecedent to, but co-terminous with marriage. Still, the moral is clear and familiar: he is blessed because he has risked everything, even complete failure.

What is more surprising, perhaps, is that, after all, Papageno also gets his girl. Why? Because he is shameless, honest, selfish and himself, because he is willing to give her up rather than lose his life.[4] The gods smile and Papageno is blessed. Wisdom he may not have, but he is granted his double, his Papagena, his happiness, and they both live, increase and multiply ever after in a naive unity with Nature, the beloved children of Eros in whom he is well pleased.

For Tamino and Papageno have two things in common. Firstly, Passion. Papageno has a passion for being immediately alive, even if that means remaining a bachelor. We may see that his emotions of boasting, hunger, terror, delight, are conditioned by objects outside himself, but to him, just because he is conscious of nothing beyond the immediate moment, there is no distinction between object and subject, a lion and a feeling of fear. Like all children, he can speak of himself in the third person.[5]

Tamino, on the other hand, has had a vision; he has seen Pamina's

177–8 has the Auden–Kallman version). For further references to the scene, see Auden's 'Address on Henry James', *Gazette of the Grolier Club*, 2.7 (Feb. 1947), 225: 'of examples of those who in their day have dared, like the Prince Tamino, the trials by fire and water and survived them to enter the Temple of Wisdom, he [the contemporary writer] will, thank God, find a number,' and n. 42 below. Auden's poem 'When rites and melodies begin' (1953) also refers to this episode (*CP91* 576).

[3] An ambivalence to the claims of art is distinctively Kierkegaardian. Auden commented on the human lovers 'Tom and Mary, for whom the curtain does not fall' in 'Eros and Agape', *Nation*, 152.26 (28 June 1941), 756; and on 'the foreshortened time of the Esthetic' in 'A Preface to Kierkegaard', *The New Republic*, 110.1537 (15 May 1944), 686. In the latter review of *Either/Or*, he quotes Kierkegaard's explanation: 'Romantic love can very well be represented in the moment, but conjugal love cannot, because an ideal husband is not one who is such once in his life but one who every day is such' (686).

[4] The preface to the Auden–Kallman translation of *The Magic Flute* comments: 'Threatened then by the Priest that if he [Papageno] refuses he will never win Papagena, he replies, ". . . In that case, I'll remain single." It is by this last answer that his humility is revealed, and for which he receives his reward' (*Libretti*, 132).

[5] Cf. Georg Groddeck, *Exploring the Unconscious*, trans. V. M. E. Collins (New York, 1933), 174: 'The child stands—or can stand—in an objective relation to itself. It sees its own being as a self and not as an "I".'

picture.[6] From that moment on, his life is dedicated to possibility,[7] to becoming worthy of her: he must look for her, whether he find her or not, whether he succeed in marrying her or not. He has a vocation.[8]

Secondly, because they both have Passion, both are willing to suffer, Tamino positively by risking his life in undergoing the ordeal, Papageno negatively by renouncing his wish for a sweetheart.

To all of us the gods offer a similar choice between two kinds of existence, between remaining Papageno the lowbrow, and becoming Tamino the highbrow.[9] What they permit to none of us, is to be a middlebrow, that is, to exist without passion and without a willingness to suffer. For the middlebrow wishes to have his cake and eat it. He is not willing to be nobody in particular, married to a vulgar little baggage like Papagena; on the other hand, he does not wish to *become* wise, only to *be* wise, to graduate cum laude. So, when he is asked if he is prepared to risk the ordeal, he shouts 'of course' and strikes a noble attitude, while thinking to himself: 'All this talk about suffering is old-fashioned rubbish. I'm smart and modern. I'll take the trial by correspondence, or buy a bottle of aspirin at the drug-store and feel nothing. After all, what are college professors and scientists for?'[10]

We are all born lowbrows and, in so far as we are physical organisms that can only function under certain physical conditions, we remain so. Sleeping, eating, fighting physical dangers and obstacles, in all our immediate existence, that is, we are Papagenos, for in the

[6] The preface to the Auden–Kallman translation of *The Magic Flute* explains that the second of the two main themes of the opera is: 'an educational one: how does a person discover his vocation and what does the discovery entail? When the opera opens, Tamino has been wandering about the desert without aim or direction, driven by some vague dissatisfaction, and is therefore, like all adolescents, in danger from forces in the depth of his nature which he cannot understand or control (the serpent). Saved from this, he is shown Pamina's picture and falls in love with her, i.e., he believes that he has discovered his future vocation, but only time will show if his belief is genuine or fantastic; he has, as yet, no notion of what this vocation will involve' (*Libretti*, 130).

[7] This word is used here in a Kierkegaardian sense: 'it is the opposite of NECESSITY, . . . it means room for FREEDOM, and therefore is like breath to a drowning man, a man "lost to the possibility", as S. K. puts it' (Lowrie, 633).

[8] In *EF* Auden wrote: 'That Ethical Hero of the Enlightenment, Prince Tamino in the *Magic Flute*, braves suffering, the ordeal by fire and water, because he knows that on the other side of it wait the Palace of Wisdom and the Princess Pamina' (111).

[9] There are comic updatings of *The Magic Flute*'s couples in 'Metalogue to *The Magic Flute*' (1955), *CP91* 580 and *Libretti*, 154.

[10] The contributions of the third son who succeeds in fairy-tales include 'a willingness, unlike his elder brothers who always carry aspirin, to accept suffering': 'In Praise of the Brothers Grimm', *The New York Times*, 12 Nov. 1944, sect. 7 (Book Review 49.46), p. 28.

immediate[11] we are not conscious of a definite self separated from the rest of reality, and the word selfish, therefor, has no meaning. Like the trolls in *Peer Gynt*, we are sufficient to ourselves.[12]

Once, however, we wake into self-consciousness, when the division between objective and subjective becomes apparent,[13] either we discover within ourselves a subjective passion for becoming, or we freeze into that passionless Great Boyg of self-love where 'Backward or forward, it's just as far. Out or in, the way's as narrow.'[14] For, in the conscious individual, passion can no longer be concerned with immediate being and the actual, only with becoming and the possible. Moreover, this change is a real mutation. There is no turning back. If we take the first step, we must take the last. Once woken, Papageno must either go forward like Tamino, or degenerate into Monostatos or Caliban.[15]

[11] Lowrie glosses 'immediacy' as 'what is apprehended in nature directly (i.e. without REFLECTION), either by the senses or by intuition . . . S. K. uses this word also to describe the sensuous life, relatively untroubled by reflection' (631).

[12] The trolls' motto in *Peer Gynt* is 'Troll, to thyself be—enough!' (Act 2, Scene 6). (The men's is 'Man, to thyself be true!') *Peer Gynt* was one of the main Romantic texts assigned in Auden's 'Poetry: Experience and Beliefs' class at the Writers' School of the League of American Writers in New York in the autumn of 1939, and he recommended the Everyman edition of the play to his students: *Peer Gynt: A Dramatic Poem*, trans. R. Farquharson Sharp (New York, 1922), in which the mottos are on pp. 61–2. (Only later, slightly revised impressions of the translation have precisely this wording.) At around this time Auden started quoting the troll king's definitions of the trolls' and humans' credos regularly: see, for example, the Cats' Creed in *Paul Bunyan*, which ends with 'Like the troll in Peer Gynt, both in hunting and love, | The cat has one creed: "To thyself be enough"' (*Libretti*, 36, 533). There are many other citations of the mottos during this period, including *DM*, where childhood is described as a time when human nature 'to itself appeared enough' (93). The whole passage from *Peer Gynt* is quoted in *EF* 85, and Auden comments that 'to be oneself is the aim of every romantic.' Auden quoted the distinction between trolls and humans on a great many later occasions, including 'Genius & Apostle', *DH* 439.

[13] In the passage in *EF* referred to in n. 12 above, Auden also writes: 'To be enough to oneself means to have no conscious ego standing over against the self, to be unable to say no to oneself, or to distinguish fantasy from reality, not to be able to lie, to have no name and answer to Hi or to any loud cry' (85–6).

[14] † 'Backward or forward . . .' is Peer Gynt's comment to himself at the points of greatest difficulty on his travels. He first makes the remark as he tries to fight the invisible troll, the great Boyg, in Act 2, Scene 7: see *Peer Gynt: A Dramatic Poem*, trans. Farquharson Sharp, 74. Auden refers to the great Boyg in 'Christmas 1940': ' "Beware! Beware! The Great Boyg has you down," | Some deeper instinct in revulsion cries' (*EA* 459); in *The Queen's Masque* (1942–3), written shortly before 'Vocation and Society', where the Queen of Dullness shouts: 'Revenge. Revenge. O Great Boyg, hear my prayer' (*Libretti*, 428); and in *The Age of Anxiety*: 'It is Bacchus or the Great Boyg or Baal-Peor, | . . . which they actually adore' (*CP91* 534).

[15] Monostatos, the High Priest Sarastro's lecherous servant in *The Magic Flute*, is described in the Auden–Kallman preface to their translation as the 'corrupted twin' of

This mutation into consciousness is beautifully described in the myth of Cupid and[16] Psyche. As long as Psyche does not know who her immortal lover is, he is immediately there, but the moment she sees him, he vanishes, and her life becomes a search, a dedication to the possible. What happens when the flash of vision fails to arouse passion, is described in another tale, Hans Andersen's *The Snow Queen*.

Kay and Gerda sat and looked at the picture book of beasts and birds. Then it was, while the clock was just striking five on the church tower that Kay said: 'Oh, something struck my heart and pierced me in the eye.' The little girl fell upon his neck; he blinked his eyes. No, there was nothing at all to be seen.

'I think it is gone,' said he; but it was not gone. It was just one of those glass fragments which sprang from the mirror—the magic mirror that we remember well, the ugly glass that made everything great and good which was mirrored in it seem small and mean, but in which the mean and wicked things were brought out in relief, and every fault was noticeable at once. Poor little Kay had also received a splinter just in his heart, and that will now soon become like a lump of ice. It did not hurt him now, but the splinter was still there.

'Why do you cry?', he asked. 'You look ugly like that. There's nothing the matter with me. O fie, that rose is worm-eaten and this one is quite crooked. After all, they're ugly roses. They're like the box on which they stand.' And then he kicked the box with his foot and tore the roses off.[17]

A vocation, then, is, if I may borrow a term from Professor Koehler, a state of 'subjective requiredness',[18] requiredness because it is

the uncorrupted child of Nature, Papageno. 'He is clearly another version of Caliban' (*Libretti*, 133).

[16] 'and' emended from the typescript's 'or'.

[17] Auden seems to be quoting from a slightly revised version of H. W. Dulcken's Victorian translation of 'The Snow Queen'. Dulcken translated Andersen's works in 20 vols. as *The Hans Andersen Library* (London, 1869–87) and many different selections from this edition were published, usually under the title *Fairy Tales and Stories*, in Britain and the United States in the last three decades of the 19th century and the first two of the 20th. For more, see pp. 200–1 of the present volume.

[18] Wolfgang Köhler (1887–1967), German scientist, Gestalt psychologist, and philosopher. He left Germany shortly after the Nazis came to power. Auden had known Köhler's work from at least the early 1930s: as Mendelson points out (*Early Auden*, 107), the geometric patterns in *The Orators* (*EA* 74) are lifted from Köhler's *Gestalt Psychology* (1929). He probably first encountered Köhler (who had joined the Swarthmore College faculty in 1935) and his second wife Lily in person on a visit he made to Swarthmore from *ca.* 2–8 April 1940. Later the same month, Auden described

indifferent to calculation of success or failure, and subjective because it is concerned with possibility; objective requiredness only concerns its How, never its Why.[19] Moreover to acknowledge a vocation is, like marriage, to take a vow, to live henceforth by grace of the Absurd,[20]

Köhler as 'one of the greatest men I've ever met' (ALS to A. E. Dodds, [?ca. 15 Apr. 1940], Bodleian). That summer the two corresponded briefly (see *Libretti*, 741) and Auden began extolling Köhler's books to his pupils and friends. He seems to have become personally close to the Köhlers shortly after he moved to Swarthmore at the end of Sept. 1942 (for observations on Auden's relations with Köhler at Swarthmore, see Maurice Mandelbaum, 'Swarthmore', in *Tribute*, 120–1) and composed a polyglot (and now lost) poem for Köhler's 56th birthday on 21 Jan. 1943, six days after he gave 'Vocation and Society'. There is general biographical information on Köhler in Ronald Ley, *A Whisper of Espionage* (Garden City Park, NY, 1990).

Auden borrowed the term 'requiredness' from *The Place of Value in a World of Facts* (New York, 1938), which he probably read during 1939. (The *OED* credits Köhler with the first use of the word 'requiredness', citing this book.) In a philosophical context, it belongs to the study of axiology or ultimate value. Köhler himself never defines 'requiredness' very pithily in *The Place of Value in a World of Facts*, but his use of it occurs when there is a value outside the present situation which requires another experience or fact for it to be fulfilled or completed—as in the case of a succession of musical notes which 'need' certain further notes in order to become a melody. Köhler writes that: 'At the bottom of all human activities are "values," the conviction that some things "ought to be" and others not' (35). See also chapter 3, 'An Analysis of Requiredness', esp. pp. 63–84, for distinctions between 'subjective' and 'objective' requiredness. Auden had been recommending *The Place of Value* to his students since at least late 1939 and it is quoted in *DM* 97–8, and listed as one of the volume's 'Modern Sources', *DM* 161. He first used the terms subjective and objective requiredness in print in 'A Note on Order', *The Nation*, 162.5 (1 Feb. 1941), 131, 132. (After that, they occur often during the following years.) Under the influence of Kierkegaard's concern with the 'required' (see *DM* 84–5), Auden uses 'requiredness' in a more speculative, 'romantic', and theological sense than Köhler, who is mostly concerned with its cognitive and philosophical implications. A contemporary definition by Auden of 'subjective requiredness' is: 'a requiredness the source of which I cannot identify with anything I call an object, and which concerns the meaning and value of my existence to myself. That is my immediate religious experience which allows me no rest until I believe I have understood it' ('Purely Subjective', *Chimera*, 2.1 (Summer 1943), 1). For Auden, then, subjective requiredness is an order from God to a human being about their personal destiny. See also Introduction, p. 4.

[19] Cf. 'For the Time Being' (*CP91* 385): 'Time is our choice of How to love and Why'. This and the following paragraph are heavily indebted to Denis de Rougemont's discussion of marriage and passion in *Love in the Western World*, trans. Montgomery Belgion (New York, 1940). De Rougemont says: 'The problematical element in marriage belongs not to *cur* but to *quomodo*, to the "how" and not the "why"' (288).

[20] Cf. de Rougemont's 'a troth that is observed *by virtue of the absurd*' (*Love in the Western World*, 290). De Rougemont in his turn is drawing on Kierkegaardian terminology. Lowrie glosses the term 'the absurd' by reference to the analogous concept of the paradox: 'Faith as such can find an appropriate object only in paradox; for if faith is reached, or subsequently justified, by demonstration, or by plausible argument, it is no longer faith but knowledge' (633). The Kierkegaardian category of the 'absurd' invaded Auden's writing during the early Forties, as for example in his Christmas 1941 letter-poem to Kallman: 'in the eyes of our bohemian friends our relationship is absurd', i.e.

to love for better or for worse, for richer or for poorer, in sickness and in health, until death do us part. No one can hope to have a vocation, in fact, if he makes a private reservation that, should circumstances alter, he can get divorced.[21]

For this reason Vocational Guidance is a contradiction in terms.[22] The only reason[s] another can give me why I should adopt this career rather than that are that I should be more successful or happier or it pays better, but such matters are precisely what I must *not* think about if I am really to find my vocation. If I say; 'Miss So-and-So is a nice girl. A bit homely, unfortunately, but she's rich and in love with me. I might as well marry her', it may show my common sense, but it certainly shows that I am not in love.[23]

There are two, and only two, possible kinds of large-scale differentiated society that can function: a static society in which each member has a fixed occupation and a fixed social status, based on the belief that requiredness is, for all except a small minority, objective, and a dynamic democratic society, based on the belief that, for all except a small minority, requiredness can be subjective, that all men are equal, not in their gifts, which they plainly are not, but in their common capacity each to recognise his peculiar vocation.*

---

* The historical relation between Vocation and Democracy as an unconditional ideal rather than, like the Greek Polis, an epiphenomenon of exceptional geographical conditions, is, I think, fairly clear. In the Middle Ages society as a whole was of the fixed status type, but there was one career, that of the priest, which was recognised as a vocation, and, in consequence, the Church was a democratic institution in the sense that anyone, irrespective of his social origin could

foolish to them, a matter for faith for us (quoted in Farnan, 66); and, most relevantly for the connection between marriage and art, in 'In Sickness and In Health' (1940): 'All chance, all love, all logic, you and I, | Exist by grace of the Absurd' (*CP91* 319).

[21] Cf. '[I]n the humblest lives the plighting of a troth introduces the opportunity of constructiveness and of rising to be a person—on condition, of course, that the pledge has not been for "reasons" in the giving of which there is a reservation allowing these reasons to be repudiated some day when they have ceased to appear "reasonable"! The pledge exchanged in marriage is the very type of a *serious* act, because it is a pledge given once and for all. The irrevocable alone is serious!' (de Rougement, *Love in the Western World*, 290–1).

[22] See Introduction, pp. 4–5, 10.

[23] There is an almost identical paragraph to this one in Auden's 'Purely Subjective', *Chimera*, 2.1 (Summer 1943), 6. De Rougemont also refers to a 'Miss So-and-So' (287–8).

In theory, either of these kinds of society is possible. What is quite impossible is a dynamic democracy based upon a trust in objective requiredness, in the effectiveness of such stimuli as happiness, success, utility, avoidance of pain, or any other of those things in which astrologers, psychoanalysts and advertising agents believe. Such a democracy is without passion[25] and must inevitably dissolve into an amorphous abstraction called the General Public[26] in which everyone is, as Kierkegaard says, 'like the interjection, without influence on the sentence, and at the very most takes a case, eg *O me miserum*, and the politicians are like Greek reciprocals ($\alpha\lambda\lambda\eta\lambda o\iota\nu$) which are wanting in the nominative singular and all subjective cases, and can only be thought of in the plural and possessive cases'.[27]

In consequence we are now faced with a large, powerful, and ruthless body of people who believe that a democratic society is

---

enter it with the possibility of rising to a high position. The breaking down of the feudal concept of status at the Reformation, the new possibility for the virtuous apprentice to marry the Master's daughter was, as Max Weber has pointed out, intimately related to the Lutheran doctrine that a 'worldly' occupation also could and should be regarded as a *Beruf*. Nor is it an accident, I think, that the social group which has, so far, both in its religious and its social life, [been] the most obviously democratic is precisely the one which has consciously based itself upon a belief in the Inner Light, the Society of Friends.[24]

[24] Auden's note alludes to Weber's *The Protestant Ethic and the Spirit of Capitalism*, trans. Talcott Parsons (London, 1930), in particular chapter 3, 'Luther's Conception of the Calling: Task of the Investigation', 79–92.

[25] Kierkegaard, *The Present Age*: 'Our age is essentially one of understanding and reflection, without passion', in *The Present Age: And Two Minor Ethico-Religious Treaties*, trans. Alexander Dru and Walter Lowrie (London, 1940), 3. (A year or so later, Auden recommended that the 'general reader', new to Kierkegaard, begin with *The Present Age*: see 'A Preface to Kierkegaard', *The New Republic*, 110.1537 (15 May 1944), 683.) *The Present Age* is an abbreviation, made by the English translators, from a longer work by Kierkegaard called *Two Ages* (1843).

[26] Kierkegaard, *The Present Age*: 'In order that everything should be reduced to the same level it is first of all necessary to procure a phantom, its spirit, a monstrous abstraction, an all-embracing something which is nothing, a mirage—and that phantom is *the public*' (37). 'The public is . . . a body which can never be reviewed, it cannot even be represented, because it is an abstraction' (38–9).

[27] † Kierkegaard, *The Journals of Søren Kierkegaard*, trans. and ed. Alexander Dru (London, 1938), 51, 56. Auden quoted parts of the same passage in *DM* 101 and included it in his anthology, *The Living Thoughts of Kierkegaard* (New York, 1952), 28 (although published in 1952, the anthology was compiled in the mid-1940s).

impossible. On one point Hitler is right, and his success is largely due to his insight that, without passion, there can be to-day, not only no democracy, but no society at all. In the struggle with Fascism it is becoming clearer daily that a) in a technical industrialised age a static society of innocent little Papagenos is no longer possible, and b) under an economy of abundance[28] where Nature no longer acts as a stimulus, if the passion necessary to make society function must be aroused from without, then it must be stimulated artificially; a Pseudo-Nature of imaginary objective dangers, Jews, plutocrats, communists, foreigners, must be consciously manufactured by the State which in the end, of course must provide real ones, the Police and finally War.[29]

It is a disquieting but necessary reflection that two of the fascist assertions, that a society without passion does not function but breaks down into economic chaos and class-war, and that, under the external stimulus of war, a society will function, have been proved correct.

We have, therefor, not only to defeat our enemies in the field, but disprove, which we have not yet done, their third assertion that there is no alternative, that war is the natural state of an industrialised society, by proving that a peaceful society can function under modern conditions. For those of us who are concerned with education, this means that our first problem is what, if anything, can we do, to make a sense of vocation the normal instead of the exceptional thing.

In a static society, the role of education is clear and positive;—to equip the young with whatever skills are necessary to exercise their occupation, the nature of which is already decided upon by the accident of their birth. In a fascist society, or in any society at war, education has a similar positive role, to teach techniques for such occupations as the State shall require, and to indoctrinate the proper passion. But in a peaceful democratic society, this is not so, and if our educational theory and practise are in the mess that they are, we have at least the excuse that our problems are much more complex and subtle.

[28] Cf. *PD* 48: 'Science . . . has created an economy of abundance'; 'Romantic or Free?' *Smith Alumnae Quarterly*, 31.4 (Aug. 1940), 356: 'Our age is unique, in that for the first time in history men have the technique to create that economy of abundance which can make an open society physically possible'; see also 'A Note on Order', *The Nation* 152.5 (1 Feb. 1941), 132.

[29] De Rougemont, *Love in the Western World*: 'a Totalitarian State is but the state of war being prolonged and renewed, and then made permanent, in a nation. But if total war abolishes any possibility of passion, politics transfers individual passions to the level of the Collective Being. Everything that a totalitarian education withholds from individuals is heaped upon the personified Nation' (252).

The negative objection of progressives to traditional education, namely, that it stunted individual growth by forcing children into moulds for which their natures were unsuited, was, in the main, sound. But they then proceeded to assume that the way to help a child to discover its vocation was to remove every obstacle, to make its life as easy as possible[.] But passion is never aroused by ease, only by obstacles.[30] The defect in traditional education was, not that it failed to arouse passion, but that this, in too many cases, was the passion of rebellion, and rebellion is not a vocation, ie, subjective, being only the mirror image of that against which it rebels. Baudelaire's classic expression of romantic revolt: 'When I have succeeded in inspiring universal horror and disgust, I shall have conquered solitude',[31] betrays a refusal to accept solitude which is essentially no different from that of the Rotarian or Fraternity Boy.[32]

If the traditionalist caused the child to stumble by putting up a barbed wire fence, the progressive has equally sinned against him by greasing the floor. The former may have been a savage old battle-axe who thundered; 'Boys, be pure in heart or I will flog you till you are',[33] but the latter is a hygienic cocotte, a Carmen in cellophane who sings of a Never-Never Land[34] where there is neither suffering nor requiredness, only the vital expressive self.

> Le ciel ouvert, la vie errante,
> Pour pays l'univers,
> Et pour loi sa volonté,
> Et surtout la chose enivrante,
> La liberté.[35]

[30] See also Auden's review of de Rougemont's book, 'Eros and Agape': 'To Tristan and Isolde love . . . can exist in the world of time only so long as there are obstacles to its physical consummation' (*The Nation*, 152.26 (28 June 1941), 756).

[31] Charles Baudelaire, *Intimate Journals*, trans. Christopher Isherwood (London, 1930), 45. Auden quoted this passage from *Fusées* in the original French in *DM* 134; and referred to it in the introduction to his *A Selection from the Poems of Alfred, Lord Tennyson* (New York, 1944), repr. in *FA* 232; and in his introduction to a new edition of Isherwood's translation, published in Hollywood in 1947.

[32] See also Auden's comments about romantic rebels, including Baudelaire, in 'Mimesis and Allegory', *English Institute Annual 1940* (New York, 1941), 15–16.

[33] In 'Tradition and Value', *The New Republic*, 102.1311 (15 Jan. 1940), 90, Auden attributed this *mot* to John Keate (1773–1852), headmaster of Eton from 1809–34, once said to have flogged 80 boys in a single day.

[34] The preface to the Auden–Kallman translation of *The Magic Flute* states: '*Die Zauberflöte* must remain in its own Never-Never Land' (*Libretti*, 129).

[35] From Meilhac and Halévy's libretto for *Carmen*: the alluring description of the wandering life sung to Don José by Carmen and the gypsies at the end of the Second Act. (Auden quotes the same passage in *EF* 17.)

And that affair, as our little Don Josés presently discover, starts out Hans Andersen but ends Grimm.[36]

Whether they define it in terms of authority and obedience, or of mutual interest and affection, both traditionals and progressives share a common assumption that there should be a direct relation between teacher and pupil. I believe this to be false. I am certain, too, that it implies on the teacher's part, which the traditionalist would admit, that he is essentially superior to the pupil he claims the right to assist. 'We are all here on earth to help others; what on earth the others are here for I don't know.'[37]

Being one myself, I glance from time to time at a journal put out for the benefit of teachers of English Literature, and what do I find? Article after article on such topics as 'How to make Dickens appeal to 12+ boys from the Bronx' or 'Poetry and the Maladjusted Girl'. Why this incessant emphasis, not on our subject, but on our relationship to our pupils? Is it not because, as a group, we English teachers have no personal passion for literature or for teaching ourselves through literature? Since we can offer no practical financial advantages for getting an A in English, except to other budding English teachers, our only assurance of our importance becomes the popularity of our courses. We become, in fact, the showmen of a parade of cultural Powers Models: 'Melville would look beautiful on Modom. The young lady would feel provocative in Proust'. It is hardly surprising, then, if we get the students we deserve, the debutante, the yearner, the woolly-minded, the domestic servant intellect.

Let not the science teacher, however, thank God that he is not as we are. We, at least have one advantage over them:[38] we are found out sooner, so that we do less harm to less valuable material. A student majors in Literature. Nothing happens. He is undeceived. A student majors in Physics. Nothing happens either. But he has learned to determine the co-efficient of expansion of brass and so gets a good job in industry. Accordingly he can go through his life without

[36] Auden had used this same turn of phrase in his Christmas 1941 poem to Kallman: 'our love, beginning Hans Andersen, became Grimm' (quoted in Farnan, 66).

[37] A favourite saying, quoted on many different occasions in private and public (and often with a satiric intention), e.g. *PD* 23, where Auden calls it: 'the conceit of the tyrant'; 'The Fabian Figaro', *Commonweal*, 37.1 (23 Oct. 1942), 13; 'The Giving of Thanks', *Mademoiselle*, 20.1 (Nov. 1944), 188; and 'Squares and Oblongs', in Donald A. Stauffer, ed., *Poets at Work* (New York, 1948), 177, where it epitomizes 'the conceit . . . of the social worker'.

[38] In the typescript 'them' has been changed to 'him' in a hand that is probably not Auden's.

realising that he is without passion, one of those trimmers in the Inferno of whom Virgil says: 'Mercy and Justice disdains them; let us not speak of them; but look and pass'.[39]

Can any of us, whatever our[40] field of learning, read this passage from Nietzsche without a red face?

Science has to-day absolutely *no* belief in itself, let alone in an ideal superior to itself, and wherever Science still consists of passion, love, ardour, suffering, it is not the opposition to the ascetic ideal, but rather the incarnation of its latest and noblest form. . . The fact of its having contented workers is absolutely no proof of science as a whole having to-day one end, one will, one passion for a great faith. When it is not the latest manifestation of the ascetic ideal, Science is a *hiding-place* for every kind of cowardice, disbelief, remorse, *despectio sui*, bad conscience—it is the very *anxiety* that springs from having no ideal, the suffering from the *lack* of a great love, the discontent with an enforced moderation. . . . The diligence of our best scholars, their senseless industry, their burning the candle of their brain at both ends, their very mastery in their handiwork—how often is the real meaning of all that to prevent themselves continuing to see a certain thing. Science as a self-anaesthetic: *do you know that*? You wound them—everyone who consorts with scholars experiences this—you wound them sometimes to the quick through just a harmless word; when you think you are paying them a compliment, you embitter them beyond all bounds, simply because you didn't have the *finesse* to infer the real kind of customers you had to tackle, the *sufferer* kind, (who won't own up even to themselves what they really are), the dazed and unconscious kind who have only one fear—*coming to consciousness.*[41]

To which of us, even the best in their weaker moments, does this not apply? Whenever the passion for vocation flags, the fire of uncertainty and the water of solitude[42] which are the trials of consciousness become intolerable; whenever the Socratic Sign disappears, the Socratic Doubt which is the weapon of honesty, must wound our-

[39] † *Inferno*, Canto 3. Auden is quoting from the Modern Library edition: *The Divine Comedy of Dante Alighieri: The Carlyle-Wicksteed Translation*, introduced by Charles H. Grandgent (New York, 1932), 23. Auden's copy of this book is now in HRC. The headnote to the canto describes these sinners as 'the unhappy people, who were never alive—never awakened to take any part in either good or evil, to care for anything but themselves' (22).

[40] In the typescript, 'our' is changed to 'his' in a hand almost certainly not Auden's.

[41] † *The Genealogy of Morals*, trans. Horace B. Samuel (New York, 1918), third essay, sect. 23, pp. 160–2. (Auden's quotation is highly condensed.)

[42] See n. 2 about *The Magic Flute*, above.

selves and corrupt the young whom we teach.[43] Whenever passion is
lacking, our intellectual life has only three alternatives; a hellenistic
specialisation upon minutiae, an indigestible digest of General Survey
Courses in Truth (Science), Beauty (Art) and Goodness (Hygiene), or
a mania for statistical classification; and our spiritual life only a choice
between Fatalism (It's smart to know you're damned), Relativism (It's
ethical to be a conditioned reflex), and Humanism (Government of
the ego by the ego for the ego).

To teach at all is hard, to teach well impossible, but at least it will
be something if we realise that without a vocation of our own, without a passion for teaching ourselves, we cannot hope to help others.
Every little Papageno knows instinctively that in becoming conscious
he will run a dreadful risk, every little Psyche guesses that her
beloved Cupid will go far away, and only the example of adults who
take this risk, whose lives are, in the words of Charles Péguy, 'a perpetual infidelity, for to remain faithful to the truth, they must make
themselves continually unfaithful to all the continuous, successive,
indefatigable, renascent errors',[44] only those who can weep and sing
simultaneously,[45] saying with Forese; 'And not once only while circ-
ling this road is our pain renewed: I say pain and ought to say
solace',[46] can help them to risk that dread,[47] that loss.

[43] The Socratic Sign refers to Socrates' *daimonion* ('divine sign'), an inner voice,
sent to him by the gods, which, as he explains in Plato's *Apology*, directed his life away
from political involvement. See also 'New Year Letter' (1940): 'Bewildered, how can I
divine | Which is my true Socratic Sign' (*CP91* 224); 'Many Happy Returns' (Feb.
1942): 'May you always, Johnny, | Manage to combine | . . . The Socratic Doubt with
| The Socratic Sign' (*CP91* 323); and 'the socratic *dubito ut intelligam*': 'Purely
Subjective', *Chimera*, 2.1 (Summer 1943), 21.

[44] †This passage comes from Péguy's *Basic Verities: Prose and Poetry*, trans. Ann
and Julian Green (New York, 1943), 51. (It is originally from *De la situation* (1906).)
The volume was copyrighted in Washington, DC, on 15 Jan. 1943, the day of Auden's
talk, but then, as now, books were available for sale in the US before their official publication date. Auden and Louis Kronenberger included the quotation, in a slightly different form, in their *Viking Book of Aphorisms* (New York, 1962), 321.

[45] Dante, *Purgatorio*, 26.142: 'Ieu sui Arnaut, que plor e vau cantan'. In the translation that Auden used (see n. 39), this is rendered as: 'I am Arnault that weep and go a-
singing' (349).

[46] *Purgatorio*, 23.70–2. Auden again quotes from the Modern Library edition (329;
see n. 39 above). This passage was a touchstone for Auden and he cited it on many
occasions around this time, for example in 'The Giving of Thanks', *Mademoiselle*, 20.1
(Nov. 1944), 189; 'The Essence of Dante', *The New York Times*, 29 June 1947, sect. 7,
p. 23; *EF* 74; 'The Ironic Hero', *Third Hour*, 4 (1949), 46; and in 'Presenting
Kierkegaard', the introduction to his anthology, *The Living Thoughts of Kierkegaard*
(New York, 1952), 4 (see n. 27 above).

[47] Kierkegaard says of 'dread' (now usually translated as 'anxiety') 'What is it? It is

Moreover it is only thus that we shall be able to restrain our natural lust for power and approval,[48] to exhibit in our relation to our pupils that careful indifference, that conscious refusal to help, (which is, of course, only genuine in the degree to which we wish to help, in the degree to which refusal causes *us* suffering), which is, I believe the proper educational obstacle to arouse subjective passion.[49] The gifts of the Spirit are not to be had at second hand, and until a child has discovered his vocation, it is neither the traditional birch nor the progressive lollipop that we should offer him, but a vacuum. Once he finds it, he is no longer a pupil but a colleague who teaches as much as he learns, and who knows that every human relationship, in work, play, or love, is a marriage of two solitudes.[50]

Why, in the last analysis, do we think it essential to abolish poverty, ignorance, disease, tyranny, if not because we know that these external sufferings deafen men to the voice of subjective requiredness.[51] If we imagine or allow others to imagine that we are thereby abolishing suffering itself, that there will no longer be a command before which a man must walk in fear and trembling,[52] then we are middlebrows and the truth is not in us.

the day to come' (quoted by Lowrie, 74). And Lowrie himself glosses it as 'an agonizing premonition prompted by nothing concrete, but by horror at . . . nothingness—like the dizziness one may experience on the brink of an abyss' (631).

[48] 'Christmas 1940': 'all Its lust to power is impotent | Unless the actual It hates consent' (*EA* 459).

[49] Parts of the lecture from its beginning until this point were revised and re-used by Auden in his 'Mozart and the Middlebrow', *Harper's Bazaar*, 80.3 (Mar. 1946), 153, 252.

[50] Auden is alluding to R. M. Rilke, *Letters to a Young Poet*, trans. M. D. Herter Norton (New York, 1934): 'this more human love . . . will resemble that which we are with struggle and endeavor preparing, the love that consists in this, that two solitudes protect and touch and greet each other' (60). Cf. a passage in the poem Auden wrote just before this talk: Ferdinand's sonnet to Miranda in 'The Sea and the Mirror', in which he calls his loved one: 'solitude | Where my omissions are' (*CP91* 412). See also the original version of 'In Sickness and In Health' (?Autumn 1940): 'lay your solitude beside my own' (*SP* 114).

[51] See also 'Prologue' in *DM*: 'neither a Spring nor a war can ever || So condition his ears as to keep the song | That is not a sorrow from the Double Man' (12). Auden's argument here is related to the overview of history he had sketched out in *Paul Bunyan* in 1939–40: first external necessity must be conquered, so that human beings can then face their own natures: 'Gone the natural disciplines | And the life of choice begins' (see *Libretti*, 45).

[52] The phrase derives from Job 4: 14: 'Fear came upon me, and trembling, which made all my bones to shake.' But by now the words have virtually been annexed by Kierkegaard, two translations of whose *Fear and Trembling* (1843) would have been available to Auden. The first version was a translation by Robert Payne (London, 1939), the second was by Walter Lowrie (Princeton, NJ, 1941; London, 1942).

What, after all, is a Democracy but a society in which each individual has the right to choose his suffering and be tormented by his own Either–Or?[53] And is not the only freedom for which it is worth dying, the freedom to risk failure continually for the sake of a Pamina of whom we have only seen a picture?[54]

It would be dishonest of me to conceal my conviction that the notion of subjective requiredness presupposes a belief that man is born in sin but may be saved by the Grace of God, but it would be presumptuous of me to pretend that I speak here with any authority.[55]

So, to modify slightly a statement of E. M. Forster's: 'Two cheers for Democracy: one because it admits vocation, and two because it permits contrition. Two cheers are quite enough. There is no occasion to give three. Only Agape, the Beloved Republic, deserves that'.[56]

[53] Kierkegaard's *Enter / Eller* (1843) was not published in an English translation until March 1944. (Auden reviewed it in 'A Preface to Kierkegaard', *The New Republic*, 110.1537 (15 May 1944), 683–4, 686.) However, he would have known this phrase by now from numerous sources, including Kierkegaard's *Journals*, *passim*, and 'Has a Man the Right to Let Himself Be Put to Death for the Truth?', included in *The Present Age: And Two Minor Ethico-Religious Treatises*, trans. Dru and Lowrie: 'the "either or" . . . either to fall down in adoration, or to take part in putting Him to death' (95; see also 90). He could also have seen it in both the main books on Kierkegaard available at the time, D. F. Swenson's *Something about Kierkegaard*, ed. Lilian Marvin Swenson (Minneapolis, 1941) and Lowrie's *Kirkegaard*, 2 vols. (New York, 1938). Auden had already used the phrase 'Either-Or' in 'In War Time' (June 1942), *EA* 461: see n. 54 below.

[54] This paragraph is foreshadowed in Auden's 'In War Time' (June 1942): 'If we are right to choose our suffering | And be tormented by an Either-Or, | The right to fail that is worth dying for' (*EA* 461). For further instances of the necessity of risking failure, see the roughly contemporary review, 'An Unbiased Biography of Yeats and His World', *Chicago Sun*, 7 Feb. 1943, Book Week, p. 6: 'to regard art as a religious ritual damages the art for it prevents the artist from taking serious risks of failure'; and 'K's Quest', in Angel Flores, ed., *The Kafka Problem* (New York, 1946): 'the successful one, the hero . . . is willing to risk failure to answer the call for help' (48). There is a change of emphasis in the later 'The Poet and the City' (?1962): 'among the half dozen or so things for which a man of honor should be prepared, if necessary, to die, the right to play, the right to frivolity, is not the least' (*DH* 89).

[55] 'Authority' is one of the main terms in Kierkegaard's thought. See, for instance, *Journals*, 322: 'the most important ethical-religious concept: authority'; and '*Authority* is the decisive quality . . . neither the poet nor the thinker has authority, even within his own sphere of relativity; their statements are judged on purely aesthetic and philosophic grounds according to the value of the form and the content. . . . Authority is a specific quality either of an Apostolic calling or of ordination': 'Of the Difference between a Genius and an Apostle' (1847), trans. Dru, in *The Present Age*, 146, 148, 149.

[56] Auden is adapting Forster's words: 'two cheers for democracy: one because it admits variety and two because it permits criticism. Two cheers are quite enough: there is no occasion to give three. Only Love, the Beloved Republic deserves that.' (Forster himself is alluding to Swinburne's 'Hertha': 'love, the beloved Republic, that feeds

And concerning that republic, I cannot conclude more fittingly than with the closing lines from the most recent poem of the greatest poet now living, one in whom America and England may both rejoice, one whose personal and professional example are to every other and lesser writer at once an inspiration and a reproach, Mr T. S. Eliot.

With the drawing of this Love and the voice of this Calling

We shall not cease from exploration
And the end of all our exploring
Will be to arrive where we started
And know the place for the first time.
Through the unknown remembered gate
When the last of earth left to discover
Is that which was the beginning;
At the source of the longest river
The voice of the hidden waterfall
And the children in the apple-tree
Not known, because not looked for
But heard, half-heard, in the stillness
Between two waves of the sea.
Quick now, here, now, always—
A condition of complete simplicity
(Costing not less than everything)
And all shall be well and
All manner of thing shall be well
When the tongues of flame are in-folded
Into the crowned knot of fire
And the fire and the rose are one.[57]

upon freedom and lives'—see the 'Bonchurch' edition of *The Complete Works of Algernon Charles Swinburne*, eds. Sir Edmund Gosse and Thomas James Wise (London, 1925), *Poetical Works*, vol. 2, 144). Auden probably knew Forster's comment from the essay published in Clifton Fadiman, ed., *I Believe* (New York, 1939), 82, to which Auden had also contributed an article (see *EA* 372–80). He admired Forster's essay and had already borrowed from it in 'September 1, 1939' (see *Early Auden*, 329–30).

[57] From *Little Gidding*, published in *The New English Weekly*, 15 Oct. 1942 and as a pamphlet on 1 Dec. 1942.

Some Letters from Auden to James and Tania Stern

EDITED BY NICHOLAS JENKINS

Introduction
'Selves, Joined in Friendship'

FOR every writer registered and discussed in even the most detailed scholarly surveys of a period, inevitably a hundred, the milling creatures of the epoch, are missed. In Valentine Cunningham's *British Writers of the Thirties*,[1] for instance, a wide-sweeping searchlight at first appears to have caught in its beam the decade's every last obscure book and neglected author. Yet, in the wake of Cunningham, a great army of lesser names from the Thirties is still hidden in the historical darkness, helplessly waiting, like the shades in Auden's elegy for Freud, 'to enter | the bright circle of his recognition'.[2] Take a single example. Of the ten contemporaries that Auden and Isherwood discussed in the optimistically titled 'Young British Writers—On the Way Up',[3] a pot-boiling article written in early 1939 during their first few months in the United States, nine have made it into Cunningham's index. Missing, though he once possessed a 'fabulous reputation',[4] is one of Auden's closest friends, the Anglo-Irish short-story writer James Stern.[5]

---

[1] (Oxford, 1988).   [2] *CP91* 273.

[3] *Vogue*, New York, 94.4 (15 Aug. 1939), 94, 156–7.

[4] See the entry on Stern in John Wakeman, ed., *World Authors 1950–1970* (New York, 1975), 1376–7; this piece contains an important autobiographical statement by Stern (1376). I am grateful to Edward Mendelson for allowing me to see notes of an extended conversation that he had with Mr and Mrs Stern during the mid-1970s. Unless otherwise indicated, the information and quotations in this introduction were supplied by Mr and Mrs Stern during their conversation with Mendelson or during discussions that they had with me on 14 July 1989 and 2 June 1992.

[5] I take Cunningham's massive typology to be the most intensive look at the period. So does the Thirties historian and memoirist Julian Symons, who calls Hugh Gordon Porteus '*the* forgotten man of the literary Thirties' (my italics), although Porteus just scrapes into Cunningham: see Symons, 'Forgotten Man of the Thirties', *TLS*, 4695 (26 Mar. 1993), 13–14. This is an unnecessary injustice to the many 'forgotten' men and women, the latter perhaps even more numerous (though, since they are forgotten, who can count them?). Stern is no more visible in other standard Thirties volumes,

Stern, a short, slender man who liked to flash a wide, ironical grin, was born on 26 December 1904 and died on 22 November 1993.[6] Despite a long life, the dates of his main publications make him more completely an artist of the Thirties than almost any other writer, just as, for years, his loathing of family and caste made him that archetypal Thirties figure, a refugee. Having started writing stories in the 1930s (he never published a novel), Stern kept at it after the Second World War, producing some more stories (and shuffling the best of his earlier work into new orders); completing a book about his time in Germany in 1945 with the United States Strategic Bombing Survey; translating many classics of German and Austrian literature (often in collaboration with his German-born wife, the physical therapist Tania Stern); and—as a guileful, self-deprecating reviewer—turning out a steady, though never large, flow of literary journalism. In this second, long, rather fallow period, as he struggled with his fiction he also made a serious private art out of his correspondence, an output that made him famous amongst the well-disposed audience of his friends. 'If I survive you,' Auden once wrote to Stern admiringly, 'I'm going to edit your letters (*profusely* illustrated by photos and maps).'[7]

But Stern's two main collections of stories, *The Heartless Land* and *Something Wrong*, came out in 1932 and 1938.[8] In these clipped, precise narratives—satiric, comic, and closely observant of British social codes—the man who grimly called himself 'a Jewish mongrel who went to Eton & Sandhurst',[9] tackles from a unique angle many of the Thirties' most familiar themes: exile, class guilt, political commit-

including Hynes's *The Auden Generation* and Bernard Bergonzi's *Reading the Thirties: Texts and Contexts* (London, 1978). Biographies of writers who lived in or visited the United States around the mid-century often mention incidents involving the Sterns in New York during the war, and there are of course reviews of Stern's books buried in old periodicals. His work is briefly considered in *The Short Story in English* (Oxford and New York, 1981), 236–40, by another Thirties veteran, Walter Allen.

[6] Obituaries include Richard D. Lyons, 'James Stern, 88, a Prolific Writer of Short Stories and a Translator', *The New York Times*, 24 Nov. 1993, p. D19; 'James Stern', *The Times*, London, 27 Nov. 1993; 'Obituary of James Stern', *The Daily Telegraph*, 27 Nov. 1993, p. 19; Alan Ross, 'Obituary: James Stern', *The Independent*, 24 Nov. 1993, p. 29; Anne Chisholm, 'Paris Spring with Le Grand Sam', *The Guardian*, 24 Nov. 1993, p. 41.

[7] ALS, [7 Aug. 1944].

[8] His third collection of fiction, *The Man Who Was Loved* (New York, 1951; London, 1952), contained twelve stories, seven of which had already been printed in the first two books. After that came *The Stories of James Stern* (London and New York, 1968), a selection of his best work. Wherever possible, I refer to this, Stern's most recent and accessible book.

[9] TLS to Humphrey Carpenter, 6 June 1980 (Rare Books and Manuscripts Room, Butler Library, Columbia University).

ment, the ordeal of the Test, antagonism towards an older generation, and the obsession with childhood and school.

'By birth and breeding Mr Stern belongs to the English upper class', Auden told a publisher, 'and few writers have a more imaginative insight into both the strength and the weakness of that extraordinary culture.'[10] His life-history in some ways resembles those of his fellow Etonians George Orwell and Henry Green, depths-seeking counterparts of the school's 'Children of the Sun'. And his work, like theirs, draws heavily on his personal background. For many years, Stern spent much of his energy passionately, almost desperately, in revolt against his past. Yet however much he was appalled and wounded by his *haut bourgeois* childhood, it was, in a way typical of many Thirties' writers, his artistic capital, his subject. And for that reason, an understanding of Stern's work is inextricably tied up with an exploration of his personal origins.

On Boxing Day 1904 James Stern was born into a world of butlers and bespoke tailoring at Kilcairne, near Navan (now An Uaimh), County Meath, the eldest of the five children of Major Henry Stern and his wife Constance. Streams of wealth flowed from both sides of his family: Stern's mother's people, the Watts of Londonderry, were 'fox-hunting Protestants from Londonderry and County Kildare', his father's 'middleclass Jews' with an extensive banking business, Stern Brothers, in London, Berlin, and Vienna.[11] Henry Stern was an oddity within his family in that, unlike all the other males, he did not go to work in the bank. Instead, this crusty, formal man lived the withdrawn, old-fashioned rustic life of a cavalry officer in the British Army. Perhaps because of a sense of only precariously maintained assimilation, he was highly self-disciplined and conformist, never telling his son that he was a Jew until after he had served his country in two wars.[12] Major Stern's brothers, both of them bankers, were knighted for special services to their country: Sir Albert for his work developing the tank, and Sir Frederick for his contributions to genetics and horticulture.

Stern's maternal ancestors, on the other hand, already stood at the

---

[10] ALS to Alfred A. Knopf, 15 Dec. 1939 (HRC).

[11] See Wakeman, ed., *World Authors*, 1376.

[12] Stern was 16 before he found out, by accident, from his grandmother that his father's family was Jewish (see 'Revelations: A Memoir of Childhood', *Quarto*, Aug. 1981, p. 12).

Anglican pinnacle of the Victorian Establishment—his maternal great-grandmother was the Duke of Wellington's mistress and, although James Stern was not informed of this until he was 50, family legend held that Stern's maternal grandfather was the Duke's son.[13] The Watts had once owned nearly a fifth of Ireland and in the nineteenth century Stern's grandfather, Andrew Watt, had reached such a level of seigneurial grandeur that his annual migration south to a summer home in Meath was made by private train.[14] After Stern's parents were engaged, there was a period of intense Trollopian bargaining between the two families as they negotiated the merger of substantial amounts of property and cash.

Major Stern, the cavalryman, 'saw all things in terms of right and wrong', his son wrote, '. . . and every yesterday through the leading editorial of today's *Times*.'[15] A gruff character (Stern once compared his father's attempt to show a smile beneath his bristling moustache to a fox baring its teeth), he was also 'a shy, reticent man. It was this shyness, this inwardness and awkwardness that made his sudden bark, for a child, so frightening. Children embarrassed him. He did not like them. Nor did my mother.'[16] The Major's two great passions, aside from soldiering and fox-hunting, were the trees of Britain and regimental uniforms, subjects which hint at carefully camouflaged reserves of artistic feeling. A talented amateur water-colourist, he toiled in secret at pictures of Army horses and officers, the only subjects that he would allow himself to execute. But in front of his sons he displayed a more professional manner, inspecting their appearance as if they were on a special kind of indoor parade: 'If he spotted a rucked stocking or a waistcoat "done-up" "*You*!" he would bark. "*You'll* never get into Eton, y'know . . . Never make a soldier!"'[17]

In the padded luxury of their surroundings, the Sterns were a family of 'almost eccentric undemonstrativeness'.[18] The only time that Stern ever remembered his father betraying any emotion at all was when his sons' hair got too long. Yet James Stern's locks had become for him a symbol of the individuality which he was terrified that his

---

[13] 'Revelations'.

[14] 'Disbeliefs', *London Magazine*, NS 22.8 (Nov. 1982), 16–27. This piece, along with 'Allergies', *London Magazine*, NS 10.3 (June 1970), 41–5; 'Highdown', *London Magazine*, NS 21.1 and 2 (Apr.–May 1981), 40–8; and 'Revelations' (see n. 12 above) is an extract from Stern's projected autobiography, *The Golden Spoon* (see Introduction, p. 62).

[15] 'Allergies', 44.   [16] 'Disbeliefs', 16.   [17] 'Allergies', 44.

[18] *The Hidden Damage* (New York, 1947), 48.

parents were trying to eradicate. In the face of the Major's fury, like a pint-sized Samson, Stern was defiant: 'to assert myself, to keep at least my mouth above the waves, there were certain commands I adamantly refused to obey.'[19] In later life he claimed that he had never once asked his parents for the loan of even 'a sovereign'.[20]

The Major's wife complemented her husband's monitoring of clothes and hair with her own obsessive attention to her children's teeth and bowels. As a result, James Stern developed intense neuroses about his appearance and body. When he met his future wife in Paris in 1934, the first thing that she noticed was how ragged and dirty he was, and how contemptuous of money. Later, just before they were married, when they were sitting one night in a French dining-car and she reached over affectionately and patted his hair, Stern leaped up like someone attacked in his sleep and hit her on the side of the head.[21]

Constance Stern was a fierce, hard-riding sportswoman, fanatically devoted to horses and clothes. Instead of a cupboard or a closet, she had a large white-washed room in her house, filled with hats, shoes, and tea-gowns. Yet the members of the household talked about little but horseflesh and Stern suspected that his mother had resented becoming pregnant with him, because it cut down the amount of time she could spend in the saddle. And although she was a figure of great bravado, he also darkly sensed that she might have been afraid of giving birth. Of all the people that he ever met, he wrote that his mother was 'the most complicated, the most unpredictable, the most inconsistent, the most difficult to please'.[22] When he was still a small child, she abandoned him to the attentions of wet-nurses and governesses while she rode back and forth across the Irish fields.

Stern spent much of his youth in Bective, not far from Navan, in a 'long, low, ivy-covered Georgian house, with the panorama from its windows over the River Boyne, the Hill of Tara, and the lush, emerald meadows of Meath'.[23] Just as the solid, unhurried directness of his prose style reflects something of the ordered military household in which he grew up, his intense, quasi-Lawrentian feeling for nature, his alertness to quirks of speech and the rhythms of story-telling, stem from the more chthonic and expressive world of the rural Irish around his home. The Stern children were allowed to roam—on horseback, of course—'in the great illusion of peace' through the Irish

[19] 'Allergies', 45.   [20] 'Revelations'.   [21] 'Allergies', 45.
[22] 'Disbeliefs', 17–18.   [23] Hidden Damage, 56.

countryside. As a result Stern came to know intimately the peasant communities scattered around the house at Bective. It was from them, he remembered, that, 'as well as the language of our parents, we learned the more vivid, poetic tongue of the people of Meath.'[24]

Stern's exotic ancestry, the ambiguities of his status as the alienated son of an aristocratic landowner in a poor, but fertile part of Ireland, and his awareness of the two social and linguistic worlds dividing the country, fed a scepticism about and a fear of tribal loyalties. 'Possibly on account of this mongrel origin, and a youth spent shunting back and forth between Ireland and England,' he once wrote, 'I have never felt that I belong to any particular place or country, never felt drawn to any creed or party. I feel as much at home in Western Europe as in English-speaking countries.'[25]

The vision of Edenic innocence he had woven round Meath's lanes and farms was torn apart in 1916. Two Easters after his father left to fight in France, the gates to the lodge of the Sterns' estate were suddenly locked and armed men arrived, apparently out of nowhere, to guard the house and its inhabitants. For a week at the start of the Irish Civil War the family were trapped inside their home, and one day not long afterwards Stern saw their chauffeur come staggering into the yard, 'his face and clothes covered with blood'. He had been ambushed by the IRA on the road to Dublin.[26] The Sterns eventually left Ireland in 1922 when the Irish Free State was created, and Stern was later to write that 'Memories of this war have had, I believe, a lasting effect upon my life.'[27]

He was at prep school at Wixenford where he was a classmate of Harold Acton and Kenneth Clark. War work for women and small boys at the time often involved knitting scarves and mufflers for the men at the front—one of whom, of course, was Stern's father. A manifestation of his festering anxieties, Stern's muffler had reached the length of 60 feet by 1918. Auden told an interviewer that when

[24] Clipping of 'Home Thoughts' [review of Mary Lavin, *Tales from Bective Bridge*], *Irish Press*, 5 Oct. 1978, [no p. no.].

[25] See statement in Wakeman, ed., *World Authors*, 1376.

[26] Stern, 'Home Thoughts'.

[27] Wakeman, ed., *World Authors*, 1376. In a piece about William Plomer, Stern mentions 'the nightmares of a Protestant youth spent in Catholic Ireland during the Troubles and the Civil War': 'Sharing the Veld', *London Magazine*, NS 13.5 (Dec. 1973–Jan. 1974), 11.

Stern heard the news of the Armistice, he put his creation in a closet and started weeping.[28]

For all his father's fierce prophecies, Stern did get into Eton, an institution that his contemporary Henry Green impassively described as being like 'a humane concentration camp'.[29] Stern stayed there from 1918 to 1923, but he seems to have passed through the school as soundlessly as a ghost through a wall: although there were many writers amongst his schoolfellows, none of their memoirs mention him in any detail. He was friendly with Cyril Connolly, with Acton (again), and with Brian Howard, but he wrote that eight years in expensive English schools had 'bored' him into a routine of golf, gambling, and eventually petty larceny.[30] A year at Sandhurst convinced his disappointed father that his eldest son would never make a soldier. So, in 1925, after a few months on a Dorset farm, Stern was packed off, like the traditional black sheep, to Southern Rhodesia, where for a year he helped a Scot manage a herd of Hereford cattle and 'acquired a hatred of colonialism and racial intolerance'.[31] Although he probably did not realize it at the time, he had also gathered the material for *The Heartless Land*.

Stern was frail,[32] and, after his turbulent childhood, prone to bouts of disabling melancholy. (Isherwood described him in 1936 shut up alone in his room all day like an invalid, 'hating his father', prostrated by nerves, and able only to see his wife.[33]) He was plagued by swarms of allergies and phobias, many of them related to his parents' surveillance of his body, and for a while was even forced to carry around a little tin of 'panic pills', which in calmer moments he would sometimes pull out of his pocket and show to friends.[34] Life in colonial Rhodesia was predictably harsh and cultureless (*The Heartless Land* describes a world of sun-baked bleakness, philistinism, and roughness, even for the landowners), and in 1926, on doctor's orders, Stern returned to England.

[28] Paul Seabury, 'Auden, Would-be Mine Operator Favors Ungodly But Intelligent', *Phoenix*, 63.3 (14 Dec. 1943), 3. (Auden and Kallman borrowed the story of the muffler for use in their libretto *Elegy for Young Lovers* (1959–60), see *Libretti*, 663.)

[29] *Pack My Bag: A Self-Portrait* (London, 1940), 93.

[30] Wakeman, ed., *World Authors*, 1376.   [31] Ibid.

[32] This frailty was probably exacerbated by an accident: he seems to have suffered some sort of serious brain concussion that periodically afflicted him with its after-effects (see ALS from Auden to Kallman, [8 Dec. 1944]).

[33] *C&HK* (US), 251.

[34] See Michael Wishart, in John Byrne, ed., *James Stern: Some Letters for His Seventieth Birthday* (London, 1974), 24.

At his parents' insistence, he agreed to become a clerk in the family bank of Stern Brothers, first in London, then in the suffocating Wilhelmine stolidity of the branches in Frankfurt and Berlin. After days in the basement clipping bond coupons, at night Stern prowled through the Otto Dix-like underworlds of these German cities, creeping from bar to bar until the last one closed, then, a few hours later, stumbling in for work at Stern Brothers.[35] 'By the end of 1928 I had become acutely aware that for two-and-a-half years I had been living the life of a sleepwalker,' he wrote. 'That I ever published a page of prose was due primarily to the dread prospect of spending the rest of my days in a bank.'[36] Bridget Tisdall remembers him lying on a bed in his paternal grandmother's Prince's Gate mansion, near Hyde Park, saying 'I refuse to be another pearl on the Stern necklace', and letting out a peal of cackling laughter.[37]

In 1929, through another Old Etonian, Alan Pryce-Jones, Stern got a job as an assistant editor at J. C. Squire's *London Mercury* where he read manuscripts in a tiny office off the Strand. Writers like Chesterton, Belloc, and de la Mare dropped into the *Mercury* offices, but Stern felt inhibited by these 'lions'.[38] So, later that year, when a friend offered him a trip, all expenses paid, to New York, Stern left his job and set off. They were in America during the first months of the Depression, but, to British eyes, the country seemed exhilaratingly open and mobile. He felt exalted by the atmosphere of apparent anonymity and classlessness, particularly in Harlem, which he visited and greatly enjoyed, rejoicing in the fact that: 'no one knew me from Adam, no one called me sir.'[39] And he vowed that he would return.

Feeling buoyed up, Stern decided to travel home round the world, returning to England via Russia. However, he fell seriously ill in Honolulu[40] and six months later was back in the *Mercury* office in London. Squire kept pressing him to write something, and one evening in desperation Stern started a description of an African veld fire that eventually metamorphosed into 'The Cloud'.[41] Inspired, but with no support from his parents, he spent 1931 virtually alone in the

---

[35] *Hidden Damage*, 83–9, and (Stern roomed with Howard in Frankfurt) Marie-Jaqueline Lancaster, ed., *Brian Howard: Portrait of a Failure* (London, 1968), 239–42.

[36] Wakeman, ed., *World Authors*, 1376.   [37] Byrne, ed., *James Stern*, 20.

[38] Wakeman, ed., *World Authors*, 1376.   [39] Ibid.

[40] See 'Next Door to Death' in Stern, *Stories*, 225–38, for a fictionalized account of the experience.

[41] *The Heartless Land* (London and New York, 1932), 1–27, repr. in Stern, *Stories*, 23–37.

Hôtel d'Alsace in Paris, in the room where Oscar Wilde had died. Avoiding friends, he wrote all day until his story drafts were bulked up to 30,000 words or more. Then he boiled them down to a fifth or a tenth of their original length and posted them off to English magazines. After what he described as the 'first happy year of my life',[42] Stern found that he had written enough about Africa to make a book of 'thinly disguised autobiographical stories'.[43] *The Heartless Land*, published in 1932, demonstrated Stern's quest for a style that his friend Constantine Fitzgibbon described as 'the terse, the pointed, and the relevant'.[44] Its publication deeply satisfied Stern, but its frank exposure of the brutal shabbiness of colonial exploitation and, worse still, the prevalence of interracial desire, further embarrassed his Pharisaical parents.[45]

All eight of the stories, which are mostly stolidly traditional in form, take place in what was then Southern Rhodesia and their unifying theme is hatred: the hatred of the white settlers for each other, and their terrified and contemptuous hatred of the Africans—a feeling that in its turn is amply repaid. Although the stories are set in Africa, *The Heartless Land* is mainly about the Europeans, specifically the dregs of the British imperial culture in its most provincial and soulless manifestations. The book dwells on the moral corruption of the older settlers and their families in their spartan outposts, and, repeatedly, on the agonized loneliness of the younger, single men in 'this wilderness'.[46] The volume as a whole conveys a deep sense of bitterness; there are frequent eruptions of melodramatic violence and many of the stories end in a sense of encirclement and futility. This feeling is only partially offset by Stern's mordant social observation; the mood of barely suppressed rage is exacerbated by the fact that, underlying the African setting, are analogies with the embattled situation of the Anglo-Irish gentry amongst whom Stern had grown up. This quasi-symbolic dimension gives *The Heartless Land* something of the quality of a dream-sequence, as if readers of the book found themselves in a huge, unfamiliar terrain suffused with some urgent but obscure message. Stern recalled that the stories were 'written in a Paris bedroom overlooking a narrow, noisy street, but in my

[42] Wakeman, ed., *World Authors*, 1376.
[43] 'Malcolm Lowry: A First Impression', *Encounter*, 29.3 (Sept. 1967), 58.
[44] Fitzgibbon, in Byrne, ed., *James Stern*, 5.   [45] 'Home Thoughts'.
[46] 'The Heartless Land', in *Heartless Land*, 66.

imagination all were composed in the silence of a room overlooking the Boyne'.[47]

The dominant literary influences, looming presences in much Thirties writing, are the stories of Maugham and Lawrence,[48] but the racial situation gives a new twist to the familiar theme of the struggle to transcend the prison of social class. Like countless other works by middle-class writers of the period, Stern's book explores the ways in which the privileged are driven by an overwhelming sense of inadequacy and loneliness to defy their own taboos: in the world of Stern's writing the system breaks down principally because of the price it exacts from its defenders. In 'The Force', for instance, a story which must be a very early example of the literary representation of sex between the races, it takes the pathetic failure of his flirtation with a married white woman for Newman, a bachelor member of the British South African Police, to realize that his isolation has been created by imperial ideology. Alone in his hotel room, and in despair, he reels involuntarily towards the servant-girl who has brought him a whisky. '[A] torrent whose power was irresistible surged up in him, possessed his stricken limbs as his arms went about her, and the rocks called colour were conquered as the man and the woman fell slowly together where they stood, on the floor.'[49]

Auden later told Stern that he thought the best piece in the book was 'Charles Congreve, Esquire', a story about the Sunday lunches that an idly pretentious settler with a faded, lower-class wife and a snobbish child gives to his seedy circle of dissatisfied employees.[50] However, the story in *The Heartless Land* most frequently mentioned by critics is 'The Man Who Was Loved', a piece with strong Oedipal undercurrents. It is the most inventive story formally—in it two narrative methods are contrasted within a single frame. The first part, a self-conscious parody of the well-made Maughamesque story with a

---

[47] 'Home Thoughts'.

[48] On 10 July 1939 Katherine Anne Porter told Glenway Wescott: 'Jimmie gave me a copy of Maugham's short stories, telling me what a great writer he was and how he Jimmie admired him' (*Letters of Katherine Anne Porter*, ed. Isabel Bayley (New York, 1990), 170). For testimony about Lawrence as an influence on Stern, see Martin Green, *Children of the Sun: A Narrative of 'Decadence' in England After 1918* (New York, 1976), 110.

[49] Stern, *Stories*, 53. This remarkable sentence is full of conflicted double meanings, not least in the Metaphysical punning of the couple 'falling' where they 'stand'.

[50] *Heartless Land*, 185–232. Auden's remark comes in an ALS, [7 Aug. 1944]. He admitted, though, that the story, which looks forward to the less hectoring social comedy of *Something Wrong*, was untypical of *The Heartless Land*.

'sting in the tail', describes the death of Major Carter, a man who has perfected the art of killing snakes with his bare hands.[51] The narrator and the Major (Stern's father was also a major) confront a green mamba, which is terrifying some tribesmen and a herd of oxen. Although no serum is available, the Major deftly grabs the snake by the tail, whirls the body round, and cracks it like a whip, so that the head is snapped off. The lifeless tail spins away into the bush, but at the same moment the Major falls to the ground: the snake's detached but still lethal head has dropped neatly down the opening of his shirt. The second half of the story, describing the day of the Major's funeral is, by contrast, slow-moving, collective, muted, epiphanic, a picture of societies rather than individuals. The settlers insist on raising money for a plaque, but once their short-lived display of grief in church has guttered out, it is left to the Africans to bury the Major's body in a ceremony of deep, heart-felt mourning. The narrator notices that the faces of the African pall-bearers, 'strangely brown, all bore a definite resemblance one with the other, and that each face shone with tears'. Left open is the question of whether the narrator's perception is a manifestation of colonial superciliousness or whether these men carrying the Major to his grave may actually be his sons. '[T]he vast procession, like one wing of a gigantic magpie, formed up behind and followed the bones of the man who was loved.'[52]

Paris during the Thirties was the capital of modernist exile and experimentation, and Stern, who was a witty talker and an uncannily sensitive listener, got to know many writers and artists, including Joyce and Beckett, with both of whom he could share an exile's fondness for cricket and memories of Ireland. Late in 1933 he came across a semi-comatose Malcolm Lowry lying on the floor of a bistro. They launched off together on a series of day-long, drunken walks round the city, forays that were to be the subject of one of the best of Stern's several excellent memoirs.[53] However, in spite of his success in getting a book published, he felt that literature alone could never cure him of his emotional turmoil. He later wrote that all his life his one 'over-riding ambition' had been 'to find someone to live with, capable of living with me'.[54]

---

[51] Isherwood records that Stern was terrified of snakes and had been bitten by one while he was in Africa (*C&HK* (US), 250).

[52] *Heartless Land*, 98; repr. in Stern, *Stories*, 22.

[53] See n. 43, pp. 58–64, 66–8.   [54] Wakeman, ed., *World Authors*, 1376.

Tania Kurella was born in Berlin in January 1904, the only daughter of the psychiatrist Hans Kurella. (She had three brothers, two of whom became prominent left-wing intellectuals, while the third, another psychiatrist, became a conservative.[55]) She died on 17 April 1995. In the city's energized, bohemian world of the 1920s, with its cults of youth, fitness, and beauty, she became a pupil of the physical therapist Else Gendler, who had evolved a technique of relaxation designed to develop *Körperbewußtsein*, 'bodily consciousness'. Later Tania Kurella started taking pupils of her own, to whom she taught methods of increasing awareness of their bodies, their sense of balance, and the development of their senses. Isherwood first met Tania and James Stern in 1936 in Sintra, Portugal.[56] In *Christopher and His Kind*, he wrote that she was

one of the most unaffected, straightforward, sensible, and warmhearted women Christopher had ever encountered. She was also one of the most beautiful: small, dark-haired, dark-eyed, and with a body as beautiful as her face . . . When she looked at you, she seemed aware of all the faults of posture which betrayed your inner tensions; but you never felt that she found them repulsive or even absurd. She was ready to help you correct them, if you wanted her to.[57]

By 1933 Tania Kurella's left-wing brothers Heinrich and Alfred had both fled Germany. Shortly after Hitler became Reichschancellor in January of that year, she was warned that she was in danger of being taken as a hostage for them. Kurella and her close friend the American writer Eda Lord managed to get out of the country and they travelled first to Ascona on Lake Locarno (where they met the Manns and the novelist and anti-Fascist Lion Feuchtwanger), and then on to Paris. There and, later, in New York, Mrs Stern helped other refugees from Hitler to find jobs, passports, and accommodation.

---

[55] One brother, Alfred Kurella (1895–1975), was an important East German Communist Party official and literary theoretician (see the entry on him in Borys Lewytzkyj and Juliusz Stroynowski, eds., *Who's Who in the Socialist Countries* (New York and Munich, 1978), 336). Auden met him by chance at a PEN conference in Budapest in early Oct. 1964 and he reported to Mrs Stern that her brother's speeches were considered to be long and exceptionally boring, even by his fellow GDR delegates.

[56] For Stern's rather flat reminiscences of Isherwood in Sintra, see *Hidden Damage*, 70.

[57] *C&HK* (US), 250. Isherwood borrowed her surname for the second violinist in Cheuret's quartet in *Lions*, 153.

The singer Hedli Anderson,[58] who had been one of Tania Kurella's pupils in Berlin, was now living in Paris. In 1934 she invited Kurella and Lord to her flat and when they arrived she introduced them to her dishevelled boyfriend, James Stern. Mrs Stern recalled that at their first meeting, elusive, shy, disdainful of grooming, 'he looked like a ragged tramp'. None the less, they became friendly. One evening, Stern, Anderson, Lord, and Kurella went to the Bal Musette in Montparnasse and on the dance-floor there, Stern suddenly swept Tania Kurella up and kissed her. It was the start of their life together and the beginning of James Stern's recuperation. He once said that 'for thirty years pills and salts of various kinds remained the most essential part of my personal luggage'.[59] A month or so before his thirty-first birthday, he got married to Tania Kurella. Thirty years later, he wrote, 'But for her I should long ago have perished.'[60]

After initial puzzlement and distress, Stern's parents were reluctantly reconciled to their son's mysterious foreign fiancée. As their concession, Stern and Kurella agreed to have an English wedding, which took place in London on 9 November 1935. None of Tania Kurella's relatives could attend the ceremony, so she was given away in church by Ernst Freud, whom she had known since her childhood. After the celebrations, the Sterns went back to Paris and their tiny flat on the top floor of a building at 31 Quai de l'Horloge, a place with a view across the Seine that, according to Humphrey Carpenter, was 'so beautiful that Stern found it almost impossible to work'.[61]

But Stern's distraction was not simply due to the sublimity of the French capital, nor to his lurking family demons. Soon after their marriage, at around the time that the Spanish Civil War broke out in 1936, the Sterns began to think about leaving Europe: James Stern was horrified by the way that the political situation was developing and he wanted to go back to America.[62] In one of Stern's stories, a wartime refugee from Europe, an Irish doctor, comments tersely that 'Only a fool or a convict could have lived in Europe and not seen things, terrible things'.[63] Many years later, when the Sterns unpacked

[58] For more on Hedli Anderson, see Donald Mitchell and Philip Reed, '"For Hedli": Britten and Auden's Cabaret Songs', AS2 61–5. See also Letter 15, n. 10.

[59] 'Allergies', 41.　　　　　　　　　　　[60] Wakeman, ed., World Authors, 1376.

[61] Carpenter, 220.

[62] According to Mrs Stern, at one stage they planned to go and live in Mexico with Isherwood and his boyfriend Heinz Neddermeyer.

[63] In 'Solitaire', Stern, Stories, 243.

some belongings that had been left in storage in a Paris warehouse, they found their china was wrapped in newspapers reporting the early fighting in Spain.

Nevertheless, Tania Stern was more reluctant than her husband to leave Paris and it took the couple two years to make the break; in the mean time Mrs Stern gave gymnastic lessons and James Stern composed more stories and eked out a living by translating German books.

It was during this period that Auden met the Sterns. He already knew Stern's work: at Isherwood's prompting he had read *The Heartless Land* in 1934.[64] Then Isherwood introduced him to the Sterns at the Café de Flore, a literary hang-out in Saint-Germain-des-Prés, probably on 12 January 1937.[65] Of the group of five or six gathered at the table that day, all were—in the melancholy grandiloquence of a phrase of Mrs Stern's—'drowning persons', part of the tide of refugees and *Wandervögel* seeping westward across pre-war Europe. Isherwood had lived abroad for most of the decade. Tania Stern had left Germany to escape Nazi persecution. James Stern, a careful and agonizingly slow worker estranged from family and background, was engaged on a new book of stories, *Something Wrong*. And Auden, believing that the time had come to 'gamble on something bigger'[66] for his poetry, was *en route* to Spain. In the next two years before he emigrated to the United States, Auden spent less than half his time in England. While the others in the group at the Left Bank café gossiped and drank liqueurs, Auden was content to read a book and sip coffee. '[H]e sat there, bent over, oblivious, absorbed', the fretful Stern wrote. 'For one who found concentration difficult, it was an envy-making sight.'[67] After meeting him in Paris in early 1937, the Sterns did not see him again until they were all in New York in 1939.

In the autumn of 1938 *Something Wrong* appeared—and a tilt away from the overtly political and towards the psychological became evident in Stern's writing.[68] Mostly set in the British Isles and Ireland, *Something Wrong* is a more detached and relaxed book than *The Heartless Land*, one much more concerned with descriptions of a

[64] See ALS to Alfred A. Knopf, 15 Dec. 1939 (HRC).

[65] On the Café de Flore, see Herbert R. Lottman, *The Left Bank: Writers, Artists, and Politics from the Popular Front to the Cold War* (Boston, Mass., 1982), 7–10. (Carpenter, probably wrongly, dates the meeting to Apr. 1937 (220).)

[66] ALS to E. R. Dodds, [8 Dec. 1936], (Bodleian).   [67] *Tribute*, 126.

[68] *Something Wrong: A Collection of Twelve Stories* (London, 1938).

world that Stern, like MacNeice, registered as 'incorrigibly plural',[69] a little universe of physical impressions, social nuances, and linguistic quirks, in particular the mannerisms of upper-class speech. *Something Wrong* is also almost wholly given over to the horrors and delights of childhood. In November 1938 Auden wrote very favourably about it during his brief stint as a reviewer with Birmingham's Labour paper, *The Town Crier*.[70] He was probably impressed by the restrained but quite unequivocal description of a young American boy's awakening homosexuality in 'Travellers' Tears', a story which he singled out for special praise.[71] And, more generally, as a connoisseur of neurotic symptoms, particularly those related to domineering mothers, Auden was excited by Stern's delineation of the sufferings that parents inflict on their children. In his discussion of a story about a boy terrified that he can never live up to the level of physical prowess demanded by his fox-hunting mother, he homed in on one of the recurrent themes in Stern's stories. It was a theme, as he must by then have known, that arose from personal experience, and with which Auden himself could identify: 'Parents are inclined to regard their children as dream extensions of their personality . . . the sensitive child is tortured only too often by the feeling that he is unworthy of his father or mother. The *Broken Leg* is a terrifying study of this common situation.'[72] Stern's intense focus on his upbringing, and his unembarrassed artistic exploration of the subject, parallel Auden's Rilkean fascination with childhood, which is such a major theme in his poems from 'This Lunar Beauty' through to his baroque hymn of praise to the baby, 'Mundus et Infans'. And especially in the year or so after Auden's mother died in September 1941, parents—sources for both writers of intensely ambivalent feeling—were to be another important topic in their talks and letters.[73]

But for all his praise of *Something Wrong*, Auden was relatively cursory in his analysis of Stern's book. His good opinion was clearly

---

[69] 'Snow', *Collected Poems of Louis MacNeice*, ed. E. R. Dodds (London, 1966), 30.

[70] Stern wrote to Humphrey Carpenter: '*Something Wrong*: Oh, what a sad story. First I ever heard of WHA's review was when Ed. M. [Edward Mendelson] sent me a copy *after W's death*. I nearly wept: I had never thanked him! The book also had a sad history: appearing during the Munich crisis, the bulk of the edition was destroyed in the Blitz!' TPCS, 20 July 1979 (Rare Books and Manuscripts Room, Butler Library, Columbia University).

[71] *Something Wrong*, 61–82; repr. in Stern, *Stories*, 189–210.

[72] 'A New Short Story Writer', *The Town Crier*, NS 996 (4 Nov. 1938), 2.

[73] It was also to the Sterns that Auden offered a description of the death of his father in 1957. See Letter 18 below.

based, at least in part, on subjective attitudes to Stern himself and not just on his enjoyment of the dry finesse of Stern's writing. One factor in this was surely the combination of Stern's Jewish ancestry and his grim childhood, the effects of which still tormented him—Stern wrote feelingly in *Something Wrong* about the 'great hollow abyss of misery that only a child can know'.[74] In a Christmas 1941 letter-poem to Kallman, Auden confessed to his class-inheritance of an 'O-so-genteel anti-semitism'.[75] But his sense of guilt was probably more specific and self-incriminating. Auden once suggested to Stern that his later fascination and friendship with Jews, particularly marked in his life after he came to the United States, stemmed from an incident during his schooldays when he had insulted a Jewish boy and soon afterwards had been overwhelmed with a sense of grief and remorse. Auden implied that his later determination to absorb Jewishness and Jewish thought into his life and poetry (and, perhaps, the lengths to which he was prepared to go to sustain his relationship with Chester Kallman) were partly an attempted reparation and atonement.

Auden's warmth also derived from his admiration for Stern's strictness of purpose. Having lived abroad for so long, Stern was completely outside the crusading London literary world of anti-Fascist writers' committees and marches. At the end of the Thirties, Auden and Isherwood's communal, myth-making imagination apparently seized on their friend in the same way that they had earlier exalted Edward Upward. And they did so as a corrective to their praise of Upward's political trenchancy. Where they had once lauded Upward's self-surrender to Party work, they now celebrated Stern's artistic self-containment and political reticence. Brian Howard once announced to Michael Wishart that, 'the one man who might *just* persuade Wystan to alter *one* word in a poem, my dear, is Jimmy Stern'.[76] Stern felt himself to be a blocked, tortured, costive writer. But, with his extremely personal subject-matter, his exile, his slow, scrupulous production, and his freedom from the taint of involvement in partisan politics, he came to represent for the campaign-weary Auden and Isherwood a new ideal: the isolated integrity of the artist. (There is a parallel here with Auden's respect for another Anglo-Irish

[74] 'The Broken Leg'; repr. in Stern, *Stories*, 135. Stern was brought up as a Protestant (see nn. 13 and 27 above) but a reference in an ALS of 21 Mar. [1955] makes it clear that Auden thought of him as a Jew.
[75] Quoted in Farnan, 65.
[76] Quoted by Wishart, in Byrne, ed., *James Stern*, 24.

contemporary, Louis MacNeice.[77]) Spender recognized this too: he has written, rather equivocatingly, that his feelings about James Stern are of the kind

one might have about a god in some shrine known to my friends and always a bit mysterious and shrouded from myself. His beard and slightly mysterious smile add to this elusiveness; the result of Auden's and Isherwood's allusiveness to him . . . I have known Jimmy and his adorable and caring wife Tania for over thirty years, yet they always remain to me legends recounted by Auden and Isherwood.[78]

Just as James Stern had no political affiliations beyond his general anti-Hitlerism and contempt for the British Establishment, he had no theory about writing, nor did he confine himself to a fashionable interest in the lives of proletarians or intellectuals. In 'Young British Writers—On the Way Up', Auden and Isherwood praised Stern as 'the best of the younger story writers', remarking that he had 'no formula, no pattern; each story is a fresh surprise'.[79] And in December 1939, Auden told the publisher Alfred A. Knopf, in a letter evidently written in an unsuccessful attempt to get Stern an American publisher:

Mr Stern is little known as yet either in England or the States. In the first place he has an artistic integrity which not only forbids him writing on subjects of which he has no experience, but also makes him reluctant to write until his experience has been completely digested . . . In the second place he is neither a journalist with a flair for news nor noisily experiment[al], so that he has missed both a Book-Club and an Avant-Garde triumph.[80]

It was the kind of writing which had become relevant to both Auden and Isherwood as they experienced a mounting sense of ideological exhaustion and doubt towards the end of the decade and it seemed to offer them a new focus for their ambitions.[81]

So popular were the Sterns, that their big farewell party at the

---

[77] See 'Louis MacNeice: 1907–63', *The Listener*, 70.1804 (24 Oct. 1963), 646; repr. in *Louis MacNeice: A Memorial Address* (London, 1963). Another quality that MacNeice and Stern shared in Auden's mind is charm, a characteristic that he often associated with the Irish. See, for instances, Auden's praise of the Ireland that gave MacNeice a 'love of the . . . disorderly charming' ('Louis MacNeice', *We Moderns: Gotham Book Mart 1920–1940*, catalogue 42 ([Dec. 1939]), 49); 'Irish charm' in 'For the Time Being' (*CP91* 365); and the 'charm' of Nevill Coghill's 'Irish provenance' in 'Eulogy' (*CP91* 764).

[78] Byrne, ed., *James Stern*, 17.

[79] 'Young British Writers—On the Way Up', 157. See n. 3 above.

[80] See n. 64.   [81] See *C&HK* (US), 332–3.

restaurant La Coupole in Paris in 1939 was attended by important literary figures such as Eugene Jolas and Caresse Crosby. It almost ended in disaster. Tania Stern got very drunk and rushed out on to the Boulevard Montparnasse emptying the contents out of her purse and scattering everything, including her passport, behind her. Fortunately her husband had seen what was happening and was running along in her wake, picking up the irreplaceable documents one after another as soon as they hit the pavement.

The Sterns arrived in New York in April or May 1939, a few months after Auden. There, in the 'electrifying atmosphere'[82] of a city already filled with European exiles, James Stern kept writing and translating, and Tania Stern gave gymnastic classes in a brownstone on East 59th Street. Soon afterwards, probably during May or early June, they arranged to meet up again with Auden, this time in a restaurant. Chester Kallman came with him. They also noticed another change: Auden had begun to drink more liberally.

The sacred Pennine landscape that Auden returned to so often in his poems was a deserted place; being shy and easily bored, he often seems to have found it difficult to blend in comfortably with other people. In his elegy for MacNeice he told the poet's ghost that 'the dead we miss are easier | to talk to' than the living.[83] But in mid-1939 Auden began seven or so years of extremely close contact with the Sterns. Isherwood had left New York that April and during the time from the writing of 'New Year Letter' to the end of work on *The Age of Anxiety*, the Sterns were amongst Auden's most important, most highly valued friends. It was an intimacy that the three sealed when they were together by lapsing into German, 'the language of our friends, the refugees'.[84] (Auden's circle in New York during the early part of the war was crowded with German-speakers; the linguistic cross-pollination is reflected in the polyglot idiom he uses in 'New Year Letter'.)

The Sterns never had children, and, perhaps because their nurturing energies were not diverted elsewhere, they functioned for Auden almost as an accepting surrogate family—a role that he was certainly aware of: he once begged Tania Stern to 'be my Big Sister always'.[85] His sexual nature was also acceptable to them, as it was not to his own family or, probably, to Elizabeth Mayer, the woman he once addressed

---

[82] *Tribute*, 126. [83] 'The Cave of Making', *CP91* 692.
[84] *Tribute*, 126. [85] TL, 29 Nov. [1941].

in a letter as 'Mutti'.[86] The Sterns were adaptable and uncensorious: in 1936 Isherwood, an inveterate wanderer and a defiant homosexual chauvinist, had believed that he and Heinz might have lived together with the Sterns 'in harmony for months or even years'.[87]

For their part, the Sterns found Auden to be immensely frank and direct, an arbiter, a seer, and, for all his idiosyncracies, someone acutely sensitive to their own psychological needs. They often had the feeling that he secretly thought of himself as a doctor or a priest. Major Stern, like Auden, had structured his days by the implacable rigours of the clock, and Auden, who was often drawn to identify with and to protect people he perceived as weak or self-destructive, seems to have seized on such similarities to act out the role of a loving, stimulating father to Stern. James Stern later remembered him as so 'imaginatively indulgent of one's weaknesses. He could express in a sentence that combination of affection, authority and encouragement which he knew the child for years had craved in vain.'[88]

But during his early years in the States, Auden was even closer to Tania Stern than he was to her husband, an intimacy that was partly rooted in her brief role as his physical trainer and partly in her personal warmth and intense, affectionate sympathy—qualities that she had radiated to many people including Spender and Isherwood. She rapidly took over from Mrs Dodds as Auden's female confidante. In May or early June 1939, Auden had apologized to Mrs Dodds for telling her in his letters about Kallman, adding 'I hope all this stuff about my private life doesnt bore you too much; but Christopher is away and I must have someone to talk to.'[89] In the summer of 1939 in Los Angeles, Auden, still heavily under the influence of Isherwood's pacifism and Gerald Heard's holistic and mystical ideas, was persuaded that he needed to undertake some form of physical training. (Kallman told Harold Norse that on their trip to California they had met Aldous Huxley 'and his alter intellectual ego: Gerald Heard who feeds him ideas and right now has everyone going on yoga—including Christopher and Harvey'.[90]) When Auden got back

[86] ALS, [16 Jan. 1943], (Berg).   [87] *C&HK* (US), 251.
[88] *Tribute*, 124. See, for instance, Letter 2, p. 69: 'Jimmy, if you start saying again that you cant write, I shall come to New York, disguised as your father, and beat you.'
[89] ALS, [May or June 1939], (Bodleian).
[90] ALS, 16 Aug. [1939], (Lilly). In a letter to A. E. Dodds, Auden wrote 'I realise that if one does take up a pacifist position one has got to go in for spiritual exercises to make oneself genuine and effective, so I suppose I shall have to look for a Yogi teacher or someone when I get back to New York'—ALS, [*ca.* 6 Aug. 1939], (Bodleian).

to New York he decided that he would try Tania Stern's classes, and soon after he started these the personal remarks and confidences in his letters to Mrs Dodds dried up.

Carpenter explains that Mrs Stern taught 'relaxation and breathing-exercises with the intention of making her pupils more aware of their bodies'.[91] Classes were held twice a week and lasted about 50 minutes; attendance was usually small, limited to around five people. Apart from Auden and Kallman, those who took part included, at one time or another, Jean Connolly and her American friend Tony Bower, the conductor Jascha Horenstein, and, sometime later, Auden's troublesome patroness, Caroline Newton.[92] Mrs Stern made her pupils stretch, lie on the floor, and play with wooden balls. Sometimes, she blindfolded them and asked them to touch different surfaces.

When he started taking her classes, Tania Stern found Auden clumsy, and very dissatisfied with his status as a pupil. She sensed that he was least 'in touch' with his hands and feet, and she felt that this was because, as an intellectual, he was cut off from the world of sensation around him. To Auden's annoyance, she insisted on taking him to an orthopaedist who told him that his arches were almost gone. So she worked especially hard on his feet, often making him stand barefoot on empty bottles. Auden did what she instructed but without really trying, and he lost patience quickly. She saw that he could understand and appreciate the reason for doing something long before his body could actually perform the task. On 26 November 1939 Auden told Mrs Dodds, in the Jungian terms which had recently entered his thinking, that he found the exercises '*most* painful, but illuminating. Apparently my solar-plexus and my head are very much alive, but not the chest centres; I suppose because I'm a thinking-intuitive.'[93]

Nevertheless he and Mrs Stern got on extremely well and enjoyed fitting their friends into various somatic templates. Auden got enough out of the exercises to continue with the classes until sometime in 1940; during that time he even composed an elaborate publicity handout for Tania Stern to use. In it he blended his own current ideas with descriptions of her practices with imperious rhetorical ease:

[91] 281.

[92] For more about Newton, see annotation to letters below, especially Letter 1, n. 2 and Letter 13, n. 2.

[93] TL, 26 Nov. 1939 (Bodleian).

Man has not two separate natures [of Body and Mind] but is an indivisible
trinity of Mind, Body, and Person . . . Mental conflicts that lead to malad-
justments in private and social life can be relieved and sometimes radically
cured through special training which, starting with bodily functions, strives to
restore and maintain that balance of Mind, Body, and Person which is the
necessary condition for a full realisation of our true possibilities.[94]

As a psychiatrist's daughter from a sophisticated, liberal background in Berlin, Tania Stern was one of the few people willing to
talk candidly, and sometimes critically, to Auden about his relationship with Kallman. Sensing that Auden was not a very expert lover,
she encouraged him to try to become more physically adept and also
more considerate of Kallman's feelings. For although Auden had
fallen deeply in love with Kallman and had endowed their relationship with a near-religious significance, he still sometimes seemed to
her to treat Kallman like an object rather than a person. Once, when
Mrs Stern had scolded him for neglecting Kallman whenever they
were together in intellectual company, he confessed to her that for a
long time he had been lazily inclined to think of his boyfriends as
'pieces of trade'. She told him she was shocked and afterwards Auden
made great efforts to compensate for this attitude. She sensed,
though, that it was too late and that the relationship was already
becoming inharmonious and competitive. (Neither of the Sterns ever
got on well with Kallman.)

Perhaps because Tania Stern already knew both Auden and
Kallman so well, her intimacy with Auden lasted through the break-
down of his 'marriage' to Kallman, his coming to terms with this sit-
uation, and the writing of the three long poems, 'For the Time Being',
'The Sea and the Mirror', and *The Age of Anxiety*, that evolved out
of this emotional turmoil and his subsequent retreat into his art.[95]
During the winter of 1941–2 while Kallman was embroiled with the
English sailor-adventurer Jack Barker, Tania Stern acted as an inter-
mediary for them: 'there's no one but you that either he [Kallman] or
I can trust,' Auden wrote to her from Hollywood.[96]

[94] An autograph manuscript, undated, in Tania Stern's collection.
[95] The Auden–Kallman 'Crisis', as Auden called it, may have erupted while they
were visiting the Sterns in Amenia in mid-July 1941: without explaining why, Elizabeth
Mayer recorded in her diary for 17 July that she had suddenly driven up to Amenia
but had been unable to find Auden or the Sterns. See also Letter 13.
[96] ALS, 30 Dec. 1941. Auden was visiting Kallman in Hollywood when Barker suddenly arrived in New York, trying to get in touch with Kallman. Auden appealed to
Mrs Stern for help in sorting out the situation.

In the first few years after he arrived in the States, Auden struck acquaintances there as a haunted, driven writer, like the bi-locating poet Clare Vawdrey in Henry James's story 'The Private Life'. MacNeice described with admiration how, while the war raged in Europe, Auden in America was 'working eight hours a day . . . getting somewhere',[97] and Alan Ansen recorded the remarks of someone who remembered Auden at Middagh Street: 'During '40 living in Brooklyn. Wild parties going on downstairs WHA writing in solitude upstairs.'[98] His poems from this time are full of self-imposed exhortations. In April 1940, at the age of 33, Auden was already contemplating what had to be done before he could meet the 'grave's dead-line'.[99] Less than a year later in a poem of personal stock-taking he prayed for help because: 'The darkness is never so distant, | And there is never much time for the arrogant | Spirit to flutter its wings.'[100] And in the first half of 1942 he told James Stern, 'Unless I write something, anything, good, indifferent, or trashy, every day, I feel ill.'[101]

Although, as with any couple, there were periodic tensions and stormy arguments, James Stern had found a happy life with Tania Stern. But his creative energies were slowly beginning to wane in the United States. Auden, on the other hand, felt his powers being unleashed with renewed force. Yet though he was writing with such seriousness of purpose, his friendship with the Sterns, with its jokes, conspiracies, and flirtations, liberated a zestful, playful side of him that seems to have become increasingly rare again in his later life (at least as it has been conveyed by the two biographies written so far). In 1940 and the first half of 1941, Auden spent a lot of time out of New York, often with the Mayers in Amityville, Long Island. The Sterns, though, tried to visit him wherever he was. During the summer of 1940, for instance, they came to see him at Mina Curtiss's home in Northampton, Massachusetts (where Auden and Tania Stern got stuck at the top of the Ferris wheel at the local fair), and later

[97] 'Traveller's Return' (1941); repr. in *Selected Prose of Louis MacNeice*, ed. Alan Heuser (Oxford, 1990), 90–1.

[98] Miscellaneous note in Alan Ansen's 'Notebook 3' about a conversation in *ca.* 1947 with 'Stringham' (Berg). Stringham told Ansen that when they met, Auden asked him 'Are you happy?'

[99] 'New Year Letter', *CP91* 242.

[100] See the original version of 'At the Grave of Henry James' in *Partisan Review*, 8.4 (July–Aug. 1941), 270; slightly revised version reprinted in *CP45* 130 and *SP* 123.

[101] See Letter 4, p. 72.

that year they often saw him at 7 Middagh Street in Brooklyn, where he was living with George Davis and Carson McCullers. James Stern recalled scenes of 'George naked at the piano with a cigarette in his mouth, Carson on the ground with half a gallon of sherry, and then Wystan bursting in like a headmaster, announcing: "Now then, dinner!"'[102] Auden also made journeys to visit the Sterns in Amenia, near Leedsville in upstate New York, where they had rented Green Cottage from the social theorist Lewis Mumford.

Generally Auden collaborated only with people whom he knew well; the works he undertook jointly were a way of furthering a personal bond.[103] 'Queers to whom normal marriage and parenthood are forbidden', he wrote in a notebook, 'are fools if they do not deliberately look for tasks which require collaboration and the right person with whom to collaborate—again, the sex does not matter.'[104] Given his closeness to Stern, it was almost inevitable that they should begin to work together. Sometime during the early part of 1941 Auden asked him for help with a CBS radio dramatization of D. H. Lawrence's story *The Rocking-Horse Winner*.[105] The project went well, though Stern remembered a conversation while they were working on the script, in which Auden said to him: 'Why are you using all those names [for the bookies' calls]? It sounds very peculiar to me, are you certain it's right?' Stern, who had grown up with horses, tactfully replied, 'Perhaps we should drop the whole thing?' To which Auden swiftly answered, 'Well, no, if you're certain . . .'

Although Auden may have wanted to make use of Stern's horse-racing expertise, *The Rocking-Horse Winner* also became a subtle gesture of warning and encouragement to his blocked friend, a bringing to consciousness of the reasons why Stern often found it so difficult to write. In a very early draft of what later became 'The Meditation of Simeon' in 'For the Time Being' (written in the winter of 1941–2)—the speech is not quite yet in Simeon's voice but still sounds very much like Auden's own—Auden used the world of Lawrence's story to declare that a writer's 'first adolescent efforts are scarcely more | Than a substitute for the nursery rocking-horse | On

[102] Quoted in Carpenter, 304.
[103] The exception is his collaboration with Brecht on *The Duchess of Malfi* in 1946, which he told Alan Ansen that he did 'for the money' (see Ansen, 2; *Libretti*, 430–2).
[104] Holograph notebook, [1964–5], (Berg), fo. 9.
[105] For the text and details of the history of the commission, see *Libretti*, 383–97, 746–50.

which we rode away from a father's imperfect justice'.[106] In the script that he and Stern wrote, the boy Paul's visionary ability evolves as a psychological compensation for his miserable childhood. As if to push home the point, Auden wrote to Stern a few months later, 'If I read your stories right, they have been your catharsis of your childhood, and that particular task is almost or quite over.'[107] The difficulties of Stern's later creative history make this an especially poignant statement.

Auden was invited to spend part of the summer of 1942 at The Maypole, the newly acquired Pennsylvania home of Caroline Newton. Probably wanting to avoid the boredom and embarrassment of being there alone with the infatuated Newton, he insisted that Kallman and the Sterns be invited there, too, and soon afterwards he wrote to James Stern, 'I would rather spend the summer with you and Tania than anyone'.[108] Kallman declined the holiday-offer, but the Sterns accepted. From late June to early August 1942, the Army Draft Board kept postponing Auden's call-up date and his sense of a drastic change looming over him, combined with the prospect of finishing work on 'For the Time Being'—which he did on 25 July 1942— apparently put him in a retrospective frame of mind. After James Stern left to attend a writers' conference in Colorado, Auden and Mrs Stern stayed on at Newton's estate, taking walks alone together, sharing jokes about their hostess, and sitting in the pool for hours telling each other their life stories.

Both the Sterns had observed that Auden had 'an amazing effect on women' and they were constantly watching with amusement as (usually rich) ladies fell in love with him—they remembered around six cases during his first eight years in the States.[109] Usually, these feelings were not reciprocated, but with Mrs Stern the situation seems to have been different. While they were marooned at Caroline Newton's stuffy bourgeois estate, feelings close to love developed between her and Auden. At the same time, Auden wrote long, relaxed

[106] Holograph notebook in use 1941–2 (Berg Collection), fo. 90. In the end Auden gave these words to Prospero, the disillusioned magician, for his speech 'Prospero to Ariel' in 'The Sea and the Mirror'. The imagery in the published version is less explicit: 'Beyond their busy backs I made a magic | To ride away from a father's imperfect justice' (*CP91* 405). Auden also worked some details into Herod's monologue, for example his description of the winter day, 'cold, brilliant, and utterly still, when the bark of the shepherd's dog carries for miles . . . and the mind feels intensely awake' (*CP91* 391) first occurs here in this Ur-Simeon speech.
[107] See Letter 4, p. 72. [108] See Letter 4, p. 74, and n. 11.
[109] See, for instance, Letter 8, n. 4.

letters to James Stern in Boulder City, working a vein of social comedy that is relatively rare in his correspondence.[110]

At the end of August, when the visit to Pennsylvania was over, Auden decided to stay in the Sterns' apartment on East 52nd Street in New York for a few days. He had finally been called-up and the Sterns had agreed to let him store some things with them. When he arrived, he simply threw a suitcase overflowing with manuscripts and old socks onto the floor. He soon returned, rejected, from his appointment with a military psychiatrist, and the Sterns remembered him saying that he had been asked if he had any girlfriends. By 1942 this was a stereotypically famous question, used by army recruiters who, in accordance with a newly codified set of military regulations, were trying to screen out gays. Auden, who would have known in advance that he was likely to be put in the position of having to lie in order to get into the Army, had replied: 'I have a lot of friends who are girls' and was excused service on the grounds of his homosexuality.[111]

Although Tania Stern had not wanted to leave Paris, at first both she and her husband greatly enjoyed New York, where they found themselves leading an energetic social life: in the circle of German emigrés and sympathizers involved with the magazine *Decision*, the Sterns were known to give 'fabulous parties'.[112] James Stern wrote relatively little fiction during the war, but he worked on a new edition of the Grimms' *Fairy Tales* and developed a reputation as a book reviewer for *The New York Times*, *Partisan Review*, and *The New*

---

[110] See Letters 5–7 below.

[111] Allan Bérubé, *Coming Out under Fire: The History of Gay Men and Women in World War Two* (New York, 1990) has a full account of the US Army's Second World War procedures for dealing with homosexuals. Bérubé points out that there had never been an official government policy for screening recruits to detect homosexuality until preparations for the US entry into this war began. The new anti-gay policy was widely publicized during 1941–2 and the military's techniques for spotting homosexuals were enthusiastically reported in news magazines. During 1942, the year Auden was called up, the Army's demand for men had increased enormously, but anti-homosexual screening by draft board doctors and psychiatrists was enforced even more vigilantly than it had been in 1941, although men with handicaps such as stuttering or marginal intelligence for which they would previously have been rejected were now being inducted (8). Bérubé's figures indicate that Auden was one of relatively few men to be rejected on the grounds of moral unfitness. Of the approximately 18 million American men summoned for service during wartime, only 4,000–5,000 (i.e. roughly 0.003%) were excluded for this reason. Most homosexuals apparently chose to lie about their sexual orientation (33).

[112] Virginia Spencer Carr, *The Lonely Hunter: A Biography of Carson McCullers* (Garden City, NY, 1975), 145.

Republic.[113] In around October 1942 he began to supplement his income by filling in as an art critic for *Time*, where he got to know the photographer Walker Evans, later the subject of another of his highly observant memoirs.[114]

The Sterns and Auden did not see as much of each other during 1943: both they and he spent a lot of their time out of New York, though he still was apt to drop in on them periodically for visits from Swarthmore.[115] However, even though they were separated, he still considered them among his closest friends and in February 1944 after he finished 'The Sea and the Mirror', which he thought was 'the best I've done so far',[116] he dedicated it to them both. It was the first time he had dedicated a work to a married couple, but he continued the practice with every collection from *Nones* (1951) to *About the House* (1965).[117] During roughly the same period, as if still haunted by the possibility, Auden also contemplated other marriages for himself.[118]

'[F]or some years now I've known that the one thing I really needed was marriage,' Auden had written to A. E. Dodds in July 1939, 'and I think I have enough experience to know that this relationship is going to be marriage with all its boredoms, troubles and rewards.'[119] During the brief period of this 'marriage' to Kallman, Auden became fascinated with the dynamics of other marriages too. Kierkegaard bolstered this interest, because for Kierkegaard a marriage is the supreme temporal expression of the eternal, the 'test case and center of ethical life'.[120] If anything, the failure of Auden's own

[113] Later on, he was responsible for some reviews that substantially raised the American reputations of important foreign authors, including Malcolm Lowry and Patrick White. In 1955, for instance, Stern wrote a long piece in *The New York Times* on White's *The Tree of Man* that proved to be the Australian's breakthrough in the US (see David Marr, *Patrick White: A Life* (New York, 1992), 303–5).

[114] 'Walker Evans (1903–75): A Memoir', *London Magazine*, NS 17.3 (Aug.–Sept. 1977), 5–29.

[115] *Hidden Damage*, 3.   [116] ALS to Elizabeth Mayer, 20 Apr. 1944 (Berg).

[117] *The Dance of Death* (London, 1933) is dedicated to Robert Medley and Rupert Doone, but this was because they had commissioned the work.

[118] In fact, his life was quite regularly complicated by possibilities of marriage of one sort or another—it was evidently a state he deeply desired for himself. In the 1920s, he proposed to Sheilah Richardson; in the 1930s he married Erika Mann; in the 1940s he declared himself married to Kallman; in the 1950s he proposed to Thekla Clark; and in the late 1960s he proposed to Hannah Arendt.

[119] ALS, [?July 1939], (Bodleian).

[120] James Collins, *The Mind of Kierkegaard* (Chicago, 1953), 76. Collins continues: 'The marriage vow is a sign that the ethical will can dominate chance and fate, and hence can liberate the individual from the confinements of esthetic existence' (77). Ideas like these underlie Auden's epithalamium for his vows to Kallman, 'In Sickness and In Health' (*CP91* 317–20).

bond with Kallman to persist in the way that he had wanted it to, only increased his fascination (just as Kierkegaard's wretched experiences during his engagement to Regine Olsen left him obsessed by matrimony afterwards). Granted a 'peep at Atlantis | In a poetic vision',[121] Auden probed intensively into other people's marriages, including those of the Sterns, the Stevenses in Ann Arbor, and the Mandelbaums at Swarthmore. Sometimes these unions were strained or tested under the raking power of his scrutiny. Perhaps partly because the Sterns survived his probing unscathed, no couple became more representative to him of the married state. In a letter written on 5 July 1944, a few months after finishing 'The Sea and the Mirror', he announced to James Stern that he had 'long cherished a secret wish to collaborate with you on a play about marriage, the *only* subject'.[122]

Auden stayed for much of the second half of the summer of 1944 in the Sterns' Manhattan apartment; they were vacationing in a rented shack called Bassetts Roost on Fire Island. While he was in the apartment, Auden got down to serious work on *The Age of Anxiety*, and in the process reduced his surroundings to a state of chaos. His chief concern, apart from the heat (he later called the first fortnight of August 1944 his 'hottest memory', and wrote: 'I had money, friends, an electric fan, a shower, a refrigerator. I lay in a stupor wishing I were dead'[123]), was the lack of ashtrays—his smoking was a constant source of friction with the Sterns—and he complained to the fastidious James Stern: 'My dear, I do love this apartment, but I can't understand why it doesn't have more *ash*trays!'[124] Stern recalled being terrified that one day Auden would set the house on fire.

---

[121] 'Atlantis', *CP91* 316.

[122] See Letter 10, p. 88, and n. 11. The phrase about marriage alludes to 'The Sea and the Mirror', finished shortly before. There Caliban refers to 'the only subject' in two different senses during the course of his monologue (just as Auden's camp italicization in this letter draws out a third): first it describes the artist's discovery of his own Caliban Nature, the ego's relationship to its own embodiment, 'the only subject that you have' (*CP91* 433). Second, it describes the absolute ontological loneliness resulting from the wish to recover the peace of unfallen flesh: the hell of unending repetition and infinite passivity where you are, as 'you have asked to be, the only subject' (*CP91* 439). Cf. also 'The Self-So which is the same at all times, | That Always-Opposite which is the whole subject | Of our not-knowing' in *The Age of Anxiety* (*CP91* 535). In 1963 Auden told the Sterns that had they not already been the dedicatees of 'The Sea and the Mirror', he would like to have dedicated 'The Cave of Nakedness', the bedroom poem in the 'Thanksgiving for a Habitat' cycle, to them (ALS, 1 July [1963]).

[123] 'I Like It Cold', *House and Garden*, 92.6 (Dec. 1947), 110.   [124] *Tribute*, 124.

Auden went back to Swarthmore in the autumn of 1944, but he saw the Sterns on and off throughout the autumn and winter, whenever he was up in New York. The three of them began a half-hearted collaboration on a translation of Brecht's *The Caucasian Chalk Circle*,[125] and in November 1944 Auden published as *The New York Times Book Review*'s leading article a laudatory piece on James Stern's revision of the translation of the Grimms' *Fairy Tales*.[126] At the end of the year, when Tania Stern and Caroline Newton got into a fight about payment for some lessons that Newton had been taking, Auden unhesitatingly took Mrs Stern's side and eventually, as they also did, he broke off his friendship with Newton—probably he was glad to be able to do so.[127]

On 5 March 1945 he arrived for one of his visits from Swarthmore at their Manhattan apartment and announced that he was applying to go to Germany on a mysteriously defined government survey.[128] He described what he thought his mission would be and when Stern asked whether he might be able to come too, Auden was surprised but encouraged him to apply.[129] Before they left the country, they had decided that they would collaborate on a book about their trip and they signed a contract with Harcourt, Brace, agreeing to a $3,000 advance.

Auden left for Europe at the end of April and Stern joined him in Germany at the end of May or the beginning of June. For nearly three months they lived and worked in extremely close confines in the ruins of large German cities, charged with interviewing civilians to ascertain the effects of Allied bombing on their morale. Both hated the official rationale for the work, but they found the conversations they had with Germans absorbing. Stern remembered only two moments of tension: one when Stern, who prided himself on his skills

---

[125] Brecht himself was unhelpful, but work seems to have continued intermittently until early 1946, when the translation was put aside. (Act 5 was published in *Kenyon Review*, 8.2 (Spring 1946), 188–202.) Then, in the autumn of 1959, at the prompting of Stefan Brecht, the translation was revised by Auden and the Sterns—in a letter to them, Auden described it as 'terrifying when a fifteen year old corpse which one has completely forgotten suddenly comes out of its grave', TLS, 13 Oct. [1959]. This version was published in vol. 1 of the Methuen edition of Brecht's *Plays* (London, 1960), 3–96.

[126] 'In Praise of the Brothers Grimm', *The New York Times*, 12 Nov. 1944, sect. 7, pp. 1, 28. There are several mentions of Grimm in Auden's writings of 1941–3 (e.g. in his poem-letter to Kallman of Christmas 1941 and in his 1943 Swarthmore Phi Beta Kappa lecture, 'Vocation and Society': see pp. 15–30 of this volume).

[127] See Letter 13, n. 2.   [128] See Letter 14, n. 2 for more details.

[129] *Hidden Damage*, 3–4.

behind the wheel, became exasperated by Auden's erratic driving, and took control of their jeep without asking Auden's permission; and another when, typing up an interview very early one morning, he interrupted Auden at his prayers.[130] Ultimately, though, as was the case with his experiences in Spain, what shocked Auden profoundly also tended to silence him.[131] He never showed any inclination to begin work on the book that he and Stern were supposed to write, nor even, after he returned to the States, to speak about what he had seen. At his agent's suggestion, Stern wrote *The Hidden Damage* alone.

The time that Auden and Stern spent together in Germany was their period of closest fellowship, an experience intensified by the horror of what they saw and by their shared frustration over the US Army's bureaucratic and ornately statistical procedures. One odd feature of *The Hidden Damage*, then, is the relatively unfocused portrait that it gives of Auden—a particular surprise because Stern's comic eye must have relished the irony of seeing the man who had enjoyed playing the role of father to him in the previous few years suddenly appearing in a Major's uniform.[132] The narrative makes it clear that Auden is a commanding figure, the civilian leader of the interviewing unit to which Stern has attached himself, a person who arranges and disposes. But, like almost all of Stern's colleagues in the book, he is a rather blurred presence.

There is a symbolic aptness to this, a way in which it was right that Auden should not fit easily into the book, because, just as the whole bombing survey itself was reminiscent of a piece of Thirties Mass Observation, so *The Hidden Damage*, filled as it is with scrupulous circumstantial descriptions and supporting documentation, reads like a late, archaic product of Thirties literary interests and methods. By this time, of course, Auden had long outgrown these concerns.[133] Everything in the anecdotal, episodic narrative in *The Hidden Damage* is coloured by Stern's self-conscious observation of his own reactions.

---

[130] *Tribute*, 127. [131] See Letter 14, n. 7.

[132] Called 'Mervyn' in the book. There is no record of what Auden thought about *The Hidden Damage*: in a letter to Stern thanking him for a copy, he avoided making any judgement about the book (ALS, 16 May [1947]).

[133] Presumably another reason why Auden became disinclined to work on the book. In 1931–2 Stern had visited, and written about, miners in South Wales and Derbyshire, in a piece of conscientious documentary prose published in Lehmann's *New Writing* (1931), repr. as 'A Stranger Among Miners', in Stern, *Stories*, 64–72. Its inclusion in a volume of stories suggests the ambiguous division between fiction and autobiography in Stern's work.

In contrast to the pseudo-objective, pseudo-scientific prose required by the Army, his memories and personal concerns claim equal prominence with the factual record of what he has seen. The effect can be rather confining: companions—not least 'Mervyn'—are peripheral, fading in and out of the story, like images of swimmers seen underwater. But, the haziness suggests one of the underlying reasons why the project seemed important enough to Stern that he pressed on and wrote the book without Auden.

As the journey from the United States back to Europe unfolds with a ramble round Stern's old pre-war Parisian haunts, a stop-off to visit his parents in their house in Somerset (one of the best set-pieces in the book is Stern's embarrassed dialogue with his parents' butler[134]), followed by a tour in memory through the Frankfurt underworld which he had frequented while he worked in the city as a bank clerk, it becomes clear that the book is a kind of Dantesque inner journey. Projected on to the map of Europe, *The Hidden Damage* is Stern's *Inferno*, an odyssey of self-discovery, a confrontation with the past and its transfiguration in the present. The outer wreckage of the landscape is counterpointed by a much more devastating sense of interior ruin, and Stern comments on a frequent sense of kinship with the defeated Germans. The theme of a country's inner devastation is one in which Stern must have heard clear echoes of his own life-story. Parts of the book are almost stiflingly sad, like the description of the afternoon that Auden and Stern spent with the parents of a young student who had been beheaded for taking part in the 20 July plot against Hitler.[135] (Auden also mentioned this interview in several letters to friends.) By the end, the experience has left Stern with a burden of knowledge that he fears might be almost unspeakable:

I tried to rehearse an imaginary conversation about the continent of Europe with my wife and friends, but I didn't know how to begin . . . I knew then that the conversation would prove futile, for I realized as never before that between those who have seen and those who haven't, there is a gulf fixed which the spoken word cannot bridge.[136]

It is a gloomy, heartfelt paragraph, and perhaps, with its suggestions of a lack of literary confidence, one shadowed with fears about his declining powers of creativity. The book as a whole marks a triumph of human empathy and attention over the literary demands of shaping and invention.

[134] *Hidden Damage*, 59–60.   [135] Ibid. 168–77.   [136] Ibid. 372.

The Sterns continued to see much of Auden after he and James Stern had returned from Germany. While the pair were away, Mrs Stern had bought the tar-paper shack on Fire Island where she and her husband had spent the previous summer. When Auden saw it, he asked if he could buy a share in the property, and this was agreed. (The hut was renamed Bective Poplars after Stern's family home in Ireland and Auden's grandmother's house, The Poplars, at Horning-low, near Repton.[137] The redeployment of a word from James Stern's miserable infancy was probably a signal of a half-acknowledged readiness to return home.) In the years until he left for his first summer in Europe in 1948, Bective Poplars, where the Sterns and Auden usually alternated in residence, was to be Auden's summer base.

But, in the aftermath of the war, and perhaps in reaction to what they had seen in Germany, both Auden and Stern were simultaneously reaching the end of a phase in their lives and careers. Perhaps this process happened independently for each of them, but, so familial had their relationship become, perhaps there was also an element of mutual influence. After the existential subjectivity of his early years in the States, his conversion to Christianity, and the struggle to adjust to the drastic curtailment of his relationship with Kallman, Auden's work was again beginning to move outwards towards the secular world of history and nature. Over the course of the next few years, he abandoned his plans for a fifth long poem, 'Underground Life', experimented with a heterosexual affair, and began *The Rake's Progress* with Stravinsky. In 1948 he spent the summer in Europe and in 1949 he told Rhoda Jaffe that his life with Kallman was really happy for the first time.[138]

After almost a decade in the United States, the Sterns too began to yearn for a change. As James Stern wrestled with his commitment to fiction, he seems to have become reconciled with much that had been painful in his sense of himself and his origins. The Sterns travelled back and forth to Europe several times in the late 1940s. Then, early in the 1950s, they decided to spend a trial two years in England.[139] After moving around the southern half of the country for some years, they finally settled near Salisbury, and in 1961 they moved into Hatch Manor, a small, Tudor manor-house in a labyrinth of sunken country lanes in Wiltshire's Nadder Valley.

[137] See 'Letter to Lord Byron', *EA* 175, for Auden's memories of travelling to 'The Poplars'.
[138] ALS from Ischia, 17 May [1949], (Berg).   [139] See Letter 15, p. 98 below.

They did not lose touch with Auden though. They kept up a regular, but lighter and breezier, correspondence with him, and saw him frequently on his annual visits to England. After settling in Wiltshire, the Sterns translated many books by major German language authors including Erich Maria Remarque, Thomas Mann, Freud, Kafka, Stefan Zweig, and Hoffmannsthal. In addition, James Stern wrote a few more stories, most of which are still uncollected. In 1968 when a selection of his best work appeared, Auden, ever practical and therapeutic, wrote to him urging him to begin an autobiography: 'Some people, like myself, have an uninteresting family background and, from a reader's point of view, an uninteresting life . . . In your case both are of the utmost interest. I implore you, therefore, to write what I know will be a document of the greatest historical and, because of your talent, the greatest literary value.'[140] Stern tried to act on his old friend's advice and, from around 1970 until his death, he worked intermittently on a book called *The Golden Spoon: Memories of Childhood and Youth*, a few fragments of which have appeared in literary magazines.[141]

Like Stern, Auden himself was struggling with resistances and compulsions at the end of his life. For all that he warned in his writings against the dangers of Manicheanism and a Gnostic hatred of the outer world, he found himself appalled by a society full of 'lasers, electric brains, | do-it-yourself sex manuals, | bugged phones, sophisticated | weapon-systems and sick jokes'.[142] In the late 1960s he spontaneously confessed to someone with whom he had struck up a conversation on a transatlantic flight: 'In our urbanized industrial society, nearly everything we see and hear is so aggressively ugly. Unless I can flee to the depths of the country and never open a newspaper, my imagination may very well take on a demonic cast and I shall ever feel that the physical world is utterly profane and shall be haunted by images of physical disgust.'[143] The final chapter of his friendship with the Sterns occurred during a frame of mind very much like this.

Auden had had a miserable Michaelmas term at Oxford in the autumn of 1972: the traffic in the city shocked him, he was robbed,

---

[140] See Letter 19, p. 104 below.
[141] See n. 14 above.
[142] 'Prologue at Sixty', *CP91* 831.
[143] A. H. Barken, 'Ageing, Anxiety & Auden', *Oxford Today*, 5.3 (Trinity Issue, 1993), 31.

he felt lonely, and he suspected that most of his Christ Church colleagues were unsympathetic to him. In November he unexpectedly
wrote to the Sterns, asking if he could come and stay with them at
Christmas.[144] For the holiday he joined Sonia Orwell (who had
already been invited) in London and they travelled down to Wiltshire
together.[145] Tania Stern remembered feeling that the letter he sent
them was 'immensely touching'.

Once he was there, as he had done when he first met them in Paris in
1937, Auden seemed to keep himself a little outside the group. Now,
whereas Stern had virtually exhausted his creative impulses but had
returned, happily, to his roots and a comfortable obscurity, Auden, a
displaced, cosmopolitan, internationally-famous poet, had almost completely absorbed himself into his artistic persona—to the detriment of his
social existence. Pleased by the heavy fog spread over the countryside,
for most of the time he sat by the fire, reading, wrapped in a blanket of
self-contemplation, or engrossed in his favourite pseudo-poetic pastime
of filling in crosswords, this time in *The Daily Telegraph*. He drank
heavily and one morning Mrs Stern found him alone in the sitting-room
totting up the number of his own works on the shelves. (Stephen
Spender remembered Auden late in his life doing something similar at
his home.[146]) She felt the sight was remarkable because they had never
before known him to show the slightest concern or pride over the
amassed bulk of his writing. It seemed clear to the Sterns that he was
deeply unhappy and that he was reluctant to leave them. Eventually he
did so, but only because he had to return to Oxford to give evidence at
the trial of the man accused of stealing from him.[147]

'Last Christmas was the first I'd spent in England since 1937',
Auden explained to Orlan Fox from Kirchstetten at the end of May
1973.[148] The same month he wrote 'Thank You, Fog', the poem that
celebrates his visit to the Sterns. It was his first work for many years to
be set in an English landscape and its alliterative reverberations evoke,
like something distant and half-remembered, the world of his earliest
writing. In its fastidious diction and details, the poem eulogizes the
Christmas holiday, the Wordsworthian 'glad circle'[149] in the Sterns'

[144] See Letter 21, p. 106 below.   [145] See Letter 22, n. 1.
[146] Quoted in Robert Robinson, 'The Auden Landscape', *The Listener*, 4 Mar. 1982,
p. 11.
[147] See Letter 22, n. 3 below.   [148] ALS, 30 May [1973], (Berg).
[149] It is, more exclusively and more crampingly, a 'close circle' in the early version
that Auden sent the Sterns. See Letter 23, p. 108. The 'glad circle' perhaps alludes to
the 'festive circle' at Cambridge in *The Prelude* 3.302 (in the 1850 version, the one

house, and the spell of stillness and arrested movement outside.[150] The tone is as muted as that of 'A Summer Night'—Auden's other great poem about guilty, private happiness in the English countryside—is buoyant. 'Thank You, Fog', with its parallel movement from the private world to the public and back to the private, reads as a wintry companion piece to the earlier poem. It is an eerie work, half-in and half-out of time, steeped in, but almost impatient with, the world of poetry; memories of the stay are condensed on the bare lines with an almost ghostly lack of ego, just as, in a beautiful figure for the poem's method, the tree-branches condense the fog's vapour into clear drops.

When Auden posted the Sterns a typescript of the poem he included no explanations or news about himself with it, but merely sent love and signed his name at the bottom of the page as if he felt that, in spite of this reticence, he were ending a letter to them.[151] (This was something he often did, particularly at the start and the finish of his career, as if he had put all he could say into his poetry.) When he sent off the poem to his friends, Auden was already as far from the Christmas fog in Wiltshire as he was near to his death in a Vienna hotel room on 29 September 1973. The next time that the Sterns heard anything about him, it was from the newspapers.

A Note on the Text of the Letters and on Annotations

The main literary relics of the 36-year friendship between Auden and the Sterns are a cache of 132 letters, eight postcards, and three telegrams from Auden.[152] After Mr Stern's death, this correspondence was donated to the Berg Collection of the New York Public Library. I have included here only some of the items of special liter-

Auden, at least late in life, claimed to prefer, see 'Remembering and Forgetting—W. H. Auden Talks to Richard Crossman about Poetry', *The Listener*, 89.2291 (22 Feb. 1973), 239).

[150] For some dissatisfied but radiantly intelligent comments on the language of this poem, see Seamus Heaney, 'Sounding Auden', *The Government of the Tongue: Selected Prose 1978–1987* (New York, 1989), 124.

[151] See Letter 23, pp. 107–9.

[152] 57 of the letters are addressed to James Stern, 20 to Tania Stern, 55 to both of them; three of the postcards are to James Stern, three to Mrs Stern, and two are to both of them; two telegrams are to him and one is to her. These items have been carefully preserved by the Sterns and many are still paired with their original envelopes. Auden threw out almost everything he got in the post, and this is a particular cause for regret in the case of James Stern because, free with the gifts of his writer's eye and ear, Mr Stern was famous amongst friends for his brilliantly rueful and witty epistles. However, like the absorbed homebody of the 'A shilling life' sonnet, Auden 'answered some | Of his long marvellous letters but kept none' (*EA* 150).

ary or biographical interest; I did so with the awareness that this small number of letters could never convey all the ramifications of an involved, often complex relationship.

Each letter is numbered here and, with varying degrees of certainty, given a date of composition. (Auden's dating is always accepted unless there is strong evidence to suggest that it is wrong.) Auden did not of course write these letters for publication and I have tried to retain as much of their original unpolished, informal texture as possible: I have not corrected spelling unless a word is unpronounceable as it stands (no editorial '[sic]'s are added either) and I have only emended the punctuation in the very few cases where leaving things as they were would, in my judgement, have caused needless confusion and aggravation for the reader. My additional punctuation points are enclosed in square brackets.

Auden's underlinings are rendered as italics except in the case of the line that he sometimes added under his signature—this has been omitted—and double underlines, which become underlined italics. Interlineations have been dropped into the text, deletions are not reproduced (none are of any substantive significance), lay-outs of addresses and valedictions have been standardized. Apart from a few instances where Auden actively sought out the left-hand margin for an address, these have also been uniformly placed on the right side of the page. Auden's habitual double quotation marks (" ") have been pared to single ones in line with the style used elsewhere in this book. At the foot of each letter, I describe its physical form (ALS, etc.), and transcribe the address and postmark on the envelope, if one exists.

In the annotations, I have tried to avoid simply repeating material from standard biographical sources like Carpenter, Farnan, and Miller. At the start of each letter—and wherever else appropriate—I supply references to passages in those works where the reader can locate the broad context of people and events into which the letter fits. The other information I give in the notes is mostly either not present in these books, is garbled there, or is present only in a vaguer form. In one or two cases—for example, in those notes about Auden's friends in the early 1940s, about the USSBS, and about the 'Œuvres du XXᵉ Siècle' conference in Paris in May 1952, which are not well covered in earlier publications—I have tried to put into print as much useful detail as is feasible.

Letters

1. *[?6–8 November 1941][1]*

1223 Pontiac Street | Ann Arbor | Michigan.

Dearest Jimmy and Tania,

Thanks ever so for your lovely long letters. Caroline Newton, as I dare say you've heard by now, had to have an emergency hystorectomy.[2] She is now back at home and I'm sure would like to see you.

[1] See Carpenter, 318–21; Farnan, 67–74; Miller, 53–5.

[2] The hysterectomy was apparently performed in early Oct. 1941. Caroline Newton (1893–1975), a rich psychiatrist and *saloneuse*, was one of Thomas Mann's earliest and staunchest friends in the US, lending him her summer house at Jamestown, Rhode Island, when he arrived in the country in 1938, and later undertaking to write a biography of him for Random House. (It was abandoned.) Mann used her as the model for Leverkühn's blushing admirer Meta Nackedei in *Doktor Faustus* (1947).

She was the daughter of the wealthy bibliophile and Johnsonian, A. E. Newton, and she had homes in Jamestown, in Manhattan, and, from 1942 onwards, in Berwyn, Pennsylvania. Her relationship with her father had been particularly troubled and she was analysed for a while by the New York physician Leonhard Blumgart and then, briefly, in 1921, by Freud in Vienna. She published translations of, amongst other things, Ferenczi and Rank's *The Development of Psychoanalysis* (New York and Washington, 1925) and Jakob Wassermann's *Caspar Hauser* (New York, 1928). In 1925 she applied to be admitted as a member of the New York Psychoanalytic Society, becoming a test case in the dispute between Freud and his American followers about whether lay analysts (like her) should be allowed to have practices. Despite Freud's protests, her membership request was denied, and even her guest privileges were withdrawn. (See Peter Gay, *Freud: A Life for Our Time* (New York, 1988), 498 and n. 499, 717–18.) Newton was later in analysis with Karen Horney in New York, and eventually she managed to set up her own practice, associated with Manhattan's Bellevue Hospital.

In the spring of 1940, probably through the Manns, Newton met Auden, and she soon appointed herself a kind of patroness to him. Before long, she also became heavily infatuated. She asked Auden to translate Goethe's poem 'Durch allen Schall und Klang' for her (published in her 'Goethe's "Reich"', a letter to *The Saturday Review of Literature*, 22.21 (14 Sept. 1940), 9) and lured him into giving her private tutoring about books and opera. Later he wrote out in longhand an extensive compilation of his favourite passages of poetry and prose. (He also gave her some old notebooks and ledgers, now in the Berg.) In return she showered him with badly-needed money and expensive presents—see Letter 13, n. 2 below. Newton's fussy, neurotic behaviour soon made her the butt of jokes between Auden and the Sterns. In the typescript draft of his memoir *Auden: An American Friendship* (New York, 1983) (now in the Berg, it is referred to hereafter as 'Miller (draft)', the published version as 'Miller'), Charles H. Miller described her during a December 1941 visit to Ann Arbor as 'short, plump, and round-faced with lots of loose brown hair, greying. Despite her furs and expensive clothing she managed to look dishevelled . . . blinking behind her glasses' (200). (For more on Miller, see Letter 2, n. 6 below.) See also Letter 6, n. 5.

(Did I tell you she sent me a cheque for my car? A 1939 Pontiac which I feel very guilty owning as I have always divided the human race into the Car-Haves and the Car-Have-Nots, and been proud to belong to the latter.).[3]

Had a letter from Chester the other day who wants to go to a secretarial school.[4] Perhaps you will scold me for agreeing to pay for it, but even if it [is] wrong to do so, I dont see how I've the right to say so, seeing as I was kept by my parents till I was 22. He sounds fairly cheerful and I think is learning things about himself.[5] I was very interested in what you (Tania) said about the effect of spinal curvatures on people.[6] I've never known any before, and his seemed to me so unimportant that I never could take it seriously, but then I suppose everyone thinks like I that they are the only one who has any defects to really complain about to Fate. He has, I think, so many wonderful qualities that it will be an awful shame if nothing comes of them, and I shall have much to answer for. But that's enough of that, I love him to distraction and cant help boring my friends about him.

Life here is a pretty settled routine now. My chief worry is gossip

[3] Miller (25–6) says that Newton sent Auden a cheque for $750 for a car, one of several large gifts around this time. Around the end of Sept. 1941 he used the money to buy the green Pontiac coupe that he drove in Michigan. Despite what Auden says here, he had already owned at least two cars, though it is possible that both were given to him rather than purchased. In Oxford during the 1926 Michaelmas term, he had his brother John's old car, a D'Yrsan, left behind when John went to India earlier in the year (see ALS from Lordswood Road, Birmingham, to John Auden [Christmas vacation 1926–7?]). He also owned a Morris-Cowley for at least part of the time when he was teaching at the Downs School from 1932–5 (see 'In Search of Dracula', *AS2* 21; Carpenter, 160; and a 7 Sept. [1933] letter from Spender to Isherwood printed in Spender's *Letters to Christopher*, ed. Lee Bartlett (Santa Barbara, Calif., 1980), 63).

[4] Kallman was in Hollywood from early Oct. 1941, trying, as Auden explained to Harold Norse, 'to find his life' (ALS, 1 Nov. 1941, Norse Mss. (Lilly)). He intended to be there eight weeks but stayed on until after Christmas (see Letter 2, n. 2 below). In the letter which Auden refers to (ALS, 3 Nov. [postmarked 4 Nov. 1941], (Berg)), Kallman says that the exotic and dissolute Denham Fouts, a friend of Isherwood (and the model for 'Paul' in *Down There on a Visit*), had told him about a 'short, efficient, and job-promising secretarial course'. Kallman started the month-long course, which cost $30, around 24 Nov. 1941, but he seems not to have completed it because by 8 Dec. he was working in a Hollywood bookshop (see Letter 2, and also ALS to Caroline Newton, [11 Nov. 1941], (Berg)).

[5] In the 3 Nov. [1941] letter, Kallman told Auden, who was sending him a small stipend, that he had been 'very poor the past few weeks through little extravagances like movies, a few good meals . . . and, I must confess, some liquor. But I feel clearer now and am beginning to visualize a gestalt in which desire and ability are closer than they were.'

[6] Tania Stern had detected the early stages of scoliosis in Kallman (see Carpenter, 316; Farnan, 92).

which means that every time I ask anyone in pants to the house, they are either hoping or dreading that I shall make a pass at them.[7]

My brightest student, who I asked in for a nice intellectual evening, took my playing of a Marlene Dietrich record as a proposal and was promptly sick. I had to give him a long lecture on his lack of intellectual self-confidence and his excess of physical vanity before I could reassure him.[8]

I am correcting the first batch of papers written by my class. O dear. O dear. Most of them appear to have been taught to regard an essay as a vehicle for self expression[.] Next Thursday I shall be like Mr Norris' friend, 'a very *severe* young lady.'[9]

I hope you can persuade C to stay here. If he really *is* thinking of going. Lincoln is the most unreliable informant in the world[.][10]

Ann Arbor is going to have a shock next week as Erika is coming to stay the night.[11]

Much love,
Wystan.

ALS (Fountain Pen).

[7] Auden was telling others besides the Sterns about this fear. In his 3 Nov. [1941] letter, Kallman wrote: 'Furious and sorry to hear about the gossip at Michigan, but that, I suppose, is university life.' See also Miller, 49.

[8] The student was Robert Hemenway and the reassuring talk apparently took place later in Angell Hall on campus (see Miller, 48–9 for details).

[9] In Isherwood's *Mr. Norris Changes Trains* (London, 1935) Norris exclaims to the flagellant prostitute Anni: 'Oh dear, I'm afraid you're in a very *cruel* mood, this evening! I see I shall be *corrected* for this. Anni is an exceedingly *severe* young lady' (47). Miller, 44–5, records Auden's comments on students' papers.

[10] I have not been able to identify 'C' with any certainty. It may be Isherwood (sometimes called 'C' by Auden in letters), who since Oct. 1941 had been at the Co-operative College Workshop in Haverford, Pennsylvania, teaching English to German refugees and helping them adapt to their new circumstances (Finney, 181). But Auden used 'C' in other contexts to refer to different people (including Kallman, and, see Letter 5, Caroline Newton, though clearly she is not the male 'C' alluded to here). Lincoln Kirstein (b. 1907), impresario, dance scholar, poet, and critic, was one of Auden's earliest friends in the US. He knew Isherwood well.

[11] Erika Mann probably arrived in Ann Arbor on 14 Nov. 1941. She came to tea and stayed to supper with Auden and Miller that day, but she slept at the Women's League on campus. The following day she lectured to the Ann Arbor Union of Women in the Lydia Mendelssohn Theatre. There was a reception afterwards at the Michigan League which Auden attended. (See 'Erika Mann Speaks to Women's Group on Youth's Future', *Michigan Daily*, 16 Nov. 1941, p. 3; Miller (draft), 165; Miller, 54–5.)

2. [?19] December [1941][1]

Dec 18th.   1223 Pontiac Street | Ann Arbor | Michigan
8.15.am.

Dearest Jimmy and Tania,

Just time to drop you a Christmas line before packing and distributing the leavings of the Ice-box to neighbours. I leave at noon for Hollywood, where, by the by, Chester has got a job in a book-shop.[2]

Jimmy's gossipy letter was a great joy. I do hope the torments of ill-natured gland have abated. Of course it's psychological, but the English are no worse at sex than anyone else. I have preached all over about the Kurella Method,[3] and there are several potential converts already.

Jimmy, if you start saying again that you cant write, I shall come to New York, disguised as your father, and beat you.

For next semester (starting Feb 12th) I have an even larger and more modern house than this.[4] I shall have a couple of P.G.'s (I suspect romantically that they are a *pair*), a blonde secretary,[5] and my

---

[1] See Carpenter, 320–1.

[2] Auden travelled to California, probably by train, to see Kallman and Isherwood. His visit was apparently not particularly happy—there were difficulties in his relationship with Kallman and tensions with members of the Mann family (Carpenter, 321), though in a letter of 10 Jan. 1942 to Caroline Newton, Thomas Mann himself described Auden as 'boyish und nett wie immer' (Thomas Mann, *Briefe 1937–1947*, ed. Erika Mann (Frankfurt am Main, 1963), 231). Auden came back to Ann Arbor with Kallman, arriving *ca.* 6 Jan. 1942. The next day they celebrated Kallman's 21st birthday together (see ALS to Caroline Newton, 10 Jan. 1942 (Berg); Carpenter (321) mistakenly says Kallman spent his birthday in New York), and then on 8 Jan. Kallman left for the East Coast to see his lover, Jack Barker. (See also Introduction, p. 51 and n. 96.)

[3] i.e. Tania Stern's therapeutic techniques.

[4] 1223 Pontiac Trail was 'an ultramodern affair of wood slats' designed and built by Jean-Paul Slusser, a professor in the School of Architecture. Slusser, who was supposed to be away on sabbatical for the whole 1941–2 university year, rented it to Auden (Farnan, 72). However, after Pearl Harbor he decided to cut short his trip and return home, and he wrote to tell Auden he would need his house back on 1 Feb. 1942. (Auden and Slusser remained friendly after Auden moved out.) The still newer house that Auden mentions here was probably 517 Oxford Avenue, the address to which he told Elizabeth Mayer he would be moving *ca.* 7 Feb. 1942 (ALS, [postmarked 14 Jan. 1942], (Berg)). In the end, he became the tenant of 1504 Brooklyn Avenue, a neat Victorian edifice belonging to Thomas A. Knott, editor of Webster's *New International Dictionary*. For descriptions of 1504 Brooklyn Avenue, see Farnan, 77–8 and Miller, 68–9.

[5] Probably the person called 'Peter Hansen' in Farnan (68, and *passim*).

indispensable Jeeves, Charlie Miller who I've told to look you up in New York this Christmas.[6] You really *must* come then.

Caroline's visit went off very well after an incident at the beginning which was so embarassing I cant write it down. (see Matthew XIV, and John XIII, and guess).[7]

Story

[*Scene.* A corridor in the English Lit building. The professor of Elizabethan Lit meets the Head of the Middle English Dictionary.]

First Prof: 'I dont like to say anything malicious about another human being, but I hear Auden is a Platonist.'[8]

Much love
Wystan.

ALS (Fountain Pen) + envelope addressed to 'Mr James Stern | 207. E. 52nd Street | N. Y. C.', postmark 'ANN ARBOR MICH. DEC 19 11 AM 1941'.

---

[6] Charles H. Miller (1913–92) (see Letter 1, n. 2 above). Miller did not move into the new house with Auden, but instead went to work on a farm as a pacifist contribution to the war effort (Miller, 67; see also my 'Charles H. Miller', *ASN*, 9 (Aug. 1992), 14). Caroline Newton lent Miller her Manhattan apartment for the Christmas 1941 holiday. Soon after he got to New York, Tania Stern phoned and invited him to a cocktail party at their apartment where Miller met several of Auden's acquaintances, including George Davis, Jack Barker, and Jean Connolly (see Miller (draft), 230–1; Miller, 64–5).

[7] Caroline Newton came to stay with Auden and Miller at 1223 Pontiac Trail from *ca.* 1 to 10 Dec. 1941 (see Miller, 59–65)—a fraught and sometimes embarrassing visit which included her presence in the front row at one of Auden's classes and a lavish surprise dinner with sirloin and old brandy that she laid on for him with Miller's help. During the stay Auden frequently had to ignore or turn aside her gushy remarks. She also persuaded him to let her publish a Christmas greetings pamphlet-version of the poem 'Three Songs for St. Cecilia's Day', which appeared in *Harper's Bazaar* while she was staying in Ann Arbor (*Bibliography*, 49–50, 194). The 'incident' that Auden is alluding to remains obscure, but the two chapters in the Gospels have in common themes of discipleship, feasting, and betrayal.

[8] The English Department at Ann Arbor was housed on the second and third floors of Angell Hall (see Mendelson's description in *Libretti*, 423). Two members of the faculty taught Elizabethan Literature at the time: Warner G. Rice and Hereward Price. The head of the *Middle English Dictionary* was Hans Kurath (d. 1992).

3. [28 January 1942][1]

Wednesday   1223 Pontiac Street | Ann Arbor | Michigan

P. S. Next week, my address will become 1504 Brooklyn Avenue.[2]

Dearest Tania,

It was grand to get your letter. I agree with evry word of it and, as you say, if anyone comes badly out of the relationship, it will be Chester, not me.

All I can say is this.

Perhaps I have too much of the English Middle Class feeling about Education. That is to say I believe that, at least for a person with Chester's intellectual gifts, the young have a right to the best academic training that one can afford and that the theory of education by contact with REAL LIFE, i.e. a job in an office or hotel or something is, in most cases, unsound. (I think you may be one of the exceptions)

If I had the money I would send him to Harvard, but I havent.[3] As it is, he has a good chance here of winning the Hopwood Prize which would give him a year's financial independance and a literary start.[4] I expect to be out of here after this semester, so that it wont be long before his discipline is entirely from strangers. I think that he really does want to work, and at least this place is so dull that there isnt much else one can do.[5]

[1] See Carpenter, 314–15; Farnan, 59, 67–8, 75–80; Miller, 68–77.

[2] See Letter 2, n. 4.

[3] At least as early as the spring of 1941 Kallman had decided that after graduation from Brooklyn College, he would spend a year at the University of Michigan (see ALS from Auden to Isherwood, [?Jan.–Feb. 1941]). This plan may have been shelved after the 'Crisis' in Auden and Kallman's relationship in the summer of 1941 (Carpenter, 311–13). Kallman graduated in the Fall term of 1941 and went off to Hollywood (see Letter 1, n. 4 above). But around Christmas 1941, he decided that, with Auden's encouragement and financial support, he would go to Ann Arbor after all for the Spring semester of 1942 and start working for an MA (see ALS from Auden to Caroline Newton, 10 Jan. 1942 (Berg)).

[4] The University of Michigan's annual Hopwood Awards, administered by Professor Roy Cowden of the English Department, had been judged by Auden in the spring of 1941, when he had wanted to award one of the poetry prizes to Charles Miller (Miller, 6). The awards, 'Major' for graduate students, 'Minor' for undergraduates, were first made in 1931. They were financed by a bequest from the playwright Avery Hopwood to encourage creative writing. In 1941–2 the Major Awards, for which Kallman could have competed while studying for his MA, ran from $400–$750. However, Kallman quickly made Cowden one of his *bêtes noires* at the University and, as a result, never submitted a manuscript (Farnan, 83).

[5] Auden left Ann Arbor *ca.* 1 June 1942. Kallman stayed on and seems to have been awarded his MA at the end of Jan. 1943. Auden returned for the ceremony; afterwards,

The trouble about this country is that the only discipline that people get from outside is of the most purely formal and negative type—clocking in, speeding up, etc. Anything important is in consequence shoved onto people like me in relationships which are too subjective to manage it without dangerous distortion.

Much love
Wystan

TL + envelope addressed to 'Mrs Tania Stern (Kurella) | 9. E. 59th Street | N. Y. C.', postmark 'ANN ARBOR MICH. JAN 30 1 PM 1942'.

4. [?25 April 1942][1]

Saturday   1504 Brooklyn Avenue | Ann Arbor | Michigan

Dearest Jimmy,

A *great* joy to get one of your famous letters. Of all the people I know, you are almost the only surviving letter-writer. Even Christopher[2] has fallen out.

I wish there was anything for me to say that I could believe would be of any help. For instance though I know it to be true that it doesnt matter a fuck, except financially, whether you or I or anyone else write another line unless we want to, it is pompous rubbish for *me* to say so to *you*, because my problem is the opposite one,—unless I write something, anything, good, indifferent, or trashy, every day, I feel ill.

To me, the only good reason for writing is to try to organise my scattered moments of living into a whole, to relate everything to everything else. All the other reasons I have are vanity, and the wish to escape *doing* anything about my life, by *looking* at it instead,—the sensual ease of je me comprends, je me regrette, je me pardonne. As long as the looking leads to real changes, and thank God in a feeble shabby way I think it sometimes does, writing is not only a pleasure but a good pleasure.

If I read your stories right, they have been your catharsis of your childhood, and that particular task is almost or quite over; so you feel stuck because the amount of resolution that writing can do is very

Kallman probably remained in Ann Arbor for a couple of months. By April 1943 he was back in New York with a job as a publicist for Victor Records.

[1] See Carpenter, 321–2; Farnan, 75–80; Miller, 68–77.   [2] Isherwood.

limited and in your case the residue of *ressentiment*[3] is still too great for you to look at your later experiences with the necessary combination of freedom and interest, while at the same time your artistic conscience is too acute to allow you to do what so many writers (eg Houseman) do, endless variations on the same theme. Maybe you will have to wait till your father dies, (it wont be long now I suppose) when you will be able to forgive him and forget him, and relive him.[4] I hope that you wont have to: its my guess that you are the kind of writer who must write directly about their own experience, so that your next stories will be about Ethel Mannin[5] and Brian[6] and Tania. Title 'It is queerer than you think', or 'Why Ireland fell'.

I interpret your dream as your saying, and, quite justly, 'Wystan may write more than I do, but he doesnt take as much trouble.' Well, I'll try to write the *long* letters, if you will try to write *lots* of short ones.

My life here with Chester has been intense. Deep down I have been happy I think, though on the surface I sometimes behave like a hysterical concierge. Not Chester's fault who has behaved wonderfully, but just the sufferings of the self-sufficient schyzophrenic caught at last.[7] I never really loved anyone before, and then when he got through the wall, he became so much part of my life that I keep

---

[3] Nietzsche's term, used in *On the Genealogy of Morals* (1887) to describe the motivation of 'natures that are denied the true reaction, that of deeds, and compensate themselves with an imaginary revenge' (first essay, sect. 10, trans. Walter Kaufmann (New York, 1967), 36).

[4] Major Stern (see Introduction, pp. 33 ff.) died in *ca.* 1958.

[5] Ethel Mannin (b. 1900), prolific Anglo-Irish popular novelist, essayist, and socialist. A friend of James Stern in the 1920s in London.

[6] Brian Howard (1905–58). Intelligent, effusively queenish in manner, Howard was the model for Anthony Blanche in Waugh's *Brideshead Revisited* (1945). He had known Stern since their days at Eton and in the late 1920s they boarded together in Frankfurt. Howard met Auden in Oxford, and admired him greatly. He was acute and had literary ambitions but experienced great difficulty in writing. He was prone to become heavily drunk and then violent and paranoid; later he succumbed to drug addiction and committed suicide in 1958 (see the sketch of Howard in *C&HK* (US), 215–18; and also Marie-Jaqueline Lancaster, ed., *Brian Howard: Portrait of a Failure* (London, 1968), *passim*).

[7] Auden was particularly interested in schizophrenia at the time and perhaps related it to some of his own character traits. Cf. remarks in an ALS to Caroline Newton, [25 Apr. 1942?], (Berg), where he wrote: 'The [*illegible*] masculine Schyz is Mother-hating—Father-loving to the point where he becomes the Almighty Father who creates all and needs no one.' Auden told Newton in the same letter that he had just been lecturing about 'Schyzophrenic and Cycloid Poetry'. He was borrowing the two basic personality types of the 'schizotheme' and the 'cyclotheme' from Ernst Kretschmer's *Physique and Character: An Investigation of the Nature of Constitution and of the Theory of Temperament*, trans. W. J. H. Sprott, 2nd edn. (London, 1925). (Auden had been interested in Kretschmer's ideas since *ca.* 1929–30. He mentions them in the 'Suggestions for a Play' that he sent to Isherwood at that time; see *PDW* 462.)

forgetting that he is a separate person, and having discovered love, I have also discovered what I never knew before, the dread of being abandoned and left alone. I am happy about him though. He has turned out a wonderful cook as I told you, he is doing all his school-work conscientiously, and writing poetry steadily and poetry which is very good, I think.[8]

He is having a[n] affair with a nice quiet musical intellectual who will suffer, poor boy, as he is wildly in love with him. The snag is that the intellectual likes to be fucked which is Chester's tour, so there are longing eyes cast at taxi drivers. Perhaps it is just as well for both of them, that it was I, and not Brian who met Chester. *Think* of the scenes. As for me, my dear, sex is a _desert_. *One* little romp in three months. When I come to New York I shall expect you all to produce something ravishing.

I dont envy the woman who has married Tony, if she has; she'll have to keep the handle of a Hoover in the house.[9]

Brogan I only know by correspondence; he sounded then as awful as you say he is now.[10]

I expect to be drafted in June. If not, I gather we are meeting at Caroline's.[11] I hope so as I would rather spend the summer with you and Tania than anyone.

Much love to you both
Wystan

ALS (Fountain Pen).

[8] Kallman's diligence did not last for long after Auden left Ann Arbor (Farnan, 82–3). His first collection of poems, *Storm at Castelfranco*, was published in 1956.

[9] 'Tony' has not been identified. Auden's 1938 New Year's Eve poem (quoted in Carpenter, 248) celebrating various friends and acquaintances refers to 'three or four Tonies' who were in his circle. These include the Connolly's American friend Tony Bower, back in California after July 1940; Brian Howard's German boyfriend Toni, who arrived in New York in 1941 and whom Auden and some of Howard's other friends in the US were trying to help (see Lancaster, ed., *Brian Howard*, 428; *C&HK* (US), 214–15); John Lehmann's 'Viennese friend, secretary and chauffeur' (Lehmann, *Thrown to the Woolfs* (London, 1978), 48); Stephen Spender's former boyfriend Tony Hyndman; and the writer Antony Bourne.

[10] Probably the British historian D. W. (and from 1963 Sir Denis) Brogan (1900–74), an expert on American and French history, author of ten books on the US, including *U.S.A.: An Outline of the Country* (London, 1941). He studied at Harvard and lived in New York for a while; from 1939–69 he was Professor of Political Science at Cambridge. It is unclear exactly what Auden and Stern disliked about him, but Brogan's *New York Times* obituary hinted at a prim, cold personality: 'Sir Denis's full face and horn-rimmed glasses gave him a solemn, owlish look. His mouth was small and tight-lipped' (7 Jan. 1974, p. 34).

[11] See Introduction, p. 54. Auden had been invited by Caroline Newton to spend

5. *[18 July 1942]*[1]

Saturday   The Elopyam | Nywreb | Ennap.[2]
3.0. pm.

Dearest Jimmy,

I have sent Tania to her room to write.[3] She tried everything to get
out of it, charm, interest in my personal life, thinking she could hear
the telephone, fearing that Caroline would miss her etc. etc. But at
last she is at her desk and we shall see.

Your masculine pride would be grossly flattered if you could see
how lost she looks. There was a thunderstorm last night and she says
she nearly came and woke me up. This little fairy would have turned
into a serpent if she had.

She will give you all the details about her tête-a-tête with Miss

---

part of the summer at her home, The Maypole, in Berwyn (the house-warming poem
he wrote for her, 'In War Time' (1942), is in *EA* 460–1). On 30 June, the day before
he was due to be inducted, the Draft Board told Auden that because they had forgotten
to give him a blood-test, they were putting off his induction until 1 Aug. 1942 (see
ALS from Auden to Norman Holmes Pearson, 3 Aug. [1942], (The Beinecke Library,
Yale University)). The induction was later postponed again, until 1 Sept. 1942. Then,
when Auden at last presented himself at Governor's Island in New York harbour, he
was turned down by an Army psychiatrist (Carpenter, 324; see also Introduction, pp.
54–5).

[1] See Carpenter, 324.
[2] i.e. The 'Maypole | Berwyn | Penna' (roughly) spelt backwards. Gurney Thomas
remembered that while Auden was a teacher at the Downs School he sometimes 'read
out words backwards and we had to write them in our exercise books the right way
round' ('Recollections of Auden at the Downs School', *ASN*, 3 (Apr. 1989), [1]).
[3] Tania Stern was legendary amongst her family and friends for her reluctance to
write letters. Her husband had left The Maypole (presumably a little earlier in July) to
take part in the thirteenth 'Writers' Conference' in the Rocky Mountains', one in an
annual series of writers' conferences held around the country (see Introduction, p. 54).
The Colorado conference was sponsored by the University of Colorado at Boulder and
was organized by an expatriate Scot, Edward Davison, a poet, and professor of English
at the University (until 1943 when he left to become a Major in the US Army). It ran
from 20 July–7 Aug. 1942 and was attended by over 100 veteran and novice authors.
James Stern was the first winner of a scholarship set up by the publishers Doubleday
Doran to enable an outstanding young writer to visit the conference (see 'Writers
Gather Here in July to CU Conference', *Silver and Gold*, Boulder, 29 May 1942).
Stern told Carpenter that at Boulder he had 'no assignment and all expenses paid. . . .
It also so happened that Edward Davidson [*sic*], the English-born poet, was President
of the University and an old friend from my Fleet Street days' (typed comments on a
draft of Carpenter's biography, *ca.* 27 May 1980 (Rare Books and Manuscripts Room,
Butler Library, Columbia University)).

Fairness.[4] She has a very nice little place. We started from here late and got lost, so C drove at sixty m.p.h. through red lights wearing a new kind of necklass, like the b[r]asses they make carthorses wear, because F doesnt like pearls. Guests. Our party, M^r and Mrs Roberts who are E. F. Benson fans, Miss Brock a semi-young pianist whose grandmother was an Anglo Catholic (but not *spiky*), and—get her— the Baron O'Shaughnessy, who arrived in brown shoes, explaining that he was so absorbed listening to a Frascobaldi Toccata on the Victrola while changing that he never noticed.[5] He once sang in Aida at Atlantic City and was rather nice. My dear, we didnt sit down till 9. Dinner not very startling. Over the men's coffee I let out *purely* by accident that I knew some of our host's friends. After that Tania took him into the next room and I sat beside Caroline's good ear ready to bawl if I could overhear anything. I'm very glad T said something. It was really getting too much, and I think he is not so unconscious of what he is doing as he pretends. In any case I dont care for amateur Disraeli's.[6]

Longing to hear what it's like being a Mountain Boy. Shall I send

---

[4] Fairman Furness was a landscape gardener who lived near Caroline Newton in Pennsylvania and was hoping to be hired by her to do some work. Although homosexual, he was carrying on a flirtation with Newton, perhaps partly for business reasons: see Auden's TL to Elizabeth Mayer, 13 July [1942], (Berg): 'There are terrible troubles looming here with Caroline and the landscape Gardener whom, poor thing, she imagines is in love with her. I am thankful that Tania is here, for when the crash comes, I am a little afraid for her sanity. La decadence Americaine is a terrifying phenomenon.' See also an ALS to Angelyn and Albert Stevens, [30 July 1942], (University of Michigan Library, Ann Arbor): 'I have done nothing except work and bathe and prepare to deal with an emotional crisis which is about to occur to my hostess. Ladies who were meant to be unselfish maiden-aunts should not read Freud' (see Letter 1, n. 2 above). In an ALS, 20 Oct. 1942, Auden told the Sterns that he had been to a dinner party at The Maypole and had met Furness there again, 'galante as ever. Hundreds and hundreds of dollars worth of shrub have been planted.'

[5] Whoever the 'Baron O'Shaughnessy' was, he is not to be identified with the third Baron Shaughnessy (b. 1922) who succeeded to the title in 1938 (information from Baron Shaughnessy given to Richard Davenport-Hines). Girolamo Frescobaldi (1583–1643) was an Italian composer and organist.

[6] Auden had been reading the novels of Benjamin Disraeli (1804–81) during the first few months of 1942. He refers here, though, to Disraeli's famous flattery of the widowed Queen Victoria, or 'the Faery' as Disraeli called her. It was a relationship, Disraeli's biographer Lord Blake has said, to which 'there is no parallel in her long reign.' Disraeli admitted that he laid it on 'with a trowel'. After she gave him a copy of her *Leaves from the Journal of Our Life in the Highlands 1848 to 1861* (1868), he (apocryphally) spoke of the two of them as 'We authors, Ma'am'. Victoria sent him valentines and when he was Prime Minister he made her Empress of India (see Robert Blake, *Disraeli* (New York, 1967), 490–3, 545, 703).

you your leather shorts? If you see any nice pieces, give them my telephone number.

Much love
Wystan

ALS (Fountain Pen) + envelope addressed to 'Mr James Stern | c/o Writers Conference | University of Colorado | Boulder City | Colorado.', postmark 'BERWYN PA. JUL 18 5-PM 1942'.

6. *[23 July 1942]*[1]

Thursday.   The Maypole | Daylesford | Berwyn | Pa.

Dearest Jimmy,

Low morale is turning me into a letter-writer, and the cause of the former is the Kafka behaviour of the Draft Board. Not having heard a *word* from them I finally wrote; now they say Sept 1st.[2] This is all very nice, but what do they expect me to live on, let alone support Chester at Michigan.[3] I was counting on being inducted July 1st, because if they had taken me then, I should have had enough money to leave for Chester, and if they didnt take me, then I could have started taking the Guggenheim money.[4] As it is, I am in the void, unable to settle down to any planned work, so that I havent the right to start exploiting the Late Mr G.

We have had a wonderful two days without Caroline[.] I agree with what you say about her. What makes it impossible to feel sorry for her, is that she pretends to suffer about one thing, when she is really suffering about something else. The day Tania was away I *nearly* broke her down to the point of admitting that she stole her niece's letters. At any rate for the first time, there was genuine pain, rage, hatred, and one could like her. Unfortunately I muffed it, with the result that I am almost *certain* that she tried to poison me mildly. My evidence. a) I had an acute attack of food poisoning, a complaint

---

[1] See Carpenter, 324.   [2] See Letter 4, n. 11 above.
[3] See Letter 8, n. 4 below for details of Emily Tompkins's assistance with Kallman's Ann Arbor fees in 1942.
[4] Auden was informed in a letter of 20 March 1942 that he had been given a Guggenheim Fellowship to work on 'For the Time Being', but in fact (see Letter 7) he finished the oratorio before he was due to start taking the money. After being refused by the Army, Auden taught part-time at Swarthmore during the Fall 1942 and Spring 1943 semesters and accepted $100 a month from the Guggenheim Foundation to supplement his income from the university.

which I am exceptionally resistant to normally. b) For some days, Tammy has been me again. 'You are cruel. You are proud of having sharp teeth when Little Fool has none. You're as bad as Hitler.' The day after my attack C said to him, 'I meant to hurt you a little.'[5]

Anyway, I cant stay here much longer, and I hope that the moment you get back, you will take Tania away.

My plans are to go up soon to Ann Arbor for a week or so, then to the Mayers in Amityville.[6] I'd like to go to Maine but cant afford it.

My dear, how *dare* you visit my dream country without me. What you describe so beautifully *is* my childhood. I shall certainly go to Black Hawk to die, it sounds just like an elephant's cemetery.[7] Why do we all love ruins so?

Delighted to hear you are already a 'top-notcher' and hope that you will soon be a 'good scout.' Do you wear your cowboy and O.E.[8] ties on alternate days?

Tania and I have a theory that you are the cause of Katherine Ann's 'Prostration', ie that she has been trying to convince you that underneath the hair-do, she is still just the simple little girl you knew in Paris, and that she has failed. Are we right?[9]

---

[5] Newton was a dog fanatic: 'I do love dogs—passionately would perhaps not be too strong a word' (a comment by her in Thomas Mann, *The Letters of Thomas Mann to Caroline Newton* (Princeton, NJ, 1971). Auden and the Sterns privately called her the 'Dog-Lady' (see Letter 7 and accompanying n. 12 below). In 1942 she had two dogs (probably poodles), Tammy and Little Fool. She liked to project her human relationships on to them: Tammy was whomever she was currently obsessed with, Little Fool was herself (see Letter 7).

[6] In mid–Aug. 1942, Auden may have made a trip to Ann Arbor to see Kallman. He came back to The Maypole, but left for good on 27 Aug. He then went to Amityville to stay with Elizabeth Mayer before returning *ca.* 29 Aug. to the Sterns' apartment in New York to prepare for induction into the Army (Introduction, p. 55, and Letter 4, n. 11).

[7] Blackhawk, a small mining town roughly 20 miles south-west of Boulder at an altitude of 5,530 feet, was the site of the first smelter in Colorado and the first mining machinery foundry in the Rocky Mountains. It was also the location of many celebrated lodes. *Colorado: A Guide to the Highest State* (New York, 1941), by the 'Workers of the Writers' Program of the Works Projects Administration in the State of Colorado', describes a highway just outside the town that 'ascends a shallow canyon dotted with ruins of abandoned mines. Here and there new mills are operating, reducing ore from the still valuable deposits of Gilpin County. Within the solid walls of many of the abandoned mills stands the original machinery, left to rust when the roofs collapsed' (267).

[8] i.e. Old Etonian.

[9] From Dec. 1932 until the spring of 1936, Katherine Anne Porter spent most of her time in Paris, where she met the Sterns for the first time. 1942 was a difficult year for Porter. In Jan. her father died and in the early summer she was divorced from her estranged husband, Albert Erskine. She had also been unable to finish a long-promised novel (see Joan Givner, *Katherine Anne Porter: A Life* (New York, 1982), 281, 324,

I dont think that either Aldington or you are completely in the right about writing.[10] I mean that his theory 'I write for myself' unfortunately seems to lead to the attitude 'Because I am a writer I am a superior being who must be supported by others, usually women.' On the other hand your theory 'I write to sell' if carried out logically, and it sometimes is, turns writers into journalists and advertisers. When I started writing I took publication as some sort of objective proof that my work had value. But since then, experiences with publishers and ladies clubs, and fans, make it so obvious that the reasons, (whatever they are I dont know), for which one is read—and so have a modest commercial value—have nothing to do with anything one is trying to say or for which one would like to be read. I cannot say therefore that I write to make money, or even to be read, though of course one hopes there are a few who really do; the money always seems to me something obtained under false pretences. It would be amusing to see how many writers would be left, if all books were published anonymously. Perhaps the real wish is not for an audience, but because one thinks one has had a vision in which suffering is turned into joy, one wants to share the joy with others, ie one would like to be able to do the same for someone else, as books which one has loved have done for oneself. The rest is bread and butter, and the desire for self-respect.

Tania is very well, but looks crestfallen whenever the mail arrives without a letter from you.

326). Porter attended the Boulder writers' conference (see Letter 5, n. 3) as the leader of the short-story group.

[10] Richard Aldington (1892–1962), English biographer, novelist, and poet. Aldington was a friend of Pound and published poems in Pound's anthology *Des Imagistes* (1913); for a while he was married to the poet H.D. He acted as literary editor of the *Egoist* and served as an officer in the First World War. He suffered severe shell-shock and described his war experiences in *Death of a Hero* (London, 1929). In 1928 he and his girlfriend Brigit Patmore left England and stayed on the Continent throughout the Thirties. In 1938 he married Netta Patmore, Brigit's daughter-in-law. They left Europe with their small daughter in Feb. 1939 and came to the US. (Like Auden and Isherwood, Aldington was criticized by English newspapers for his absence from England during the war.) He lived on the East Coast, in and around New York, until March 1941 when he moved to Florida. Just before going to the writers' conference in Colorado—where he served as one of two 'general advisers' to the conference— Aldington had begun work on *The Duke* (London, 1943) a biography of the Duke of Wellington which won the James Tait Black Memorial Prize. In Aug. 1942, after the conference was over, he moved to Hollywood where he turned out films scripts for three-and-a-half years before, in Aug. 1946, returning to France (Norman T. Gates, ed., *Richard Aldington: An Autobiography in Letters* (University Park, Pa., 1992), 161–3, 364; see also Letter 7, n. 5 below).

You cant imagine what a source of strength your marriage has been to me during the past year, a bright little light in a naughty world of greedy romantics,[11] and castrated pussy-cats.

Much love
Wystan

ALS (Pencil) + envelope addressed to 'Mr James Stern | c/o Writers Conference | University of Colorado | Boulder City | Colo', postmark 'PHILADELPHIA PA 30 JUL 23 7 30 PM 1942'.

7. [30 July 1942][1]

Thursday   The Maypole | Daylesford | Berwyn | Pa

Dearest Jimmy,

Excuse the pencil but it is your fault for taking your typewriter away: all the nibs in this house are impossible.

Tania read me bits of your letter. In case you should be afraid that she has become a paragon, let me say that the Air-Mail and Writers Conference were *my* ideas.[2]

I laughed a lot at your description of the School Feeling. When I first started to teach I couldnt really believe that it was now I who caused the bells to ring, I whose voice made others start guiltily. I wish I were with you to invent torments for Enemy Shaw (Schorr?).[3] You should get into drag, I would disguise myself as a Taxi-driver and tell him I knew of a hot piece of skirt. Then we would watch the conditioned reflexes go into action till they reached the Fairies' Paradise and He-mans Hell.

Remember me to Aldington. Funnily enough I have just been read-

---

[11] Cf. 'For the Time Being', Semi-Chorus: 'Pray for us romantics' (*CP91* 366).

[1] See Carpenter, 324.

[2] As mentioned above (Letter 5, n. 3), Tania Stern disliked writing (and sending) letters. Auden is referring to the fact that Letter 6 was sent to James Stern by air (rather than surface) mail and was properly addressed.

[3] Harry Lee Shaw, Jr. (1905–*ca.* 1989?), who was leading the non-fiction prose section of the Boulder writers' conference, taught English at New York University and had been, since 1938, Director of the Federal Writers' Project in New York. He had also recently been made an associate editor of *Look* magazine. Shaw later worked as an editor at many New York publishing houses, including W. W. Norton. Auden's phrasing 'Enemy Shaw' is a play on George Bernard Shaw's famous inscription in T. E. Lawrence's copy of *Saint Joan* (1924), 'To Pte Shaw from Public Shaw', a joke about Lawrence's alias of 'Private Shaw' in the Royal Air Force (see Michael Holroyd, *Bernard Shaw*, vol. 3: *1918–1950: The Lure of Fantasy* (New York, 1991), 88).

ing, with great pleasure, his translations of Renaissance poetry.[4] I liked him very much as a person when I met him. As a writer, I feel he has got struck in the Lawrence–Douglas LIFE religion.[5] In 1912, it was a real vision to discover that God loves a Pernod and a good fuck, but in 1942 every maiden aunt knows this and it's time to discover something else He loves. 'Cruelty and destruction', say Max Ernst[6] and Adolph Hitler, but since they hasten to add 'for you but not for me', I see no reason to believe them.

Well, as you will have heard by now, the bubble burst on Tuesday. Alas, though, in appearance only. In reality there was nothing there but a craving to be interesting to herself, and that, I'm afraid, remains, ie F[7] was always, like everything else in her surroundings, to[o] animal, vegetable and mineral, too unreal to cause any suffering.

It's been really rather a terrifying experience to see how someone

[4] Probably Aldington's book of translations, *Latin Poems of the Renaissance* (Cleveland, 1916), but possibly his *Fifty Romance Lyric Poems* (New York, 1928).

[5] Aldington wrote four books on D. H. Lawrence, edited or introduced many others, and, in *Life for Life's Sake: A Book of Reminiscences* (New York, 1941), called him 'a remarkable man, the most interesting human being I have known' (334). During the early 1920s Aldington had been one of the leading literary journalists in London and was thought likely one day to become the editor of *The Times Literary Supplement*. However, talks with Lawrence in England in 1926 inspired him to emigrate in 1928 in search of the wandering, creative life Lawrence had described. Aldington's subsequent work, including a long poem, *Life Quest* (1934), and *Life for Life's Sake*, reflects this Lawrentian vision. Because Aldington was out of England for most of the Thirties (see Letter 6, n. 10), it seems likely that he and Auden met either in Paris, or in New York during 1939–41. Stern shared Aldington's enthusiasm for Lawrence, and Stern and Aldington remained friendly long after the end of the writers' conference (for some details of later contacts, see Ian S. MacNiven and Harry T. Moore, eds., *Literary Lifelines: The Richard Aldington–Lawrence Durrell Correspondence* (New York, 1981), 13–14).

Norman Douglas (1868–1952), British novelist, travel writer, and essayist, lived abroad much of his life, mostly on the shores of the southern Mediterranean. He was best known for his novel *South Wind* (1917), a hedonistic challenge to the rigours of Christian morality. Huxley portrayed him as Scrogan in *Crome Yellow* (1921) and Lawrence, with whom he quarrelled, put elements of him into Argyle in *Aaron's Rod* (1922). Aldington wrote about him in *Pinorman* (1954). For an earlier reference to Douglas, 'last of the Ancient Greeks', see 'Auden and MacNeice: Their Last Will and Testament', *LFI* 244.

[6] The surrealist artist Max Ernst (1891–1976) arrived in New York in July 1941. Auden probably met him or knew of him through Gypsy Rose Lee, occasionally a housemate at 7 Middagh Street. In 1941 Gypsy Rose Lee commissioned Ernst to paint her portrait and she painted his in return (see Denis de Rougemont, *Journal d'une époque 1926–1946* (Paris, 1968), 470). Auden may have got the suggestion for the title of *The Age of Anxiety* from a frottage by Ernst, 'L'Âge de l'angoisse' (1925), no. 851 in Max Ernst, *Werke 1925–1929*, eds. Werner Spies, Sigrid and Günter Metken [vol. 3 of *Max Ernst Œuvre-Katalog*] (Köln, 1976), 31.

[7] Fairman Furness (see Letter 5, n. 4 above).

82 SOME LETTERS FROM AUDEN TO THE STERNS

will demand of the universe to prove that they themselves exist; her parents, her money, her diseases, her china, her crushes, all of them are to be slaves who cry night and day 'Yes, my dear, you really *are* there. We can see you,' and that is their *only* function.[8]

I wish you were here to get the data first-hand for a wonderful story, which I hope you'll write anyway. As you know she talks to the two dogs all the time. Little Fool is always herself, and Tammy is always The Other. I'm sure she's done this for years, ie Tammy has been Glenway Wescott,[9] Leslie Higham,[10] Thomas Mann, W H Auden, Fairman Furness, and no doubt many others. (*not* a very virile crew I fear)

Dont you think a fascinating Novella could be written in which a woman's life was shown entirely through her conversations with her dogs?[11]

eg. For the past two days we have [been] told ad nauseam what a wonderful person F is ('greater than Thomas Mann')[.] Last night however after supper we were having coffee when Tammy barked. 'I wish you were dead' she shouted. Later she took him on her knee and said, 'You a lovely doggie really. The nicest doggie I've ever had except one (ie Little Fool). You *do* love me though you love others as well. I'm a possessive old dog-lady.'[12]

Glad you have found a nice warm womb in the Rice family.[13] Dont be too uncritical, though.

[8] Cf. the reproving talk of the dresses, pills, and potions in Auden's 1937 ballad, 'Sue' (*AS2* 93).

[9] The American writer Glenway Wescott (1901–87) was another homosexual friend of Caroline Newton.

[10] I have not been able to identify Leslie Higham, though Lincoln Kirstein told me in conversation (May 1993) that he believed Higham might have been an auctioneer.

[11] Auden's suggestion to Stern is similar to the idea used in Woolf's *Flush* (London, 1933), the novel about Elizabeth Barrett Browning's spaniel which is written from the dog's point-of-view. Auden had been reading Virginia Woolf at The Maypole. He told Elizabeth Mayer in a TL, [13 July 1942], (Berg): 'Have just re-read *To The Lighthouse* after many years. Its a masterpiece, I think.'

[12] Auden and the Sterns liked this pet-name, the 'Dog-lady', and used it amongst themselves to refer to Caroline Newton. In their sense, the 'Dog-lady' plays on the pseudonyms of Freud's famous 'Rat Man' and 'Wolf Man' patients, mockingly turning Newton into another exemplary psychopathological case. (In 1921 she had briefly been Freud's patient (see Letter 1, n. 2).) The Sterns were as familiar with the Freudian universe as Auden was: Ernst Freud had given Tania Kurella away at her wedding to James Stern in 1935 (see Introduction, p. 43) and the Sterns later translated the *Letters of Sigmund Freud 1873–1939* (New York, 1961; 2nd edn., New York, 1975).

[13] Accommodation for men attending the writers' conference was with families or in the campus fraternity houses. Stern was staying in Alpha Tau Omega house. There were no faculty members with the surname 'Rice' in 1942, but Bruce P. Montgomery

It's a pity we cant swap childhoods for a week; you would be surprised how unpleasant too much parental love and interest can be, and what a torture of guilt it makes breaking away.[14] When I was 6 years old I used to play the love-potion scene from Tristan and Isolde with my mother.[15] When I was 15 I was on a walking-tour with my father, and we were sharing a bed: I suddenly had a violent longing to be fucked by him.[16] (Not being a novelist, I have to confess that he didnt).

I've finished the Oratorio on Saturday,[17] and have been suffering from the usual depression after finishing something, when one doesnt know what to think about, and puts off the dreadful task of beginning something else. Lucky lucky Trollope; to be able to finish one novel at 4.30 and start the next at 4.35. Have passed most of the time with Tania by the pool telling each other the story of our lives. My only real contribution to her knowledge of life was the importance to the male of s i z e. (I seem to remember that the psychologists call it penal envy, but that cant be the right word).[18]

of the Western Historical Collection at the library of the University of Colorado at Boulder has suggested to me that the 'Rice family' may refer to the brothers James and Jack Rice, who lived nearby.

[14] Auden told Daniel Halpern, 'Like every adolescent one had to fight with one's mother for one's independence' ('Interview with W. H. Auden', *Antaeus*, 5 (Spring 1972), 142). For more on Auden's highly charged relations with his mother, see Katherine Bucknell's introduction to Auden's *Juvenilia*, pp. xxvii–xxxii.

[15] See 'As It Seemed to Us' (1965), repr. in *FA* 501; Ansen, 24; Carpenter, 11; Farnan, 32.

[16] Psychically and creatively, this trip into Wordsworth country was evidently very important for Auden. In Aug. 1922 he, his brother John, and their father spent a holiday at Derwentfolds Farm in the Lake District (two or three miles west of Wesco, the cottage which the family bought in 1924 or 1925). They made a series of excursions, one of them presumably to Blea Tarn, a small lake, which, late in life, Auden remembered as the setting of his first poem (see the 'Foreword' to Bloomfield, *W. H. Auden: A Bibliography: The Early Years through 1955* (Charlottesville, Va., 1964), p. ix). Blea Tarn, about 12 or 15 miles south of Derwentfolds Farm and about 4 or 5 miles southwest of Dove Cottage, is the site of the Poet and the Wanderer's visit to the Solitary in books 2–5 of *The Excursion* (1814), 'a beautiful abyss', Wordsworth wrote, 'By Nature destined from the birth of things | For quietness profound!' (5.9–11) The only lines that Auden could recall from his own poem were the final ones: 'and in the quiet | Oblivion of thy waters let them stay' (quoted in Carpenter, 28, and also in Paul Hirschhorn, 'And in the quiet oblivion of this water, let them stay', *Penumbra*, 1.3–4 (1968), 37; Auden's memory was probably re-ordering the sequence of these early events: in her edition of Auden's juvenilia, Katherine Bucknell suggests that Auden either wrote at least a few poems before the Blea Tarn sonnet or that it had 'another, previous inspiration', see *Juvenilia*, 3.

[17] 25 July.

[18] Auden's joke turns on a misuse of the term 'penis-envy', first used by Freud in the 1925 paper 'Some Psychical Consequences of the Anatomical Distinction between the Sexes', *SE* 19, 248–58.

Many many thanks for the map which Tania only remembered to give me to-day. I shall learn to draw it from memory,[19] and then when we meet again we'll have another competition[.]

Dont forget Oklahoma next time[.]

Much love
Wystan

ALS (Pencil) + envelope addressed to 'Mr James Stern | Writers Conference | Alpha Tau Omega House | University of Colorado | Boulder | Colorado.', postmark 'BERWYN PA. JUL 30 1-PM 1942'. Quoted in *Juvenilia*, pp. xxix, l.

8. *[1 November 1942]*[1]

Sunday Afternoon   Sunnybank | Vassar Avenue | Swarthmore | Pa

Dearest Tania and Jimmy,

It is three o clock on sunday afternoon, ie the worst time of the day on the worst day of the week, added to which I have caught a bad cold through having holes in my shoes, and since there is no shop in Swarthmore, I suppose I shall continue to have them.

Thanks ever so for your newsy letters which are a great comfort in a place where everyone is extremely nice but no one is naughty or gay, where the few beauties are in engineering and there isnt even a bar to get acquainted in.

Dont bother about the coffee. I wouldnt have [asked] if I'd realised that New York was in the same boat, I thought it was just Main Line obstinacy; it seems to have swept down on us very suddenly, and now next month. . . . I cant make up my mind whether to have a cup a day every day or none until the last few days and then a real caffeine debauch.[2]

---

[19] For other instances of this love of maps, see the 'Prologue' to *O*: 'With the finest of mapping pens he fondly traces | All the family names on the familiar places' (*EA* 61) and 'Amor Loci': 'I could draw its map by heart' (*CP91* 779). In 1947 Auden had a large map of the Pennines hanging on the wall of the Fire Island shack that he shared with the Sterns.

[1] Auden had arrived in Swarthmore at the end of Sept. 1942; see Carpenter, 324–7.

[2] In 1942 submarine warfare began depleting the coffee shipments reaching the US from Central and South America. Stocks dwindled while demand increased. By the beginning of Oct. 1942 coffee was scarce throughout the country, with many stores either sold out or restricting sales to 1lb. per customer. In an ALS, [20 Oct. 1942], Auden told James Stern that he was enclosing $10 and he asked Tania Stern to buy him some

Terribly sorry to hear about Shrecker's miscarriage; he sure has his troubles. I havent got his adress so will you tell him when you see him that if he is free any time I would love a visit from him.[3]

Sorry to hear about Emily. What does William think of her himself?[4]

Glad you didnt let the kind Lady-dog get away with her charity. By the way, you never told me, and I didnt like to ask her, what happened about her lessons[.] Did she give way.[5]

---

coffee in New York because it was so hard to obtain any in Swarthmore. But by 26 Oct. the general situation had become bad enough to make the front page of *The New York Times* and the Federal Office of Price Administration announced that from midnight on 28 Nov. coffee would be rationed to 1lb. per person every 5 weeks, an average of slightly over one cup a day. There were no easy alternatives for the caffeine lover: tea and cocoa were also being rationed. Shortly afterwards, Tania Stern was apparently able to find some coffee for Auden—in an APCS to her, [4 Nov. 1942], he sent thanks from 'your devoted addict'. (It is also possible that she had just resupplied him with benzedrine.) Auden had another source too. The historian Daniel Boorstin was an assistant professor at Swarthmore at the time, and he and his wife donated their coffee ration coupons to Auden. In *The Queen's Masque*, probably mostly written in Dec. 1942, Mabel sees a crowd of happy people and asks: 'Has Hitler died? Is coffee to be had? | What's going on here?' (*Libretti*, 425).

[3] Dr Paul Schrecker (1889–1963), married Anne Martin in 1951. They had one son, Theodore Franz Schrecker. Paul Schrecker was a philosopher with doctorates from the Universities of Vienna and Berlin. He was on the staff of the University of Paris from 1933–40. After coming to the US in 1940, he was a visiting professor at the New School for Social Research in Manhattan from 1941–5, and at the École Libre des Hautes Études in Manhattan from 1942–5. He later became a professor at Swarthmore and Bryn Mawr and, finally, from 1950 until his retirement, at the University of Pennsylvania. Schrecker edited the works of Leibniz (1929–33) and Nicolas Malebranche (1934–40). No details about the miscarriage of a child have been uncovered.

[4] Emily Tompkins, a Philadelphian, a friend (and possibly a patient) of Caroline Newton, had apparently spent time in Bellevue Hospital and was unstable. She was present occasionally at The Maypole and seems to have been in love with Auden (see Introduction, p. 54). She had approached him at the New School for Social Research and at first Auden seems to have taken an interest in her problems, bringing her to Tania Stern to see if she could offer any help. Tompkins rented an apartment for herself and her cats above the Sterns on East 52nd Street in Manhattan. (Auden and the Sterns nicknamed her the 'Cat-lady' to parallel Caroline Newton, 'the Dog-lady', see Letter 7, n. 12 above). In Aug. 1942 Tompkins lent or gave Auden $350 for Kallman's Fall 1942 semester at Ann Arbor (see ALS from Auden to Chester Kallman, [25 Aug. 1942].) But around Oct. 1942 she seems to have become vicious and irrational when she felt that she was being rejected by the Sterns and Auden. Elizabeth Mayer's husband, the psychiatrist William Mayer, who had experience with the insane, was called in to treat her.

[5] Caroline Newton was taking lessons from Tania Stern. See Letter 13, n. 2 below for a description of the row about money which took place in Nov.–Dec. 1944 and which led to the end of Auden's friendship with Newton.

Very tired of reading 'creative' mss, each more infantile than the last. At my last Thursday Evening At home, my room was packed to capacity with girls who wanted to know if I felt inspired when I wrote. How Yeats would have enjoyed himself. I didnt. Really, if I'm not careful, I shall end as a traitor to the flag.

Much love
Wystan

ALS (Pencil) + envelope addressed to 'Mrs Tania Stern | 207. E. 52nd Street | New York City. | N. Y.', postmark 'SWARTHMORE PA. NOV 2 8 30 AM 1942'.

9. *[3 November 1942]*[1]

Tuesday   Sunnybank | Vassar Avenue | Swarthmore | Pa

Dearest Jimmy,

  Strictly confidential. Could you find out for me the details of where and how to get into the Merchant Marine. The more I think about the future and how they are going to take the adolescent and the married, the more uncomfortable I feel about sitting back on my 4F bottom (Sore but sound).[2] Also, all these girls are stifling my genius.

  But please dont breathe a word to anyone.

Much love
Wystan

ALS (Fountain Pen) + envelope addressed to 'Mr James Stern | 207. E. 52nd Street | New York City | N. Y.', postmark 'SWARTHMORE PA. NOV 3 6 30 PM 1942'.

---

[1] See Carpenter, 324–7.

[2] A reference to Eliot's suggestion that in the 'Journal of an Airman' in *The Orators* Auden substitute 'the June bride' for the original reading of 'the fucked hen' (see *EA* xxii, 81, and Carpenter, 124). Auden told an interviewer that he hadn't understood until Eliot explained that after a local election the press asked the victor how he felt: 'Like a June bride—sore but satisfied.' Then they asked the loser how he felt: 'Like a June bride—I knew it was coming but I didn't know it would be so big' (Michael André, 'A Talk with W. H. Auden', *Unmuzzled Ox*, 1.3 (Summer 1972), 5).

10. [5 July 1944][1]

Wednesday
Hotel Layette | Caut Indeed Avenue | Sale Ville | Wrong Island.[2]

Dearest Jimmy,
Chester must have been transferred to the Post Office as your letter didnt get here till 11.0 am. to-day.[3] It cheered me up a great deal, as accounts of misery always do. It is not so good here. The clientele is very lower middle-class indeed, the food is terrible and never less than ¾hr late, served by sluts whose insolent clumsiness is all too American, and I cant get a comfortable chair in my room. There is a nice café when its juke-box is not going, but that isnt often. The only decent beach is restricted to 'nice Christian people'.

Still, I've managed to start working, and it would be no better anywhere else.[4] O Why, why why, did Mina Curtis have to be a shit.[5]

The more I think about it, the less I feel like facing another year at Swarthmore.[6] I am, after all, a crook, and need a more baroque and louche habitat to breathe in, than the Quaker's provide.[7] Also I feel

---

[1] See Carpenter, 331–2; Farnan, 104–6.

[2] James Stern, who had been out on Fire Island earlier in the summer, had found Auden a room at the Hotel Lafayette, Caudee Avenue, Sayville, Long Island, near ferry-points to Fire Island.

[3] During the first half of 1944 Kallman's friend Mary Valentine persuaded him to take a civil-service examination with her. They both passed and were given work in the Bureau of Censorship on West 25th Street in Manhattan, inspecting wartime letters to and from GIs overseas. The job ended with the war in mid-1945 (Farnan, 100, 105, 114, 129).

[4] Probably on *The Age of Anxiety* (see Carpenter, 331).

[5] Auden had enjoyed his summer 1940 visit to Ashfield, Mina Curtiss's country home in Massachusetts (see Introduction, p. 52). In Jan. 1942, though, he broke off with her after she referred to Kallman, unrepentantly, as a 'Brooklyn kike' (Carpenter, 315).

[6] Auden had vented his dissatisfaction with life in Swarthmore in 'A Healthy Spot' (*CP91* 328), written in ?Feb. 1944. However, despite an offer of a one-year appointment from Aug. 1944–July 1945 at Bennington College, he stayed at Swarthmore until late in April 1945 (see Carpenter, 333, and the Introduction to 'Vocation and Society' in this volume, p. 5).

[7] The Sterns remember Auden telling them in conversation, 'Queers are members of the criminal class.' For other instances of his linkage of homosexuality and criminality (factually the case at the time when he was writing), see the inscription in a copy of Bridges's *The Testament of Beauty* that Auden gave Isherwood *ca.* 1929: 'He isn't like us | He isn't a crook | The man is a heter | Who wrote this book' (quoted by Isherwood in 'Postscript' to 'Some Notes on the Early Poetry', *Tribute*, 79). In 'Ode to Gaea' (1954), the lines about 'certain Southern countries "whose | status and moral climate | we have no desire, sir, to emulate"' (*CP91* 554) are taken, slightly rearranged, from the Hansard report of Earl Winterton's highly censorious speech during the

an attack of wanderlust coming on. (Perhaps all this is only the effect of reading *A Coffin for Demetrius*).[8]

You _must_ write your story of Caroline and her dogs. As Dear H. J. would say, the subject bristles with importance and the blest spirit of composition begins most startlingly to throb.[9]

Delighted about Esquire. Which story was it?[10] You know, I've long cherished a secret wish to collaborate with you on a play about marriage, the *only* subject[.][11]

Much love and come down quickly.

Wystan.

ALS (Pencil) + envelope addressed to 'Mr James Stern | 207. E. 52nd Street | New York City | N. Y.', postmark 'SAYVILLE N. Y. JUL 5 5 30 PM 1944'.

11. [?14 October 1944][1]

Saturday   16 Oberlin Avenue | Swarthmore | Pa

Dearest Jimmy,

Many thanks for your letter. Enclosed is cheque for the amount you mention.[2] I hope you havent cheated yourself at all. Evidently Emily's fan ate up the current.[3]

House of Lords Debate on Homosexuality on 19 May 1954—see Great Britain, *The Parliamentary Debates (Hansard)*, 5th ser., vol. 187, The House of Lords (27 April 1954–18 June 1954), col. 741. Auden quoted the Earl's remarks in a letter to the Sterns from Forio, ALS, 1 July [1954].)

[8] Eric Ambler's thriller of international intrigue, *A Coffin for Dimitrios* (New York, 1939), takes place in Istanbul, Sofia, and Paris. (The title of the British edition is *The Mask of Dimitrios* (London, 1939).)

[9] Cf. in 'Caliban to the Audience' in 'The Sea and the Mirror', 'the heady wine of amusement is distilled from the grape of composition' (*CP91* 430) and 'the Good Right Subject that would never cease to bristle with importance' (*CP91* 434).

[10] Stern's 'The Man Behind the Bar' was published in *Esquire*, 23.6 (June 1945), 52–3, 116, and reprinted as 'The Face Behind the Bar' in his *The Man Who Was Loved* (New York, 1951; London, 1952), 193–201, and Stern, *Stories*, 252–9.

[11] See Introduction, p. 57 and n. 122. Auden had also told Isherwood that 'One day we have to write a play about Marriage' (ALS, 23 June 1943).

[1] See Carpenter, 332.

[2] From Aug.–mid-Sept. 1944, while the Sterns were staying out on Fire Island in the shack that they bought with Auden in 1945 (see Introduction, pp. 57, 61), Auden lived in their apartment at 207 East 52nd Street in Manhattan.

[3] Emily Tompkins, the woman who lived above the Sterns at 207 East 52nd Street (see Letter 8, n. 4, and Introduction, p. 54).

As things have turned out, I'm glad, I think, I didnt go to Eton, but if one had a son, it would be a difficult problem to decide.[4] Given English society, I think one must give the maximum amount of emotional security one can, and maybe that includes Eton. The trouble always is that every insecurity is a blessing *if* one survives it, yet you cannot deliberately put obstacles in other people's way.

Income from home is quite another matter. I'm sure that, however rich a family may be, the moment education is finished, the parents should not give their son an allowance, as that is really a castration.

Fancy *Time* having nothing on McCabe: it really sounds a most promising field.[5] A propos of cranks I've just got *Prelude to Sanity* by S. Greiner who you may remember advertised himself in the Nation with an ad starting 'The Piddling Nation' and including a letter from Claire Booth. *Well*, you wait till you see the book.[6]

I'm coming up next Friday or Saturday because Harvey Breit is giving a party for Haggin whom I would rather like to meet.[7]

Could you get me some reproductions of a) The photo of me we

[4] In an ALS, [9 Oct. 1944], Auden had told Stern: 'as I once confessed to Tania, for years I resented not having gone to Eton. I envied that rich well-fed laugh it seems to develop.'

[5] James Stern had been working for *Time* as an art critic from about the beginning of Oct. 1942. From early Sept. 1944, he had been pestered there by a transplanted Englishman called Joseph McCabe (1867–1955), a former Franciscan priest who had become a rationalist and freethinker. McCabe, who referred to himself as the 'Universal Sage', was the source of a gigantic torrent of books and pamphlets, including *George Bernard Shaw: A Critical Study* (London, 1914), *The ABC of Evolution* (New York, 1921), an eight-volume *Key to Love and Sex* (Girard, Kan., 1929), *Our Wonderful Glands* (Girard, 1938), and *The History of Flagellation* (Girard, 1946).

[6] S[amuel] Greiner, *Prelude to Sanity* (Fort Lauderdale, 1943). Greiner, a successful restaurateur in Fort Lauderdale, Florida, developed a theory that civilization was merely the outgrowth of a world-wide schizophrenic condition, an individual's personality just 'the pus exuding from a cyst within the racial organism' (p. xii). By turns racist, paranoid, and megalomaniacal, *Prelude to Sanity* is a genuinely mad book. (Its tone is sometimes strangely close to the Vicar's Sermon in the first published version of *DBS* (*PDW* 575–9), which may account for some of Auden's fascination.) Greiner described himself as a 'racial pathologist' (154) who believed that what he called 'the racial persona' was 'ageless, unbiased, unsophisticate, yet illimitably wise' whereas the ego was 'an opportunistic parvenue, a cantankerous upstart, an amalgam of rags and patches, a motley of inadequacies and incompetencies, a fortuitous harlequin, a leper, an excrement of racial trauma' (149).

[7] Harvey Breit (1909–68), an interviewer, critic, novelist, and poet, wrote for *The New York Times* from 1943 to 1957. B. H. Haggin (1900–87) was one of the country's most famous writers on music and dance; he was at the peak of his influence as music critic for *The Nation* from 1939 to 1957. In a profession known for its recourse to the windy and impressionistic, he was celebrated for his tart, lucid prose. He wrote many books, including *Music on Records* (1938) and *Music in the Nation* (1949), a collection of his magazine pieces.

had enlarged. (For 2nd papers).[8] and b) The one on the ferry (for friends).

Much love to you both
Wystan

ALS (Fountain Pen) + envelope addressed to 'Mr James Stern | 207. E. 52nd Street | New York City | N. Y.', postmark 'SWARTHMORE PA. OCT 15 5 30 PM 1944'.

12. [18 October 1944][1]

Wednesday   16 Oberlin Avenue | Swarthmore | Pa

P. S. I wrote a letter to *The Nation* the other day about Jim's Film column, which I hope they will publish.[2]

Dearest Jimmy,

Thanks for letter. The McCabe saga becomes more and more like a Graham Greene novel.[3] I hope you've bought a revolver and poison in case of being trapped. I look forward to reading the Well's which I suspect of being poor. There is plenty to chalk up against Mother Church, but if I had to choose between the Inquisition and the World State run by Wellsian experts, I would take the first.[4] The first will

---

[8] Probably the second round of forms and interviews for naturalization as an American citizen. Auden's second hearing took place on 11 Jan. 1946 and he finally changed nationalities on 20 May 1946 (Carpenter, 339).

[1] See Carpenter, 332.

[2] James Agee (1909–55) was a feature writer and the principal film critic at *Time* from 1941 to 1948, where he was friendly with his colleague, James Stern. His work there was, like everything else in the magazine, unsigned. However, during the same period, from 1942 until 1948 Agee was allowed to write a signed film column for *The Nation*, where the brilliance of his reviewing quickly gave him a cult status among *The Nation*'s 60,000 readers (see Laurence Bergreen, *James Agee: A Life* (New York, 1984), 263, 272–3). Auden had been seeing a lot of Agee during the summer of 1944. His letter about Agee's *Nation* film column, 'Agee on Films', *The Nation*, 169.21 (18 Nov. 1944), 628, is dated 16 Oct. In it, he declares: 'In my opinion, his [Agee's] column is the most remarkable regular event in American journalism today . . . his articles belong in that very select class—the music critiques of Berlioz and Shaw are the only other members I know—of newspaper work which has permanent literary value.'

[3] See Letter 11, n. 5 above.

[4] Wells's short, fiery *Crux Ansata: An Indictment of the Roman Catholic Church* (New York, 1944), published in the US on 5 June 1944, was part of his crusade against Catholicism. The book attacks the 'strangling octopus of Catholic Christianity', charges it with a tradition of cannibalism, and of being an 'open ally of the Nazi–Fascist–Shinto axis', and ends by accusing Rome of attempting 'a final world-wide St. Bartholemew's

say: 'Sleeping with boys is a sin for which you are responsible. Give it up if you can; if not, at least repent.' The second will say, 'Of course we understand. It's not your fault that your heredity and environment have made you queer, but we can settle this. Now, just a teeny weeny operation and you'll be quite cured.'[5]

Can I stay Saturday night in your back room? Dont bother to answer unless this is impossible. I hope to catch the 9.00 am train on Saturday morning.

So glad the LW is cheerful again.[6]

Much love
Wystan.

ALS (Fountain Pen) + envelope addressed to 'Mr James Stern | 207. E. 52nd Street | New York City | N. Y.', postmark 'SWARTHMORE PA. OCT 18 1 PM 1944'.

13. [30 December 1944][1]

Saturday   16 Oberlin Avenue | Swarthmore | Pa

Dearest Tania,

A letter from Jimmy saying you have had one from Caroline. My dear, I do hope you arent contemplating re-opening relations, even for $500 a year, as I'm convinced it will not end well for either of us if you do.[2] (I enclose $44.00 as promised).

Eve'. Wells's notion of a World State was one of his oldest and most famous ideas. He began pushing the concept in 1892 in his essay 'Ancient Experiments in Co-operation' and it became familiar in later works like *A Modern Utopia* (1905), *Outline of History* (1920), and *The Shape of Things to Come* (1933) (see Peter Kemp, *H. G. Wells and the Culminating Ape* (New York, 1982), 174).

[5] Cf. in 'Epistle to a Godson', 'I've beheld in nightmares || . . . Herod's genetic engineers commanded | to modify the Innocents' (*CP91* 833).

[6] 'LW': 'the Li'l Woman', one of James Stern's nicknames for his wife.

[1] See Carpenter, 332–3.

[2] In the first half of Nov. 1944, Newton precipitated a crisis in her relationship with Tania Stern by refusing to pay for some physical education lessons she had been taking. Unlike the Sterns, Newton had plenty of money, but she maintained that because they were all friends the lessons should be free. There was a fierce argument between the two women, and Auden soon learned about it. In an ALS, 2 Dec. 1944 (Berg), Newton asked him to stay out of the fight. He refused, insisting in two letters to her that she apologize to Tania Stern (ALS, [4 Dec. 1944], (Berg), and ALS, 7 Dec. 1944 (Berg)). Newton was unwilling to do this. In an ALS, [8 Dec. 1944], to Kallman, Auden wrote: 'Tania (and through her me) have had our final break with La Carolina.' Later that month Newton wrote to him and phoned him again, apparently hoping to

Apropos of our last talk about Romance; it is not my natural cup of tea at all for, as you know, what I like is humdrum certainty, the same person, the same times. It was chiefly, I think, because I had come to realise the danger of this attitude, that, when Chester and I reached a sexual impasse,[3] I chose, against my natural inclination, to persevere with the relationship rather than drop it. I am more glad than I can say that I did so, dangerous as it has been and still is for both of us[.] There is of course, the element of romantic magic uncertainty still there, but it is not really to my liking, and the more he finds himself and so *can* be relied on, the more warmly I feel (Believe it or not).

I had a lovely Christmas. Thanks ever so for your large share in it.

love for 1945 and always
Wystan

ALS (Fountain Pen) + envelope addressed to 'Mrs Tania Stern | 207. E. 52nd Street | New York City | N. Y', postmark 'SWARTHMORE PA. DEC 31 5 30 PM 1944'.

---

repair relations. In an ALS, 18 Dec. [1944], Auden told James Stern, 'I hope T realises now that her position is more like mine was than she realised, ie T wants a professional relationship for money. C wants free love.' Finally, before a poetry reading which she had organized on 20 Dec. at the Cosmopolitan Club in Philadelphia, Auden told Caroline Newton that their friendship was over. (Carpenter, 332–3, gives an inaccurate account of this episode.)

[3] In mid-July 1941: see Carpenter, 312–13; Farnan, 53–66.

14. 20 May [1945][1]

May 20th   Somewhere in Germany[2]

Dearest Tania,

I havent written before because I've been waiting every day for Jimmy to arrive. I hope nothing has gone wrong about his papers.[3]

The town outside which we live was 92% destroyed in 30 minutes—You cant imagine what that looks like unless you see it with your own eyes.[4] We are billeted in the house of a nazi who committed suicide and also poisoned his wife, children and grandchildren.[5] It

---

[1] See Carpenter, 333–7, and in *Tribute*: James Stern, 'The Indispensable Presence', 123–7; Lincoln Kirstein, 'Siegfriedslage', 128–33; Nicolas Nabokov, 'Excerpts from Memories', 133–6, 145–8.

[2] Auden left the US by air on *ca.* 23 April 1945. After spending a few days in England, he arrived in Germany around the beginning of May (Carpenter, 334) and probably wrote this letter from Darmstadt (not specified by Auden in his letter in accordance with military regulations, but see Stern in *Tribute*, 127), where he (and later Stern) were based for part of their tour with the United States Strategic Bombing Survey. For the founding of USSBS in the Autumn of 1944, see books by two of its three former co-directors: John Kenneth Galbraith, *A Life in Our Times: Memoirs* (Boston, Mass., 1981), 196–9; and George W. Ball, *The Past Has Another Pattern: Memoirs* (New York, 1982), 42–53. (The third co-director was Paul H. Nitze, later one of the US's leading nuclear arms negotiators.) The so-called Morale Division of the operation was headed by Rensis Likert (1903–81), a social scientist and pioneer in public opinion research. He may be the recruiter 'Mr Nesbit' whom Stern describes in *Hidden Damage*, 4–6. Auden was recommended for the job by a professor of social psychology at Swarthmore, Richard S. Crutchfield, and recruited by Otto S. Klineburg. Everyone was given a rank theoretically corresponding to his previous station in civilian life (Auden became a Major), and was told to buy his own uniform. The Division actively recruited Britons living in the US, because many of them knew Germany well and were eager to serve the war effort (Galbraith, *Life in Our Times*, 196–9).

[3] Auden apparently made contact with Stern on the 25 or 26 May, when Auden phoned him in the evening at the USSBS headquarters at Bad Nauheim and told him to come over to Darmstadt and join Auden's interviewing unit (*Hidden Damage*, 82).

[4] Although undefended, Darmstadt was subjected to saturation bombing on 11 Sept. 1944 in a raid lasting 51 minutes. According to local figures, 8,433 people were killed and 2,439 were seriously wounded. After the raid, 49,000 people, nearly half of the survivors, fled from the town into the surrounding countryside. More than half of the city's 8,400 homes were destroyed and its entire centre was levelled (*Hidden Damage*, 94). Stern recalled pre-war Darmstadt as 'a pink city, built of the local "red" sandstone'. When he got there in 1945, what he saw was 'a high sea, a tempestuous ocean of pink rubble with jagged, perforated walls sticking up between the great waves' (*Hidden Damage*, 93, 95).

[5] Towards the end of his life, Auden told a *New York Times* interviewer that he had stayed in the Darmstadt house of a Nazi couple who had gone into hiding, leaving their children with the grandparents. The grandparents had killed the children and then themselves. This presumably means that on 20 May 1945 (when he wrote his letter) Auden was unaware that the couple were not in fact dead but missing. He told the interviewer that when the couple came back, he had to break the news to them about

was very comfortable but now too many people have arrived. We are a mixed lot but most of them are very nice.[6]

The work is very interesting but I'm near crying sometimes.[7]

Have been to Heidelberg and had some fascinating talks with people who were concerned in the July 20th affair last year.[8]

Now I have a chore for you. One of our sergeants (a refugee who was in Dachau) has a sick wife in N.Y who needs money to get into the country. Could you therefore send a hundred dollars to.

> Mrs Evelyn. T. Blitz
> c/o Dr Brull
> 316 W. 85th. N.Y.C 24. N.Y

Am very well and longing for Jimmy to come. Got a letter yesterday from Helen Sonthoff[9] dated May 3rd which is rather quick judging by most peoples experiences.

Good Rhine whine costs 35 cents a bottle[10] and the weather is wonderful. The people, though, are sad beyond belief.

Much love
Wystan

the suicides and murders (see Alan Levy, 'On Audenstrasse—In the Autumn of the Age of Anxiety,' *The New York Times*, 8 Aug. 1971, *Magazine* (sect. 6), p. 42, repr., enlarged, in Alan Levy, *Auden: In the Autumn of the Age of Anxiety* (Sag Harbor, NY, 1983), 26).

[6] By the time Auden's team transferred from Darmstadt to Heidelberg on 29 May, it consisted of Auden, the civilian 'leader' of the unit; 'Dudley', a 6-ft, wise-cracking private who before the war had worked on the San Francisco waterfront; 'Frank' a German-American sergeant recently out of college; 'John', a former minister of the American Church in Munich; a Major, the military 'leader' of the unit, who had been a clinical psychologist before the war; the 'Professor', a corporal, formerly a social scientist at a south-western university; and Stern (*Hidden Damage*, 92–3).

[7] See also ALS to Elizabeth Mayer, 9 May 1945 (Berg): 'I keep wishing you were here with us to help and then I think perhaps not, for as I write this sentence I find myself crying' and ALS to Wolfgang and Lily Köhler, 14 May [1945], (Library of the American Philosophical Society): 'The work is extremely interesting but I am sometimes very near crying . . . July 20th was more terrible than we knew.'

[8] Probably the anti-Nazi professors Emil Henk and Alfred Weber (1868–1958), a sociologist. Stern printed Henk's summary account of the 20 July conspiracy in *Hidden Damage*, 385–90.

[9] Helen and Herbert Sonthoff were friends of the Sterns and of Auden. (Mr Sonthoff had been a political dissident in Germany until he was obliged to flee the country. Auden apparently met him in Swarthmore, *ca.* 1944.) They lived now in Cambridge, Mass., and in late Aug. 1945, shortly after returning to the US, Auden paid them a visit in a house they were renting there. For a few more details about the friendship, see remarks in Jane Rule, '"Silly like us," a Recollection', *A Hot-Eyed Moderate* (Tallahassee, Fla., 1985), 205–14.

[10] German wine was not available in the US during the war, but in 1945 moderately

P. S Hope you managed—at my expense—to get the records. Where are you going for the summer[?]

ALS (Fountain Pen) + envelope addressed to 'Mrs Tania Stern | 207. E. 52 Street | New York City | N. Y. | U. S. A.', postmark 'U. S. ARMY POSTAL SERVICE A. P. O. MAY 20 1945 206'.

15. 6 June [1952][1]

June 6th   Via Santa Lucia 14 | Forio d'Ischia.

Dearest Jimmy and Tania,

At last a moment to write. I was *so* disappointed at just missing you like that. I arrived May 17th. I so wished you could have been there to share the fun and instruct me about Paris. I had a lovely

priced bottles of Californian table wine cost between 70¢. and $1 (see also *Hidden Damage*, 30). James Stern commented that in Germany Auden 'never went to bed with less than one full bottle of the local wine' (*Tribute*, 127) and in his poem 'Siegfriedslage' Lincoln Kirstein records that amongst the assorted dreck in Auden's Army jeep was a 'crate of wine' (ibid. 128). In his memoirs (see Letter 14, n. 2 above), George W. Ball claims that at the USSBS Headquarters at Bad Nauheim, Auden 'dined with us drunk several times' (49). Wine was not only cheap, but Auden suddenly had more money than usual to spend: his rate of pay doubled when he went into the Army. At Swarthmore he had been earning $2,000 per year. His USSBS salary was fixed at $4,300 per year and for his roughly three-and-a-half months of service in Germany he received $1,433.33.

[1] See Carpenter, 374. Auden was in Paris from 17 to *ca.* 30 May 1952 to take part in a huge festival of the arts called 'Œuvres du XXe Siècle', which included performances of opera and ballet, exhibitions of painting, and literary readings and colloquia. Based at the Théâtre des Champs Elysées, the conference was organized by Nicolas Nabokov and paid for by the American baking goods magnate Julius Fleischmann under the aegis of the Congress for Cultural Freedom. The aim was to demonstrate the greatness of art created in the free countries of the world. Many French intellectuals, including Sartre's *Temps modernes* circle, boycotted the events, which they viewed (with good reason) as CIA-sponsored cultural imperialism; Malraux was virtually the only leading French writer to take part in the conference. (For reports on the festival, see Genêt [Janet Flanner], 'Letter from Paris', *The New Yorker*, 28.15 (31 May 1952), 72, 74, 76–7; and Hellmut Jaesrich, 'Brief aus Paris: Töne und Theorien', *Der Monat* (Berlin–Dahlem), 4.86 (Juli 1952), 345–52. See also Peter Coleman, *The Liberal Conspiracy: The Congress for Cultural Freedom and the Struggle for the Mind of Postwar Europe* (New York, 1989), 55–6, 253.) Auden spoke to at least two sessions: a symposium on 'Rebellion and Communion' with Czeslaw Milosz, Glenway Wescott, Guglielmo Petroni, and Roger Caillois; and the final meeting in the Salle Gaveau, where he shared the microphone with William Faulkner, Salvador de Madariaga, Denis de Rougemont, and André Malraux (see Jaesrich, 'Brief aus Paris', 349, 350–1). He also went to a great many festival exhibitions and performances while he was in Paris, and on 28 May attended a cocktail party at Mme Grillet's (see Julien Green, *Journal 1950–1954* (Paris, 1955), 164).

time though *prodigiously* expensive, (as bad as N.Y.) but I still feel
Paris is not my city in the way that, for instance, Rome is. The
Amerloque writers contingent consisted of Katherine Anne (who kept
having heart attacks), Glenway Westcott (who seemed to know some
very grand people)[2] Allen Tate, Robert Lowell, me and Faulkner.[3]
We had an anxious time with the last for he went into a bout on
arrival, shut up in his hotel throwing furniture out of the window and
bottles at his ladies and saying the most *dreadful* things about coons.
However we managed to get him sober and onto the platform on the
last day to say that the Americans had behaved badly but that he
hoped they would behave better in the future and sit down.[4] Malraux
looks and speaks rather like Hitler but the public loved it.[5] I was the
first speaker at that meeting and as I rose a shower of pamphlets
descended from the gallery. Naturally, I thought it was the Commies
starting up, but it turned out to be les lettristes[6] accusing Malraux of
being a sous-Gide and Faulkner of being a sous-Joyce.[7] Cyril was
there with Barbara who is *so* rude that it is rather endearing.[8] Louis

[2] Including Philippe de Rothschild, whom Wescott probably knew through
Rothschild's American wife, Pauline Potter, who had worked on *Vogue*.

[3] See Ian Hamilton, *Robert Lowell: A Biography* (New York, 1982), 178; and *Letters
of Katherine Anne Porter*, ed. Isabel Bayley (New York, 1990), 421–2.

[4] Faulkner embarked on a wild drinking bout when he arrived in Paris, but his
behaviour was aggravated by the fact that he was suffering from several fractured verte-
brae. (This was only diagnosed and treated after the conference was over.) One of the
women who came to see him in Paris was the Swede Else Jonssen (see Joseph Blotner,
Faulkner: A Biography (New York, 1974), vol. 2, 1421–2, and Frederick R. Karl,
William Faulkner: American Writer: A Biography (New York, 1989), 814, 839). Blotner
says that when the unpopular secretary of the conference came to visit Faulkner, who
was laid up in bed in his hotel room, he hurled a bottle at her (1421–2). Karl adds that
there was a powerful Faulkner mystique in Paris at the time. When he rose to speak in
the Salle Gaveau (see Letter 15, n. 1 above), he was greeted by a lengthy ovation. His
'déclaration' was published as 'Tous les hommes libres doivent un petit quelque chose
à la France', in *Arts* (Paris), 362 (5–11 Juin 1952), 6.

[5] Malraux's speech was published as 'Ce que nous avons à defendre', in *Arts* (Paris),
362 (5–11 Juin 1952), 1, 6.

[6] Lettrisme was a post-war, concrete poetry movement, that forswore all relation to
semantical sense and relied instead on effects of onomatopoeia. (See Isidore Isou,
Qu'est-ce que le lettrisme? (Paris, 1947).) Sartre wrote: 'le lettrisme est un produit de
remplacement, une imitation plate et consciense de l'exubérance dadaïste' (*Situations II*
(Paris, 1965), 241).

[7] Jaesrich, 'Brief aus Paris', 550–1, has a brief report on the incident.

[8] Cyril Connolly and Barbara Skelton, who was his wife from 1950 to 1954. Skelton,
an Englishwoman and a denizen of bohemian Soho during the war, had been King
Farouk of Egypt's mistress. Subsequently, after her long affair and short marriage with
Connolly, she became involved with Lord Weidenfeld, to whom she was married from
1956 to 1960. Edmund Wilson reported that Skelton ruled Connolly 'with an iron
hand, and can, I am told, be exceedingly truculent.' Connolly described her to Edmund

and Hedli of course, too.[9] I suppose I shouldnt say anything against one of your 'ex'-s[10] but I think Hedli has become quite impossible—the *airs*, my dear. Peter Watty as nice as ever.[11]

I got back last night after spending three days with an old lady at Kitzbühel whom I hadn't seen since 1927.[12] A wonderful old thing who had Jews during the war and after had Alphonse Chateaubriand for six years till he died.[13] He had been condemned to death by the

Wilson as 'a lioness—her silvery hair and her greenish and feline eyes'. Wilson, however, wrote that he found 'no response in her face, a simple narcissistic mask, petrified by a fundamental sullenness' (Edmund Wilson, *The Fifties: From Notebooks and Diaries of the Period*, ed. Leon Edel (New York, 1986), 106, 373, 374). For a few anecdotes about Connolly and Skelton's stay in Paris, see Barbara Skelton, *Tears Before Bedtime* (London, 1987), 131–2.

[9] Louis MacNeice and his wife, the singer Hedli Anderson (1907–89). MacNeice mentioned his visit to Paris in 'Notes on the Way' [1] (28 June 1952), repr. in *Selected Prose of Louis MacNeice*, ed. Alan Heuser (Oxford, 1990), 176–7. For more on Anderson, see Donald Mitchell and Philip Reed, '"For Hedli": Britten and Auden's Cabaret Songs', *AS2* 61–5.

[10] James Stern and Anderson had lived together in Paris in the mid-Thirties. See Introduction, p. 43.

[11] Peter Watson (*ca.* 1908–56), a wealthy supporter of the arts, and the principal backer of *Horizon*. In an obituary in the *Guardian*, Connolly wrote: 'Mr Peter Watson, who died unexpectedly at the age of forty-nine, held a unique place in the world of modern art. As a young man he stepped, gay and delightful, out of a charmed existence like a Mayfair Buddha suddenly sobered by the tragedy of his time, to become the most intelligent, generous and discreet of patrons, the most creative of connoisseurs' (quoted in Barbara Skelton, *Weep No More* (London, 1989), 14; see also Michael Shelden, *Friends of Promise: Cyril Connolly and the World of Horizon* (London, 1989), *passim*).

[12] Hedwig Petzold was the widow of the Austrian poet Alfons Petzold (1882–1923). They were married in 1915 and had three children. Frau Petzold was from a middle-class family, but Alfons Petzold came from a working-class background and was known for his writings about proletarian life. He was a highly religious Protestant, a prolific writer, and a friend of Rilke, Hofmannsthal, Gerhart Hauptmann, and Hesse. After his marriage, he ran a bookshop in Kitzbühel until his death, which was caused by flu. His works include a famous autobiographical novel published posthumously, *Das rauhe Leben* (1932). After her husband died, Frau Petzold began taking paying guests at her home in Kitzbühel; Auden and his father lodged with her in the summer of 1925. Auden and his friend William McElwee returned to stay with her in the winter of 1926–7, when she seems to have gone to bed with Auden, and he may possibly have seen her again in the summer of 1927 on his way to Yugoslavia (Carpenter, 41, 69). They had corresponded occasionally since then.

[13] Alphonse de Chateaubriant (1877–1951), an aristocrat from Nantes whose novel *Monsieur des Lourdines* won the Prix Goncourt in 1911. He became increasingly Catholic and right-wing as he grew older. In *La Gerbe des forces* (1936) he advocated collaboration with Nazi Germany and in 1940 he founded *La Gerbe*, a collaborationist daily paper. He fled to Austria in 1944 and was condemned to death in his absence in 1945. For most of the rest of his life he lodged with Hedwig Petzold in Kitzbühel under the pseudonym of Wolf and continued writing until his peaceful demise in 1951.

French for collaboration. I had forgotten just how lovely the Tirol is.[14]

The kittens have grown marvellously during my absence and are now at their most enchanting stage.

What are your plans? Your two years will be up soon wont they?[15]

lots of love.

Wystan

ALS (Fountain Pen) + envelope addressed to 'James Stern Esq | Bottle Knap | Long Bredy | Dorchester | Dorset. | Inghilterra', postmark 'FORIO D'ISCHIA (TELEGRAFO) -6. 6. 52'.

16. 28 February 1953[1]

Feb 28th 1953   61 Paradise Rd | Northampton | Mass

Dear Jimmy and Tania,

Many thanks for your wire. As a whole the production of The Rake was good[2]—Blanche Thebom was our only real headache for she was determined to play the bearded lady for cheap laughs (which she got) and no one could stop her.[3] The reviews were just what one

---

[14] Auden got a letter from Hedwig Petzold in late April 1952 and he decided to make a detour to visit her in the Tirol on his way back from Paris to Ischia after the 'Œuvres du XXe Siècle' conference (see Letter 15, n. 1 above). This trip initiated a series of visits to Austria during the 1950s: Auden made further journeys to the Tirol in at least 1953, 1954, 1956, and 1957. By March 1957, he had decided to move there, complaining about tourists and, to Petzold, about the lack of water in his Ischian cistern: 'Another reason to move from Italy to Austria. Alas, my lease here lasts till 1960, but then . . .' (ALS, 19 March [1957], (Berg)). In the summer of 1957 Christa Esders, Frau Petzold's daughter, helped Auden look for a property outside Vienna, and it was she who spotted the newspaper ad for the Kirchstetten house that Auden later bought (Carpenter, 387; see also Letter 18, n. 3 below).

[15] The Sterns had gone back to live in England for two years as an experiment. They considered returning to the US but eventually decided to stay in England (see Introduction, p. 61).

[1] See Carpenter, 374–5.

[2] The Rake's Progress, conducted by Fritz Reiner, staged by George Balanchine, and starring Hilde Gueden as Anne Trulove, Mack Harrell as Nick Shadow, and Eugene Conley as Tom Rakewell, opened at the Metropolitan Opera House on 14 Feb. 1953. Although he had a generally negative reaction both to Stravinsky's music and to Auden and Kallman's libretto, The New York Times critic Olin Downes wrote 'the production was in every respect first class—in scenic settings and costuming, carefully co-ordinated action, choreography, and singing throughout of a high rank' ('Rake's Progress Has U.S. Première', The New York Times, 15 Feb. 1953, p. 61; see also Farnan, 190–1).

[3] Downes, The Times's critic, wrote: 'the strongest impersonation was Miss Thebom's

would like, ie wildly enthusiastic or violently anti.[4] You may have
seen the *Time* piece—clearly an offensive in its anti-Homintern campaign.[5] However, Time notwithstanding, the booking is so good that
the Met is putting on a number of extra performances.[6]

My job here is a sinecure—no teaching. I have a nice apartment
and a nice office in the library.[7]

Noemi is better but I am at a loss to know what to do about her.[8]
At D[r] Gourevitch's request I saw as much of her as I could manage. I

Baba the Turk, flaunting, insolent, monstrously exhibitionistic, also irresistibly comical
and burlesque' (ibid. 61).

[4] For a positive review, see Virgil Thomson, 'Music: "The Rake's Progress"', *New
York Herald Tribune*, 15 Feb. 1953, sect. 1, p. 34: 'Few composers in our time have
been served by an English libretto so high class all through.' Thomson ended his piece
by saying that of all Stravinsky's works, *The Rake's Progress* 'is probably among his
finest'.

[5] The unsigned review, 'Rite of Autumn', *Time*, 51.8 (23 Feb. 1953) allowed some
faint praise for Stravinsky's music but was caustic about Auden and Kallman's work:
'Igor Stravinsky's new opera, *The Rake's Progress*, headed into the Metropolitan Opera
for its U.S. première last week and there, before a large audience of well-wishers (and
an estimated 9,000,000 who listened on radio), fell flat on its libretto . . . [A]s the first
modern work the Met had produced in five years, it seemed pretty effete. Written by
Poet W. H. Auden and Chester Kallman as an 18th century moral fable, *The Rake*'s
book pointed its moral more in irony than in earnestness, had a minimum of dramatic
action onstage, and for its biggest bit of comedy wagged its lean finger at a bearded
lady' (59–60).
For *Time*'s solidly pro-Republican and anti-intellectual viewpoint during the 1950s,
and especially after Eisenhower's election as President in 1952, see James L.
Baughman, *Henry R. Luce and the Rise of the American News Media* (Boston, Mass.,
1987), esp. ch. 9, 'The Lucean Decade and Its Detractors 1950–1959', 158–79.
Baughman describes *Time* as reporting stories in a style 'full of "knowing" detail, possessed of an omniscience tinged by or dripping in biases' (166) and Arthur M.
Schlesinger, Jr. quotes *Time* on the 'wide and unhealthy gap' between American intellectuals and the American people in '*Time* and the Intellectuals', *The Politics of Hope*
(Boston, Mass., 1963), 230–6. In the early months of 1963, Auden and some of his
friends were interviewed extensively for a planned *Time* cover story on him. He also sat
for a cover portrait (paintings were used then, not photographs). When the interviewer
T. G. Foote went to see Auden in late Jan. 1963, he noted that 'Auden is enormously
gun-shy about inquiry into his private life (which is understandable)' (unpublished
interview and notes by T. G. Foote, p. 2; parts of this and later interviews were finally
used in Foote's obituary, 'Auden: the Sage of Anxiety', *Time*, 102.15 (8 Oct. 1973),
113–14). The story was cancelled when *Time* executives learned about Auden's domestic arrangements and decided that they did not want a homosexual on their cover.

[6] *The Rake's Progress* was performed at the Metropolitan Opera on 14, 19, 27 Feb.,
and 4 and 16 Mar. 1953.

[7] Auden was at Smith from late Feb.–mid-May 1953, living in Paradise Road. See
Carpenter, 374, and, for recollections of Auden at Smith, Wendell Stacy Johnson,
W. H. Auden (New York, 1990), *passim*.

[8] Noemi Kenmore, a woman with whom Auden and the Sterns had been friendly
and who, like several others (see Introduction, p. 54; Letter 1, n. 2; and Letter 8, n. 4),

should have followed my own intuition which is to have nothing to do with people who go off their rockers. (There has been another one, a complete stranger, who kept calling in the middle of the night, then arrived one morning, said she was 'spiritually married' to me and refused to leave. I had to call the cops in. Ugh).

My Papa was taken ill at Christmas and the doctors gave up hope. However he recovered; luckily we have been able to find a house-keeper for him as he cant now look after himself.

How did you like *Hemlock and After?*[9] I thought it awfully good and much kinder than his short stories. The reviewers here were horrified, not at the subject, but at his portrayal of queers as no more unhappy than anyone else.[10]

When you return and if it is still running, as I expect it will be, you *must* go and see *Pal Joey*.[11] Its the best musical I ever saw.

Heard Emlyn Williams the other night doing his Dickens readings.[12] Loved it.

I suppose you heard that George Davies was beaten up last September and left for dead.[13] (He [is] quite patched up now, though

had fallen in love with Auden. He probably had a brief affair with her. In late 1952 she had a serious collapse: a 'schyzy paranoia, hearing voices etc' Auden told the Sterns (ALS, 20 Dec. [1952]).

[9] Angus Wilson's first novel was published in 1952. Geoffrey Gorer brought it to Ischia with him on a visit during that summer and Auden read and admired the book. He met Wilson for the first time in London in the later part of June 1953, a few months after he wrote this letter (see ALS to Wendell Stacy Johnson, 4 July [1953], (Berg)).

[10] See, for example, the unsigned review in *Time*, 60.97 (29 Sept. 1952), 97–8: 'Sands [the book's protagonist], it turns out, is a homosexual and almost proud of it . . . Yet compared with the moral termites around him, he seems a fair sort' (97).

[11] *Pal Joey*, starring Vivienne Segal and Harold Lang, was playing at the Broadhurst Theater in New York.

[12] The Welsh actor, director, and playwright Emlyn Williams (1905–87) began his successful one-man shows, *Emlyn Williams as Charles Dickens*, in 1950. He appeared on stage dressed like Dickens and sitting at a Dickensian lectern. In the spring of 1953, Williams travelled around the US with his version of *Bleak House*, winding up in New York in mid-April. 'L. F.' wrote in a review, 'Mr. Williams is an actor of tremendous range and his voice has an amazing flexibility. He can roar with fury and whisper so that pathos overwhelms an audience. His eyes can flash with anger and become soft with pity. His virtuosity can traverse a galaxy of thirty-six characters' ('At the Theater', *New York Times*, 21 Apr. 1953, p. 33).

[13] Auden had met the American writer and editor George Davis (1906–57) in London in 1937. In 1938, on their way back from China, Auden and Isherwood were entertained by him in New York (see *C&HK* (US), 313–15). During Auden's early years in the US, Davis, who came from Detroit and had lived in Paris, was one of his closest friends. Described by Isherwood as 'Small, plump, handsome, sparkling' (*C&HK* (US), 313), Davis had written a successful novel, *The Opening of a Door* (New

one eye is a little displaced). I went with him and Lotte to the trials. One of the defense lawyers tried to make as much stink as possible but the Judge was very sensible. From the lawyers questions, I gather that to the courts the most suspect literary activity is poetry, then short stories, and then, least compromising, novels.

Much love to you both

Wystan

ALS (Fountain Pen) + envelope addressed to 'James Stern Esq | Rowbarrow Farm | Adber | N^r Sherborne | Dorset. | England', postmark 'NORTHAMPTON MASS. MAR 2 9 AM 1953'.

17. [?] 1 May [1955][1]

Via Santa Lucia 14 | Forio d'Ischia | Prov. di Napoli | Italy

May 1st:

Dearest Jimmy and Tania:

Many thanks for your letter and the heavenly p.p.c.'s. It's extraordinary what you may send through the mails if its archaeological—at least I *hope* I shant be prosecututed.

re B-P: I has a letter from Mrs Giroudette[2] just before I left in which she couldnt tell me just what would have to be done as she

York, 1931), but then suffered from a long creative block. Despite that personal crisis, he was responsible for getting serious writing into the high-paying fashion magazines for the first time, from 1936 to 1940 as fiction editor at *Harper's Bazaar*, and from 1941 to 1949 as fiction editor at *Mademoiselle*. In 1940 he found the house at 7 Middagh Street, Brooklyn, after seeing a vision of it in a dream, and he invited Auden and Carson McCullers to move in with him (Virginia Spencer Carr, *The Lonely Hunter: A Biography of Carson McCullers* (Garden City, NY, 1975), 116–17; Carpenter, 303–4). Davis was drawling and immensely explicit in his conversation—Auden described him as the wittiest person he had ever known (quoted in Gerald Clarke, *Capote: A Biography* (New York, 1988), 88)—and he had a passion for kitsch Victoriana, which he seems briefly to have passed on to Auden *ca.* 1943 (see Carpenter, 329).

Lotte Lenya (1898–1981) was in the first Berlin production of Brecht and Weill's *Die Dreigroschenoper*, which ran at the Theater am Schiffbauerdamm in Berlin in 1928, where Auden saw it. She was married to Weill until his death in 1950. The next year she married George Davis and he encouraged her to try to revive Weill's work and to sing again, both of which she did very· successfully. Davis died of a heart attack in Berlin in 1957, where he was helping Lenya with a recording session.

[1] See Carpenter, 378–80.

[2] The Giroudettes, a local couple, looked after the Bective Poplars shack on Fire Island for Auden and the Sterns (for details of later events concerning the Giroudettes, see Farnan, 127).

had not been out yet. I have written to her again now that she is in Cheery Grove to say that if she will engage someoné and send me his estimate I will send her a cheque for that at once. I hope the old ruin doesnt just crumple.

Berlin was fascinating: you cannot *imagine* what the new soviet architecture of the workers flats in the Stalin Allee is like—a sort of 1907 Comfort Station style.[3] And its really true what the reporters say: if you sit in a restaurant in the East Sector, no one talks above a whisper. My name having appeared in the papers, I got a letter from a boy-friend of 1929, then a sailor, beautiful as the dawn, who behaved very badly to me. I went to see him, and nearly fainted—He had not just put on weight, he was grotesque like something in a circus—also owns a lamp-shade factory and is obviously pretty rich.[4] However he did take me to a dive near the Gorlitzer Bahnhof which was exactly like it used to be in the old days.[5] You really must go there (Berlin, I mean, of course) if you get a chance; as it is the most extraordinary city in the world.

I've never thanked you for the wonderful time I had in Dorset.

much love to you both
Wystan

TLS + envelope addressed to 'James Stern Esq | Stourminster Newton | Dorset | Inghilterra', postmark 'FORIO D'ISCHIA (TELEGRAFO) 2 -5 55'.

---

[3] The *OED* defines 'comfort station' (early uses date from the 1920s) as a US genteelism for a public lavatory. See *The Age of Anxiety*: 'Ingenious George reached his journey's end | Killed by a cop in a comfort station' (*CP91* 482).

The Stalinallee, later renamed the Karl-Marx-Allee, was the site of a huge and prestigious workers' housing project started in the 1950s.

[4] Gerhart Meyer. See David Luke, 'Gerhart Meyer and the Vision of Eros', *AS2* 103–11.

[5] The Görlitzer Bahnhof, demolished in 1967, was in south-west Berlin on Wienerstraße, in the American sector of the post-war city. For details from the period when Auden was first in Berlin, see Karl Baedeker, *Berlin and Its Environs: Handbook for Travellers*, 6th edn. (Leipzig, 1923), 169. Auden told Lincoln Kirstein: 'Berlin was fascinating, and the old life still goes on among romantically ruined slums, at least in *our* sector' (ALS from Forio, 26 April [1955]).

18. 9 May [1957][1]

May 9th   CHRIST CHURCH, | OXFORD.

Dearest Jimmy and Tania:

Thank you very much for your note and for thinking of sending it to Repton where I got it just before the funeral.[2]

Also for your letter which I should have answered before, but what with finding a place to live, going to a niece's wedding, visiting Papa, I have been rushed.[3] He had no pain at all, thank goodness, but simply sank slowly away. Do you know that the novelists are right, and that dying people really *do* pluck at the bed-sheets.[4]

When dead, he looked immensely old and eternal, and less like himself, than an archetypal ancestor of the Audens.

My first lecture went off well, I think, last Monday.[5] Am reviewing a terribly bad biography of Houseman which does, however, contain one curious fact. When the first volume of his scholarly magnum opus, his critical edition of the eighth rate poet Manilius appeared, Houseman hired a press-cutting agency![6]

Have also got to review for the *New Yorker*, a new piece of old Bernard Shaw, *Miss Dorothea* advice to young girls, which I havent yet opened.[7]

I hope very much to be able to pay you a visit but dont yet know

---

[1] See Carpenter, 383–4.

[2] Auden arrived in Repton to see his father, Dr George A. Auden, *ca.* 1 May 1957. Dr Auden died two days later on 3 May. After the cremation, Auden and his brothers went by train with their father's ashes to the Lake District, where the family scattered Dr Auden's remains.

[3] The reference to 'finding a place to live' suggests that Auden already knew that he had been awarded the Premio Feltrinelli (although this was not announced publicly until 4 June 1957) and that he had decided to buy a home with the prize money. Carpenter (386) says that Auden first considered purchasing the villa in Forio where he had spent the winter of 1956–7, and on which he had a lease until 1960 (see Letter 15, n. 14 above). In June, though, Auden wrote to Hedwig Petzold to give her the news about the prize and to tell her that he wanted to move to Austria immediately, rather than in 1960 as he had originally planned (ALS, [?20 June 1957], (Berg)).

[4] For some other remarks by Auden about his father's death, and for John Auden's comments, see Carpenter, 383, n. 1.

[5] On Robert Frost, first printed in *DH* 337–53. On 13 May Auden lectured on D. H. Lawrence, and on 20 May on music in Shakespeare (*DH* 277–95, 500–27).

[6] Auden's review of G. L. Watson's *A. E. Housman: A Divided Life* was published as 'Straw without Bricks', *New Statesman and Nation*, NS 53.1366 (18 May 1957), 643–4. He mentions the press-clipping agency in the review as well.

[7] His review of Shaw's *My Dear Dorothea* was 'Crying Spoils the Appearance', *The New Yorker*, 33.29 (7 Sept. 1957), 130–4 (New York edn., 142–6).

when, as there is going to [?be] all the problem of dividing father's things and scattering his ashes in the Lake District.

Much love to you both
Wystan

ALS (Fountain Pen) + envelope addressed to 'James Stern Esq | Sturminster Newton | Dorset', postmark 'OXFORD A 1 15 PM 9 MAY 1957'.

19. 1 March 1968[1]

77 St. Mark's Place | New York City | New York 10003

March 1st, 1968 9 p.m.

Dearest Jimmy:

I have just been sent Calder-Marshall's selection from your Short Stories.[2] (please forgive the typing but I am a little drunk) You don't need me to tell you how first-class they are. What concerns me is what you should do now. Your 'drying up' since you returned to the Old Country has worried me as I am sure it has worried many others.[3] I am convinced that what you should do now is write a straightforward and truthful autobiography. For a poet like myself an autobiography is redundant since anything of importance that happens to one is immediately incorporated, however obscurely, in a poem. With a novelist or a short-story writer like yourself this is not so.

Some people, like myself, have an uninteresting family background and, from a reader's point of view, an uninteresting life (except as a 'queer' which is nobody's business.)

In your case both are of the utmost interest. I implore you, therefore, to write what I know will be a document of the greatest historical and, because of your talent, the greatest literary value.

I have heard that you had a heart attack. I hope it is all over. I'm

[1] See Carpenter, 426–8.

[2] *The Stories of James Stern*, published in Feb. 1968 in the UK, does not mention any role played by Arthur Calder-Marshall. Calder-Marshall (1908–92) was a novelist, short-story writer, biographer, and essayist. He was educated at Oxford and, after Auden went down, was part of Spender's circle (see *WWW* (US), 64). He became a master at a minor public school, Denstone College, Staffordshire, in the first half of the Thirties, and is best known for his novel *Dead Centre* (London, 1935), a story told through a composite arrangement of the voices of pupils, masters, and staff at 'Richbury School' (see also Cunningham, 33). For brief comments by Auden and Isherwood on Calder-Marshall, see their 'Young British Writers—On the Way Up', *Vogue*, New York, 94.4 (15 Aug. 1939), 94.

[3] See Introduction, pp. 61–2.

fine, except that for the first time in my life I notice that most of the people on the street are younger than I.

> Much love to you both
> Wystan

P. S. If there is anything you and Tania wish to translate, I am quite a power on the Ford Foundation Translation Committee.[4]

TLS + envelope addressed to 'James Stern Esq | Hatch Manor | Tisbury | Wilts | England', postmark 'AL NEW YORK N. Y. PM 2 MAR 1968'.

20. 13 March [1968][1]

77 St Mark's Place   March 13th

Dearest Jimmy:

Thank you so much for your wonderful letter. I think I always guessed why you stopped writing.

I am convinced, however, as I wrote you, that your greatest work lies ahead of you, thrombo or no thrombo, and what it will basically be is an act of *thanksgiving* for your marriage.

Ageing is a funny business, isn't it, and perhaps a little harder for me than for you. As the youngest child, youngest grandchild, and usually the youngest boy in my form, I always assumed I was the youngest in any company. This year, for the *first* time, I notice, with some shock, that most of the people on the street are my juniors. Another odd thing: I find I need more sleep than I used to.

As Chester spends the winter in Athens, in the winter I have to cook for myself.[2] I find that, when I do, I develop sudden and quite irrational passions for certain foods. Last winter it was turnips; this winter it is fish.

[4] On 17 Dec. 1964, while he was in Berlin, Auden agreed to become a member of the Board of Trustees of the Ford Foundation's new National Translation Center, which had its headquarters at the University of Texas at Austin. (Other trustees at various times included Robert Fitzgerald, Roger Shattuck, and Robert Lowell.) Auden published some translations and a short prose piece in the Center's magazine *Delos* and he remained a trustee until the Center was wound up in 1969. The Sterns do not seem to have received a grant from the Center.

[1] See Carpenter, 426–8.

[2] Kallman had begun to spend periods out of New York from *ca*. 1961 onwards (Carpenter, 407–8; Farnan, 230; Miller, 130). From 1963 until 1971 (when he returned to New York for a month or so), he spent each winter in an apartment in Athens (Farnan, 227, 238–9).

Have you read *Black like Me* by John Howard Griffin?[3] If not, you must.

much love to you both.
Wystan

ALS (Biro) + envelope addressed to 'James Stern Esq | Hatch Manor | Tisbury | Wilts | England', postmark 'NEW YORK, NY OK MAR 14 PM 1968'.

21. 18 [or poss. 19] November 1972[1]

Christ Church | Oxford | Tel. 43450   Nov 18th.

Dearest Jimmy and Tania:
Could I possibly come and stay with you for Christmas and New Year?

love
Wystan

ALS (Biro) + envelope addressed to 'Mrs James Stern | Hatch Manor | Tisbury | Wilts', postmark 'OXFORD D. 3. 6 45 PM 19 NOV 1972'.

22. 8 January [1973][1]

Christ Church | Oxford   Jan 8th

Dearest Jimmy and Tania,
    The train to Waterloo was hell: not one seat to be had.[2]
    The trial of my thief was last Thursday.[3] To my amazement and,

---

[3] *Black Like Me* (Boston, 1961; London, 1962) by John Howard Griffin (1920–80). The novelist Griffin was Texan, Catholic, and white. In 1959 he decided to have his skin-pigment temporarily darkened and in 1960 he wandered through the racially segregated American South for six weeks, experiencing the humiliations of life for African-Americans. 'I wanted to test whether we really judge men as humans or whether we draw up an indictment against a whole group' he said later. 'I kept my name and changed nothing but my pigment.' Griffin's book was a sensation and eventually sold over a million copies. It was also made into a film.

[1] See Carpenter, 443–4.

[1] See Carpenter, 442–6.
[2] Auden stayed with Sonia Orwell in London on 22 Dec. 1972, and the next day they travelled from Waterloo Station to the Sterns' home in Wiltshire. Orwell left shortly after Christmas but Auden stayed on until 2 Jan. 1973, when he returned to Oxford via London.
[3] A labourer, Keith Tilley, was alleged to have stolen £50 from Auden at All Souls on 18 Oct. 1972. His trial took place on 4 Jan. 1973, and Auden was in court to give evidence (see Carpenter, 442).

apparent[ly], to the amazement of many in court, the jury acquitted him. I can only conclude that modern juries are violently anti-police and Establishment.

How is the fog in Hatch? It is bad here.

I had such a wonderful time with you both and can't thank you enough[.]

love
Wystan

ALS (Biro) + envelope addressed to 'M^r and Mrs James Stern | Hatch Manor | Tisbury | Wiltshire', postmark 'OXFORD D. 3. 9 45 AM 8 JAN 1973'.

23. [7 May 1973][1]

THANK YOU, FOG

Grown used to New York weather,
all too familiar with Smog,
You, Her unsullied Sister,
I'd quite forgotten and what
You bring to British winters:
now native knowledge returns.

Sworn foe to festination,
daunter of drivers and planes,
speeders, of course, will curse You,
but how delighted I am
that You've been moved to visit
Wiltshire's witching countryside
for a whole week at Christmas,
that no one can scurry where
my cosmos is contracted
to an ancient manor-house
and four selves, joined in friendship,
Jimmy, Tania, Sonia, Me.

[1] See Carpenter, 448–50.

Outdoors a shapeless silence,
for even those birds whose blood
is hot enough to bid them
sojourn here all the year round,
mavis and merlex, for instance,
at your cajoling refrain
their jocund interjections,
no cock considers a scream,
vaguely visible, tree-tops
rustle not but stay there, so
efficiently condensing
Your damp to definite drops.

Indoors specific spaces,
cosy, accomodate to
reminiscence and reading,
crosswords and laughter and chat:
refected by a sapid
supper and regaled by wine,
we sit in a close circle,[2]
each unaware of our own
nose but alert to the others,
making the most of it, for
how soon we must re-enter,
when lenient days are done,
the world of work and money
and minding our p's and q's.[3]

No summer sun will ever
dismantle the global gloom
cast by the daily papers,
vomiting in slip-shod prose
the facts of filth and violence
that we're too dumb to prevent:
our earth's a horrid mess, but
for this holy interim,

[2] See Introduction, pp. 63–4.
[3] Cf. 'Homage to Clio' (*CP91* 612): 'all wise | Castellans will mind their p's and q's'.

so placid yet so festive,
Thank You, Thank You, Thank You, Fog.

———————

with love and gratitude,
Wystan

TLS + envelope addressed to 'M^r and Mrs James Stern | Hatch Manor | Tisbury | Wilts | England', postmark 'KIRCHSTETTEN BEZ. ST. PÖLTEN 3062 -7.-5.73-17'.

The Fall of Rome (1966)

INTRODUCTION

G. W. BOWERSOCK

WHEN the editors of *Life Magazine* proposed that W. H. Auden write an essay on the fall of Rome,[1] they caught the poet at a moment when this subject was much on his mind. Someone perhaps knew this, and knew as well that it was a subject that had occupied him on and off over several decades. Auden wrote the essay in March 1966, but, regrettably, *Life* rejected the piece, and it is published now for the first time.[2]

Writing in *The New Republic* in September of 1944, Auden had offered his observations on the long road that led from Augustan Rome to the Augustinian city of God. He was reviewing a reprint of a book by Charles Norris Cochrane entitled *Christianity and Classical Culture*, first published in 1940. Auden acknowledged having read this book many times, and he added, 'my conviction of its importance to the understanding not only of the epoch with which it is concerned, but also of our own, has increased with each rereading.'[3] With its high-flying ideas, abstract thought, and murky argumentation, Cochrane's book was heavy going even at the time, but it was widely

---

[1] A series of essays under the collective title, 'The Romans,' ran in *Life* from 3 Mar.–17 June 1966.

[2] Auden typed the text himself double-spaced on 17 folios of 8½ × 11 inch paper, and, either then or later, made some corrections, deletions, and additions in pen. Although his essay was rejected (and presumably sent back to him), *Life* retained a xerox of the piece for their records. The magazine had a policy of burning all defunct files once they were ten years old. The text of this essay comes from the *Life* xerox of the original typescript, retrieved from the magazine's archives by a senior editor around the end of 1976, shortly before the files for 1966 were due to be destroyed. (The original typescript probably does not survive.) The title is not written in Auden's hand, though the words may be Auden's. The xerox from which this text is taken is now in the collection of Robert A. Wilson. After *Life* had rejected the essay, Auden's New York agents, Curtis Brown, tried to get it into print elsewhere: they submitted the piece to *The Atlantic Monthly* on 25 Aug. 1966. But on 13 Sept. 1966, that magazine also declined it.

[3] 'Augustus to Augustine', *FA* 33.

admired in a world that showed great respect for Toynbee's *A Study of History*.

In the last years of the Second World War and the years that followed, any synthesis that appeared to offer a comforting, yet profound explanation of the violent upheavals of history provided welcome reading. There can be few today who read Cochrane's book, despite the obvious importance of its theme. The grand progression that he postulated from 'reconstruction' to 'renovation' and on to 'regeneration' is hardly likely to persuade a historian of the 1990s. But it clearly spoke to Auden and, in particular, to Auden the Christian. Whenever he returned to the theme of the Roman Empire and its apparent collapse, the shadow of Cochrane was all too visible.

In 1944 Auden believed that the present time was 'not so unlike the age of Augustine'.[4] He drew attention to the planned society, rampant criminality, bureaucracy, religious persecution, and even 'a new Constantinism', which would impose religious instruction in the schools in order to cure juvenile delinquency. Self-satisfied Christians of the fifth century AD were presiding over the dissolution of the world they thought they had saved, and the parallel that Auden saw with his own time soon found poetic expression in his poem 'The Fall of Rome' (1947). There, for example, he represented self-righteousness, selfishness, and bureaucracy in tough and sardonic verses:

> Cerebrotonic Cato may
> Extol the Ancient Disciplines,
> But the muscle-bound Marines
> Mutiny for food and pay.
>
> Caesar's double-bed is warm
> As an unimportant clerk
> Writes *I DO NOT LIKE MY WORK*
> On a pink official form.[5]

Auden shared with the twentieth-century Greek poet C. P. Cavafy a poetic interest in the declining Roman Empire and an awareness of its relevance to contemporary events. It is not surprising to find Auden writing a preface for a new translation of Cavafy's work in 1961. He was clearly impressed by Cavafy's perception, highly unusual when he wrote, that the Christians enjoyed a traditional pagan way of life with considerably more brio than most of the

---

[4] 'Augustus to Augustine', *FA* 39.   [5] *CP91* 333.

pagans who struggled against them in late antiquity. 'After Constantine,' wrote Auden, 'it was the Christian who had a better chance than the Pagan of getting on in the world, and the Pagan, even if not persecuted, who became the object of social ridicule.'[6] Like Auden himself, Cavafy was both Christian and homosexual, and explicit about both. It is clear that Auden detected a kindred spirit, even if he was unable to read the Greek poet in his original language. The encounter with Cavafy evidently moved Auden to adopt a noticeably more positive view of the early Christian Empire than he had formed from his repeated readings of Cochrane's work.

In late 1965 the editors of the newly established *New York Review of Books* had the inspired idea of inviting Auden to review a recent set of lectures delivered in Belfast by the Regius Professor of Greek at Oxford, E. R. Dodds, under the title *Pagan and Christian in an Age of Anxiety*.[7] This book paid obvious tribute to Auden's *Age of Anxiety*, and it took up Cochrane's themes in a far more lucid and original way than Cochrane's own work. Dodds allowed Auden to find a middle ground between his original rejection of the Christian Empire and the more sympathetic treatment evoked by Cavafy. Dodds had proclaimed, in fairness to his readers, that he was an agnostic who could not share 'the standpoint of those who see the triumph of Christianity as the divine event to which the whole creation moved'.[8] In his review, published early in 1966, Auden responded to Dodds's challenge by declaring at the outset that he was an Episcopalian but did not believe that Christianity triumphed either.[9]

A clear echo of Auden's reading of Cochrane can be heard in his judgement, 'I consider the adoption of Christianity as the official state religion, backed by the coercive powers of the state, however desirable it may have seemed at the time, to have been a "bad", that is to say, an un-Christian thing.'[10] But he then went on to put in a good word for Irenaeus, who came to the defence of the heretical Montanists 'not, surely, because he agreed with them but because, gentle soul that he was, he disliked persecution, even of cranks'.[11]

Towards the end of the Dodds review, Auden returned to the positive side of the Christianization of the Roman world. He emphasized that the Church was open to all men, 'without regard to social class, education, or their past lives'.[12] In a truly Cavafian spirit, he declared

[6] 'C. P. Cavafy', *FA* 342.   [7] (Cambridge, 1965).
[8] Quoted by Auden, 'Heresies', *FA* 41.   [9] Ibid.   [10] Ibid.
[11] Ibid.   [12] Ibid. 47.

that the Christian faith was really a more 'this-worldly' religion than any of its competitors. It was obvious that, in reflecting on Dodds's lectures, Auden had enlarged his positive assessment of Christianity in the final epoch of the Roman Empire.

Clearly Auden was a brilliant choice for the *Life* essay, and it is sad that the editors found the piece he provided unsuitable for their audience. The essay is a thoughtful and exciting extension of Auden's previous reflections. Some parts of it, especially the pages on classical idealism, are warmed-over Cochrane without much change from what Auden had written in his review of 1944. But there is much that is fresh and original. Auden himself saw fit to link this essay with his earlier work by ending it with a complete quotation of the poem 'The Fall of Rome' from 1947.

In 1966 people could still talk about the fall of Rome without embarrassment. The expression came straight from Gibbon, and for two centuries historians took it for granted that Rome had declined and fallen. Most would probably have agreed with Gibbon in blaming the Christians and the barbarians for what happened. But with the publication of Peter Brown's *The World of Late Antiquity* in 1971[13] and a rising tide of relativism in historical interpretations of the Roman Empire, the Gibbonian view of decline and fall soon yielded to a vision of restructuring, regrouping, shifting of boundaries, and the emergence of new perspectives that transformed the end of Rome into the rise of late antiquity. Transformation replaced decline and fall.

Auden's essay stands interestingly on the brink of this great change in the historical interpretation of Gibbon's problem. He knew his *Decline and Fall* well and borrowed, although with evident discomfort, from Gibbon's rosy account of the Antonine age. He cites Gibbon on occasion and even rephrases the famous lines at the end of chapter two of the *Decline and Fall* on the poverty of social and intellectual life in the second and third centuries AD.[14] Two hundred years earlier Gibbon himself would have had no difficulty in subscribing to Auden's observation, 'the price paid for this tranquillity was a general decline in intellectual curiosity and invention.'

---

[13] (London).

[14] Edward Gibbon, *The History of the Decline and Fall of the Roman Empire* (Everyman Edition, London, 1974) vol. 1, 57–8: 'If we except the inimitable Lucian, this age of indolence passed away without having produced a single writer of original genius. . . . The decline of genius was soon followed by the corruption of taste.'

But, significantly, amid the echoes of Gibbon and Cochrane, there are unmistakable adumbrations of the new view of late antiquity that was to emerge in the 1970s. Auden was making his way towards this interpretation by way of Cavafy and the lectures of Dodds. Both are quoted in his essay for *Life*—with reference to Neoplatonism (Dodds was, in fact, among the most distinguished scholars of Neoplatonism in his day), and with reference to the puritanical views of Julian the Apostate as ridiculed in a poem by Cavafy. Auden had already quoted this poem in his introduction of 1961:

Was it possible that they [the Christians of Antioch] would ever renounce
Their lovely way of living; the variety of their
Daily amusement; their magnificent
Theatre where they found the union of art
With the erotic propensities of the flesh![15]

Auden now gives the translation of John Mavrogordato, rather than the Rae Dalven version for which he had provided an introduction. Although the poem has been still better translated by Edmund Keeley in recent years, the Mavrogordato translation well conveys Cavafy's admiration for the sensuality of Christian life when it was threatened by the pagan austerities of Julian. This positive view of the early Christian Empire clearly found a resonance in Auden.

Still more arresting is Auden's own assessment of the role of Christianity in reviving the cultural life of the Empire from the torpor into which both Gibbon and he believed that it had fallen. In his essay for *Life*, Auden, the avowed Episcopalian, declared with pride, 'One may like or dislike Christianity, but no one can deny that it was Christianity and the Bible which raised western literature from the dead.' In a fervent reformulation of the argument at the end of his review of Dodds, he developed the social implications of Christian doctrine:

A faith which held that the Son of God was born in a manger, associated himself with persons of humble station in an unimportant Province, and died a slave's death, yet did this to redeem all men, rich and poor, free men and slaves, citizens and barbarians, required a completely new way of looking at human beings; if all are children of God and equally capable of salvation, then all, irrespective of status or talent, vice or virtue, merit the serious attention of the poet, the novelist, and the historian.

---

[15] 'C.P. Cavafy', *FA* 343.

These lines, like virtually all Auden's critical prose, reflect his personal tastes. It is where these tastes are kept from view, as in the routine paragraphs on ancient technology or the comments on classical idealism borrowed straight from Cochrane, that Auden's piece becomes disappointingly pedestrian. But the passion and originality that suffuse most of it show him grappling with issues that had concerned him deeply for at least twenty-five years (after he first read Cochrane). Several important themes that show up here were to reappear again in the poetic work of Auden's final years.

Some of these themes are so prominent that the *Life* essay can serve as a kind of commentary on them. For example, in the second paragraph of the essay on the fall of Rome, Auden admits, 'By heredity and temperament, I think of the Romans with distaste.' But he then goes on to say, 'The only classical latin poet I *really* like is Horace.' He denounces Roman architecture and expresses a preference for the 'rolling English road'. It is perhaps not surprising that the greatest master of twentieth-century lyric in English should have admired the undisputed master of Latin lyric in antiquity. But this casual remark serves as a kind of prelude to a poem that Auden wrote two years later, 'The Horatians'. Here he competes with Horace on his own turf by writing verses based on a complex Horatian metre (Asclepiadean stanzas). His taste for the 'rolling English road' is reaffirmed in this tribute to Horace as a poet with a knowledge of local topography, whose tastes 'run to | small dinner-parties, small rooms, | and the tone of voice that suits them.' He even manages to link his favourite poet with his Anglican faith:

> how many have
> found in the Anglican Church
> your Maecenas who enabled
>
> a life without cumber.[16]

This luminous tribute to Horace of 1968 was echoed again in one of Auden's last poems, entitled 'A Thanksgiving'. These are lines in which Auden contemplates the poetic models that had inspired him over the years and those whom he now requires:

> Who are the tutors I need?
> Well, *Horace*, adroitest of makers,
> beeking in Tivoli.[17]

---

[16] *CP91* 772.   [17] *CP91* 892.

Apart from Horace, Auden confesses that in his opinion there were not many interesting writers in the Roman Empire or late antiquity. He does manage to single out the *Pervigilium Veneris* as a little masterpiece (a judgement in which most critics would concur). But the great surprise in his review of Latin literature is his praise for the poet Maximian: 'finally, in the sixth century after the West has fallen, one really remarkable poet, Maximian'. Auden strengthens his observation by quoting from one of Maximian's elegies just before the concluding section of his article. A girl in Constantinople bursts into tears upon discovering the ageing poet impotent. When the writer tells her that his personal inadequacy need hardly cause her such grief, she admits that her tears are really not for her own deprivation but for 'the general chaos'. She represents Maximian's failure as a symbol of the creative failure of the world at large.

It is nothing less than astonishing that Auden should see in Maximian one of the few great poets of the late age of Rome. Many learned classical scholars have gone to their graves without ever having read a line of Maximian's verses or even having heard his name. Possibly the brief account in F. J. E. Raby's *History of Secular Latin Poetry in the Middle Ages* (1934) led Auden to this highly obscure poet. It is not easy to come by a text of his verse in Latin, let alone in translation. Classical scholars who have actually studied the elegies of Maximian have generally not thought much of them. The standard classical encyclopaedia pronounces this poet *ein mittelmässiger Kopf* ('a mediocre fellow').[18] But it is easy to see why he appealed to Auden. This is a poet of declining powers, who sees himself and the world around him disintegrating, who tries to live with the passion he once felt and can no longer express. There is something unmistakably Horatian about the elegies of Maximian (who looks superficially more of an Ovidian). His complaint that he is no longer what he once was echoes the famous words of Horace in the first poem of the fourth book of *Odes* to the same effect, '*Non sum qualis eram*' (cf. Maximian, less stylishly, '*non sum qui fueram*'). These words must have spoken eloquently to Auden, who, at the end of his life, left those heart-breaking lines, first published by Edward Mendelson in the preface to *Thank You, Fog*:

> He still loves life
> But O O O O how he wishes
> The good Lord would take him.[19]

---

[18] Pauly-Wissowa, *Realencyclopädie der classischen Altertumswissenschaft* 14.2 (Stuttgart, 1930), 2533.   [19] (London, 1974), p. viii.

The quotation from E. R. Dodds in Auden's essay on the fall of Rome arose from a long-standing interest in Neoplatonism and Gnosticism. In 1966 he was convinced that the social unrest of the day—especially the drug culture of the hippies—bore some resemblance to the peculiarities of the philosophical movements of late antiquity that became, for most purposes, substitutes for religion. In 1972 Auden composed a poem for Dodds under the title 'Nocturne'. This poem, invoking young radicals plotting to blow up a building and airplanes imagined as metal mosquitoes, cries out for a lost innocence. There is a sense of doom, the advent of night, that echoes the pessimistic conclusion of the *Life* essay. There Auden wrote, 'I have no idea what is actually going to happen before I die, except that I am not going to like it.' The beginning of the poem for Dodds asks:

> Do squamous and squiggling fish,
> down in their fireless houses,
> notice nightfall? Perhaps not.[20]

In the following year, the year of his death, Auden took up the subject again in 'No, Plato, No', a kind of poetic reprise of all that Cochrane had taught about Matter and Mind. In fact the pessimism with which Auden ends his *Life* essay includes a condemnation of public taste for prehistoric archaeology. This judgement is, in its way, as deeply felt as Auden's condemnation of heroin addicts and beats. For him it was Graeco-Roman archaeology that held human interest. The taste for the prehistoric (Neolithic or Bronze Age) represented yet another departure from the humanity he prized above all.

This passing reference to archaeology foretells another of Auden's latest poems. In *Thank You, Fog* there are verses from 1973 entitled simply 'Archaeology'. It becomes clear here that what directed Auden to the whole subject of excavation was the problem of ascertaining from the remains left behind what people long ago were really like:

> From murals and statues
> we get a glimpse of what
> the Old Ones bowed down to,
>
> but cannot conceit
> in what situations they blushed
> or shrugged their shoulders.

[20] *CP91* 879.

What can one infer about rituals—some abominable, but some perhaps not?

> There's nothing the Crucified
> would like less
> than butchery to appease Him.[21]

How, in short, do we know the past? History may not be the answer. In his last years, Auden seems to have suspected that history was apt to get everything wrong. He did not want succeeding generations to believe everything they read in history books. He must have remembered that Gibbon had defined history as 'little more than the register of the crimes, follies, and misfortunes of mankind'.[22] Archaeology of the right kind could therefore be a kind of consolation:

> From Archaeology
> one moral, at least, may be drawn,
> to wit, that all
>
> our school text-books lie.
> What they call History
> is nothing to vaunt of,
>
> being made, as it is,
> by the criminal in us:
> goodness is timeless.[23]

---

[21] *CP91* 895–6.   [22] *Decline and Fall*, vol. 1, 77.   [23] *CP91* 896–7.

The Fall of Rome

W. H. AUDEN

The Roman Empire is an historical phenomenon towards which no Westerner can feel either indifferent or impartial. My distant ancestors were barbarians from Scandinavia, which was never under Roman rule. I was born in Britain where the Roman culture was not strong enough to survive the Anglo-saxon invasions, and which broke away from the Roman Church in the sixteenth century. It must be significant, I think, that the countries which went Protestant at the Reformation were precisely those which had been least influenced by the culture of *pagan* Rome.

By heredity and temperament, I think of the Romans with distaste. The only classical latin poet I *really* like is Horace. I find their architecture, even in ruins, as oppressive and inhuman as the steel-and-glass buildings of to-day. I prefer 'the rolling English road' made by 'the rolling English drunkard' to the brutal straight line of the Roman road or the thru-way. One reason why I like Italy and the Italians so much is that, aside from their unfortunate addiction to rhetoric, I cannot imagine a people *less* like the Romans of antiquity.

* * *

We open a classical atlas and note that the Roman Empire stretched from the Scotch Border to the Euphrates. We tour Europe and look at the ruins of gigantic buildings, acqueducts, roads, fortifications. We read descriptions of Roman banquets. On the basis of such evidence, it is natural to imagine the Empire as a society like our own: highly affluent, humming with industry, and bustling with commerce. Such a picture, however, is false.

By modern standards, the population figures were small. In the early fourth century the population of Rome itself was between one half- and three-quarter million, that of Antioch, the third city in the Empire, about two hundred thousand. Though the Empire contained one or two industrial and trading cities, its economy was based on agriculture, and its agricultural techniques were primitive. The only technical advance made by the Romans was the application of dry-farming methods in North Africa. They possessed no plough capable of cultivating heavy clay soils, and no wheel-barrow. Rotation of crops had not been discovered, so that the fields had to lie fallow every other year. It would seem that some kind of reaping machine was invented, but it was hardly used; the standard harvesting tool was the sickle. Before the time of Augustus an efficient water-mill had been invented, but in most of the lands round the Mediterranean the water-supply was neither copious nor constant enough to permit of its use. In the Second century Rome ground its wheat by donkey-mills and it was not until the Fourth that these were replaced by water-mills supplied from the acqueducts. In the country wheat continued to be ground in hand querns. Techniques of manufacture were equally primitive; spinning was done on distaff and spindle, cloth woven on hand-looms, pottery moulded on the wheel, metal hammered out on the anvil.

The Empire possessed an excellent road net-work but, since the horse-collar had not been invented, goods could only be transported by ox-waggons moving at the speed of two miles an hour. Perishable goods, like fruit and vegetables, therefore, could not be transported at all, meat could only be transported salted or on the hoof, and transport costs were high; a journey of three hundred miles doubled the price of wheat. Nor was transport by sea much easier. The techniques of ship-building and navigation were such that the Mediterranean was closed to shipping from mid-November till mid-March, and for only two months in the year was sailing considered fairly safe. Under such conditions only the State could afford to transport necessities for any great distance; private trade was either in luxury goods or for a local market.

Under the Empire, wealth was probably more evenly distributed than it had been in the late days of the Republic when, according to Gibbon, 'only two thousand citizens were in possession of any independent substance.' There must have been a number of small landowners like Horace, whose Sabine farm was run by a foreman and eight slaves, and had five tenant farms attached to it. The disparity of wealth between the classes, however, remained very great. Rome in the fourth century contained eighteen hundred family houses and forty-five thousand tenement buildings. There were a small number of immensely wealthy men, most of them senators, and a vast number of slaves, peasants, small tenant farmers, living near the subsistence level. The precarious situation of the small man was aggravated by the tax system. The financial needs of the Government were mostly met by a tax on land, levied at a fixed rate. A big landowner with estates scattered over the Empire could suffer a loss here through civil disturbance, a loss there through a bad harvest, and still be able to pay his taxes and show a profit; a tenant farmer with a single piece of land, visited by similar misfortunes, could easily be ruined and forced to sell.

All of this meant that the Empire operated on a narrow margin of financial safety. The wars of the Republic had been wars of shameless aggression in which, as Gibbon says, 'the perpetual violation of justice was maintained by the political virtues of prudence and courage', but they had paid: money, slaves, plunder of all kinds, had poured into Italy. The stabilisation of the frontiers under the Emperors put an end to such adventures; henceforth the Roman army was maintained for the purposes of defence, and a defensive war, though normally more commendable than an offensive, is a dead financial loss.

So long as the barbarians outside the frontiers remained too weak or too afraid to attack, so long as no ambitious army commander started a civil war in a bid for power, so long as it suffered no natural catastrophe like an epidemic of plague, the Empire could just manage. But any prolonged war or serious catastrophe strained its resources to breaking-point.

*   *   *

Political stability depended upon the Emperor being approved of both by the senate and by the army. So long as he commanded the loyalty of the army, an emperor could, of course, ignore the wishes of the senate or cow it into submission, and some emperors did, but such a procedure was always risky. By tradition, senators of pretorian rank were put in command of all the legions except the one in Egypt, and senators of consular rank were appointed as governors of all the major frontier provinces, so that they were in a good position, if they found an emperor really intolerable, to start a military revolt; if that failed, senators were rich enough and influential enough to hire an assassin.

It was also highly desirable that an emperor should reign for a long time, on account of the custom of the donative. Upon his accession an emperor was expected to present every soldier in his army with a substantial sum in cash; consequently, a succession of short reigns meant a ruinous drain on the Treasury.

In every respect the age of the Antonines was lucky. The senate, who distrusted the hereditary principle, and the army, who tended to be loyal to the last emperor's legitimate heir, were able to agree because the Antonine emperors were childless. Each was able to please the senate by nominating as his successor someone from among their members of proven ability and, by adopting him into his family, to secure the support of the army. Furthermore, most of them lived to a ripe old age. In the hundred-and-twenty-one years between the accession of Vespasian and the death of Marcus Aurelius, there were only eight emperors, the average length of a reign was fifteen years, and only one, Domitian, died a violent death.

Even during this period of peace and tranquility, however, there were signs that all was not well economically. Since the reign of Augustus, the State had kept down the expenses of administration by entrusting local government to city councils who served without pay, on the assumption that in every city there were enough persons of substance with the civic pride and patriotism to undertake the task willingly. The pride and patriotism were there alright, but there was less money than either the State or the cities imagined. The sums spent by the city councils, in jealous competition with each other, upon public buildings, water-works, free public entertainment, exceeded their resources and, by Trajan's time, the State found it necessary to appoint auditors to keep a check on extravagance. The two campaigns, lasting less than a year each, in which Trajan conquered Dacia, were small-scale affairs, but to pay for them, he had to debase the coinage, a practice continued by his successors with the inevitable results.

Culturally, too, something was lacking. The Augustan settlement had put an end to an intolerable state of anarchy and, for two centuries at least, made it possible for a citizen to live what the Greeks would have called an 'idiotic' life, that is to say, a private life free from political cares, but the price paid for this tranquility was a general decline in intellectual curiosity and invention. In the field of technology, for example, the characteristic Roman contributions, the use in architecture of the arch, the vault and concrete, the use of pumps and archimedian screws for draining mines, the arts of surveying and road-making, the military techniques of the legion, the techniques of organising large disciplined bodies of men for labor or war, all of these ante-date the Empire. During the five centuries that it lasted, the only new inventions we hear of are an improved siege-engine and the use of heavily-armed cavalry. In 370 an anonymous inventor of a portable pontoon bridge and a paddle-wheel war-ship driven by oxen offered his services to the State but was, apparently, ignored.

Then, in the arts, where there can be no progress, only blossoming or sterility, the Imperial flowers, it must be admitted, are few. The poets, for example, who are still widely read with both admiration and pleasure are Lucretius, Catullus, Virgil, Horace, Propertius, Ovid. All of them grew up under the Republic, and the youngest of them, Ovid, is dead by A.D.17. After them, who is there? Seneca (d. 65), Martial (c. 104), Juvenal (c. 140); readable, but hectic, strained, and basically unpleasant. Then nobody for two hundred years. In the fourth and fifth centuries, a mysterious little masterpiece, the *Pervigilium Veneris*, and some poets, Pagan and Christian, like Prudentius, Ausonius, Paulinus of Nola, Claudian, who wrote one or two nice pieces, but are very minor figures. Finally, in the sixth century after the West has fallen, one really remarkable poet, Maximian. The list is not long.

* * *

Serious trouble began during the reign of Marcus Aurelius with a long campaign along the Danube and an outbreak of plague. After his death, disaster followed disaster. Invasion by Frank and Goth and Berber, peasant revolts in Gaul, frequent civil war, anarchy and galloping inflation.

The picture drawn by St. Cyprian (200–258) is probably not much exaggerated.

The world to-day speaks for itself; by the evidence of its decay it announces its dissolution. The farmers are vanishing from the countryside, commerce from the sea, soldiers from the camps; all honesty in business, all justice in the courts, all solidarity in friendship, all skill in the arts, all standards in morals—all are disappearing.

For the next hundred years few of the emperors were even competent and none were nice. In the seventy-three years between the death of Severus and the accession of Diocletian there were twenty legitimate emperors, not counting their nominal co-regents, and a host of usurpers. The average length of a reign was two-and-a-half years. Claudius died of the plague, Valerian was taken prisoner by the Persians, Decius fell in battle against the Goths; all the rest, and almost every usurper, were assassinated or lynched or killed in civil war. Great areas of land went out of cultivation—they may have been of poor quality, but hitherto they had been found worth cultivating—, and the denarius sank to 0.5% of its value in the second century.

Diocletian, Constantine and his successors managed for a time to stop the anarchy, but at the cost of a wholesale regimentation and immobilisation of society under which any personal freedom ceased to exist, a rate of taxation which destroyed all private initiative and sense of civic responsibility, and forcible conscription of peasants, who were branded like cattle so as to make it easier to recognise deserters. The main victims of the inflation were the city governments whose income was derived from long-term mortgages and fixed rents, and government employees on salary. Diocletian increased the size of the army, but attempted to cut down expenses by paying it in kind. During the first two centuries, equipment and rations were issued to a soldier against stoppage of pay, yet he could still hope to save half of his pay, and requisitions of food or material from the cities were paid for. Under Diocletian promotion in the army was rewarded by an increase not in pay but in rations, and requisitions were not paid for. Both the soldier and the civil servant were much worse off than they had been earlier, and the temptation to plunder and peculation became correspondingly greater.

The time was long past when candidates eagerly stood for election to municipal office. Men had now to be compelled by law to serve, and edict after edict, threatening with fines and confiscations officials who evaded their responsibilities by hiding out in the country, show that this was in fact what was happening.

By 380 the Government had to forbid the construction of new city buildings until the old ones had been repaired; in 385 it had to undertake to pay a third of the cost of such repairs. Some idea of what it must have been like to be a citizen in the time of Theodosius can be gained from the following edicts.

Landowners found harboring persons who have left their legal domicile, or evaders of military service, shall be burned alive. (379)

Anyone who cuts down a vine or limits the productivity of fruit-trees with the intent of cheating the tax-assessors shall be subject to capital punishment, and his property shall be confiscated. (381)

Anyone who thrusts himself into a position to which he is not entitled shall be tried for sacrilege. (384)

By 404 the State had become impotent to maintain even elementary law and order, for an edict of that year authorises all persons to exercise with impunity the right of public vengeance against the common enemy 'by exterminating malefactors, brigands, deserters, wherever they may be found.'

The partition of the Empire into an Eastern half and a Western half did not take place officially until after the death of Theodosius in 395, but from the time of Diocletian they had begun to go different ways, and, once they did so, the collapse of the West could only be a matter of time. The West was much poorer than the East, and its frontiers much longer and more difficult to defend. Invasion followed invasion. In 410 the Goths under Alaric entered and sacked Rome. In 476 a boy who bore the names of the founder of the Republic and the founder of the Empire, the emperor Romulus Augustulus, was deposed by the barbarian king Odoacer and retired to a villa in Ravenna. Turnus was avenged at last.

* * *

The decline of the Roman Empire has been attributed to many causes: defects in the economy, a falling birth-rate, the dessication of the grasslands in Asia which set the barbarians in motion, Christianity, etc, and there is something to be said for them all. The question remains, however, whether there was not some radical defect in the fundamental principles upon which the Empire was originally based which in the long run were bound to bring it to disaster.

The Imperial civilisation derived its categories of thought, its concepts of Nature, Man and Society from Greek idealist philosophy. (Epicurean materialism of the Lucretian kind died an early death.)

Classical idealism postulates two co-eternal principles, Mind and primordial Matter. Matter-in-itself is an amorphous meaningless flux upon which Mind imposes forms or patterns, aside from which, Matter is nothing or all-but-nothing. The imposed forms which impart to Matter the nature of body do not in the process lose their formal character but remain timeless and immutable. Matter-in-motion, moreover, resists the imposition of forms, and can never furnish perfect copies. The material cosmos is a world of becoming which never quite becomes; it remains an inadequate reflection of the truly real and intelligible world. The latter, the divine and truly real, whether as Plato's Ideas or as Aristotle's Unmoved Mover, is self-sufficient, without either knowledge of or concern for anything but itself. To account for the existence of form and order in the cosmos, Platonism postulates an intermediary demiurge, the World Soul, which looks upward to contemplate the archetypes and downward to impose them on Matter; Aristotelianism postulates an inherent wish for order in Matter. While 'God has no need of friends, neither indeed can he have any', all things are 'in love' with God and become as orderly as it is possible for things in motion to become, inanimate beings like the stars by making their movements regular, living beings by trying to live an existence in conformity to the species or type to which they belong. For man alone, by virtue of his reason, the divinely real can become an object of experience and through that experience the master of his destiny. To live according to reason is, however, immensely difficult and calls for a heroic effort by the 'super-ego'. The 'Id', the energies of the body are hostile, and no help can be expected from the Divine. Knowledge of the true and the good, which are not apparent to the senses, presupposes a longing for it, and this longing is to be found only in a few individuals. Plato's Philosopher and Aristotle's Great-Souled-Man are both social freaks.

To classical idealism, motion, processes, change as such are misfortunes: the perfect does not move. The consequences of such a view for science, politics, art and history are serious. It permits the study of mathematics and logic, and the classification of biological and social types, but experimental investigation of nature must be a waste of time, since the real truth cannot be found in the imperfect copy. Corresponding to the antithetical pair Mind–Matter, in its cosmology, classical idealism sees history and politics as an interaction between timeless Virtue and mutable Fortune. To call the historical circumstances in which man finds himself Fortune, implies that, like primordial matter, they are unintelligible; to attempt to discover what has caused them to be what they are or to predict what may follow from them must be a waste of time. Then, since few men possess Virtue, the majority must be persuaded to lead a life they do not and cannot understand by habituating them to laws and telling them 'noble lies'. The peace and happiness of mankind depend upon a tiny élite. On them falls the task of discovering and maintaining the perfect form of State, of which there can be only one, under which human beings will lead the life proper to their species. All that is essential about an individual is the 'type' to which he belongs, and this type cannot change, only repeat itself. An individual can progress from ignorance to knowledge, but communal or social development is ruled out. The goal of 'creative' politics is to conquer Fortune and so put an end to history, a task so formidable that only a superman can accomplish it.

Supermen the Roman Emperors tried to be. Cicero and others might make fine speeches about Natural Law before which all men were equal, but their words had very little to do with Roman reality. Roman Law may be a fascinating subject of study for lawyers, and, since I know nothing about them, I am willing to believe that in certain sectors of Civil Law, like laws of contract and testament, the Romans made great advances. What I do know is that debtors were treated as criminals. In the two legal domains of most concern to the average man, Criminal Procedure and Administrative Law, that is to say, decrees concerning taxation, military service, the rights and limits of freedom of speech and movement, I cannot see that the Roman record is anything to boast about. Its criminal procedure was brutal and inefficient, relying largely upon informers and torture, and did not make the faintest pretence at equal treatment for all. If, in its later days, the Empire became legally more democratic, this was a democracy of slavery; the use of the lash was no longer confined to the lower orders.

As for Administrative Law, the citizen had no say whatsoever in its decrees, and no right of protest. Since the emperor was both the executive and the legislative head of the State, there was nothing, theoretically, to stop him issuing any decree he liked; 'what is pleasing to the Prince', says Ulpian, 'has the force of law.' Moreover, since he was regarded as a sacred being, any violation of his decrees could be interpreted as an act of treason or sacrilege, the one offence for which a member of the *honestiores*, or upper classes, could be tortured and executed; a number of emperors made use of this legal possibility.

Classical idealism cannot tolerate the arts as gratuitous activities; either they must be reduced to didactic instruments of some ethical or political purpose, or they must be suppressed. Plato had the intelligence to see this clearly; Aristotle in his *Poetics* merely betrays his utter misunderstanding of his subject.

Roman literature, both in verse and prose, was an aristocratic art addressed to a small highly sophisticated audience. This in itself was not a fault. Once the age of the bard reciting tribal lays in the hall of his chief is over, and until printing has been invented and literacy has become common, literature cannot be anything else. Indeed, a 'courtly' period is probably necessary if a language is to realise its full possibilities. In writing for a small critical circle, the classical Latin authors discovered what could be done with Latin, the wealth of its conjunctions and subordinate phrases, the flexibility of its tenses and word-order, which make it such a superb instrument for organising facts into a logical and co-herent whole. The defect of Latin literature was not its way of treating facts, but the extraordinar[il]y small number of facts it considered worth treating. It averts its face from all experience save that of the highly educated and the politically powerful. The literature of the middle-ages had an equally small audience, but readily drew its material from popular sources. *The Canterbury Tales* were written for a courtly audience, but its characters are neither courtiers nor figures of farce. As W. P. Ker has written:

Classical literature perished from a number of contributory ailments, but none of these was more desperate than the want of romance in the Roman Empire, and especially in the Latin Language. . . . 'The Gothic mythology of fairies', as Dr Johnson calls it, was no less the property of Italy than of the North. In any mountain village the poets might have found the great-great grandmothers of those story-tellers for whom Boccaccio in his *Genealogy of the Gods* offers a courteous defence. The elves and fays of Italy, *Lamiae*, as Boccaccio calls them, might have refreshed the poets. But the old wives and their fairy tales are left unnoticed, except by Apuleius.

And Apuleius, one must add, was only interested in their gruesome or grotesque elements.

What was a limitation in the poets was quite fatal to the historians. It is significant that history was regarded by the Romans, not as the matrix from which all literature is derived, but as a handmaid to literature. One may admire the Roman historians for their style, or enjoy their scandalous gossip, but for historical understanding one looks to them in vain. As Gibbon remarked: 'They said what it would have been meritorious to omit, and omitted what it was essential to say.' Conceiving of the human individual as a specimen embodying a type, in abstraction from all those concrete features and relations which give him an historical existence, they assumed that men are free to choose between arbitrary and abstract alternatives of 'vice' and 'virtue', that there is nothing to stop them, if they wish, from living the life of their great-grandfathers. Of their historical approach, Erich Auerbach says:

It does not see forces, it sees vices and virtues, successes and mistakes. Its formulation of problems is not concerned with historical developments, either intellectual or material, but with ethical judgements. It shows an aristocratic reluctance to become involved with growth processes in the depths, for these processes are felt to be both vulgar and orgiastically lawless . . . The ethical and even the political concepts of antiquity (aristocracy, democracy, etc) are fixed aprioristic model concepts.

One symptom of this approach is the complete lack of interest shown by the classical historians in what people actually say, all the idiosyncracies of phrasing and vocabulary which reveal the personality of the speaker. Face-to-face dialogue goes unreported by them. When they do employ Direct Speech, it is a set piece of oratory written in the style of the historian himself.

One may like or dislike Christianity, but no one can deny that it was Christianity and the Bible which raised Western literature from the dead. A faith which held that the Son of God was born in a manger, associated himself with persons of humble station in an unimportant Province, and died a slave's death, yet did this to redeem all men, rich and poor, freemen and slaves, citizens and barbarians, required a completely new way of looking at human beings; if all are children of God and equally capable of salvation, then all, irrespective of status or talent, vice or virtue, merit the serious attention of the poet, the novelist and the historian. St Jerome, trained in the classical rhetorical tradition, might find the Bible 'uncouth', but in his translation he made no attempt to 'classicalise' it. (Only the sixteenth century humanists were crazy enough to try that.) Old Testament stories, like Abraham and Isaac, or David and Absalom, New Testament stories like Peter's denial, did not fit into any of the classical stylistic categories; to translate them called for a quite different vocabulary, even a different syntax.

*   *   *

Most of the writings which have survived from the third and fourth centuries are polemic theological journalism, Neo-platonists versus Christians, Christians with one interpretation of their faith against Christians with another. From being an obscure sect, disliked by the mob, as oddities always are, and suspected of horrid secret rites, but people no man of education would give a thought to, by the reign of Marcus Aurelius Christians had become numerous enough and influential enough to be taken seriously both by the authorities and by intellectuals. Persecution, hitherto sporadic and incoherent, became a deliberate planned policy under the more serious-minded emperors. Intellectuals like Celsus and Porphyry felt that Christianity was a cultural threat serious enough to deserve attack, and, on the Christian

side, there were now converts like Tertullian and Origen educated
enough to explain and defend their beliefs. Reading their polemics to-
day, one is more struck by the points upon which they agreed than
by their differences.

Wilt thou yet take all, Galilean? but these thou shalt not take,
The laurel, the palms and the paean, the breasts of the nymphs in the brake:
Breasts more soft than a dove's, that tremble with tenderer breath;
And all the wings of the Loves, and all the joy before death.

So Swinburne. But his contrast between jolly, good-looking, sexy,
extrovert Pagans on the one hand, and gloomy, emaciated, guilt-
ridden, introvert Christians on the other is a romantic myth without
any basis in historical fact. The writings of Christian and Pagan alike
during this period seem to indicate that, as Joseph Bidez says;

Men were ceasing to observe the external world and to try to understand it,
utilise it, or improve it. They were driven in on themselves. The idea of the
beauty of the heavens and of the world went out of fashion and was replaced
by that of the Infinite.

Such an attitude is consonant neither with orthodox Platonism nor
with orthodox Christianity. Despite its latent dualism, orthodox
Platonism held that the material universe was in some manner a
manifestation of the Divine. The cosmos, says Plato in the *Timaeus*,
'is the image of the intelligible, a perceptible god, supreme in greatness and excellence and perfection'. For the orthodox Christian, God
created the world 'and saw that it was good', and 'The heavens
declare the glory of God and the firmament showeth His handiwork.'
But in the third century, both among Pagans and among those who
imagined themselves to be Christians, radical dualistic theories began
to take hold. 'Some held that the cosmos had been created by an evil
spirit, or by an ignorant one, or by bodiless intelligences who had
become bored with contemplating God and turned to the inferior;
others concluded that it had somehow fallen into the power of star-
demons.' (*E. R. Dodds*) The incarnation of the human soul in a fleshly
mortal, body was felt by many to be a curse and accounted for as
being either a punishment for an earlier sin committed in heaven, or
the result of a false choice made by the soul itself. Consequently, to
an increasing number, the body became an object of disgust and
resentment. Among some Christians there was a tendency to make a
heretical substitution of Lust for Pride as the archetypal sin, and to
see in violent mortification of the flesh, not a discipline, but the only

road to salvation. A fascination with the occult, with astrology, spiritualism, magic, was wide-spread. Both Pagans and Christians took oracles and 'belly-talkers' seriously. Reading the Christian polemics of the third century, one gets the impression that the Church was in grave danger of going crackpot. Only one writer, Irenaeus, can be called orthodox, as orthodoxy was to be defined in the next two centuries. The fact that the Councils of Nicea and Chalcedeon were able to arrive at the credal definitions they did, suggests, however, that the most vociferous and articulate Christians were not typical of their third century brethren. Not all, not even the majority, can have been Gnostics who believed that Christ's body was an optical illusion, or crypto-materialists like Tertullian, or crypto-idealists like Clement, or indulged in glossolalia like Montanus, or castrated themselves like Origen, or behaved like the Marcionite, who always washed his face in his spittle to avoid using water, the creation of the demiurge.

* * *

The fiasco of Julian's attempt to establish his solar monotheism, and the ease with which his successors suppressed pagan worship—there were very few Pagan martyrs—suggests that, by the time of Constantine's so-called conversion, Christianity as a faith had already won out over its competitors, Neo-platonism, Manicheeism and Mithraism. For this victory many explanations can be given;—the impression made by the courage of the martyrs, the refusal of the Church to limit its membership to a spiritual or intellectual élite, or to make mystical experience necessary to salvation, the opportunities it offered to any man of talent and character to rise to high office in its hierarchy, its superior ability to give its converts a sense of belonging to and being needed by a community, and its philosophical superiority. *Credo ut intelligam* is a maxim which applies to all experiences except that of physical pain, and the Christian creed made better sense of human experience than the others. Far from Constantine and his successors contributing to this victory, they very nearly ruined it. The greatest disasters which have befallen the Church, disasters for which we have not yet finished paying the price, were the adoption by Theodosius of Christianity as the official State religion, backed by the coercive powers of the State, and the mass, often forcible, conversions of the barbarians in the centuries that followed.

Constantine and Theodosius took up Christianity for a purely pagan reason; they hoped that the 'Christian' God would ensure them political and military success; a view neatly diagrammed by Blake in his re-translation of Dr Thornton's translation of the Lord's Prayer.

Our Father Augustus Caesar, who art in these thy Substantial Astronomical Telescopic Heavens, Holiness to thy Name or Title, a reverence to thy Shadow. Thy Kingship come upon Earth first & then in Heaven. Give us day by day our Real Taxed Substantial Money bought Bread; deliver from the Holy Ghost whatever cannot be Taxed; for all is debts & Taxes between Caesar & us & one another; lead us not to read the Bible, but let our Bible be Virgil & Shakespeare; & deliver us from Poverty in Jesus, that Evil One. For thine is the Kingship, or Allegoric Godship, & the Power, or War, & the Glory, or Law, Ages after Ages in thy descendants; for God is only an Allegory of Kings & nothing else. AMEN.

As Charles Cochrane has written:

To envisage the faith as a political principle was not so much to christianise civilisation as to 'civilise' Christianity; it was not to consecrate human institutions to the service of God but rather to identify God with the maintenance of human institutions, represented in this case by a tawdry and meritricious empire, a system which, originating in the pursuit of human and terrestrial aims, had so far degenerated as to deny to men the very values which had given it birth, and was now held together only by sheer and unmitigated force. So far from rejuvenating *Romanitas*, the attempted substitution of religion for culture as a principle of cohesion served merely to add a final and decisive element to the forces making for the dissolution of the Roman order.

The eremitic movement, and the monastic movement which succeeded, it, were essentially movements of protest not against Paganism but against worldly Christianity. Before we condemn the desert hermits, as the humanists of the eighteenth and nineteenth century did, for refusing to accept their civic responsibilities, we must remember what, especially for the better educated and better off, who might have become magistrates or civil servants, taking such posts involved. A magistrate had to inflict torture; a bureaucrat could not live without taking bribes. Even what seems to us their most peculiar and repellant trait, their horror of washing, might be more understandable if we knew more about how men and women behaved in the public city baths. To anyone who took his faith seriously, the urban life of the 'Christian' Empire must have seemed an appalling spectacle. It was now worldly advantage to be labelled a Christian, and there must have been a great multitude who, counting upon a death-bed repentance to cancel their sins, continued to enjoy gladiatorial shows, wild-beast fights, obscene mimes, etc. Cavafy's description of the reaction of the citizens of Antioch to a visit from the emperor Julian is probably not far from the truth.

Was it possible that they would ever deny
Their comely way of living; the variety
Of their daily recreations; their splendid
Theatre where they found the union of Art
With the erotic propensities of the flesh!

Immoral to a certain, probably to a considerable extent,
They were. But they had the satisfaction that their life
Was the much talked-of life of Antioch,
The delightful life, in absolutely good taste.

Were they to deny all this, to give their minds after all to what?

To his airy chatter about the false gods,
To his annoying chatter about himself;
To his childish fear of the theatre;
His graceless prudery; his ridiculous beard.

Most certainly they preferred the letter CHI,
Most certainly they preferred the KAPPA—a hundred times.

(translated by John Mavrogordato)

Most people's idea of the Desert Fathers is derived from what they have heard about Simeon Stylites, and this is unjust to them. To begin with, few of them were mendicants; most earned their modest keep by weaving palm-leaf baskets and mats. Lunatics and spiritual prima donnas were, it is true, to be found among them, but many anecdotes reveal that they were recognised for what they were by their saner and humbler brethren. At its best the movement produced characters of impressive integrity and wisdom, with great psychological understanding, charity and good-humor. Nor was excessive mortification ever encouraged by the Church authorities. An early canon condemns those who abstain from wine and meat on fast-days for 'blasphemously inveighing against the creation.' We owe the Desert Fathers more than we generally realise. The classical world knew many pleasures, but of one which means a great deal to us, it was totally ignorant until the hermits discovered it, the pleasure of being by oneself. Nothing could better illustrate the relentlessly public character of classical civilisation than an anecdote of Augustine's, in which he tells of his utter astonishment when he saw a hermit reading to himself without pronouncing the words aloud: this was a new world. Again, they seem to have been the first people in history to appreciate the beauties of wild nature, and the first to make friends with wild animals instead of hunting them.

Though it did not reach its full development until after the collapse of the West, the monastic movement had already started. It began to be realised that, while solitary withdrawal could be valuable for certain exceptional persons and for certain periods in their lives, man was a social animal who normally needed to live with others. The problem was one of devising a kind of social organisation which would be neither totalitarian, based on collective egoism, nor competitive, based on the egoism and ambition of the individual. At its best, the monastic movement solved this problem better than any other social form before or since. Its drawback is of course that it has been limited so far, to the celibate. Perhaps it has to be: perhaps family life and communal life are incompatible, except under catastrophic conditions. But the matter deserves more attention than we give it.

* * *

'Histories of the downfall of Kingdoms', said Dr Johnson, 'and revolutions of empires are read with great tranquility.' I am not sure that to-day it would not be more accurate to say 'with great excitement'. On the evidence of contemporary historical novels (a surprising number are concerned with the fall of Rome) and science fiction, it would seem that what really fascinates us to read about is a post-catastrophic society and landscape—abandoned ruins of once great cities, bad lands, roads overgrown with grass, individuals and small groups, which have been brought up in a civilised society, learning how to cope with life under barbaric conditions. It is noticeable, too, that there is a far greater public interest in neolithic or bronze-age archaeology than in Graeco-roman archaeology.

I can guess at various reasons for this change of taste, some good, some alarming. Compared with our great-grandfathers, we are far more suspicious of worldly success, far less willing to believe that economic, social and racial inequalities are in conformity with the laws either of nature or of God. When we read the *Aeneid*, we can recognise as they did the magnificence of the verse, but we are repelled, as, apparently, they were not, by Virgil's identification of Right with Might. We agree with Burckhardt.

'This or that hall-way would have to be the most beautiful if only because it leads to our room.' What coldness and heartlessness there is in this attitude:

the ignoring of the silenced moans of the vanquished who, as a rule, had wanted nothing else but to preserve what had come into being. How *much* must perish so that *something* new may arise.

How much more moving to us than Virgil's description of the military triumphs depicted on Aeneas' shield is the following incident in one of Maximian's elegies. Sent by Theodoric as an envoy to Constantinople, he picks up a girl. He is getting on in years and proves impotent. The girl starts to cry. He tries to comfort her by assuring her that she can easily find a more adequate lover. 'It's not that,' she says, 'it's the general chaos of the world.'

I think a great many of us are haunted by the feeling that our society, and by ours I don't mean just the United States or Europe, but our whole world-wide technological civilisation, whether officially labelled capitalist, socialist or communist, is going to go smash, and probably deserves to.

Like the third century the twentieth is an age of stress and anxiety. In our case, it is not that our techniques are too primitive to cope with new problems, but the very fantastic success of our technology is creating a hideous, noisy, over-crowded world in which it is becoming increasingly difficult to lead a human life. In our reactions to this, one can see many parallels to the third century. Instead of gnostics, we have existentialists and God-is-dead theologians, instead of neo-platonists, devotees of Zen, instead of desert hermits, heroin addicts and beats, (who also, oddly enough, seem averse to washing), instead of mortification of the flesh, sado-masochistic pornography; as for our public entertainments, the fare offered by television is still a shade less brutal and vulgar than that provided by the amphitheatre, but only a shade, and may not be for long.

I have no idea what is actually going to happen before I die except that I am not going to like it. Some ten years ago I tried to express my forebodings in a short lyric entitled *The Fall of Rome*:

> The piers are pummelled by the waves;
> In a lonely field the rain
> Lashes an abandoned train;
> Outlaws fill the mountain caves.
>
> Fantastic grow the evening gowns;
> Agents of the Fisc pursue
> Absconding tax-defaulters through
> The sewers of provincial towns.

Private rites of magic send
The temple prostitutes to sleep;
All the *literati* keep
An imaginary friend.

Cerebrotonic Catos may
Extol the Ancient Disciplines,
But the muscle-bound Marines
Mutiny for food and pay.

Caesar's double-bed is warm
As an unimportant clerk
Writes I DO NOT LIKE MY WORK
On a pink official form.

Unendowed with wealth or pity,
Little birds with scarlet legs,
Sitting on their speckled eggs,
Eye each flu-infected city.

Although elsewhere, vast
Herds of reindeer move across
Miles and miles of golden moss,
Silently and very fast.

———

Principal Sources

Auerbach, Eric	Mimesis
Cochrane, Charles N.	Christianity and Classical Culture
Dodds, E. R.	Pagans and Christians in an Age of Anxiety
Gibbon, E.	Decline and Fall of the Roman Empire
Jones, A. H. M.	The Later Roman Empire
Ker, W. P.	The Dark Ages
Rostovtzeff	The Social and Economic History of the Roman Empire
Singer, Charles (editor)	The History of Technology, Vol II.

Phantasy and Reality in Poetry (1971)

EDITED BY KATHERINE BUCKNELL

Introduction
'Freud's Not Quite O.K.'[1]

FREUD, although he wrote no poetry, was one of Auden's most important poetic fathers. He made possible for Auden a way of thinking about personal experience which liberated and enlightened Auden's outlook, and enormously influenced his work. Yet Auden was never entirely at ease with Freud's doctrines. He argued with Freud from youth to maturity, sometimes ferociously, sometimes graciously, often covertly. In his lecture 'Phantasy and Reality in Poetry' delivered at the Philadelphia Association for Psychoanalysis in March 1971 and published here for the first time, Auden summarized many of his views on Freud developed over the course of his career. Taken as a whole, the lecture demonstrates a complex and enormously illuminating ambivalence in Auden's mature attitude to Freud. For as Auden picks apart Freud's theories—in particular the ones on art and artists—he offers episodes from his own creative life and passages from his poetry to support his arguments. His personal reflections reveal a characteristic longing to be understood by his audience, which, on this particular occasion, must certainly have included a number of professional psychoanalysts, so that even as he subtly and with a certain sly brilliance exposes inadequacies in Freud's thought, Auden seems to be putting himself forward, rather trustingly, as a subject for analysis. The lecture is loosely arranged and hardly makes a coherent argument; in places, it almost wanders from point to point as if by a process of free association. And yet it contains scattered moments of illumination—insights into Auden's artistic nature and into his work. In this essay I will try to outline the main objections to Freud's theories that Auden articulates in the lecture and also try to sketch briefly the evolution of Auden's more general argument with Freud from the 1920s onward. (In my notes to the lecture itself I point out numerous places in his work where Auden makes the same arguments—about Freud and about a few related subjects—as he makes in the lecture and readers will

---

[1] 'Letter to Lord Byron', *EA* 198.

notice some overlap with Auden's 1970 Neulengbach speech, printed on pp. 224–30 of this volume; the lecture also contains new observations and personal recollections that are otherwise unknown.) Later on in this essay I will suggest ways in which the lecture invites us to re-examine, even to reinterpret, some of Auden's writing in the light of the very theories of Freud which Auden seems to debunk. In particular, I will discuss a few striking connections between Auden's adult work and the childhood reading which he describes in the lecture. According to Auden's own mature myth about the genesis of his poetic personality, the stories and poems he read as a child enormously influenced him, and their ever-changing but persistent echoes in his writing illuminate his growing understanding of his creative temperament and of his role, as an artist, in society.

Auden's recognition of Freud's failings did not come about painlessly. Although he politely forgets it in the 1971 lecture, Auden was psychoanalysed in 1928 and the process was a failure. The analysis may have taken place in two phases, certainly during a week in the Easter holidays and perhaps again over a period of three weeks in the summer when he visited a psychoanalyst in Belgium. However brief the analysis may have been, Auden's few references to it in letters from the period make clear that he planned and looked forward to it for many months and that he hoped it would materially alter his personality. He wrote to his brother John about it eight or nine months beforehand in July 1927, 'I am probably going to be psycho-analysed next vac; by a lady who analysed a friend of mine with the most astonishingly good results. I wish to improve my inferiority complex and to develop heterosexual traits.'[2] The 'lady' Auden refers to may have been Margaret Marshall who had informally analysed Cecil Day-Lewis, but it is not certain that she did eventually analyse Auden; nor is it clear whether she or another analyst Auden may have had, followed anything like orthodox Freudian practices.[3] The smattering of

[2] ALS to John B. Auden, from Hotel Esplanade, Zagreb, Croatia, [July 1927].

[3] In his memoir Day-Lewis recalls long talks, tantamount to analysis, that he had in the 1920s with his close friend Margaret Marshall who was 'trained as a psychiatrist'; see The Buried Day (London, 1960), 149 ff. Margaret Marshall later became John Auden's first wife, and Anita Money, John Auden's younger daughter with his second wife, had the impression that Margaret Marshall may have been a follower of Emile Coué, a French chemist who taught self-improvement through auto-hypnosis. Even if she was a Couéist, Margaret Marshall may also have had some other genuinely psycho-analytic training.

psychological terminology in Auden's letters of the period may reflect
his reading more than any sessions of analysis (for instance, Adler's
term, 'inferiority complex' appears in a letter to John Auden that pre-
dates the analysis); still, Auden's subsequent remarks imply the analysis was, broadly speaking, Freudian.

At first Auden's reaction to the sessions was enthusiastic. He wrote
to Isherwood: 'Had a most pleasant week with my analyst. Libido, it
is proved, is towards women. The trouble is incest.'[4] And he over-
came his fear of mother-incest sufficiently to consider himself bisexual
for a time. Later he wrote to David Ayerst: 'I have just been in Spa
for 3 weeks staying with a psychoanalyst; quite an amusing place, full
of lesbians weighing 110 kilos. I find I am quite ambidextrous now.'[5]
But in the end his optimism gave way to disillusionment. Sometime
during the second half of 1928 he became engaged to a nurse, but by
late July 1929 he broke off the engagement and vowed he would
never marry. Meanwhile, in the spring of 1929 he had begun to make
detailed notes in his journal as to what was wrong with Freud's theories, taking on parts of Freud's works one page at a time. He rejected
the repetition compulsion and the death-wish, arguing that Freud
failed to recognize the true nature of creative pleasure:

The error of Freud and most psychologists is making pleasure a negative
thing, progress towards a state of rest. This is only one half of pleasure and
the least important half. Creative pleasure is, like pain, an increase in tension.
What does the psychologist make of contemplative joy?

The essence of creation is doing things for no reason, it is pointless.
Possessive pleasure is always rational: Freud you see really believes that pleasure is immoral, ie happiness is displeasing to God.

If you believe this of course the death wish becomes the most important
emotion, and the 'reinstatement of an earlier condition.' Entropy is another
name for despair.[6]

Auden also focused on the inadequacy of Freud's remarks about the
nature and causes of homosexuality, chafing in particular against the
implication of selfishness and even solipsism in Freud's emphasis on
the role of narcissism in the evolution of the homosexual personality.
By 1930, when Auden wrote the poem beginning 'Get there if you

[4] ALI, on Lordswood Rd. letterhead and attached to a draft poem beginning 'In
your house came a voice' (eventually revised as 'The Spring will come'), [Mar.–Apr.
1928].
[5] ALS, on Lordswood Rd. letterhead, [Aug. 1928].
[6] 1929 journal (Berg); this passage printed with some variants in EA 299.

can and see the land you once were proud to own', Freud was listed among the 'boon companions' who 'lured with their compelling logic' and then 'betrayed us'.[7]

And yet Auden continued to think and work under a psychological rubric that he associated with Freud. His obsession with Homer Lane and John Layard, for instance, was a new version of his infatuation with Freud, and he used Lane's theories to help him formulate his own objections to Freud. Later there would be other psychological gurus, notably Jung. At home, Auden had first discovered Freud in his father's library, and the charged attitude with which Auden regarded each of his psychological mentors in turn seems to draw on his feelings towards his own father who had read widely in psychology and published articles in the field. George Auden's published work makes clear that he was convinced by and drew on aspects of Freud's thought, but that he also disagreed with much of it. He regarded past experience as the source of behavioural problems in juvenile delinquents and he believed childhood emotional experience shaped the mature emotional attitudes of adults, but he did not accept Freud's exclusive emphasis on the sexual instinct as the source of emotional conflicts. Auden himself ultimately took a similar view. In a 1921 article George Auden wrote,

I am more and more convinced of the paramount part which is played by the repressed complexes of childhood, not necessarily sexual, in the often strangely perverse conduct of children. These actions are not unequivocal evidence of moral turpitude, but are associated with the emotional elements of consciousness . . . it is the experience of childhood that gives colour to the whole emotional content of the outlook on life and the resulting behaviour of the adult.[8]

Dr Auden had command of the theories of a great many other psychologists besides Freud. A 1926 article 'Exogeneous and Endogenous Factors in Character Formation' cites works by, among others, Freud, Jung, Kretschmer, MacDougall, and Rivers. Auden probably read the article, but certainly he at least followed his father's work on it, for during the 1920s Auden read or dipped into almost all of the same works that his father cites by these particular psychologists; later Auden drew on them for a number of the poems he wrote in the

---

[7] *EA* 48.

[8] 'The School Medical Service in Relation to Mental Defect', *The Journal of Mental Science*, 77.8 (1921) 479–80. I am extremely grateful to Richard Davenport-Hines for showing me this and other articles by George Auden.

1930s. Nevertheless, despite the breadth of Auden's reading, Freud's theories, more so than those of any other psychologist, gripped Auden's imagination. As early as 1939 when Auden wrote the elegy 'In Memory of Sigmund Freud', the pain of his personal disillusionment with Freud had dissolved into forgiveness and even love. This, too, may in part reflect Auden's changing attitude towards his own father:

> If some traces of the autocratic pose,
> the paternal strictness he distrusted, still
> > clung to his utterance and features,
> > it was a protective coloration
>
> for one who'd lived among enemies so long:
> if often he was wrong and, at times, absurd,
> > to us he is no more a person
> > now but a whole climate of opinion
>
> under whom we conduct our different lives:[9]

Leavening Auden's grateful praise for the new intellectual atmosphere he suggests Freud brought about, are gentle, affectionately trivializing points of ridicule: Freud was often wrong, sometimes even absurd. Auden's mature antagonism is candid, reasonable, prosaic, like that of a grown son who teases his father as a peer, even as a senile old fool, a clown; the father in the position, now, of child.

Auden's assertion that Freud's fatherly attributes—'the autocratic pose', 'the paternal strictness'—were only 'protective coloration' for one living among his enemies reflects a crucial and perhaps surprising aspect of his attitude towards Freud: Auden looked upon Freud both as the established authority that Freud became with age and renown, and also as a rebel striving to bring about intellectual change. He was captivated by the figure of Freud poised in an attitude of revolt against the society that had produced him. Perhaps this was in part because Freud was a Jew and Auden, newly in love with Chester Kallman when he wrote the elegy, felt a kind of tenderness towards the difficulty of being Jewish. But more broadly, Auden admired Freud for his courage in opposing the world-view of the generations of doctors, scientists, and thinkers who had preceded him. Reviewing the first volume of Ernest Jones's biography of Freud in 1953, Auden said of the young Freud who had yet to publish *The Interpretation of*

[9] *CP91* 275.

Dreams: 'No wonder Freud was frightened, for the people he was going to outrage were not the general public but the very men who, intellectually, he most admired.'[10] Later, in his 1971 lecture, Auden remarked: 'Speaking for myself what I admire most about Freud the man is that his love of truth was great enough to give him the courage to transcend the materialist even mechanistic scientific philosophy which went almost unchallenged when he was growing up.'[11]

Auden continued to borrow from Freud and to argue with him throughout his career, but he came to regard Freud's work as belonging not to his father's realm of medical science but to the realm of history. In his 1953 review of the Jones biography, Auden wrote:

The great revolutionary step taken by him, one that would make him a very great man still if every one of his theories should turn out to be false, was his decision—I am not perfectly sure that he ever quite realised what he had done—to treat psychological facts as belonging, not to the natural order, to be investigated according to the methodologies of chemistry and biology, but to the historical order.[12]

He repeated and elaborated upon this opinion in a 1954 review of Freud's letters,[13] and it is a central tenet of the 1971 lecture where Auden also adds that poets have known all along what Freud was the first psychologist to discover—'that the life of the mind was a historical life.'[14] In the lecture, Auden also describes Freud as one of 'the three great masters of the German language in this century'[15]—praise that tends to categorize Freud as a literary figure more so than a scientist. In such a capacity Freud's errors are not harmless, but certainly a poet might be as well qualified to expose them as a scientist. Thus Auden begins by debunking Freud's 'absurd' conviction that the Earl of Oxford wrote all of Shakespeare's plays, and progresses to weightier objections; yet his attack is oblique and equivocating.

Auden's claim never to have been analysed is not the only disingenuous assertion in the 1971 lecture. He seems perhaps to have been motivated by a wish to make himself pleasant to his audience. By saying he had never been analysed he excluded himself from being

---

[10] 'The Greatness of Freud', review of Ernest Jones, *Sigmund Freud: Life and Works*, vol. 1: *The Young Freud 1865–1900*, in *The Listener*, 50.1284 (8 Oct. 1953), 593.

[11] See p. 179 in this volume.

[12] 'The Greatness of Freud', 593.

[13] 'The Freud–Fleiss Letters', review of Sigmund Freud, *Sigmund Freud's Letters: The Origins of Psychoanalysis*, in *The Griffin*, 3.6 (June 1954), 8.

[14] See p. 179 in this volume.   [15] Ibid. 177.

entitled to pass what must have been a fairly negative judgement on the practice of psychoanalysis. Possibly he had come to regard his early analysis as not meeting any orthodox Freudian criteria anyway, and indeed he *may* have forgotten about it. When in the lecture he addresses other aspects of Freud's theories, he similarly tends to understate the nature and significance of Freud's errors, as well as the strength of his own objections to them. For instance, Auden remarks that he found *Totem and Taboo* 'impossible to swallow',[16] but he does not mention that his own 1932 work, *The Orators*, in so far as it addressed the same problem of the relation between the leader and the group, had been in some sense an attempt to rewrite Freud's theory of the primal horde in terms that might have had actual relevance for contemporary English society.[17]

Later in the lecture Auden argues that Freud, in an effort to ground himself scientifically, often used 'a Descartian vocabulary, which one has to translate in order to understand him'. Thus, Auden continues, when Freud describes a mature sexual relation as 'object love', what he really means is 'subject love'; for, Auden asks, 'Is it not the mark of maturity to be able to recognize others as persons, as subjects, in their own right?'[18] But is there any evidence that when Freud said 'object love' he did not *mean* 'object love'? Freud's theory of love focuses on the lover, not the beloved. Auden, rather remarkably, attributes to Freud a concern for the subjectivity of the love object that Auden himself had learned only through painful personal experience. In one 1939 poem Auden had said the state of being in love was all that mattered to him; the object of his love could be anything at all:

> Love requires an Object,
> But this varies so much,
> Almost, I imagine,
>   Anything will do:

---

[16] Ibid.177.

[17] Auden's doubts about *Totem and Taboo* were at least partly based on his own amateur anthropological studies, and probably reached back to his Berlin friendship with John Layard and to his reading in the 1920s of W. H. R. Rivers and Bronislaw Malinowski, among others. In his review of the second volume of Ernest Jones's Freud biography he wrote, 'I think [Jones] dismisses the anthropologists' objections to *Totem and Taboo* too cavalierly, but I am not a competent judge' ('The History of an Historian', *The Griffin* 4.11 (Nov. 1955), 9).

[18] See pp. 180–1 in this volume.

> When I was a child, I
> Loved a pumping-engine,
> Thought it every bit as
> Beautiful as you.[19]

The initial capital on 'Object' suggests Auden may have been using Freud's own technical term, but the crisis in Auden's relationship with Chester Kallman, which occurred a few years later in the summer of 1941 when Auden discovered that Kallman had taken another lover, made it clear to Auden that he had, in a sense, been living on fantasy. He had allowed himself to treat Kallman as a sacred object, a symbol, rather than recognizing him as an autonomous person. Auden's rhetorical strategy in the 1971 lecture is eccentric, as if he either did not believe or, before this particular audience, did not wish to suggest that Freud might have regarded other people as objects rather than as subjects. And yet by raising the issue in this apparently generous way, he suggests precisely that. Throughout his career, Auden was persistently, guiltily preoccupied with the moral necessity of noticing other people as subjects in their own right, and he made this obligation, and the frequent failure of human nature (including his own human nature) to meet it, a theme of some of his best work, both before meeting Chester Kallman and after.

In a broad sense, the 1971 Freud Memorial Lecture is a prolonged outcry against an accusation Auden had long recognized and objected to in Freud's theories, that the artist is at best a near neurotic, selfish and immature, who uses his fantasies to gratify appetites he has been unable to satisfy in the material world. In the lecture, Auden quotes a passage from Freud's *Introductory Lectures on Psychoanalysis* which he had already objected to in print many years before in 'Psychology and Art To-day' (1935). In 1935 Auden implied the passage was infuriating; in 1971 he more calmly and impersonally states that it is 'if not totally erroneous, at least a grave distortion of the truth'.[20] Here is the part of Freud's lecture that Auden quotes:

An artist is once more in rudiments an introvert, not far removed from neurosis. He is oppressed by excessively powerful instinctual needs. He desires to win honour, power, wealth, fame and the love of women; but he lacks the means for achieving these satisfactions. Consequently, like any other unsatisfied man, he turns away from reality and transfers all his interest, and his libido too, to the wishful constructions of his life of phantasy, whence the

---

[19] 'Heavy Date', *CP91* 261.   [20] See p. 181 in this volume.

path might lead to neurosis . . . and he has thus achieved *through* his phantasy what originally he had achieved only *in* his phantasy—honour, power, and the love of women.[21]

The artist, Auden insists in his lecture, seeks none of the worldly things Freud has suggested. He has a vocation to contemplate or discover 'hitherto unrealised truths'[22] (this is much the same vocation that Auden asserts Freud had). In the particular form of poet, Auden's artist is in love with language, which does not and cannot ever belong to him anyway.

By 1971, Auden had earned the right to say these grandiose things about the vocation of the poet, for he had indeed pursued his vocation at the cost of other real possibilities. He had admittedly received by 1971 a great measure of honour and fame, and it is impossible to know what he would have said and how he would have fared without these. But even in youth, it is plain that Auden made material sacrifices in order to write poetry. Certainly he sometimes tried to attract contemporaries or impress friends with his work, but otherwise he did not use his poetry as a means by which he might obtain something else; on the contrary, he was far more interested in poetry than in any of the things that Freud suggests the artist longs for. For instance, though he was an excellent student and went up to Oxford with an Exhibition in biology, Auden sacrificed the Exhibition in order to read English. It is well known that he fared disappointingly in his final exams, and a contemporary recalls that he wept after one of the papers.[23] He had been irresponsible about his academic work, but he had not been wasting his time: during his years in Oxford he wrote roughly one hundred poems, edited two volumes of *Oxford Poetry*, contributed widely to undergraduate magazines, read a great deal of modern literature not admitted to the undergraduate syllabus as well as many other works not assigned to him by any of his tutors, and talked, talked, talked to his contemporaries about poetry. For long periods he staked his life, both practically and aesthetically, upon

[21] Part 3, 'General Theory of the Neuroses', Lecture 23, 'The Paths to the Formation of Symptoms', *SE*, vol. 16, 376–7. When he quoted the passage in 1935, Auden was apparently drawing on the text of the 1922 edition of Freud's *Introductory Lectures on Psycho-Analysis*, but in the 1971 lecture he drew, loosely, on the version in *SE*, paraphrasing some of it and perhaps relying on memory.

[22] See p. 182 in this volume.

[23] See Carpenter, 80. William McElwee 'found Auden in his rooms weeping' after the Anglo-Saxon paper, but Stephen Spender thought this was because Auden had overworked preparing for finals so that his eyes watered throughout all his papers.

an ascetic regime of self-sacrifice and self-discipline. In 1927 he twice
wrote to his brother John explaining that in order to succeed as an
artist he was prepared to forego in life the very pleasures that Freud
suggests an artist desires, 'all the pleasant material things'. He was
celibate at the time, and he told his brother he never would marry,
not only because he was homosexual, but also because 'the insistent
craving for money would mean artistic deterioration'.[24] In late 1926
and throughout 1927 Auden strived with growing success to make
even his poetry disciplined and spare; he later recalled in 'Letter to
Lord Byron' of his taste during the Oxford period: 'Good poetry is
classic and austere.'[25]

The need for self-denial and self-sacrifice was fundamental to
Auden's nature. In the 1971 Freud lecture, he traces this back to his
childhood imaginative play, explaining that when he constructed his
mines and chose machinery to work them, he instinctively imposed
upon himself a law of scientific reality. Indeed, his mature description
of his childhood play is framed as if specifically to overturn Freud's
argument that the artist 'turns away from reality and transfers all his
interest, and his libido too, to the wishful constructions of his life of
phantasy'. Auden's discussion of his childhood play is evidently
informed by Freud's treatment of the subject in 'Creative Writers and
Day-Dreaming' (1908) where Freud compares the play of the child to
the imaginative work of the poet:

every child at play behaves like a creative writer, in that he creates a world of
his own, or, rather, re-arranges the things of his world in a new way which
pleases him. It would be wrong to think he does not take that world seriously;
on the contrary, he takes his play very seriously and he expends large amounts
of emotion on it. The opposite of play is not what is serious but what is real.
In spite of all the emotion with which he cathects his world of play, the child
distinguishes it quite well from reality; and he likes to link his imagined
objects and situations to the tangible and visible things of the real world. This
linking is all that differentiates the child's 'play' from 'phantasying'.

The creative writer does the same as the child at play. He creates a world
of phantasy which he takes very seriously; that is which he invests with large
amounts of emotion, while separating it sharply from reality.[26]

[24] Both quotations are from an ALS, probably from Christ Church, [summer term
1927]; Auden's thoughts are reiterated in another ALS, from Christ Church, [June? or
more likely Dec. 1927].
[25] EA 195.
[26] SE, vol. 9, 143–4. Auden may have known I. F. Grant Duff's 1925 translation of the
essay, 'The Relation of the Poet to Day-Dreaming', included in Freud's Collected Papers,
authorized trans. under supervision of Joan Rivière, vol. 4 (London, 1925), 172–83.

Rejecting Freud's emphasis upon the separation between fantasy and reality, Auden focuses on the child's impulse, described by Freud, to link his play *to* reality. He says in the 1971 lecture that he forbade himself 'magic means' to operate his mines, and that he disciplined himself to choose practical machinery over beautiful machinery: 'I had to choose between two types of a certain machine for separating the slimes, called a buddle. One type I found more sacred, but the other type was, I knew, from my reading, the more efficient. At this point I realized that it was my moral duty to sacrifice my symbolic preference to reality or truth.'[27] Thus, he suggests that he had experienced Freud's childhood transition from the pleasure principle to the reality principle as a moral event in which he voluntarily renounced the pleasures of pure imaginative beauty for the requirements of material reality. (Arranging his imaginary world according to the reality principle may indeed have given him more pleasure, but a different kind of pleasure.) For Auden, reality offered a severe discipline to the imagination, and the impulse on which he asserts he founded his imaginative life was not an impulse to indulge fantasy, but an impulse to restrain it.

He had described this childhood renunciation in the same way several other times,[28] and whether or not the account accurately presents his pyschological development in childhood, it tells a great deal about his mature outlook and it helps to explain the trajectory of his career. Absorbed in his private fantasy world, he reacted against the whole idea of fantasy: the conflict reverberates through the length and breadth of his poetry. It is the basis of Auden's obsession with telling the truth in poetry, and it partly explains why he rejected or rewrote some of his most celebrated works. When Auden described this childhood experience in his 1971 commonplace book, he linked it directly to a view of poetry he often expounded elsewhere:

When, later, I began to write poetry, I found that, for me at least, the same obligation was binding. That is to say, I cannot accept the doctrine that in poetry there is a 'suspension of disbelief.' A poet must never make a statement simply because it sounds poetically exciting; he must also believe it to be true.[29]

In the lecture printed here, Auden makes a further understated but powerful attack upon Freud's thought when he mentions in passing,

---

[27] See pp. 188–9 in this volume.
[28] See 'Hic and Ille', *DH* 102; and 'Writing', *ACW* 425.   [29] *ACW* 425.

as if it were hardly significant, that he disagrees with Freud about why human beings make symbols: 'Experience convinces me that however the process of symbol formation occurs, the main impetus behind it is not repression: it is something much more like a passion for not minding one's own business. The other animals may find eating and mating sufficient for a lifetime: we do not.'[30] Freud theorized that the purpose of symbol formation, in dream work in particular, was to disguise the dreamer's own unacceptable wishes—in other words, to conceal repressed, fundamentally sexual, instincts. Auden suggests that mankind, far from being unconsciously always preoccupied with such basic drives, would grow bored with continually satisfying them, and so has devised other pastimes, such as making symbols—for which we may justifiably also read 'works of art'. Auden's artist makes symbols not to conceal his sexual or other impulses from himself, or even as a substitute form of gratification, but for the greater pleasure he can find both in the symbol itself and above all in the activity of creation. This goes back to the theory of creative pleasure that he first posed against Freud in 1929, 'The essence of creation is doing things for no reason, it is pointless.'[31] In his 1935 essay 'Psychology and Art To-day' Auden had made clear his view that Freud did not sufficiently distinguish between art and fantasy because he did not understand the poet's art. Auden emphasizes in that essay, in the sections entitled 'Craftsmanship' and 'The Conscious Element', that the poet is not an inspired madman, but labours to exercise conscious and deliberate technical control over his fantasies:

The poet is inclined to retort [to the psycho-analyst] that . . . in his own experience, what he is most aware of are technical problems, the management of consonants and vowels, the counterpointing of scenes, or how to get the husband off the stage before the lover's arrival, and that psychology concentrating on the symbols, ignores words; in his treatment of symbols and facts he fails to explain why of two works dealing with the same unconscious material, one is aesthetically good and the other bad; indeed that few psycho-analysts in their published work show any signs of knowing that aesthetic standards exist.[32]

Much of Auden's 1971 Freud Memorial Lecture presents an autobiography of his own creative life as evidence that his version of the

---

[30] See p. 186 in this volume.   [31] 1929 journal (Berg); see p. 141 above and n. 6.
[32] EA 336–7.

creative process, and not Freud's, is the correct one. In his conclusion, Auden throws doubt on the whole enterprise of psychoanalysing art by arguing that in the successful poem any contribution that an analyst might make is already complete: 'A good poem, one might say, is like a successfully analysed patient: both have become, what the Psalmist says of Jerusalem, "A city that is at unity in itself." '[33] Only a bad work of art, he argues, can be illuminated by psychoanalysis, and his analogy implies that the unity of the poem as it leaves the poet's hands or of the successfully analysed patient as he or she leaves the analyst's couch, is sacred, like the holy city of Jerusalem. Still, Auden offers no objection to psychoanalysing the artist, nor to examining the creative process. On the contrary, with the self-contradictoriness that reveals his profound ambivalence, he undertakes in the lecture what he calls 'a little self-analysis'. Of his fascination with a favourite symbol, the mine-riddled limestone landscape, he observes that 'the cross-sectional diagrams of mines in my books . . . are like stylised pictures of the internal anatomy of the human body . . . that the word *lead* rhymes with *dead* and that lead is or was used for lining coffins . . . that mining is the one human activity that is by nature mortal.'[34] During the lecture, Auden read out 'In Praise of Limestone', 'Amor Loci', and the Rookhope passage from 'New Year Letter'. In these poems, the themes of love and death, human frailty and inspiration, so richly play over the topography that to him resembles 'the internal anatomy of the human body' and where as a child he mined entirely alone, as to make his presentation of them in the lecture seem like a provocation to the analyst or literary critic for whom the process of interpretation is, after all, as pleasurable as the process of creating art is for the artist. And his gesture at self-analysis confirms that however emphatically Auden pronounced against Freud, he was, even at the end of his life, still fascinated by the promise of the methods Freud had devised for studying the psyche.

If Auden felt that Freud was mostly wrong about the artist and the creative process, he certainly acknowledged that Freud had understood and helped to illuminate the method by which an artist such as Auden seeks to discover for himself his true nature—by exploring his past, his personal history. And this appears to have been the emphasis in Freud's thought that Auden's father most fully accepted and drew on. In his elegy for Freud, Auden writes:

[33] Psalms 122: 3; see p. 195 in this volume.   [34] Ibid. 187.

> . . . as they lie in the grass of our neglect,
>   so many long-forgotten objects
> revealed by his undiscouraged shining
>
> are returned to us and made precious again;
>   games we had thought we must drop as we grew up.[35]

By rediscovering his childhood games and preoccupations Auden endeavoured, like Wordsworth and so many others, to understand himself as a poet and also as a human being; eventually, he came to regard his childhood experiences as the spring of his creative life. In some respects writing poetry was for him a continual process of self-analysis, and one over which he perhaps preferred to keep exclusive control. Yet despite his reservations about Freud's theories, Auden seems to have wished to open this process of self-analysis to his audience at the Philadelphia Association for Psychoanalysis, and moreover, he seems to have expected that his listeners might, like Freud himself, be able to understand and to interpret the details of his personal history that he laid before them. For he took out and showed off in his lecture some 'long-forgotten objects' from his own childhood.

Perhaps the single most important of these 'long-forgotten objects' is his nursery library. Auden had drawn attention before to the books he remembered reading in childhood, and by producing the list yet again, he seemed to be insisting that his audience attend to it. The list is incomplete because one page of the lecture is lost, but he published a similar one in *A Certain World* and mentioned items from it in other places as well, so it may be fairly reliably reassembled.[36] The most eccentric and most talked-about items in Auden's nursery library are the technical books on mining which he often referred to and drew upon in his adult career, but the more conventional selection of prose fiction and poetry is equally revealing. Most are classics, some still widely read. In these poems and stories lie clues to the character of many of Auden's lifelong preoccupations and habitual patterns of thought. For instance, George MacDonald's fairy-tale, *The Princess and the Goblin* helps to explain why for so many years Auden confused his vocation as poet with the vocation of mining engineer. *The Princess and the Goblin* takes place in Auden's sacred landscape of

---

[35] *CP91* 275.

[36] The list appears in *ACW* on 291–2. A similar list appeared in Auden's introduction to John Betjeman's *Slick but Not Streamlined* (Garden City, NY, 1947); a few of the books are also mentioned in 'Making, Knowing and Judging', *DH* 34, and in other places. See Appendix for the full list and some annotations.

mountains and valleys, filled with underground caves and mines; and the hero of the story, a young boy called Curdie Peterson, is both a miner and a poet. Curdie's task is to rescue the princess from the goblins who live in the mines. At first it seems he may achieve this by virtue of his ability to rhyme, because the goblins are repelled by rhymes, and for a time Curdie uses his rather crude verses successfully against them. Eventually though, the rhymes prove inadequate. He is captured and has to be rescued by the princess through genuinely magic means. In the end, it is Curdie's practical skills as a miner which enable him to foil the goblins' plan of flooding the princess's house with an underground river and kidnapping her as a bride for their grotesque prince. Curdie works the underground passages in such a way as to direct the flood into the goblins' own quarters, drowning some and driving out the rest.[37]

We don't know exactly how old Auden was when he read the story or had it read to him, so we cannot know whether the landscape was sacred to him already, or whether this may have been the tale that first lodged the landscape in his mind. We do know that it was his early reading rather than any outdoor experience that impressed him. He told Alan Ansen in 1947: 'My landscapes aren't really the same as Wordsworth's. Mine, and that's a point I haven't written about yet, come from books first.'[38] We also cannot know whether this story helped to generate Auden's self-imposed prohibition against using magic means in his own mines, but according to that prohibition, Auden would have permitted himself to identify with the hero's practical ability as a miner rather than with his more romantically striking attribute of being a poet. In any case, the 'magic' of Curdie's poetry proves inadequate to the task required of the hero in the tale.

In maturity, Auden always described his decision to become a poet as sudden. In 1936 in 'Letter to Lord Byron' he wrote:

> . . . indecision broke off with a clean-cut end
>> One afternoon in March at half-past three
> When walking in a ploughed field with a friend;
>> Kicking a little stone, he turned to me
>> And said, 'Tell me, do you write poetry?'
> I never had, and said so, but I knew
> That very moment what I wished to do.[39]

[37] I am grateful to Richard Davenport-Hines for allowing me to read in a draft chapter of his forthcoming biography of Auden his suggestive discussion of George MacDonald's influence on Auden.

[38] Ansen, 15.   [39] *EA* 194.

Twenty years later in 'Making, Knowing and Judging' he described the moment in much the same way in prose, commenting 'the suggestion that I write poetry seemed like a revelation from heaven for which nothing in my past could account'. But in the 1956 lecture he added that on subsequent reflection he had come to see that he had all along been experiencing the language of his technical books on mining in a particular way: 'A word like *pyrites*, for example, was the Proper Name of a Sacred Being.' Thus, 'without knowing it, I had been enjoying the poetic use of language for a long time.'[40] Mining was a symbolic activity that stood for something else, or, as Auden might have preferred to put it, that was a preparation for something else: in order to get ready to make poems he had been making mines. Thus, Auden's decision to become a poet was not so sudden after all. Indeed, it was not perhaps a decision so much as a relenting. The regime of self-denial he had imposed upon his imagination in childhood gave way in this momentous instant to the force of his imaginative desire, as if all along the practical vocation of the boyhood hero, Curdie, had only concealed the more beautiful one. Almost certainly Auden relented partly under the spell of romantic intoxication; for he was in love with the boy, Robert Medley, who asked him if he wrote poetry and this was the first time Auden had fallen in love with a boy his own age who might be able to return his feelings.

Auden's mature poetic treatments of the themes of mining and underground life are certainly among his most beautiful work. In order of composition, the Rookhope passage from 'New Year Letter', 'In Praise of Limestone', and 'Amor Loci' offer, among other things, an almost narrative account of his evolving experience of love in all its forms, human and divine. Far from concealing repressed instincts or unacceptable memories, the symbolic elements of these poems articulate something far more complex than the fundamental drives on which they undoubtedly draw. In all three poems, Auden is moving towards memory, towards the past, in order to draw it out for his readers; to mine it, and to forge a new, more elaborate artefact. In his 1935 lecture 'Psychology and Art To-day', Auden wrote 'Creation, like psycho-analysis, is a process of re-living in a new situation;'[41] each of these poems revisits his symbolic landscape at a different phase in his adult creative life, and the 'meaning' of the landscape is transformed and augmented each time he writes about it. The

[40] *DH* 34–5.   [41] *EA* 337.

Rookhope passage in 'New Year Letter' refers to an experience Auden had there in adolescence: he dropped a stone into an empty mineshaft and felt deeply awed when he heard it splash in the distant bottom of the shaft. He had written about this experience already in 1924, 1925, and 1930.[42] In 'New Year Letter', he sets the experience into a richly allusive context which universalizes his sense of fear and inspiration. Auden certainly had other traumatic experiences—and probably more wounding ones—but in the poem, he suggests the way in which this moment at Rookhope stands for them all. In a 1941 book review, he explained that the child covets an overwhelming experience like the one he had at Rookhope, because, he asserts, the psychological wound that might result has a purpose. He was writing about Kafka, but as is characteristic of his most striking intuitions about other artists, he may as well have been describing himself:

Psychotherapy will not get much further until it recognizes that the true significance of a neurosis is teleological, that the so-called traumatic experience is not an accident, but the opportunity for which the child has been patiently waiting—had it not occurred, it would have found another, equally trivial—in order to find a necessity and direction for its existence, in order that its life may become a serious matter. Of course it would be better if it could do without it, but unconsciously it knows that it is not, by itself strong enough to learn to stand alone: a neurosis is a guardian angel; to become ill is to take vows.[43]

This passage makes clear that in objecting to Freud's view that the artist is a near-neurotic—as Auden did in his 1935 essay 'Psychology and Art To-day' and in his 1971 lecture 'Phantasy and Reality in Poetry'—Auden was objecting to the way in which Freud theorized the artist *responded* to his near-neurosis, not to the idea of neurosis at all.

---

[42] Auden's adolescent poems, 'The Old Lead-mine' and 'Like other men when I go past' (*Juvenilia*, 29–30, 82) both describe dropping a stone down a mine-shaft; he used the experience again in the 1930 poem beginning 'Get there if you can and see the land you once were proud to own' (*EA* 48). Another adolescent poem, 'Rookhope (Weardale, Summer 1922)' suggests the actual experience may have occurred in the summer of 1922 (*Juvenilia*, 54), but in the Freud lecture Auden says that the Rookhope passage in 'New Year Letter' refers to him at 12 years old, which would have been in 1919.

[43] 'The Wandering Jew', review of three translations of Kafka (*Amerika, A Franz Kafka Miscellany, The Castle*) in *The New Republic* 104.1367 (10 Feb. 1941), 186.

Another favourite nursery tale that Auden recalls in the 1971 Freud lecture is Hans Andersen's *The Snow Queen*.[44] As with the limestone landscape, his childhood affinity for this tale resonates throughout his work. *The Snow Queen* might be summarized as follows. An evil troll makes a distorting mirror in which everything good appears as nothing and everything bad is emphasized. The mirror breaks, and two slivers lodge in the eye and heart of a boy called Kay, so that everything good looks ugly to him and everything bad takes on exaggerated prominence. He is cruel to his beloved playmate, Gerda, and to his grandmother, and runs off in the snow with his sledge, whereupon he is kidnapped by the Snow Queen who makes him forget everything with her kiss. Eventually Gerda makes her way to the Snow Queen's castle and finds the Snow Queen sitting on a frozen lake which is cracked into thousands of pieces all exactly alike, 'a perfect work of art'. The Snow Queen—perversely alluding to the distorting mirror that has transfixed Kay—calls the lake 'the mirror of reason'.[45] Kay, blue with cold, is absorbed in playing 'the icy game of reason' in which he uses the ice fragments as puzzle pieces to form words. He is stuck trying to form the word 'eternity', and the Snow Queen has promised to free him if he can succeed. Kay does not recognize Gerda, and so she weeps. Her hot tears 'penetrated into his heart, and they thawed the lump of ice, and consumed the little piece of glass in it.' Then Kay looks at Gerda and she sings a little verse about spiritual renewal that refers to the rose trees the playmates cultivated together at home: 'Roses bloom and roses decay | But we the Christ child shall see one day!'[46] (Roses serve as a symbol of faith between the two throughout the tale.) At this, Kay himself begins to weep and the second splinter of glass is flushed out of his eye so that he at last recognizes Gerda. Their mutual joy overflows into the scene around them, and even the blocks of ice begin to dance, forming themselves into the word 'eternity'. Thus, the playmates are set free and make their way home through scenery now transformed by the arrival of spring flowers and foliage.

The Snow Queen offers a flat, rigid, and frozen landscape that is very nearly the perfect opposite to the mountainous, multi-layered

---

[44] In 'Letter to Lord Byron', Auden wrote, 'My favourite tale was Andersen's *Ice Maiden*' (*EA* 191). This is a different story with its own importance for Auden's work. See Appendix, pp. 200–2.

[45] Hans C. Andersen, *Stories and Tales*, trans. H. W. Dulcken (London, 1864), 293.

[46] Ibid. 294.

and fertile one of *The Princess and the Goblin*, and Auden frequently drew in his adult work on the imagery in *The Snow Queen* of freezing and thaw. If a limestone landscape symbolized for him the changing and self-conscious experience of love, a frozen landscape tended to symbolize the failure of love and the impossibility of compassion. In two adolescent poems, 'Frost' and 'Christmas Eve', Auden used wintry scenes to comment on the way in which pleasure ignores the suffering of other people. 'Christmas Eve' achieved this with a moralizing juxtaposition of images:

> Along the wrinkled roads come bands
> Of shouting boys, skates in their hands
> Watching them pass a beggar stands.[47]

Winter pleasures, by their very nature, are oblivious to the seasonal experience of death that surrounds them. In the December 1933 poem beginning 'The earth turns over, our side feels the cold' the skating boys are again contrasted with the certainty of mortality foreshadowed by the season: 'The ticking heart comes to a standstill, killed, | The icing on the pond waits for the boys'.[48] Later, in 'Musée des Beaux Arts', which takes as its main theme the way in which suffering usually occurs unnoticed, the skating boys again reappear as 'Children . . . skating | On a pond at the edge of the wood' in order that they may ignore both the season and the birth of Christ, just as they would probably ignore 'even the dreadful martyrdom' which the poem also mentions.[49]

In his 1939 elegy for W. B. Yeats, Auden used the imagery from *The Snow Queen* far more redemptively. The elegy begins in a frozen landscape (Yeats died, as the poem says, 'in the dead of winter') and ends with images of cultivation, growth, and flowing water. The idea of the ice splinter informs the lines 'And the seas of pity lie | Locked and frozen in each eye,'[50] and Auden calls upon the poet, with his voice and verse, to release these tears, just as Gerda releases Kay's tears when she sings of the roses and the Christ child:

> Follow, poet, follow right
> To the bottom of the night,
> With your unconstraining voice
> Still persuade us to rejoice;

---

[47] *Juvenilia*, 118; for 'Frost', see *Juvenilia*, 113.   [48] *EA* 144.
[49] Ibid. 237.   [50] Ibid. 243.

> With the farming of a verse
> Make a vineyard of the curse,
> Sing of human unsuccess
> In a rapture of distress;
>
> In the deserts of the heart
> Let the healing fountain start,
> In the prison of his days
> Teach the free man how to praise.[51]

The 'poet' here is not necessarily Yeats, but any poet, and presumably Auden himself. For the stanzas outline the task that, in Auden's view, remains for poetry after Yeats's death. In the context of the 'nightmare' of coming war in Europe and the shame this casts upon every European, Auden's phrase 'the seas of pity' clearly alludes to Wilfred Owen's 1918 preface to his war poems. Owen wrote 'My subject is War, and the pity of War. The Poetry is in the pity.'[52] Auden had quoted the phrases already in his 1933 poem beginning 'Here on the cropped grass of the narrow ridge'.[53] Now he calls upon the poet to 'persuade' even though he cannot constrain. Presenting Yeats's poetry as a river ('it flows south | From ranches of isolation and the busy griefs'[54]) and Yeats himself as a 'vessel' now emptied— as if poetry were a liquid, pity a tear—Auden urges the poet to unlock with his tragic song the 'healing fountain' in the heart, the redemptive overflow of human pity.

When Auden later used imagery from *The Snow Queen* it was with a colder purpose. The troll's distorting mirror appears a few months after the Yeats elegy in 'They', suggestively in the hands of a mother rather than a troll: 'in a mother's distorting mirror | they discovered the Meaning of Knowing.'[55] And the idea that 'one could weep because another wept' is presented as an impossibility in 'The Shield of Achilles'.[56] Auden used the image of the ice splinter again in part two of *The Age of Anxiety*—'The Seven Ages'—to describe the emotional condition of the successful public man in his Sixth Age. The speech is Malin's:

---

[51] *EA* 243.

[52] See *The Complete Poems and Fragments*, ed. Jon Stallworthy (London, 1983), vol. 2, 535.

[53] '"The poetry's in the pity", Wilfred said' (*EA* 144.)

[54] *EA* 242.

[55] *CP91* 254.

[56] Ibid. 598.

                                    Feverish in
        Their bony building his brain cells keep
        Their hectic still, but his heart transfixed
        By the ice-splinter of an ingrown tear,
        Comatose in her cave, cares little
        What the senses say; at the same time,
        Dedicated, clandestine under
        The guilt and grime of a great career,
        The bruise of his boyhood is blue still,
        Horrid and hurting, hostile to his life
        As a praised person. He pines for some
        Nameless Eden where he never was
        But where in his wishes once again
        On hallowed acres, without a stitch
        Of achievement on, the children play
        Nor care how comely they couldn't be
        Since they needn't know they're not happy.[57]

As the epigraph—from George Herbert's 'Miserie'—to this second
part of the poem implies, the unhappiness of this public man in some
respects is Auden's own unhappiness:

            A sick toss'd vessel, dashing on each thing;
                    Nay, his own shelf:
                My God, I mean myself.[58]

And there is an element of autobiography in Malin's longing for a
symbolic Edenic landscape and for a mind not yet so engaged in the
tasks of reason that it has lost all ability to feel, burying the 'bruise of
boyhood' rather than healing it.

    By the time he wrote *Elegy for Young Lovers* (1959–60) with
Chester Kallman, Auden had objectified the character of the successful public artist so completely that with Kallman he could openly
attribute to the poet, Mittenhofer, the 'guilt and grime' of ruthlessly
exploiting those around him for the sake of his work. Mittenhofer's
artistic aspiration to 'freeze' Elizabeth and Toni in his elegy about
them, articulates as an achieved crime the Snow Queen's sinister
attempt to keep Kay her prisoner in her 'perfect work of art', 'the
mirror of reason'.[59] The opposing spheres of frozen art and warm life

[57] Ibid. 477–8.
[58] See ibid. 465; I have printed the excerpt of Herbert's poem from *Poets of the
English Language*, eds. W. H. Auden and Norman Holmes Pearson (London, 1952),
vol. 2, 459.
[59] Andersen, *Stories and Tales*, 293.

persistently inform the language of the libretto, but two passages in particular demonstrate its debt to Andersen's tale. In Act 2, Scene 10 Mittenhofer sings the following:

> Out of Eden, bringing Eden
> With them, the young lovers come
> Hand in hand to the cold lands.
> The snow falls. There is no welcome.
> Their singleness reproaches our mingled
> Isolations, their love our songless
> Ice-altars; we refuse the rose
> Of Heaven's children. Nevertheless,
> One who dare not break the barrier . . .
> His own . . . who only will turn, will move to
> Reach for and bless their happiness,
> Shall heedlessly enter Eden too.
> They bring us a gift from afar:
> A fragile and eternal flower.[60]

Here from Gerda's song is the redeeming rose of the Christ child, associated in Andersen's tale with the innocent love of children and with the natural order of the ordinary world; Mittenhofer rejects it for the icy white edelweiss. He sends Elizabeth and Toni to collect this flower on the mountain and when they die in the blizzard (echoing the fate of Lamp as he reaches for the Polus Naufrangia in *The Ascent of F6*) he is able to form his own Eden, a perfect artifice, in his poem. As Elizabeth and Toni set off for the mountains, having agreed to spend one more day in Mittenhofer's service before leaving together, Elizabeth sings: 'One day? How light a fee | To bribe eternity!'[61] 'Eternity' is the word Kay must spell in order to win his freedom from the Snow Queen; here the Mephistophelian pact works in reverse. Whereas in Auden's 1939 Yeats elegy, poetry is imaged as a river and a fountain which may flush its audience with pity, in this later work, poetry, like the sliver of glass from the distorting mirror, is the vision that transfixes the eye and freezes the heart. In their account of writing the libretto, Auden and Kallman explained, 'The Theme of *Elegy for Young Lovers* is summed up in two lines by

---

[60] *Libretti*, 226. No evidence survives on which to attribute composition of this passage either to Auden or to Kallman (see *Libretti*, 645–6). It is possible that Kallman wrote it, but probably Auden had directed him to Andersen's fairy-tale anyway—the whole conception of the libretto is informed by the idea of *The Snow Queen* and details are also borrowed from *The Ice Maiden*.

[61] Ibid. 228.

Yeats: "The intellect of man is forced to choose | Perfection of the life or of the work." '[62] Yet these lines hardly address the exceptionally heavy burden of guilt that the libretto in fact lays upon Mittenhofer for choosing art over life. He is depicted not as merely cold-hearted but as a murderer. This is a disproportionately harsh judgement against what, in his 1967 T. S. Eliot Memorial Lectures, Auden called 'the European Romantics' myth of the Artistic-Genius' who 'is not to be judged by the moral standards we apply to ordinary mortals.'[63] Although Auden ostensibly rejects this grotesque role for himself, he none the less seems to accept the burden of guilt attached to it; moreover, he seems to desire this guilt.

Auden's appetite for such harsh self-criticism, his deep sense of guilt, and even his apparent streak of masochism, may be better understood by a further look at the nursery library to which he drew the attention of his listeners at the Philadelphia Association for Psychoanalysis in March 1971. All of the poetry—as distinct from prose—that Auden recollected from his early reading is about crime and punishment. He lists Hilaire Belloc's *Cautionary Tales*, Harry Graham's *Ruthless Rhymes for Heartless Homes*, and Heinrich Hoffmann's *Struwwelpeter*. Belloc's rhymes are ironic and witty and the crimes grow more outlandish and unlikely as the book progresses: James is eaten by a lion at the zoo because he strays from his nurse; Henry King chews bits of string and dies from knots in his tummy; Matilda burns to death after issuing too many false alarms to the fire brigade; Rebecca slams doors for fun and is killed when a heavy object falls on her from a plinth; George bursts a balloon so large that it knocks out the lights and windows, topples the house, and kills him and several others. By contrast, the empty success of Charles Augustus Fortescue highlights the excitement and pleasure of naughtiness and its consequences. (The relation among these rhymes is recaptured in Auden's 1953 description of *The Rake's Progress* as 'a bourgeois cautionary tale' whose 'twin is the story of The Virtuous Apprentice who is never late for work, saves his pennies and finally marries the master's daughter.'[64]) Harry Graham's rhymes make fun of the selfishness and folly of grown-ups as well as the misdemeanours of children, but the events in them are incidental and eccentric rather than archetypal or

[62] Ibid. 246.
[63] 'The World of Opera', *SW* 102–3.
[64] 'The Rake's Progress', *Harper's Bazaar* (Feb. 1953); repr. *Libretti*, 617.

easily recognizable, and the punishments which they describe bear no necessary relation to the crimes. In fact sometimes perfectly innocent people meet with disaster. Thus, despite their sometimes shocking sadism, Graham's verses have far less moral punch than the two other collections Auden mentions. By comparison, Heinrich Hoffmann's stories seem not funny but grotesquely frightening. The sins they describe are common and venial, likely to have been committed by many children, and a young child would have to be brave indeed to laugh them off altogether. 'Shock-headed Peter' is taunted by other children for refusing to have his hair or nails cut; 'Cruel Frederick', malicious towards animals, is bitten by a dog which then takes his place at the family table; Edward, William, and Arthur who tease a black boy are dipped in black ink by 'Big Agrippa'; Augustus who will not eat his soup wastes away to nothing and dies.[65]

The ostensible point of all these rhymes is to admonish children, as Belloc's title makes clear. The stories depend on the convention that the children in them will be naughty and break the rules laid down for them; their interest lies in the way the author invents the appropriate punishment for the crime. Indeed, the arrival of the suitable retribution is the climax of almost all the tales and the moment in which the reading or listening child is apparently meant to take the greatest pleasure.

Auden describes in the 1971 lecture one childhood episode during which he himself was disciplined. He and his brother were told to be quiet because a visiting uncle was ill in bed; Auden replied 'I wish he would die' and was spanked. As an adult he professes the view that the spanking was called for, though he argues that he felt, even at the time, that he had been misunderstood; for, in fact, the Uncle, Harold Allden Auden known as Uncle Harry, was his favourite and he did not really wish him dead. In the lecture Auden uses the episode to formulate a distinction between a wish and a desire. A desire, he urges, is based in reality and means what it says, but a wish—such as his wish for his uncle's death—refuses to accept reality. The form the wish takes, Auden argues, is not important because all wishes mean the same thing; they wish for things to be other than they are. In Auden's example, he wished not that his uncle was dead but simply that things were different so that he could go on playing. He says that he expressed his wish as a wish for his uncle's death simply

---

[65] It is not known which of the numerous English editions of *Struwwelpeter* Auden possessed; see Appendix, pp. 205–6.

because he liked to shock his elders. In telling the story Auden does not mention that in *The Orators*—a work for which the underlying motivation to shock his elders is as true as it was of Auden's wish at six years old—he finally did indulge his childhood wish in fantasy, for the Airman's Uncle Henry, considered by the Airman to be his true ancestor, does die. The Airman, obsessed with this fact, shapes his life around understanding and honouring the meaning of his uncle's death: 'In hours of gentleness always to remember my Uncle.'[66]

Though Auden insists in his lecture that the murderous formulation of his childhood wish was not important, in fact the sense of guilt apparently associated with the wish suggests, like the guilt associated with the character Mittenhofer, that, in some sense, it *is* important. In his 1953 poem beginning 'Make this night loveable,' Auden acknowledges the murderous wish that even the lover may feel toward his beloved, and he asks the moon to illuminate the night, as if its light could keep such a wish at bay:

> Shine lest tonight any,
> In the dark suddenly,
> Wake alone in a bed
> To hear his own fury
> Wishing his love were dead.[67]

Probably the lines refer to an impulse Auden felt towards Chester Kallman when he first discovered Kallman's infidelity in 1941; certainly they articulate a kind of ambivalence which Freud would have recognized and which Auden, as if conforming to a pattern of repression that Freud often described, glossed over in the 1971 lecture. Auden recalls in the lecture that the Uncle Harry episode happened at Christmas time, the season of the year he often used in his later poems to reflect upon the way that human beings, especially children, so easily ignore the sufferings of other people, just as he had been punished for doing. In respect of Auden's distinction between a wish and a desire, one lesson of the episode must have been that making fantastic wishes, such as the wish that Uncle Harry would die so that Auden could go on playing without restraint, was somehow wrong; in other words, the punishment may have served as another spur to Auden's childhood reaction against fantasy.

---

[66] *EA* 90. Isherwood also had an Uncle called Henry and the Uncle Henry in *The Orators* in some respects resembles him.
[67] *CP91* 577.

Auden read aloud during the lecture one of the poems from Hoffmann's collection *Struwwelpeter*, 'The Story of Little Suck-a-Thumb', perhaps partly because he assumed it might be familiar to his audience. Freud cites the verses as an example of a story that, in disguise, threatens castration to little boys who play with themselves: 'In *Struwwelpeter*, the famous work of the Frankfurt paediatrician Hoffmann (which owes its popularity precisely to an understanding of the sexual and other complexes of childhood), you will find castration softened into a cutting-off of the thumbs as a punishment for obstinate sucking.'[68] Auden clearly knew this passage in Freud; it appears in the same lecture from which he quoted in 1935 and again in 1971 the objectionable passage characterizing the artist as a neurotic. Moreover, Auden understood 'The Story of Little Suck-a-Thumb' according to Freud's interpretation, for in *A Certain World* he included the poem under the heading 'Castration Complex' and noted 'it's not about thumb-sucking at all, but about masturbation, which is punished by castration.'[69] Auden was a life-long nail-biter; he says in the 1971 lecture that in childhood he ignored his mother's attempts to stop him, but he never feared that the great long red-legged scissorman would cut off his thumbs because he knew that the scissor-man was only a figure in a poem. In other words, the sort of admonitions presented to him by the poetry he knew in childhood did not persuade him to behave differently—in this case to cease biting his nails—but rather they taught him to recognize, once again, the importance of the distinction between fantasy and reality. Thus, the same principle that required Auden to choose a utilitarian rather than a beautiful machine to work in his imaginary mines, and that perhaps led him to believe his vocation was to be a mining engineer rather than a poet, also helped him to defend himself from the threat offered by the scissor-man.

What can he have felt when, having successfully fortified his childish psyche against the scissor-man, he was in fact circumcised at seven? He later told Alan Ansen that the experience had been 'really something'.[70] It occurred around the same time that his father left home to join the RAMC, leaving Auden alone with his passionate and

[68] 'The Paths to the Formation of Symptoms', *SE*, vol. 16, 69.

[69] *ACW* 52–3.

[70] Recorded in Ansen's unpublished notes of their conversations during 1946 or 1947 (Berg; this passage is not included in the selection *Table Talk*) and quoted in Carpenter, 21.

puritanical mother to serve as his only parent for the next five years. Auden states in the Freud lecture that he finds crabs, spiders, and octopi far more frightening than the great long red-legged scissor-man in *Struwwelpeter*; they represent to him, he conjectures, the castrating, toothed female genitals (presumably this is the background of Alonso's lines in 'The Sea and the Mirror', 'In their Royal Zoos the | Shark and the octopus are tactfully | Omitted'[71]). In fact, the image of the scissor-man, with his blades spread wide, is as much like a pinching red crab as any part of the female anatomy.[72] In any case, the sexual identity of the figure of retribution Auden evokes from his childhood is a shifting one, and not long before the Freud lecture he told an interviewer that he had once been deeply frightened in childhood by seeing his parents dressed in one another's clothes: 'I remember at the age of seven seeing my Ma and Pa in drag and bursting into tears. She had on his clothes and a false moustache and he was wearing hers. They were going to a masquerade I think, and I suppose they thought it would amuse me. I was terrified. It was one of the last times I saw him as a child.'[73] John Auden, sufficiently older to have a more reliable memory, recollected that in fact the incident occurred in 1912 when Auden was five, but Auden came to think of it as one of the last times that he saw his father before his father left for the war.[74]

In the 1971 Freud Memorial Lecture Auden discusses at length his 1932 poem beginning 'O what is that sound which so thrills the ear', which he read out or recited for his audience. Although he does not say so, the situation in the poem closely resembles 'The Story of Little Suck-a-Thumb'. In the poem, a voice reassures then vanishes,

[71] *CP91* 416.

[72] All the English editions of *Struwwelpeter* that I have seen have the same illustrations (the earlier ones brilliantly hand-coloured). The scissor-man is depicted leaping through the door, his long hair streaming back from a cruel and sensual face, his red legs spread as wide as the scissors he carries; the scissors are almost as big as Conrad. Conrad's mother appears in only one of the pictures with her back, not her face, showing. But at the rear of three of the four pictures in 'The Story of Little Suck-a-Thumb', faces look down from the wall decoration as if standing in for her watchful presence; each face has a different expression. After Conrad's mother leaves, two faces which are bearded in the first picture move to the centre of the wall and become one face without a beard. And once his thumbs are off, this face smiles with wicked contentment on the humbled boy.

[73] Jon Bradshaw, 'W. H. Auden and His Graffiti', *The Observer* Colour Magazine, 7 Nov. 1971, p. 43. Bradshaw had published two other versions of the same interview early in 1970.

[74] Carpenter, 13.

like Conrad's admonishing mother; the victim is left alone, like Conrad, to face a fleet and mysterious retribution; and a troop of 'scarlet soldiers'[75] arrive like the red-legged scissor-man to carry out the punishment. Auden explains that he intended readers to experience the poem as if it were a dream, and while this statement might have seemed to his audience at the Association of Psychoanalysis like an invitation to analyse the poem's latent meaning, he pointedly went on to describe to them some of the conscious work he had done to try to achieve the dream-like effect. The poem was suggested to him, he says, by a painting of Christ's agony in the garden.[76] He imagined seeing the painting as a film rather than a still image, so that the group of soldiers shown marching over a nearby bridge would draw closer and closer to Christ as he waits with the sleeping disciples who are soon to forsake him. Then Auden says, he recalled a nightmare in which he was pursued by a steam-roller. He presumed that most people have had such a dream about being pursued by a malignant power, but the soldiers seemed to him a better, more universal symbol for such a power than the steam-roller he actually had dreamed about himself, and so he used them in the poem. He repeatedly emphasizes that he has never had such a dream of soldiers himself, implying that whatever symbolic impact the soldiers might have upon a reader of the poem is put there deliberately by the poet, and is not the result of undirected fantasy or of repression. Nevertheless, he also tells his listeners about the steam-roller, inviting another kind of analysis. The steam-roller in Auden's own nightmare seems to embody in the form of the machinery he loved as a child some attributes of the overbearing and overloving mother he clearly also loved. However much he may have feared to be crushed by such a phenomenon, he also apparently relished it, just as he relished being underground or confined in a small space. In 'Letter to Lord Byron' he wrote:

> Today I like a weight upon my bed;
> I always travel by the Underground;
> For concentration I have always found
> A small room best, the curtains drawn, the light on.[77]

[75] EA 125.
[76] As Richard Davenport-Hines has discovered, this is probably the one by Giovanni Bellini in the National Gallery, London; see p. 193 and n. 25 in this volume.
[77] EA 192.

As a houseguest Auden was even known to take curtains off the windows, pictures off the walls, or carpets off the stairs and pile them on top of himself before going to sleep.[78]

A point that Auden omits from his 1971 account of writing 'O what is that sound which so thrills the ear' is that the poem draws not only on the painting he describes and on his nightmare of the steam-roller, but also on a poem by Thomas Hardy entitled 'On the Portrait of a Woman about to Be Hanged'. Hardy presents the threat of execution hanging over his subject and the military feel of its dreadful advance in the first stanza of his poem:

> Comely and capable one of our race,
> Posing there in your gown of grace,
>   Plain, yet becoming;
>   Could subtlest breast
>   Ever have guessed
> What was behind that innocent face,
>   Drumming, drumming![79]

According to the syntax of the poem, the 'drumming' behind the woman's face must be her racing blood; but it also implies soldiers. Auden picked up the haunting repetition with his refrain-like second line, 'Down in the valley drumming, drumming?'[80] The Hardy influence perhaps accounts for the fact that Auden's poem does not feel as much like a dream as Auden says he meant it to; it is more like a ballad, with its jaunty air. The title of Hardy's poem ('On the Portrait of a Woman about to Be Hanged') suggests that he, like Auden, was inspired by a painting as much as by an actual experience. Thus, although Auden does not mention Hardy's poem when he describes writing his own (he may not, by 1971, have remembered it) it is striking that in 1932 he appears to have been reminded of the feelings evoked by Hardy's poem when he was looking at another painting—of Christ's agony in Gethsemane. Hardy's poem makes clear that although his victim looks innocent she is indeed guilty of something. And the dream experience that Auden meant his poem to suggest seems to be the experience of profound guilt and the expectation of retribution. But in his 1971 lecture, Auden describes the pursuing power as malignant, and to emphasize the innocence of the

---

[78] Carpenter, 45.
[79] *Human Shows, Far Phantasies, Songs, and Trifles* (London, 1925), 169 ff.
[80] *EA* 125.

pursued he associates him or her with Christ. His 1932 poem, Auden is thereby asserting to his lecture audience, is about unjust persecution, not about just retribution; the subject is not a criminal but a blameless victim whose goodness and high spiritual purpose have been somehow, bewilderingly, betrayed. None of this is evident in the text of the poem; it is supplied only in 1971, long after Auden had returned to the church and in many respects undergone complex personal transformation.

The scissor-man haunted Auden. In his second letter to Erika Mann in *Letters from Iceland*, he described a nightmare had while travelling which was not about the threat of castration, but about an appendectomy awaited in hospital. Many years later, in his commonplace book, he recorded the 1936 nightmare again, and he apparently refers to it in his 1971 lecture when he explains, 'Only once in my life have I had a dream which, on conscious consideration, seemed interesting enough to write down.'[81] In the nightmare Auden manages to escape before the operation is performed, and he has 'a vision of pursuit like a book illustration and, I think, related to the long red-legged Scissor Man in *Shockheaded Peter*.' His pursuer has a pseudo-Icelandic name, Giga, which strengthens his association with Auden's nursery library, and the dream characters generally reflect Auden's childhood family circle. These include for Auden's mother 'an old lady who was going to do me an injury' but who has her arm cut off before she can;[82] for his father, doctors who are at first 'inattentive' but subsequently concerned for the patient; his actual father who shares his food with Auden when the brothers in the dream greedily seize the rest; the brothers themselves, of whom Auden is uncertain whether there are two or three and whether they are friends or foe. There is also a 'companion' who has 'green eyes and a terrifying affection for me' who is either the third or the fourth brother and apparently represents Auden's alter ego. (Constance Auden's third pregnancy ended in miscarriage before she had Auden, and the confu-

---

[81] See p. 190 in this volume.

[82] Leon Edel suggests that the amputation of the woman's arm is a substitute for the castration threatened to the dreamer in the looming appendectomy and expresses Auden's 'fear of his own anger and aggression against the woman with whom he has also identified himself, and whom he counter-attacks by dreaming that *her* arm is cut off instead of *his* appendix.' See 'Wystan Auden and the Scissors-Man', *Stuff of Sleep and Dreams: Experiments in Literary Psychology* (London, 1982), 211. I am grateful to Richard Davenport-Hines for reminding me of Edel's discussion, related to my own, of the scissor-man in Auden's work.

sion in the dream over the number of brothers may refer to this.) It is the green-eyed 'companion' who cuts off the old lady's arm and for whose 'bad influence' over the dreamer the doctors eventually express their concern.[83]

A few years later, in 1939, the scenario of betrayal in 'O what is the sound which so thrills the ear', along with elements from the painting on which Auden says the poem is based, appeared in another poem, 'The Riddle':

> Down in order from a ridge,
> Bayonets glittering in the sun,
>   Soldiers who will judge
> Wind towards a little bridge.

In the concluding stanza of 'The Riddle' Auden suggests that the lesson of love is perfect self-containment:

> Nowhere else could I have known
> Than, beloved, in your eyes
>   What we have to learn,
> That we love ourselves alone:
> All our terrors burned away
> We can learn at last to say:
> 'All our knowledge comes to this,
> That existence is enough,
>   That in savage solitude
>   Or the play of love
> Every living creature is
>   Woman, Man and Child'.[84]

The conviction offered in the poem, of the completeness and self-sufficiency of every living creature, responds to the anxiety of betrayal by eliminating any love object outside the ego. Despite the triumphant tone of the poem, such a view barely transmutes the narcissistic, self-pitying state of mind of the speaker in 'Letter to a Wound' who prefers to love his injury rather than to risk being afflicted by anything in the world around him.

Auden frequently treated in other works the themes of abandonment

---

[83] *LFI* 148–9 and *ACW* 126–7. In the same letter to Erika Mann, Auden also included a favourite childhood fairy-tale, 'Gellivör', which he says his father often read to him and which first gave rise to his interest in Iceland. The imagery in 'Gellivör' has illuminating links with some of Auden's early poems, but Auden does not mention the tale in his 1971 nursery library list.

[84] *CP91* 257–9.

and betrayal so telling raised in the Freud lecture. For instance, his 1940 radio play, *The Dark Valley*, rewrites 'Letter to a Wound' as the monologue of an old woman to a goose with which she is neurotically obsessed. She addresses the goose as confidante, pet, child, and victim; it absorbs her entirely. The goose is her vocation; yet she would rather kill it than allow it to fly away and leave her. Thus, in her final speech she assumes the voice of a patriarchal god figure, the 'All-Father', stroking and coddling the goose, as she prepares to take the knife to it. Like the figures of retribution evoked by Auden elsewhere, the woman adopts a man's identity, and her final speech casts a sinister shadow of desertion backward onto the beautiful childhood relationship with her own father which she describes earlier in the play. Once the dark valley was alive with miners, her father the best of them; then he was killed in an explosion. The mine was abandoned, and she was left alone with her mother in a forbidding and silent landscape. Perhaps the treatment in *The Dark Valley* of desertion and betrayal draws on Auden's own experience of being left alone with his mother when his father went away to the war; in any case, it has close thematic links with psychological preoccupations presented elsewhere in Auden's work. The old woman with the knife might be compared for instance, to any of the following: the scissor-man; to Auden's poetic representation of his doctor father of whom he says in 'Letter to Lord Byron', 'My earliest recollection to stay put | Is of a white stone doorstep and a spot | Of pus where father lanced the terrier's foot;'[85] to the figure of the surgeon in 'Letter to a Wound' and elsewhere in Auden's work; to Auden's dream image in the poem beginning 'The earth turns over and our side feels the cold' of 'My mother chasing letters with a knife'[86] (which perhaps suggests by synecdoche some threat he sensed in her attitude to him as a writer, for he had regularly sent letters to her from school enclosing his poems); or to the figure of the poet himself poised in an anxiety of self-betrayal over his gift, over the innocent possibility of his artistic future, or even over the future of his Christian soul.

The deserted mining landscape that the old woman describes in *The Dark Valley* is Auden's own imaginary childhood playground; indeed, her recollections closely echo adolescent poems such as 'The Old Mine', 'The Old Lead-mine', 'Allendale', 'Lead's the Best', and especially 'Rookhope (Weardale, Summer 1922)'.[87] The re-emergence

[85] *EA* 191.   [86] Ibid. 145.   [87] *Juvenilia*, 29, 31, 70, 127, 54.

in *The Dark Valley* of Auden's abandoned mining landscape—he had not written about it for roughly a decade, but he was to write about it more and more in the years to come—is deeply poignant. For as Auden explains in his 1971 lecture, the landscape was associated for him with the interior of the human body, and mining with mortality. In *The Dark Valley*, the death of the miner-father and the desertion of the mine signify the departure of the god of love from the landscape and from the household. The old woman recollects: 'O but it was otherwise, Nana, when I was born. Then love was a God who drove men mad . . . mother watched every movement I made, afraid that father's passionate blood would appear in his daughter. For the god of love was father's friend—yes and mine.'[88] Auden knew by adolescence that his father, while away at the war, had had an affair with a woman colleague and that he had continued to correspond with her for years afterwards. Conjugal relations with Auden's mother had, in some respect and perhaps for some time, been abandoned.

In the 1971 lecture Auden describes his inability to see why his parents had chosen to marry each other as if it were a universal blindness in all children's understandings of their parents' relationships; elsewhere he more simply remarked that his parents did not seem to him to belong together.[89] He appears to have understood his own intense intimacy with his mother during childhood not as an attempt on his part to make up for the difference he perceived between his parents, but as a relationship initiated by her and to which he had submitted. Probably influenced as much by D. H. Lawrence as by Freud or any other psychologist, Auden wrote in 'Psychology and Art To-day': 'The possible family situations which may produce an artist or intellectual are of course innumerable, but those in which one of the parents, usually the mother, seeks a conscious spiritual, in a sense, adult relationship with the child, are probably the commonest.'[90] If his mother's high-minded affection helped to raise Auden's exceptional natural ability towards artistic achievement it also placed on him an immense burden of response, especially in his father's absence during the war. Auden recognized the value of this early experience, but he also felt the cost. He told a friend in 1942: 'You would be surprised how unpleasant too much parental love and interest can be, and what a torture of guilt it makes breaking away.'[91] When Auden emigrated to America, his sense of guilt over

---

[88] *Libretti*, 376.   [89] See p. 183 and n. 9 in this volume.   [90] *EA* 334.
[91] ALS to James Stern, from Berwyn, Pa., see p. 83 in this volume.

breaking away seems to have welled-up again, perhaps combined with fears about his destiny in a new country, alone and far from home. But after his emigration Auden began to write about the mining landscape again, and in a sense the god of love returned to it through the intensity of his own poetic attentions.

In his 1939 elegy for Freud, Auden attributed to him the powers of a father confessor. He wrote:

> he merely told
> the unhappy Present to recite the Past
> like a poetry lesson till sooner
> or later it faltered at the line where
>
> long ago the accusations had begun,
> and suddenly knew by whom it had been judged,
> how rich life had been and how silly,
> and was life-forgiven and more humble,
>
> able to approach the Future as a friend . . .[92]

'Like a poetry lesson' suggests the way in which Auden sometimes used his poetry to examine and even to exorcise his past, and the lines together suggest that Freud helped Auden to a sense of self-understanding that to some degree released him from his own characteristically harsh self-judgement. In fact, 'accusations' begin to be made in childhood by the parents, but the child identifies with the parent and soon takes over the parental role; the super-ego learns to criticize in place of the parents so that the psyche is divided against itself, epitomizing the struggling of the young child against the parents. The independent, self-criticizing child is cut off also from the love once shared with the parents; Freud's theories, the poem suggests, aim to help the child experience this love again in his independent state:

> He would unite
> the unequal moieties fractured
> by our own well-meaning sense of justice,
>
> would restore to the larger the wit and the will
> the smaller possesses but can only use
> for arid disputes, would give back to
> the son the mother's richness of feeling:[93]

[92] *CP91* 274.   [93] Ibid. 276.

These lines apparently allude to the opening scene of *King Lear* (a scene Auden knew well and on which he also drew elsewhere) in which Gloucester describes Lear's division of his kingdom between his elder daughters' husbands as being too equal to show which Duke he favours: 'neither can make choice of either's moiety.' (Earlier the poem uses 'duchy' and 'State': 'Duke' and 'state' also appear in the first scene of *Lear*.) Shakespeare's theme of near-senile patriarchy passing on both its wisdom and its folly to its knowing heirs resonates throughout the elegy. In this passage Auden seems to be referring in particular to the way that Lear, by giving away his kingdom to his children, precipitates a train of events that corresponds to the pattern of the development of the super-ego as Freud describes it: Lear forces his children to become independent authorities over themselves, and to do without his parenting or justice. Goneril and Regan quickly become divided against themselves and behave towards Edmund as if they were indeed starved of love. Lear's fracturing of his kingdom makes him go mad, and the fool famously describes his madness as an equal dividing of the psyche that echoes the division of the kingdom: 'Thou hast pared thy wit o' both sides and left nothing i' th' middle.'[94] The restoration of feeling between mother and son longed for in the Freud elegy comes about between Lear and his favourite but silent third daughter just before their deaths; their final moments might be compared to Ransom meeting his mother on the mountain top in *The Ascent of F6* or to the old woman preparing to kill her goose in *The Dark Valley* (the switch in sexual identities is a familiar transformation in Auden's work). Auden was the third son in his family, and always believed he was the favourite; though he once called Cordelia 'a silly little bitch',[95] he evidently in some sense identified with the role of the best-loved child who becomes alienated through its wish to follow its own true nature and whose return to parental grace is linked inextricably with its destruction.

In *A Certain World* Auden observed:

Freud recognized that there was a profound difference between the Voice of Conscience, i.e., the Voice of the Holy Spirit, and the Voice of the Superego, but was too inclined, in my opinion, to identify the former with the Voice of Reason. The superego speaks loudly and either in imperatives or interjections—'DO THIS! DON'T DO THAT! BRAVO! YOU SON OF A BITCH!' Conscience speaks softly and in the interrogative—'Do you really think so? Is that really true?'

[94] 1.4.   [95] Ansen, 55.

To say that their voices are different does not mean, of course, that they never coincide; indeed in a perfect society they always would coincide.[96]

He sometimes defied the bullying voice of the super-ego, but Auden sought more and more as he grew older to follow the voice of conscience; and for him both voices were somehow always inextricably mingled with the voices of his parents, for they had had highly developed consciences before him. On one of his first trips to England after his mother's death, Auden went to Birmingham especially to collect her ivory crucifix.[97] Of all her possessions, he wanted the one which represented her piety, and in particular her devotion to the idea of Christ's passion. (When he was a boy, she had given a wooden crucifix for the chapel at St Edmund's School.[98]) Auden always suspected himself of somehow turning away from the idea of such suffering. About a year before the 1971 Freud lecture, he imagined how he would have behaved in Jerusalem on Good Friday:

In my most optimistic mood I see myself as a Hellenized Jew from Alexandria visiting an intellectual friend. We are walking along, engaged in philosophical argument. Our path takes us past the base of Golgotha. Looking up, we see an all too familiar sight—three crosses surrounded by a jeering crowd. Frowning with prim distaste, I say, 'It's disgusting the way the mob enjoy such things. Why can't the authorities execute criminals humanely and in private by giving them hemlock to drink, as they did with Socrates?' Then averting my eyes from the disagreeable spectacle, I resume our fascinating discussion about the nature of the True, the Good, and the Beautiful.[99]

As in 'Musée des Beaux Arts' the world turns away from the disaster, and Auden implicates himself in this crime. Yet 'Musée des Beaux Arts' is a kind of icon for Auden's uncertainty about his role as a poet, for his many works on the theme of abandonment and betrayal make clear that he would also have identified with the lost son, the

[96] 87–8.

[97] Natasha Spender recollects that when Auden stayed with the Spenders in London near the end of the war or soon after it, he was preoccupied with getting to Birmingham to collect the crucifix, which he brought back and showed to them: 'It was a terribly important almost ritualistic thing for him. It was as if he wanted her, or her bones—something like that.' (Conversation with Katherine Bucknell, 4 June 1992.) This may have been during Auden's brief visit on the way to Germany in 1945 or more likely in 1948.

[98] Recorded in *The St. Edmund's School Chronicle*, 7.6 (Nov. 1919), 90. The crucifix was hung near St Edmund's window, though it is now gone.

[99] *ACW* 169.

innocent victim, the insignificant winged figure plunging into the sea. Icarus aspired to fly too high while the father that he had meant to follow, the gifted technician of the myth, apparently went on more cautiously without him, not noticing his fall, and indeed not even present in Brueghel's painting or in Auden's poem. Auden's father, as a doctor, devoted his life in a different way than Auden's mother directly to the problem of human suffering. For all his faults, so did Freud. However much he admired or meant to emulate them, Auden also looked upon them as betrayers; they left him to find his own way out of the labyrinth of himself, if he could. He argues at the end of the 1971 lecture that the tasks of the analyst and the poet are the same in so far as both are trying to make human life more bearable. And yet so much of Auden's work demonstrates that conscience made him humbly doubt whether the poet could alleviate anyone's suffering but his own.

A Note on the Text

'Phantasy and Reality in Poetry' was delivered at the Philadelphia Association for Psychoanalysis as the Freud Memorial Lecture, 12 March 1971. Auden's text is mostly in his autograph with one type-script folio; it is unsigned and has no date. The title does not appear on Auden's manuscript, but it was used by the organizers to announce the lecture, and it may have been Auden's own title. There are thirty-five folios numbered 1 through 30. Fo. 13 is missing. Auden accidentally repeated the numbers 18 and 19 (the sequence should have run to 32) and there are four additional folios: fo. 4a apparently intended for insertion on fo. 5; fo. 13a (the typescript folio) apparently intended for insertion on the missing fo. 13 (see lecture note 10); and fos. 24a and 25a intended for insertion on fo. 24. I have transcribed the lecture as nearly as possible as Auden left it, correcting spelling (including use of apostrophes) and obvious slips of the pen and typos, and closing quotes and parentheses. I have not altered Auden's punctuation except for a small number of marks supplied in square brackets. A few words in the manuscript are illegible and they are represented in this transcription by empty brackets. A few other words are nearly legible, and they are represented by a likely guess preceded by a question mark and surrounded by brackets. In the very few places where Auden's clear intention deviates from what he actually wrote, I have supplied the missing or correct word surrounded by brackets but without a question mark; I have used the same marking in the even fewer number of instances where I have supplied or altered a word to try to clarify an apparent nonsense. A few cancelled passages are printed in the footnotes to the lecture.

Phantasy and Reality in Poetry

W. H. AUDEN

In inviting me to deliver the Freud Memorial lecture, you have done me a great honor, but one, also, for which I am only too conscious of my lack of qualifications. As regards Freud himself, there are only two points upon which, as a poet, I have the authority to pass judgements, one positive, and one negative. Firstly, his command of German. Here I would say, without hesitation, that the three great masters of the German language in this century, all of them, curiously enough, from the Hapsburg Empire, have been Freud, Karl Kraus and Kafka. Secondly, as you know, Freud believed that Shakespeare's plays were written by the Earl of Oxford. Here, again, I can say categorically that he was mistaken. I have read many of Freud's [?early] [?writings], as well as other psychoanalytic literature—some, like *The Interpretation of Dreams* and *On Wit*, have made a lasting impression and I think I understand them. Others, like *Totem and Tabu* and *Moses and Monotheism* I have found impossible to swallow.[1] In the case of most human activities, they cannot be fully understood except from the inside, and this is always presumably the case in psychoanalysis. Anyone like myself who has not had the experience of being analysed,[2] is in no position to assess the truth or falsehood of its findings.

It seems to me therefore I must confine myself in this lecture to the one subject, I do know from the inside, namely the Art of Poetry. This also entails that much of what I have to say must be autobiographical, for which I must ask you to excuse. I should like to believe

---

[1] *The Interpretation of Dreams* (*Die Traumdeutung*, 1900) first appeared in English in 1913; this was A. A. Brill's authorized translation of the 3rd German edition. *On Wit* is probably Freud's 1905 work *Der Witz und seine Beziehung zum Unbewussten*, usually translated as *Wit and Its Relation to the Unconscious*; this was first published in English in 1916. *Totem und Tabu* (1913) first appeared in English in 1918. *Der Mann Moses und die Monotheistische Religion: Drei Abhandlungen* appeared in German and English in 1939; it is difficult to imagine why Auden lists it with Freud's early works, but the syntax that implies this may be inadvertent.

[2] Auden was analysed in the spring of 1928 and possibly further in the summer of the same year. See my Introduction, 'Freud's Not Quite O.K.', pp. 140–1 in this volume.

that my experiences are not peculiar to myself but are fairly typical of all poets, but I cannot be certain.

Freud remarked once that poets had anticipated many of his findings.[3] To what extent is this true? Well, poets, and indeed, all artists, have always known that every human being is an individual member firstly of the biological species, Homo Sapiens, subject to the drives innate to that species, and a member of various social groups, cultural, and occupational, that have conditioned him to typical social behaviour, but that at the same time every human being is a unique person who can say I and is capable of deeds, that is to say, of choosing to attend to this rather than that, to do this rather [than] that, and accept personal responsibility for the consequences, whatever they may be, and they are never fully predictable.[4]

If we were not both individuals and persons there could be no Art. If we were only individuals, we should all be the same, and art could tell us nothing. If we were only persons, everyone's experience would be unique, and communication would be impossible.

This is also the case, surely, in most Medicine and above all in psychotherapy. It is possible, maybe, for a surgeon to assume that all human beings are the same or ought to be, that is to say, when he

---

[3] Lionel Trilling reported this remark in his 1940 essay 'Freud and Literature', where Auden may have read it: 'When on the occasion of his seventieth birthday, Freud was greeted as the "discoverer of the unconscious," he corrected the speaker and disclaimed the title. "The poets and philosophers before me discovered the unconscious," he said. "What I discovered was the scientific method by which the unconscious can be studied"' (*The Kenyon Review* (Spring 1940); revised and repr. in *Horizon* (Sept. 1947); repr. in Lionel Trilling, *The Liberal Imagination* (New York and London, 1950), 33). Trilling referred to the remark again in 'Art and Neurosis' (1945; repr. *The Liberal Imagination*, see p. 153).

[4] Here Auden has cancelled the following passage:

These two aspects of human life, may be seen in the two accounts of the creation of man, given in the first and the second chapters of Genesis. In the first chapter it is said 'Male and female created He them and God blessed them and said "Be fruitful and multiply.[" '] In the second chapter the plural has been replaced by the singular Adam, and the reason given for there being two sexes is not biological but psychological. 'It is not good for man to be alone.' The myth of our common descent from a single ancestor is a way of saying that, as persons we are called into being, not by any biological process, but by other persons, our parents, our siblings, our teachers, our friends, who address [us] by name or by a Thou, and to whom we respond with a name or an I.

This passage and the sentences preceding it in Auden's main text are condensed from a longer paragraph in 'Words and the World', the fourth of Auden's 1967 T. S. Eliot lectures; see *SW* 119–20. There Auden provides references to Genesis, respectively 1: 27–8 and 2: 18.

finds a body that is abnormal, this is his reason for operating. But no physician, still less a psychotherapist can work with such an assumption. If all your patients were the same, the process of analysis, by which the patient discovers things for himself, would be unnecessary. You could tell him at once what was wrong. But if every patient were only unique, you would be helpless, for neither your own experiences as an analyzand, nor anything you have learned from treating another patient, would be of any help to you, in treating this one.

Secondly, poets have always [known] that the life of the human mind was a historical life which cannot be reduced to or explained in terms of physics or chemistry. That is to say the word *cause* has a different use [in] history than it has in the physical sciences. In physics, to say A is the cause of B is to say if A then necessarily B. But in history it means that the occurrence of A provided B with a motive for occurring. That is why history can be understood backwards, but the future is never predictable with any certainty.[5]

Freud was perhaps the first psychologist to realise this. Speaking for myself what I admire most about Freud the man is that his love of truth was great enough to give him the courage to transcend the materialist even mechanistic scientific philosophy which went almost unchallenged when he was growing up. Had one asked a doctor in the 1880's or 90's to forecast the future of psychology, he would almost certainly have replied somewhat as follows. It seems probable that we shall soon be able to describe all mental events in terms of physical events in the brain, but even if we cannot, we may safely assume

1) The behaviour of the mind can be explained in terms of stimulus and response. Similar stimuli will necessarily produce similar responses.

2) Mental development is like physical growth, ie the mind passes from [a] younger or earlier phase into an older or later one. The process can be arrested or become morbid, but two phases cannot exist simultaneously any more than an oak can be an acorn at the same time.

---

[5] The argument Auden makes in this paragraph and in the next originated in his 1953 review of Ernest Jones, *Sigmund Freud Life and Work*, vol. 1: *The Young Freud 1856–1900*; see 'The Greatness of Freud', *The Listener*, 50.1284 (8 Oct. 1953), 593. Auden repeated the argument in his 1954 review of *Sigmund Freud's Letters: The Origins of Psychoanalysis*; see 'The Freud–Fliess Letters', *The Griffin*, 3.6 (June 1954), 8–9.

3) The neuroses and psychoses must be typical diagnostic entities, identical in every patient. To discover the cure for one means to discover the procedure which is effective independently of the individual doctor or individual patient.

One has only to read a few lines of Freud to realise that one is moving in a very different world, one in which there are decisive battles, defeats, victories, where things happen that need not have happened and even things which ought not to have happened, a world where novelties coexist with ancient monuments, a world, [?whatever] [?happens], that has to be described with analogical metaphors. Given his upbringing, one would have expected Freud to become a behaviourist. But as we know, he did not. About understanding history backwards he wrote:

So long as we trace the development from its final stage backwards, the connexion appears continuous and we feel we have gained an insight which is completely satisfactory and even exhaustive. But if we procede in the reverse way, if we start from the premises inferred from the analysis and try to follow these up to the final result, then we no longer get the impression of an inevitable sequence of events which could not be otherwise determined. We notice at once that there might have been another result, and that we might have been just as well able to understand and explain the latter.[6]

For instance when he first heard patients tell him that in early childhood they had been sexually assaulted by their parents, he very naturally assumed that this had been the case. It must have required enormous courage to come to the conclusion that such tales were phantasies, for if an imaginary event can be as effective as a real event, then one is out of the realm of physics and determinism altogether.

To break with the Weltanschauung in which one has been raised is never easy, and for Freud it must have been particularly difficult because a psychology without a secure scientific basis can all too easily become woozy like Christian Science or Theosophy. For this reason, he often, I think, uses, what I would call a Descartian vocabulary, which one has to translate in order to understand him. For

[6] Freud, 'The Psychogenesis of a Case of Homosexuality in a Woman' (1920), trans. Barbara Low and R. Gabler, *Collected Papers*, authorized trans. under supervision of Joan Rivière, vol. 2 (London, 1924), 226–7; Auden quotes verbatim from this early translation and he may have owned some of the five volumes of Freud's *Collected Papers* which were published in London in the 1920s, but for the same passage see also Freud, *SE*, vol. 18, 167.

example, he speaks of a mature sexual relation as 'Object love'. In my vocabulary what he really means is Subject love. That is to say, is it not precisely the neurotic who regards other people, both sexually and socially as objects, either to be exploited, or as objects, whom he can endow with any imaginary personality, that he prefers. Is it not the mark of maturity to be able to recognize others as persons, as subjects, in their own right?

The second link between poetry and psychoanalysis is that poets have always understood—it is intrinsic to their art [—] the importance of symbolic and metaphorical language, though, as I hope to explain later, our conception of the symbol and the metaphor differ in some respects from yours.

Well, then, what kind of persons become poets. Freud has a passage on this which, I am sorry to say, I consider if not totally erroneous, at least a grave distortion of the truth. He says

An artist is in rudiment an introvert, not far removed from neurosis. He is oppressed by excessively powerful instinctive needs. He desires to win honor, power, wealth, fame and the love of women: but he lacks the means for achieving these satisfactions. Consequently, like any other unsatisfied man, he turns away from reality and transfers all his interest and his libido too, to the construction of his life of phantasy. In this way he achieves, *through* his phantasy, what originally he had achieved only *in* his phantasy.[7]

When I look at my fellow human beings, I see first that they divide into two classes. Firstly those, and they are the lucky minority, who discover, usually in adolescence, what occupation in the world they feel they must devote their lives to. Then there is the majority who, whether for psychological or social reasons have no marked preferences, and accept whatever jobs their education and social circumstances suggest.

[T]hose who do discover a vocation, fall roughly into two classes which one might call extrovert and introvert, though I don't think the terms are accurate. There are those [who] feel called to a life of

[7] See Freud, 'The Paths to the Formation of Symptoms', in *Introductory Lectures on Psychoanalysis*, *SE*, vol. 16, 376–7. Auden's quotation is closer to the translation in *SE* than to the one in the individual edition of the *Introductory Lectures* published from 1922 onwards, but it strays far enough from the text published in *SE* to suggest he was recalling it from memory or even, though it seems less likely, working from some other translation, perhaps his own. The last sentence he quotes should be preceded by ellipses as he omits a substantial amount of intervening text and moves into the realm of paraphrase. See also *Introductory Lectures on Psycho-analysis*, trans. Joan Rivière (London, 1922), 314.

action, either among other human beings, like the politician, or into nature like the engineer. There are those whose interest is not in action, but in contemplation and discovery of hitherto unrealised truths. To this group I think, poets and scientists and psychologists belong.

Now it is clear that an adolescent who feels called to be either [a] man of action or a man of contemplation, whatever he may hope for if he is successful, has not yet obtained his reward. The great difference between the man of action and the man of contemplation, is that the former must receive public recognition in his lifetime, or if he doesn't he is simply a failure. The man of action, therefore, can truthfully be said to desire public power and fame[.] With the man of contemplation it is otherwise. What matters to him most is that he should perceive some new aspect of truth which he is convinced is of permanent importance. So far as recognition in his lifetime is concerned, of course he hopes for it, but the only judgement that matters is those of his peers. Public fame is of minor importance. In old age Freud did, as a matter of fact, become a world-famous figure, but suppose he had died shortly after the publication of *The Interpretation of Dreams*, which as we all know, at first hardly sold any copies. He would have died in relative obscurity. But any disappointment he may have felt at the time at not being recognised, was obviously a very minor matter compared with his conviction—that he had written a book of permanent importance—so it is with artists. Cézanne, for example, was unrecognized in his life time, but he knew he was a great painter.

In addition to honour, power, fame, Freud mentions wealth and the love of women. Aside from the obvious fact that for a would-be poet to hope for wealth would be insane, I very much doubt if wealth is a common ambition. Naturally, we all hope to earn enough money to keep ourselves and our families decently housed, clothed and fed, and of course, our standard of what is decent can vary considerably, but how many people really want more than that. As for the love of women, surely most people's idea of a satisfactory sexual life, is a happy marriage, however difficult that may be to achieve, rather than to [?pursue] a lot of women in succession.

If you ask me[,] what distinguishes a poet from other people is not, as Freud seems to think, excessively powerful instinctual needs—but rather an exceptional love of and mastery of language, and language is not his private property, but the [?creation] of the linguistic group

into which he is born. Further the poet, as distinct from the magician
[ ] oppose to an or [ ] [ ] whose imagination is stimulated by
arbitrary restrictions.[8]

And now I must start getting autobiographical. My father was a
physician and a classical scholar, and my mother had a university
degree at a time when it was very rare for a woman to have one. I
was the youngest of three brothers, and, I think the favorite child.

My parents, of course, sometimes had their rows, but I would say
that their marriage was reasonably happy. What connection, if any,
with the Oedipus complex, the following observation has, I don't
know, but I have often asked friends the following question. 'Suppose
you had been an intimate male friend of your father, or an intimate
female friend of your mother; your father comes to you and says, 'I
am thinking of marrying this girl. What do *you* think.' And your
mother asks, 'I am thinking of marrying this man. What do you
think.' And I find my friends agreeing with me that one would have
said, 'I don't think she is the right girl or he is the right man for
you.' This seems to me rather odd because of course, if they had followed one's advice, one would not exist.[9]

Anyway, I was born, thank goodness, and had the luck to grow up
in a house full of books, both scientific and literary, so that I always
knew that art and science were complementary and equally humane.

I was read to, and taught myself to read when I was four years old.
As a reader, one remains in what I would call the nursery stage, so

---

[8] Here the following passage is cut:

Thus, if one is given a poem to read and asked to guess the name of the poet who
wrote [it], one is much more likely to guess rightly from examining its style, its
handling of language, than from attending to the subject matter[.] A poet has to woo
not only his own Muse but also Dame Philology, and for a beginner, the latter lady
is the more important. The surest sign that a beginner has a genuine original talent
is that he shows more interest in playing with words than in saying something original, and even when he has found his own poetic self, it is still true that he is the
father of his poems, while their mother is his mother-tongue, and we all know the
greater role played by the mother. All poems could be listed as race-horses are—out
of L. by P.

Auden had already used parts of this passage in his 1962 essay 'Writing' (see *DH* 22)
and he returns to the ideas below (see p. 191).

[9] Auden said something related to this in a 1970 interview: 'Ma should have married a
robust Italian who was very sexy and cheated on her. She would have hated it, but it
would have kept her on her toes. Pa should have married someone weaker than he and
utterly devoted to him. But, of course, if they had, I shouldn't be here. It's quite
absurd.' Jon Bradshaw, 'W. H. Auden and His Graffiti', *The Observer* Colour Magazine,
7 Nov. 1971, pp. 41, 43; two earlier versions of the interview appeared in 1970.

long as the only judgment one passes on a book is: I like this I don't
like that, so long, that is to say, as one has not yet come to the point
of passing an aesthetic judgment. Here, then are some of the favourite
items in my nursery library

Poetry   H. Belloc   Cautionary Tales
    Harry Graham   Ruthless Rhymes for Heartless Homes
    Hoffmann   Shock-headed Peter
Prose Fiction   All of Beatrix Potter.
    Hans Andersen   The Snow Queen
    George MacDonald   The Princess and the Goblin
    Jules Verne.   The Child of the Cavern,
                        Journey to the Centre of the Earth
    Rider Haggard   King Solomon's Mines

    . . . *[Here a folio, almost certainly numbered 13, is missing and a
typed folio of verse, as follows, is interleaved, numbered 13a for insertion
on the missing page. The text picks up mid-sentence at the top of the folio
numbered 14; see below.*[10]*]* . . .

> One day, Mamma said: 'Conrad, dear,
> I must go out and leave you here.
> But mind now, Conrad, what I say,
> Don't suck your thumb while I'm away.

[10] The missing page of Auden's manuscript apparently described the rest of his early
reading. Auden had included virtually the same list and introductory remarks under the
heading 'My Nursery Library' in his commonplace book, *ACW* 291–2, and he mentions
some of the items elsewhere, for instance in 'Making, Knowing and Judging', *DH* 34.
See Appendix for a full list of the nursery books and some annotations. For a discussion of some of the items in the list see my introduction, 'Freud's Not Quite O.K.',
pp. 152 ff in this volume.

After the nursery library list, the missing folio of Auden's lecture probably introduced 'The Story of Little Suck-a-Thumb', the poem which Auden read out in the
lecture from Heinrich Hoffmann's *Struwwelpeter*. The single line, 'spiders, crabs,
octopi', after the stanzas of verse appears to be Auden's note to himself as to how to
pick up the thread of his main text after reading out the poem; Auden had printed
'The Story of Little Suck-a-Thumb' in *ACW* under the heading 'Castration Complex',
and some of the remarks missing here may be surmised from what he said there:

Reading the poem today, I say to myself, 'Of course, it is not about thumb-sucking
at all, but about masturbation, which is punished by castration.' But if so why did I
enjoy the poem as a child? Why was I not frightened? In so far as it did arouse fear,
it was a wholly pleasing fictional fear. It so happened that I was a nail-biter, but I
knew perfectly well that Suck-a-Thumb's fate would not be mine, because the
scissor-man was a figure in a poem, not a real person.
    Very different is the fear aroused in me by spiders, crabs, and octopi, which are, I
suspect, symbols to me for the castrating *Vagina Dentata*. (52–3)

The great tall tailor always comes
To little boys who suck their thumbs;
And 'ere they dream what he's about,
He takes his great sharp scissors out
And cuts their thumbs clean off—and then,
You know, they never grow again.'

Mama had scarcely turn'd her back,
The thumb was in, Alack! Alack!
The door flew open, in he ran,
The great long red-legged scissor man.
Oh! children, see! the tailor's come
And caught out little Suck-a-Thumb.
Snip! Snap! Snip! the scissors go;
And Conrad cries out—Oh! Oh! Oh!
Snip! Snap Snip! They go so fast,
That both his thumbs are off at last.

Mamma comes home; there Conrad stands,
And looks quite sad, and shows his hands;
'Ah!' said Mamma, 'I knew he'd come
To naughty little Suck-a-Thumb.'

Spiders, crabs, octopi.

. . . happened that I was a compulsive nail-biter—my mother would
put bitter-aloe on my fingers, but I simply licked it off, and got down
to work but I knew perfectly well that Conrad's fate would not be
mine, because the scissor-man was a figure in a poem, not a real person. Very different is the fear aroused in me by spiders, crabs, and
octopi which are, I suspect, symbols to me of the castrating vagina
dentata[.]

Before discussing the significance of my prose-reading, I should
like to mention an incident which happened when I was six. It was
Christmas time and my favourite uncle was staying with us. He came
down with influenza. I and my next brother were playing rather noisily. My mother came in and said 'You must be quiet because Uncle
Harry is ill.' Whereupon I said 'I wish he would die.' When I was
very properly spanked for this, I remember feeling: 'But they don't
understand. Of course I don't really wish him dead. I am very fond
of him.'

Later reflection on this incident, has taught me the profound difference between wish and desire. A desire, like hunger or lust, is real,
that is to say grounded in the present state of the self, and if I

express it, I mean exactly what I say. But all wishes are fantastic, a refusal to accept reality, so that however varied the form of expression the wish takes, all wishes have the same meaning. 'I wish that things were other than they are.' In saying that I wished my uncle would die, I simply meant, 'I wish that circumstances were not as they are, and that I could go on playing.' If you ask me why my wish was expressed as a wish for his death, I would answer: because when I was little I loved shocking my elders. I should like to think I have outgrown that, but my friends assure me I haven't[.]

This leads me to think that a wish expressed in sexual terms, does not necessarily mean what it seems to mean.

It is in the light of these remarks, that I would have [you] see, how poets regard the symbol. For us, what is important is the manifest object itself, which has completely absorbed its latent meaning if any, and frankly [the latter] does not interest us much. Then I would say that to the degree that, in analysing dreams, you can ignore the manifest content and concentrate upon the latent, you are dealing not with true symbols but with allegorical signs.

For instance I like tall factory chimneys. If you tell me that they are phallic symbols, you may be right but all I can say is that if such a factory chimney were to turn before my eyes into a phallus, I should not be shocked, but I should be very cross.[11] Which reminds me of a remark Freud once made which has always enchanted me: there are times when a cigar is simply a cigar.[12] Experience convinces me that however the process of symbol formation occurs, the main impetus behind it is not repression: it is something much more like a passion for not minding one's own business. The other animals may find eating and mating sufficient for a lifetime: we do not[.]

But to return to my books about mining. Most of what I know about the writing of poetry, or at least of the kind I am interested in writing, I discovered long before I thought of becoming a poet. Between the ages of six and thirteen I spent a great many of my waking hours in constructing a private secondary sacred world, the basic elements of which were a) a limestone landscape mainly derived from the Pennine Moors in the North of England, though until I was 12 I only knew these from photographs, and b) an industry—lead-

[11] Cp. 'The Well of Narcissus', *DH* 102.
[12] This remark is commonly attributed to Freud, though I have found no printed source.

mining[.][13] Trying my hand at a little self-analysis, I note, firstly that, even aside from the man-made caverns of mines, a limestone country is full of natural caverns and underground streams. Then, looking at the cross-sectional diagrams of mines in my books, I realize that they are like stylised pictures of the internal anatomy of the human body. As for my passion for lead-mines, I note, firstly that the word *lead* rhymes with *dead* and that lead is or was used for lining coffins: secondly, that mining is the one human activity that is by nature mortal. Steam-engines may render stage-coaches obsolete, but this cannot be foreseen. But when a mine is opened, everyone knows already, that however rich it may turn out to be, sooner or later it will become exhausted, and be abandoned.

Of this constructed world I was the only human inhabitant. Although I equipped my mines with the most elaborate machinery, I never imagined any miners. Indeed when I visited real mining areas, I preferred abandoned mines to working ones. Yet, whatever the unconscious relation between my sacred world and death may have been, I contemplated it not with fear or grief but with intense joy and reverence.

Though constructed for and inhabited by myself alone, I needed the help of others, my parents in particular, in collecting the raw materials for its construction. Others had to procure for me the necessary textbooks on geography and mining machinery, maps, catalogues, guide books, photographs and, when occasion offered, to take me down real mines, tasks which they performed with unfailing patience and generosity.

From this private activity, I learned various things which I was later to discover also applied to the fabrication of public works of art[.] Man possesses two quite different kinds of imagination which, following Coleridge, I will call the Primary Imagination and the Secondary Imagination.[14] The concern of the Primary Imagination, its only concern, is with sacred beings. The sacred is that to which it is obliged to respond: the profane is that to which it cannot respond and

---

[13] Auden described his childhood obsession with mining many times: for instance, see *PD* 120; 'Making, Knowing and Judging', *DH* 34; 'The Well of Narcissus', *DH* 102; 'Landscape: Limestone', *ACW* 216–18; 'Writing', *ACW* 423–5; 'As It Seemed to Us', *FA* 502.

[14] See the *Biographia Literaria: or, Biographical Sketches of My Literary Life and Opinions*, ch. 13. Auden first used these terms and his ensuing discussion of them in 'Making, Knowing and Judging' (*DH* 54–6), and he often introduced the same ideas in other lectures.

therefore does not know. A sacred being cannot be anticipated: it must be encountered. All imaginations do not recognize the same sacred beings, but every imagination responds to those it recognizes in the same [way]. The impression made upon the P.I[.] by a sacred being is of an overwhelming but undefinable importance—I am that I am is what every sacred being seems to say. The response of the P.I. is a passion of awe, which may range in tone from joyous wonder to panic dread. Some sacred beings seem to be sacred to all imaginations at all times. The Moon for example, Fire, Snakes and those four important beings which can only be defined in terms of non-being: Darkness, Silence, Nothing, Death. Some, like Kings, are only sacred to all within a certain culture, some only to members of a social group, like the Latin language among humanists. An imagination can acquire new sacred beings, and it can lose old ones to the profane. Sacred beings can be acquired by social contagion, but not consciously. One cannot be taught to recognize a sacred being: one has to be converted[.]

To return to my early private world. In constructing it, I learned certain principles which I was later to find applied to all artistic fabrication. Though every work of art is a secondary world, such a world cannot be constructed ex nihilo, but is a selection and recombination of elements taken from the primary world we all live in.

Then, in constructing my private world, I discovered that though this was a game, ie something I was free to do or not as I chose, no game can be played without rules. A secondary world must be as much a world of law as the primary. One may be free to decide what these laws shall be, but laws there must be.

In my case I decided, or rather without conscious decision, I instinctively felt that I must impose two restrictions upon my freedom of phantasy. In choosing what objects were to be included, I was free to select this and reject that on condition that both were real objects in the primary world, to choose for example between two kinds of water-turbine, which could be found in a textbook on mining machinery or a manufacturer['s] catalogue: I was not allowed to invent one. In deciding how my world was to function, I could choose between two practical possibilities—a mine can be drained either by an adit or a pump—but physical impossibilities and magic means were forbidden. When I say forbidden, I mean that I felt, in some obscure way, that they were morally forbidden. Then, there came a day when the moral issue became quite conscious. As I was

planning my Platonic Idea of a Concentrating Mill, I ran into difficulties. I had to choose between two types of a certain machine for separating the slimes, called a buddle. One type I found more sacred, but
the other type was, I knew from my reading, the more efficient. At
this point I realised that it was my moral duty to sacrifice my symbolic preference to reality or truth.[15]

The kind of activity I have been describing is the work of what I
call the Secondary Imagination, which is of another character and at
another mental level—for it is an activity of the conscious mind. It is
active not passive, and its categories are not the sacred and profane
but the beautiful and the ugly. Beauty and Ugliness pertain to Form
not to Being. The P.I[.] only recognizes one kind of being, the sacred
but the S.I[.] recognizes both beautiful and ugly forms. A beautiful
form is as it ought to be, an ugly form as it ought not to be.
Observing the beautiful, the S.I[.] has the feelings of satisfaction,
pleasure, absence of conflict. Observing the ugly, the contrary feelings. It does not desire the beautiful, but an ugly form arouses in it a
desire to correct its ugliness and make it beautiful. It does not worship the beautiful; it approves of it and can give reasons for its
approval. It approves of regularity, spatial symmetry, temporal repetition, law and order; it disapproves of loose ends, irrelevance, and
mess. In addition it has a sense of humor and a love of play.[16]

Lastly, it is social and craves agreement with other minds. If I
think a form beautiful and you think it ugly, we cannot help agreeing
that one of us must be wrong, whereas if I think something sacred
and you think it is profane, neither of us will dream of arguing the
matter.

If symbols are the creation of the P.I., metaphors are the creation
of the Secondary. A metaphor is a conscious analogy, and is judged
by other conscious minds by its aptness. Since it is a conscious creation, the question of repression cannot arise. We can and often do
use sexual language to describe the non-sexual. For instance, one
metaphor from agriculture, ploughing the ground and planting seed
in Mother-Earth. Even more striking is the extremely daring language
used by the mystics like St John of the Cross, who openly use the
orgasm, an experience which most people have had[,] as a metaphor

[15] For the material in this paragraph, cp. 'As It Seemed to Us', *FA* 502, and 'Hic
and Ille', *DH* 102.
[16] This paragraph and the short one following are drawn from 'Making, Knowing
and Judging'; see *DH* 56–7.

for the union of the soul with God, an experience which very few people have had, because, common to both, is the experience of total self-forgetfulness.

Perhaps nothing is more repugnant to the Secondary Imagination than dreams. Speaking for myself, I find my own dreams, however physiologically and psychologically necessary, seem to me boring in exactly the same way that lunatics are, that is to [say,] repetitive, devoid of punctuation or any sense of humor, and insanely egocentric. Only once in my life have I had a dream which, on conscious consideration, seemed interesting enough to write down[.][17]

Given my passionate interest as a boy in mines, both I and my parents naturally assumed that, when I grew up, I would become either a mining engineer or a geologist. So at Public school I studied science and won a scholarship to Oxford in biology. It was not [to] be. One Sunday in March 1922, I was walking across a field with a school friend, when he asked me if I ever wrote poetry. Good God, no I said. The idea has never occurred to me. Why don't you he replied, and at that moment I discovered my vocation.[18]

When I ask myself why my friend's suggestion met with such an unexpected response, I [now] realize that, without knowing it, I had been enjoying the poetic use of language for a long time. I had read the technological prose of my books on mining in a peculiar way. A word like *pyrites*, for example, had not, to me, been simply an indicative sign, it was the Proper Name of a Sacred Being so that, when I heard an aunt pronounce it as *pirrits*, I was shocked. Her pronunciation was more than wrong; it was ugly; ignorance was impiety. Proper Names in the strict sense are poetry in the raw. What I think the poet attempts to do is to [give] experiences their Proper name[.] Language is prosaic to the degree that it does not matter what particular word is associated with an idea, provided the association once made is permanent. Language is poetic to the degree that it does

---

[17] Evidently, this is the nightmare that Auden had on board the *Nova* while returning from Seydisfjordur to Reykjavik in August 1936; he describes it in his second letter from Iceland to Erika Mann Auden; see *LFI* 148–9. He also recorded the nightmare in his commonplace book (see *ACW* 126–7) where he expressed the same sentiments about it as he does here in the lecture. See also my Introduction, pp. 168–9, in this volume. It seems likely that Auden did record at least one other dream; there is a one-page typescript in the Berg Collection on which he based the poem beginning 'Dear, though the night is gone', written March 1936.

[18] Auden frequently described this moment. See 'Letter to Lord Byron', *EA* 194, and see also 'Making, Knowing and Judging', *DH* 34 ff, for this and for the following two paragraphs.

matter. In Genesis Adam was told by God to give names to all crea-
tures: Adam the namer was the proto-poet, not the proto prose
writer.

The immediate consequence of deciding to write poetry was that I
had to forget my personal fantasies completely, and concentrate on
learning how a poem is written. Before, that is to say, I could woo
my own Muse, I had to woo Dame Philology.[19] A beginner's efforts
can[not] be called bad. They are imaginary, an imitation of poetry in
general. The next stage for the young poet is to get a transference
upon some particular poet, with whom he feels an affinity—in my
case it was Thomas Hardy[—]whose work he imitates.[20] It is impossible to do a recognizable imitation of a poet without attending to every
detail of his diction, rhythms and habits of sensibility. In imitating his
Master, the young poet learns that, no matter how he finds it, there is
only one word or rhythm or form that is the right one. The right one
is still not yet the real one, for the apprentice is ventriloquizing, but
he has got away from poetry in general; he is learning how *a* poem is
written. Then if the apprentice is destined to become a poet, sooner
or later—in my case when I was twenty—a day arrives when he can
truthfully say for the first time: All the words are right and all are
genuinely mine.

But it was still to be many years before I could do anything with
my lead-mining world of my childhood. My first attempt was in 1940
when I was 33; I tried to describe what I had felt at the age of 12,
when I first saw my sacred landscape with my own eyes. Needless to
say, my description of my experiences is, historically a fiction: what I
wrote was an interpretation of them, in the light of, as you will see,
later reading in Theology and Psycho-analytic literature. Here it is.

> Whenever I begin to think
> About the human creature we
> Must nurse to sense and decency,
> An English area comes to mind,
> I see the nature of my kind
> As a locality I love,

[19] This idea is put forward in 'Writing', *DH* 22, as well as in 'Making, Knowing,
and Judging' (see next note).

[20] For Auden's relation to Thomas Hardy, see (in addition to 'Making, Knowing
and Judging', *DH* 37–8) 'A Literary Transference', *The Southern Review*, 6.1 (Summer
1940), 78–86; repr. in Albert Guerard, ed., *Hardy: A Collection of Critical Essays*
(Englewood Cliffs, NJ, 1963), 135–42.

Those limestone moors that stretch from *Brough*
To *Hexham* and the *Roman Wall*,
There is my symbol of us all.
. . .[21]
Always my boy of wish returns
To those peat-stained deserted burns
That feed the *Wear* and *Tyne* and *Tees*,
And, turning states to strata, sees
How basalt long oppressed broke out
In wild revolt at *Cauldron Snout*,
And from the relics of old mines
Derives his algebraic signs
For all in man that mourns and seeks,
For all of his renounced techniques,
Their tramways overgrown with grass
For lost belief, for all Alas,
The derelict lead-smelting mill,
Flued to its chimney up the hill,
That smokes no answer any more
But points, a landmark on *Bolt's Law*
The finger of all questions. There
In *Rookhope* I was first aware
Of Self and Not-Self, Death and Dread:
Adits were entrances which led
Down to the Outlawed, to the Others,
The Terrible, the Merciful, the Mothers;
Alone in the hot day I knelt
Upon the edge of shafts and felt
The deep *Urmutterfurcht* that drives
Us into knowledge all our lives,
The far interior of our fate
To civilise and to create,
Das Weibliche that bids us come
To find what we're escaping from.
There I dropped pebbles, listened, heard
The reservoir of darkness stirred:
'O deine Mutter kehrt dir nicht
Wieder. Du selbst bin ich, dein' Pflicht
Und Liebe. Brach sie nun mein Bild.'
And I was conscious of my guilt.

[21] Here the intervening passage of 'New Year Letter' is written out and cancelled; see *CP91* 227–8 for the whole passage.

Then in 1948, I visited Italy for the first time, and in Florence, wrote a poem, In Praise of Limestone which again was related to my childhood phantasies. The lead-mines, of course, could not come in, because there aren't any in Florence, but the limestone landscape was important to me [   ] as a connecting link between two utterly different cultures, the northern guilt culture, I grew up in, and the shame-culture of the Mediterranean countries,[22] to which I was now exposed for the first time. Here is the poem.[23]

Then in 1965, I tried again to write directly about my original sacred landscape.

Amor Loci[24]

I have however once written a poem which I intend every reader to read as if he or she were dreaming it. The initial idea came, not from a dream, but from a painting I saw of Christ's Agony in the Garden.[25] In the foreground was the kneeling figure of Christ; near by, on the ground, the disciples asleep. In the background some soldiers were crossing a little bridge. Visually they look quite harmless and there is nothing to show whither they are going. It is only because one has read the Gospel story, that one knows that, in fact, they are coming to arrest Jesus: I thought then that, suppose instead of a static painting, one were to make a film of this event. Then one would see the soldiers getting nearer and nearer until they reached a point where it would [be] obvious what they were coming to do. Before this, according to the gospel, Jesus had woken his disciples, and then, after his arrest, they all forsook him and fled. It occurred to me then, but not before, that I and I fancy, nearly everybody, have had a nightmare in which one is pursued by some malignant power, and that since this was a general experience, not private to myself, a poem might be based [on] it. In my own case, the pursuer used to be a steam-roller. That obviously might not be felt by readers as hostile. I have never dreamed of being pursued by soldiers, and I don't know

---

[22] Here the manuscript shows Auden first thought of these two cultures as further opposed in religion; he wrote 'the northern ~~protestant~~ guilt culture, I grew up in, and the ~~Mediterranean Catholic~~ shame culture of the Mediterranean countries'.

[23] Here Auden read out or recited from memory 'In Praise of Limestone', *CP91* 540–2.

[24] Here Auden read out or recited 'Amor Loci', *CP91* 779–80.

[25] This is a common subject, but Richard Davenport-Hines has plausibly suggested that the painting is likely to be Giovanni Bellini's *The Agony in the Garden*, bought by the National Gallery, London in 1863.

whether others have, but since soldiers are by profession aggressive, it
seemed to me that they could function for all readers as a symbol.
For dramatic purposes, I wanted a second person in the poem besides
the dreamer, so, for those disciples who ran away, I substituted a single figure, whom the dreamer loves and trusts, ie the reader can
choose whatever image suits him or her—but who in the end deserts
the dreamer leaving him to face the terror alone. Again I have never
personally had this experience in dreams of this kind. Well here is the
poem.[26]

If you ask me to describe the process of poetic composition I would
say this—The subject matter of a poem is comprised of a crowd of
historical occasions of feelings and thought recollected from the past.
The poet presupposes that this crowd is real, ie, a real disorder, but
should not be, and attempts to transform it into a community by
embodying it in a verbal society. In this he differs from the scientist
whose subject matter is [a] crowd of natural events at all times, but
who presupposes that this crowd is not real but only apparent, and
seeks to discover the true place of events in the system of nature.[27]

The verbal society of a poem, like any society in nature, has its
own laws: the laws of syntax are analogous to the laws of physics:
metrical and rhyme schemes are more like the laws of biology.

The nature of the final poetic order is the outcome of a dialectical
struggle between the recollected occasions of feeling and thought and
the verbal system. As a society the verbal system is actively coercive
upon the occasions it is attempting to embody; what it cannot
embody truthfully, it excludes. As a potential community, the occasions are passively resistant to all claims of the system to embody
them which they do not recognise as just: they decline all unjust persuasion.

In writing a poem, the poet can work in two ways. Starting from
an intuitive idea of the kind of community he desires to call into
being, he may search for the verbal system which will most justly
incarnate that idea, or starting with the idea of a certain kind of verbal system, he may look for the community which it is capable of
embodying most truthfully. In practice he nearly always works simul-

[26] Here Auden apparently read out or recited 'O what is that sound which so thrills
the ear', written October 1932; *EA* 125–6. For more about this poem, see my
Introduction, pp. 165–9, in this volume.

[27] For this and the following four paragraphs Auden draws closely on 'The Virgin
and the Dynamo', *DH* 66–9.

taneously in both directions, modifying his conception of the ultimate nature of the community at the immediate suggestions of the system, and modifying the system in response to his growing intuition of the future needs of the community.

A verbal system cannot be selected completely arbitrarily, nor can one [?say] that any given system is absolutely necessary. The poet searches for one which imposes just obligations of feeling and thought. 'Ought' always implies can, so that a system whose claims cannot be met must be scrapped. But the poet has to beware of accusing the system of injustice, when what is at fault is the laxness and self-love of the feelings upon which it is making its demands[.] A poem can fail in two ways: it may exclude too much and so be banal, or it may attempt to embody more than one community at once and so be disorderly.

The two great dangers against which a poet has constantly to guard against, are what I would call autoeroticism and narcissism.

A poet must never make a statement simply because he thinks it sounds poetically exciting or effective: he must also believe it to be true. This does not mean of course that one can only appreciate a poet whose beliefs happen to co-incide with one's own: It does mean however that one must be convinced that the poet really believes what he says, however odd the belief may seem to oneself.[28]

The second danger lies in the poet['s] imagination that an experience is of any poetic importance simply because he personally has had it. A valid experience is some perception of a reality common to all men: it is only mine in that it is perceived from a unique perspective which nobody but myself can occupy, so that it's my pleasure and duty to share it with others[.] From the poet's point of view, the ideal response of a reader to his poem is 'Why, I knew that all the time, but never realised it till now.' A good poem, one might say, is like a successfully analysed patient: both have become, what the Psalmist says of Jerusalem, 'A city that is at unity in itself.[']'[29] For this very reason I am sceptical as to the value of trying to psychoanalyse a successful work of art as if they were patients. It is only in the case of bad works of art, that I can conceive of analysis throwing light on the reason why it is bad.

---

[28] Auden expressed a similar conviction in his 1962 essay 'Writing', *DH* 19, and in the entry in his commonplace book also entitled 'Writing', *ACW* 425.

[29] Auden seems to have had in mind the text of *The New English Bible*; see Psalms 122: 3: 'Jerusalem is built to be a city where people come together in unity.'

As to our purposes in what we [do], they are not, I believe, too dissimilar. At least we both can or should be modest about what we can achieve. The sole aim in writing, wrote Dr Johnson, is to enable readers a little better to enjoy life or a little better to endure it.[30] Is that so different from what Freud once said to someone who consulted him upon whether to be analysed or not. 'I don't suppose,' he said, 'we can do much for you, but perhaps we can turn your hysterical misery into ordinary human unhappiness[.'][31]

---

[30] Auden cited the same remark—more accurately—in *ACW* 418; it is from 'A Free Enquiry into the Origin of Evil', Johnson's review of Soame Jenyns's *A Free Enquiry into the Nature and Origin of Evil*; see *The Literary Magazine or Universal Review*, vol 2 (1757), 302.

[31] Freud reported this remark in his conclusion to *Studies on Hysteria* (1893–5), written with Josef Breuer: 'No doubt fate would find it easier than I do to relieve you of your illness. But you will be able to convince yourself that much will be gained if we succeed in transforming your hysterical misery into common unhappiness. With a mental life that has been restored to health you will be better armed against that unhappiness.' (*SE*, vol. 2, 305) A version of the book first appeared in English in 1909 (omitting some of the case histories and Breuer's theoretical chapter, trans. A. A. Brill), though Auden may have known it from one of the volumes he apparently possessed of Freud's five-volume *Collected Papers*, where it appeared in vol. 1, trans. J. Rickman (London, 1924).

Appendix
Auden's Nursery Library

This list of Auden's nursery library books follows the one that he printed in *A Certain World*.[1] Only a partial list survives in Auden's Freud Memorial Lecture of 1971. There are slight differences between the lists, and also errors and omissions, all of which apparently result from Auden's having written out the lists from memory. For example, in the Freud lecture he calls Heinrich Hoffmann's collection of verses *Shock-headed Peter* while in *A Certain World* he calls it by a slightly inaccurate version of its German title, *Struwel Peter*. None the less in the sections of the lists that can be compared, nearly every book is the same, despite differences in the way they are titled.

Following Auden's own description of each book, I have given a corrected or completed description including publication details, so that the books may be easily found. For some of the items, for instance a few which may now be less widely-read, I have also offered additional information or comments. Among these is a brief discussion of a favourite childhood story of Auden, Hans Andersen's *The Ice Maiden*, which he did not include in the list, and which has sometimes been confused with *The Snow Queen*.

In his introduction to John Betjeman's *Slick But Not Streamlined* (Garden City, NY, 1947, p. 16). Auden offered an earlier version of this list which included two items not mentioned in *A Certain World* or in 'Phantasy and Reality in Poetry'; he describes these as *Mrs. Beaton's Book of Household Management* (the 1869 edition) and *Hymns Ancient and Modern* (with tunes). The first item is evidently Isabella Mary Beeton, *Mrs. Beeton's Book of Household Management* (London, 1868). I have been unable to find an 1869 edition, but the 1868 edition is the first to bear the exact title he recalls; earlier editions were titled *Beeton's Book of Household Management*, and before that the first edition was simply *Book of Household Management* (London, [1859–61]). *Hymns Ancient and Modern* exists in many versions, but apparently only one from the period includes the tunes: *Hymns Ancient and Modern . . . with Accompanying Tunes. Historical edition, with notes on the origins of both hymns and tunes and a general historical*

[1] *ACW* 292.

introduction (by the Rev. W. H. Frere), illustrated by facsimiles and portraits (London, 1909).

Nonfictional Prose

T. Sopwith   *A Visit to Alston Moor*

Thomas Sopwith's only book-length work on Alston Moor is *An Account of the Mining District of Alston Moor, Weardale and Teesdale, in Cumberland and Durham; Comprising Descriptive Sketches of the Scenery, Antiquities, Geology, and Mining Operations, in the Upper Dales of the Rivers Tyne, Wear, and Tees* (Alnwick, 1833). The book includes a section entitled 'Visit to a Lead Mine'[2] which Auden printed in *A Certain World*,[3] so it seems certain this is the book he was referring to. Auden also possessed John Postlethwaite, *Mines and Mining in the (English) Lake District*, 3rd edn. (Whitehaven, 1913), which he and someone else (possibly John Auden) lightly annotated, and into which he pasted six and dropped in two photographs of area mines, labelled in his autograph. (This volume is now in the Keswick Library, Cumbria.)

?   *Underground Life*

Louis Simonon, *Mines and Miners; or Underground Life*, trans. from the French, ed. and adapted to the present state of British mining by H. H. Bristow (London and Glasgow, 1869).

?   *Machinery for Metalliferous Mines*

Edward Henry Davies, *Machinery for Metalliferous Mines: A Practical Treatise* (London, 1894).

His Majesty's Stationery Office   *Lead and Zinc Ores of Northumberland and Alston Moor*

Stanley Smith, with contributions by R. G. Carruthers ([London], 1923).

?   *The Edinburgh School of Surgery*

Alexander Miles, Surgeon to the Royal Infirmary, Edinburgh, *The Edinburgh School of Surgery Before Lister* (London, 1918). This pre-history of surgery at Edinburgh—before the revolutionary changes wrought by Joseph Lister (1827–1912)—describes a succession of medical men as heroes advancing the techniques of surgery with each operation: the patriarchs of modern medicine. Many of the

---

[2] Sopwith, 135–42.   [3] *ACW* 219–25.

surgeons are the actual sons or sons-in-law of their predecessors, so
that the book is a kind of genealogy of early surgery, filled out by
biographical details and gory descriptions of celebrated operations—
amputations of limbs, removal or draining of tumors and abscesses.
Chief among the pre-Lister heroes is Joseph Syme—'The Napoleon
of Surgery'[4] and Lister's father-in-law—attractive as a renegade
who achieved his many unconventional successes, somewhat like
Freud, in the face of opposition from other doctors and from the
press.

? *Dangers to Health* (a Victorian treatise, illustrated, on plumbing,
good and bad)

T. Pridgen Teale, M.A., Surgeon to the General Infirmary at
Leeds (London and Leeds, 1879). Teale blames bad drainage for a
third of the illnesses in the United Kingdom at the time, and
depicts the foul water and air lurking in the drains of nearly every
room of nearly everyone's house: 'very few houses are safe to live
in.'[5] Under headings such as 'How People Drink Sewage', he diagrams and describes unsatisfactory drainage and ventilation and
offers practical advice on constructing improvements. Despite his
cheerful approach, the book is most striking for its representation
of the poisonous vapours seeping into houses and invisibly surrounding the inhabitants with danger. Many diagrams show houses
in cross-section, with evil gases making their way in at cellar level
and rising undetected through the very pipes intended to carry
away filth. Some of the pictures resemble, as Auden said his diagrams of mines did, the internal anatomy of the human body; they
also suggest the relation between the conscious and unconscious
mind.

Fiction

Beatrix Potter   All her books

Beatrix Potter's *The Tale of Peter Rabbit* (London, 1902) was the
first of her books to appear, followed by twenty-two others; but a
few were published only in the 1920s and afterwards, too late to be
included in Auden's nursery library. The ones he is least likely to
have known are *Appley Dappley's Nursery Rhymes* (1917), *The Tale*

[4] Miles, 174.   [5] Teale, 5.

of Johnny Town-Mouse (1918), *Cecily Parsley's Nursery Rhymes* (1922), and *The Tale of Little Pig Robinson* (1930).

Hans Andersen   *The Snow Queen*

Auden may have read one of the several translations of Andersen published by H. W. Dulcken, Ph.D. towards the end of the nineteenth century. Clearly he knew other tales by Andersen as well, and he alludes to some in his work; for instance, an adolescent poem, 'Pride' takes 'Big Claus and Little Claus' as its theme (*Juvenilia*, 180). Although *The Snow Queen* was a favourite, so for a time was *The Ice Maiden*, as Auden noted in 'Letter to Lord Byron': 'My favourite tale was Andersen's *Ice Maiden*.'[6] Contrary to what Charles Osborne says in *W. H. Auden: The Life of a Poet* (London, 1980, p. 12), this is not another translation of *The Snow Queen*, but a different story. One of the earlier Dulcken selections that contains most of the tales Auden seems to have read is *Stories and Tales* (London, 1864); another, *Stories for the Household* (1866) contains both *The Snow Queen* and *The Ice Maiden* in a single volume.

In *The Ice Maiden*, a young widow and her baby son, Rudy, fall into a snow-covered crevasse among the glaciers near Grindlewald. By the time they are rescued the mother is dead and Rudy, always merry before, is somehow changed and sobered by his experience. He is raised by his grandfather among mountains and goats and later apprenticed to a cousin who is a chamois hunter. The chamois hunter dies in an avalanche and Rudy becomes the mainstay of his family, dashing, brave, and widely admired. He sets his heart on a wealthy miller's daughter and willingly performs the dangerous challenge the miller sets him in exchange for her hand. But throughout the tale, a threat hangs over Rudy, for in the crevasse with his mother he was kissed by the Ice Maiden who lives in a crystal palace in the glacier, and the Ice Maiden wants him back: 'To crush and to hold, mine is the power!' she says. 'They have stolen a beautiful boy from me, a boy whom I have kissed, but not kissed to death. . . . He is mine and I will have him!'[7] Repeatedly during Rudy's childhood, the Ice Maiden sends 'Giddiness' to seize him as he works and plays on the mountain heights, but Rudy

[6] *EA* 191.

[7] Andersen, *The Ice Maiden*, in *Stories for the Household*, trans. H. W. Dulcken (London, 1866), 653.

becomes ever more surefooted and never loses his balance nor fears abysses. Later the Ice Maiden tempts him in the guise of a young girl offering to guide him over the mountains in bad weather. Her frustration grows as Rudy prepares to marry the miller's daughter and she brings avalanches down on the valley folk by laughing. Rudy and the miller's daughter quarrel, and Rudy goes to the mountains where he again meets the young girl and, this time, drinks her wine. Overcome, he receives the Ice Maiden's painful kiss and loses his betrothal ring before he tears himself away. When at last Rudy and the miller's daughter prepare to marry, they go by boat on the eve of their wedding to an island in Lake Geneva near Chillon. They are so blissful that the boat floats away unnoticed. Rudy plunges in to retrieve it and then sees a golden ring, like his betrothal ring, opening ever wider beneath him until it becomes an abyss filled with all those ever lost in the crevasses, and the Ice Maiden pulls him down at last: '"Mine! Mine!" sounded around him and within him. "I kissed thee when thou wert little, kissed thee on thy mouth. Now I kiss thy feet, and thou art mine alto-gether!" And he disappeared under the clear blue water.'[8] With the bridegroom drowned, the bride is left alone in despair. Later she recognizes the germ of sin in her heart which brought about the quarrel with her lover, and she is grateful for her enlightenment.

   The Ice Maiden offers a tragic counterpoint to *The Snow Queen*. Despite the spiritual illumination afforded to the miller's daughter by her loss, the main theme of the tale is that the gifted hero can-not elude his fate. In *The Snow Queen*, on the other hand, simple children find spiritual redemption through Christian love. The tales correspond to opposing emphases in Auden's own poetic preoccu-pations, *The Ice Maiden* more clearly resonating with the first half of his career, *The Snow Queen* with the second half. Auden uses mountains, avalanches, and threatening glacial ice in many of his early poems, often associated with the inevitability of fate or with the idea of the past overwhelming the present and obliterating the possibility of hope or change. These sorts of images culminate with the grand conception of *The Ascent of F6* in which the figure of Mrs Ransom, like the ghost of the hero's past or like the Ice Maiden herself, chillingly greets her son on the mountain top which, in a sense, he has climbed to escape her. Before that, in the

[8] Ibid. 689.

1929 poem beginning 'It was Easter as I walked in the public gardens', Auden drew on *The Ice Maiden* imagery to evoke his fatalistic attitude towards marriage. The mysterious and serene conclusion to the poem, 'deep in clear lake, | The lolling bridegroom, beautiful there,'[9] is based on Andersen's description of Rudy's death and articulates Auden's recognition, achieved through months of painful self-examination in Berlin and the failure of his engagement, that for him conventional heterosexual marriage would be a kind of death, and that he would never be a bridegroom. At the same time, it also suggests his fascination with the idea of a complete and self-immolating submission to his own fate—some difficult end for which he had been early and indelibly marked. Indeed, the drowning imagery reaches back to the very fount of Auden's poetic life, for as he once explained, the first poem he ever wrote was a Wordsworthian sonnet on Blea Tarn which concluded with a plea for a similar watery destiny: 'and in the quiet | Oblivion of thy waters let them stay.'[10]

Morris and Magnusson *Icelandic Stories*

Three Northern Love Stories, and Other Tales, trans. Eiríkr Magnússon and William Morris (London, 1875; new edition London, 1901). The most engrossing and the saddest tale in this collection is the first, 'The Story of Gunnlaug the Worm-Tongue and Raven the Skald' who quarrel during a poetic competition before the King of Sweden and then become rivals in love, fighting to the death over the most beautiful woman in Iceland and leaving her to die unhappily in the arms of another husband. A minor character in this tale has the name Audun Festargram, the Icelandic name from which Auden thought his own might be derived. The book also contains 'The Story of Frith the Bold' and 'The Story of Viglund the Fair' which similarly tell of continual feuding, mostly over women. There are also two shorter stories, 'The Tale of Hogni and Hedinn', about dwarves living in a rock, and 'Sorli slays the King Haldan' which features a Long Worm or dragon. Many aspects of these tales have parallels in Auden's work, from his juvenilia and *Paid on Both Sides* onward, especially the

---

[9] *EA* 40.

[10] The poem does not survive; see B. C. Bloomfield, *W. H. Auden: A Bibliography: The Early Years through 1955* (Charlottesville, Va., 1964), p. ix.

persistent themes of unrequited or destructive love, and, formally, the use of passages of poetry in the prose narrative.

Lewis Carroll   The two *Alice* books

Charles Dodgson's *Alice's Adventures in Wonderland* was first published in 1865, but if Auden read both books, he must have had *Alice's Adventures in Wonderland and Through the Looking-Glass and What Alice Found There* (London and New York, 1893) since the second book was not published on its own.

George Macdonald   *The Princess and the Goblin*

George MacDonald, *The Princess and the Goblin* (London, 1900).

Jules Verne   *The Child of the Cavern* and *Journey to the Centre of the Earth*

Voyage au centre de la terre was first published in English in 1872, trans. [Frederick Amadeus Malleson]. *The Child of the Cavern, or Strange Doings Underground* was first translated from the French *Les Indes-Noir* by W. H. G. Kingston in 1877. It is easy to see why Auden liked these books about life and exploration underground and in mines. The less well-known story, *The Child of the Cavern*, plays upon the resemblance, which Auden extrapolates in the 1971 Freud lecture, between Auden's symbolic landscape and the internal anatomy of the human body. An exhausted mine is brought back into work by a devoted mine foreman despite the sinister counter-plotting of a disgruntled former fireman: 'The old mine will grow young again, like a widow who remarries!'[11] And the fireman's great granddaughter, raised by him in the mine, emerges from it into the daylight for the first time ever, as if born of the mine, to become the bride of the foreman's son.

Rider Haggard   *King Solomon's Mines* and *She*

H. Rider Haggard, *King Solomon's Mines* (London, 1885); and *She: A History of Adventure* (London, 1887).

Dean Farrar   *Eric, or Little by Little*

Frederick W. Farrar, *Eric or Little by Little: A Tale of Roslyn School* (Edinburgh, 1858). This public-school novel elevates the conventions of the verse tales of Belloc, Hoffmann, and Graham onto a religious and highly sentimental plane apparently thought suitable for admonishing slightly older children. Despite his

---

[11] *The Child of the Cavern*, 82.

Christian piety and his love for his family, the hero, Eric Williams, goes slowly to the bad along with most of his schoolfellows. Among the novel's outstanding features are the close friendships formed between some of the boys—apparently sexually innocent, though clearly romantic and dangerous in the sense that the strength of their attachments again and again leads the boys into reckless behaviour[12]—and the dramatic disciplinary confrontations between the boys and the masters. Two boys suffer accidental deaths in the book—Eric's closest friend and his younger brother—but though the deaths screw up the pitch of the melodrama and add sentimental weight to the question of Eric's own reformation, neither one is quite so intensely described as the scene in which Eric defies his favourite master, Mr Rose, who has caned him, nor the scene in which Mr Rose flogs another boy, Brigson, until Brigson rolls on the floor in agony with Rose standing over him crying out 'Miserable coward' before all the other boys.[13] In the latter scene, Rose then forces Brigson to bear the other boys on his back while each of them is beaten in turn. The mass-beating is presented as a great good, the master as a reluctant and suffering, even Christlike, instrument of justice; astonishingly, the boys cheer him afterwards while he retires to pray. Thus the culmination of the boys' bad behaviour is a thrilling moment of physical violence during which they experience admiration and group joy and are gratified that their evil ways have at last received suitable attention. Of course, their depravity is not stopped by the beatings; on the contrary, it is made worse. Drinking and disobedience spread everfaster through the school, and after one incident at a local pub, the Headmaster addresses the school suggesting that those few boys who escaped uncaught should be longing for punishment, 'they will be more likely to sin again. In cases like this, punishment is a blessing, and impunity a burden.'[14]

Though it aimed to warn boys to be pious and behave well at school, *Eric, or Little by Little* now reads as an exposé of the savagery of nineteenth-century public schools. The book would leave

---

[12] Sexual activity of any kind is not addressed in the book, although there is one boy called Bull, described as the most corrupt boy in the novel, who has already been expelled from another school and who 'dropped into their too willing ears the poison of his polluting acquirements' (92)—a sinister but unspecified body of knowledge related by Farrar to indecent language and to which Eric cannot resist listening in his bed at night.

[13] *Eric, or Little by Little*, 254.   [14] Ibid. 241.

any but the most monkish and self-denying boy riddled with a sense of guilt and inadequacy, and perhaps also with a taste for physical punishment, if he took it all seriously—which Auden may well have done before he learned to laugh at it. In *A Certain World* Auden used a passage from the book as an example of 'Purple Prose'. The two paragraphs he selected are a *tour de force*, concluding with an invocation of the ghosts of all the schoolboys who have sinned and fallen: 'From the sea and the sod, from foreign graves and English churchyards, they start up and throng around us in the paleness of their fall. May every schoolboy who reads this page be warned by the waving of their wasted hands, from that burning marle of passion, where they found nothing but shame and ruin, polluted affections, and an early grave.'[15]

Ballantyne   *The Cruise of the Cachelot*

The Cruise of the Cachalot: Round the World after Sperm Whales is not by the prolific writer of boys' adventure stories, R. M. Ballantyne, but by Frank T. Bullen, First Mate (London, 1898). A cachalot is a sperm whale, and Auden may have confused the book with Ballantyne's on the same subject, *The Red Eric: or, The Whaler's Last Cruise. A Tale* (London, 1861). *The Cruise of the Cachalot* is a brightly written and technically detailed account of, evidently, a real cruise, including aspects of flora and fauna, and a gripping description of harpooning a whale from a tiny boat, during which several of the whalers are killed.

Conan Doyle   *The Sherlock Holmes* Stories

Conan Doyle, *The Adventures of Sherlock Holmes* (London, 1892).

Poetry

Hoffmann   *Struwel Peter*

Probably *The English Struwwelpeter or Pretty Stories and Funny Pictures for Little Children*, anonymously translated from the German of Dr Heinrich Hoffmann, who wrote the book for his own young son in 1844. I have seen the twelfth English edition (Leipzig and London, [1860]), which follows the twenty-ninth German edition; the first English edition appears to have been published in 1848, translated from the fourth German edition. It is not known which of the numerous English editions of *Struwwelpeter*

[15] *ACW* 311; *Eric, or Little by Little*, 101.

Auden possessed, though it must have been an early one. In the later editions, the names of the children are generally changed from Latin and German to English ones. The version of 'The Story of Little Suck-a-Thumb' which Auden read out in the 1971 lecture uses the name 'Conrad'; 'Conrad' becomes 'Jimmy' in later editions.

Hilaire Belloc   *Cautionary Tales*

Hilaire Belloc, *Cautionary Tales for Children* (London, 1908).

Harry Graham   *Ruthless Rhymes for Heartless Homes*

Harry Graham, *Ruthless Rhymes for Heartless Homes* (London, 1899). In a 1972 foreword, Auden quoted the following rhyme from Graham, saying 'When I was a child, this was the kind of poetry I most enjoyed':

> In the drinking-well
>   Which the plumber built her,
> Aunt Eliza fell . . .
>   . . . We must buy a filter.[16]

---

[16] *Ruthless Rhymes*, 60–1; Auden quoted the verse slightly wrongly in his foreword to Angus Stewart, *Sense and Inconsequence* (quoted in Carpenter, 9).

Auden in Kirchstetten

STELLA MUSULIN

LEAVING my car on a patch of deeply rutted ground near the garage, I always approached Auden's house from the field below rather than from the upper lane; there was a steep climb up through the orchard with a risk of slithering down the slope to the right. A wicket gate next to the woodshed led to the vegetable garden. Then the ground levelled off and the long, low house stood straight ahead. To the left, at the foot of the outside staircase and below the window of his work-room, were the white table and comfortable garden chairs with red cushions. Then the green front door with its bell, the kind that you pull. I seldom did so, feeling that the clamour spoke of altogether too much aggressive jocularity. Seeing the light through the sitting-room window, it seemed best to walk straight into the small entrance hall—coats hanging on the wall ahead, a clutter of books and papers on a nearby ledge—and to shout. That heart-warming bellow from Wystan: 'Ah!' And here is the familiar scene, one is enveloped again in the unchanging fug. The shelves of records and the record-player on the left, the big square dining table with its stained cloth. Centre back, the Austrian peasant cupboard, then the corner seat, the table and chairs: the *Sitzecke*. To our right a tumble of books on an invisible surface; within a matter of hours, Auden could make any volume look like a lending library reject, the content was all, the package irrelevant. And now the stove, country style, one of the glories of Austrian *Wohnkultur*.

Many were familiar with the peaceful routine at Kirchstetten, the obsession with timetables—time for a drink, time to eat, time to go to bed—and the conversation which, as so often between people who know one another as well as Auden and Chester Kallman did, took on something of the nature of a ritual. As I begin to collect my thoughts to write about those years, I almost despair. What can I say without lapsing into triviality and gossip, without calling down on my head Wystan's wrath? Think for a moment of *Forewords and Afterwords*. Of Richard Wagner he writes, 'On principle, I object to biographies of artists, since I do not believe that knowledge of their private lives sheds any significant light upon their works.[1] Chester told me that it was an obsession with him, a phobia, and the only time that Auden ever came near to snapping at me was when he spoke once, affectionately, of Tolkien, saying that he was going to speak, or perhaps it was to write, about him. I asked whether he would say anything at all about the man as the creator of the world of Tolkien, of the Lord of the Rings, and he said 'Certainly not! I shouldn't dream of saying anything about Tolkien himself.'

The second time I was invited to Kirchstetten, Auden asked me to come over and stand by him because he was giving a little tea-party. He had invited the parish priest, Father Lustkandl, and the local school-mistress and her husband. As I came in I ran into Auden who was shuffling out to the kitchen. 'Thank goodness you've come', he hissed, 'go and look after them, will you, keep the conversation going and hand round the cakes.' So saying he shot into the kitchen for more hot water. It was some time before he could abandon the role of the flustered host. But his guests were quite at their ease, and as the years went on they became his friends. Their composure on that first meeting was, I am sure, partly due to their personal qualities, but partly, too, to the fact that in Josef Weinheber they had had a local poet laureate before, and now, in Auden, they had one again. This was a cause for great satisfaction but not for any transports of ecstasy over the celebrity in their midst.

Auden was one of the most truly courteous men I ever met: he liked to follow the customs of the country he lived in and he had no special voice for inferiors. He got on well with Austrian people, who sometimes, as I discovered after his death, had no idea of the calibre of the man they were having lunch with. The only thing he could not bear was pretension. So one would have supposed that writers young and old would have lost no time in driving out to Kirchstetten. On the contrary, I sometimes see Auden's relationship with the literary scene in Austria—in so far as such a scene existed—as a string of wasted opportunities. Yes, he was interviewed, he was filmed, and the *Gesellschaft für Literatur* did its duty by him. But in the 1960s, there was really no group of people, no meeting-place to which Auden himself could naturally gravitate.

I once tried to entice Thomas Bernhard to Kirchstetten but he

---

[1] 'The Greatest of the Monsters', *FA* 244.

refused. But Bernhard was a recluse. Still, apart from lack of time, it is hard to discern any reason why Auden's translators should have shunned him. During his early years in Kirchstetten he did feel slighted by some of his translators in Austria and in Germany. They would publish their work in literary magazines, but if Auden himself ever heard about it, it was by pure chance. (A friend of Bernhard's, the young poet and author Gerhard Fritsch who committed suicide, also refused an invitation; Fritsch translated Auden's Christmas oratorio 'For the Time Being' into German.[2] 'They don't,' Auden said indignantly, 'even send me a copy.')

Latterly, matters improved a lot, and although Auden did not live to see the volume *Gedichte—Poems*[3] published in the two languages in Vienna, he did check the proofs and a few of the translators went to see him.

What became of the Ford Foundation translation scheme? Some time in the late 1960s Auden was thinking about a project to bring all the main literary works in German under review in so far as they exist in English translation, to judge their quality and to discover the gaps. The real purpose of the exercise was one Auden enthusiastically supported: to encourage professional writers of the first order to take part in the re-creation of German literature in English. To this end the Ford Foundation would make funds available. Of course nothing came of it, but we had fun making lists on the backs of envelopes and lamenting the impossibility of sharing playwrights such as Raimund, Nestroy, and Grillparzer and novelists like Adalbert Stifter with the English-speaking world. Auden knew quite well that it is not so much the language barrier as a fatal lack of universality which has made so many Austrian writers—as used to be said less justifiably of Austrian wines—travel so badly.

Auden seemed to enjoy working on Goethe's *Italian Journey* and he was always delighted when he came upon errors caused by Goethe's own faulty editing of his original diary. Certainly, Goethe as a man fascinated Auden. It cannot have been later than 1962 when there was a ring at the doorbell of my flat in Vienna. I opened the door and there was Auden, panting, as well he might, because he had just climbed ninety steps from street level. His shirt was grubby, his hair was matted, and before he was half through the door and with no further greeting he gasped out: 'I have come to the conclusion that

[2] *Hier und Jetzt: ein Weihnachtsoratorium* (Salzburg, 1961).
[3] *Gedichte—Poems* (Vienna, 1973).

Goethe was a very lonely man.' Auden knew loneliness, that 'Gate-crashing ghost, aggressive | invisible visitor.'[4]

It was while Auden was spending six weeks in Berlin as a guest professor that he remarked in a letter to me that he was lonely—as who would not be in the circumstances.

It *was* sweet of you to think of me at Christmas, especially since it's a little *einsam* here. Am beginning to know some local inhabitants. Oddly enough, the ones I can talk to most easily are from Ost-Berlin. The most awful thing about the Bifkes[5] is that they are so much nicer under a little *Druck*.[6] When they feel their oats they are so apt to become uppish.[7]

The letter goes on to throw light on a passage in Auden's long poem to Josef Weinheber. I had been reading a paperback, *The Rise of the South African Reich* by Brian Bunting, and mentioned it in my letter with particular reference to torture. After a sharp comment on the American magazine *The National Review*, he took up my complaint that certain attitudes found in liberal circles tended to push one further to the right than one wished to go. He wrote:

Of course you're right about the lib-labs' ostrich-like attitude to those who wish to destroy them, but one cannot let ones name be associated with shits. Torture is the iniquity which utterly bewilders me. I know something about the evil in my own heart and in the sort of people I meet, but I cannot conceive of myself or them torturing anybody. Where do the torturers come from? What class? Whom do they marry?

Here the words 'Have you ever met one?' are deleted. This comment found its place in the long poem addressed to Josef Weinheber, which contains the passage:

> never as yet
> has Earth been without
> her bad patch, some unplace with
> jobs for torturers
> (In what bars are they welcome?
> What girls marry them?)[8]

When I told Chester about how Auden's letter to me had made its own infinitesimal contribution to English literature, Chester snapped: 'Wystan never wastes anything!'

---

[4] *CP91* 866.   [5] Auden's version of Piefke, the Austrian word for Germans.
[6] Pressure.   [7] ALS, from Berlin–Dahlem, 23 Dec. 1964.
[8] *CP91* 758.

There is a prose translation of the poem to Weinheber, made by Auden and a German friend, which he sent to me for checking together with some amendments to stanza 3. As the poem was written to commemorate the death of Weinheber, the prose translation was for general information. 'Herewith my effort', Auden wrote, 'to do my Gemeindepflicht' (his civic duty).[9] Auden's interest in Weinheber went far beyond a mere civic duty. It was part of his whole relationship with Lower Austria, his feeling for the landscape, for its history, for the history of the people who lived, or had lived there. Auden felt at home in Lower Austria and it satisfied him to live next door to the house where Weinheber had lived, a man for whom he apparently felt a remarkable empathy and a strange compassion. An element in his sense of identity might have been this: that he himself had once changed his mind. He, like Weinheber, had made a political commitment and had then entirely turned away from it. Weinheber had allowed himself to be wooed by the Nazis, but later on he rejected them and, finally, he committed suicide.

A certain amount of Auden's working correspondence with me has survived. By far the most valuable items are, to me, the typescripts of new poems with brief letters scribbled in the margins, one of which is the text of 'Stark bewölkt', on the back of which he wrote: 'Overleaf a poem which I want to dedicate to you. Firstly because of its subject, secondly because it is written in an imitation of a medieval Welsh metre called a Cywydd'.[10] And there are announcements of domestic disasters and requests for help, written from New York. For instance, the well-known poem to Frau Emma Eiermann asking how could she go and die when they were both away—and what about the cats? The cats had in fact already been destroyed. But Wystan did not know that yet, and he wrote an urgent request for me to hurry over to Kirchstetten and find out what on earth was happening to them. He couldn't bear to think—it was November—that they were prowling around, unfed and shut out of her cottage.[11]

Auden would often lend his car out during the winter, and when he and Chester arrived one day for lunch with my mother-in-law he showed me, with some amusement, a bullet-hole just above the bonnet of his VW beetle, on the driver's side. Having already had a little experience, later to be added to, of Chester's friends in Vienna, I was not altogether surprised. It was never possible, even in the Austrian era, to keep

---

[9] ALS, from Berlin–Dahlem, postmarked 23.12.64; the original typescript of the Weinheber poem and the prose translation are still in my possession.

[10] ALS, from London, 15 Oct. 1971.   [11] ALS, from New York, 9 Nov. 1967.

Chester in purdah for long, and whenever there was a visitor from Athens there could be tension. Auden gave orders to Yannis Boras[12], who often stayed in Kirchstetten, in the abrupt tones of a colonial Englishman of yore speaking to the 'boy', and when I asked one day at lunch: 'Where is, er . . .', he said with a smirk of satisfaction: 'I sent him up on to the roof to mend tiles.' In the end, the VW became the subject of various sad letters to me before and after Christmas 1968. In December Yannis Boras was in Vienna and using the car. One day on the road to Kirchstetten he collided with a lorry and was killed instantly. Several of the letters show Wystan's desperate concern for Chester, and when we met in Kirchstetten in April, Wystan muttered to me: 'I don't know how he's going to get through the summer.'

It struck me then, though not for the first time, what a contrast there was between the two writers: the much younger man, cooking too much rich food for the sedentary existence that they both led, but otherwise with little purpose left in life, and the greater, older poet with his regular hours of work and his considerable output. They did fruitfully collaborate on opera libretti; and there always remained the *Times* crossword.

It was so easy to make fun of the slightly old-maidish ways of the house. In all the entertaining articles about Auden, the tendency has been to leave out one salient fact: Auden was a hard-working, systematic, self-disciplined writer, who knew, none better, how nice it is to sit sipping a cool drink in the shade of a tree, looking with contentment at his flowers and asparagus beds. He did this only after he had worked steadily from 9 a.m. until lunchtime and then again throughout the afternoon. And much of the bosky idyll atmosphere was simply due to the presence of guests including the sharp-eyed journalist. Furthermore, the sacred beast in his lair was probably much wittier than most strangers who came to view the set-up.

I once mentioned in a letter to Auden that a friend of his had quoted him as using the term, as a definition of humour, 'Serious insistence on unseriousness.' His response was that his friend had

a genius for subtle misrepresentation. Serious insistence on unseriousness telescopes two distinct convictions of mine, falsifying both.

One. I believe it to be a serious moral error when an artist overestimates the importance of art and, by implication, of himself. One must admit that the political history of Europe, with the same horrors, would be what it has

---

[12] In an ALS, from New York, 13 Dec. 1968, Auden calls him Jean.

been, if Dante, Shakespeare, Titian, Mozart et al, had never existed. [Of course he often said this.]

Two. I believe that the only way in which, today at any rate, one can speak *seriously* about serious matters (the alternative is silence) is comically. I have enormously admired—and been influenced by—the tradition of Jewish humor. More than any other people, surely, they have seen in serious matters, that is to say, human suffering, the contradictions of human existence, and the relation between man and God, occasions for humorous expression. e.g. 'If the rich could hire other people to die for them, the poor could make a wonderful living', or, 'Truth rests with God alone, and a little bit with me', or 'God will provide—ah, if only he would till He does so.'[13]

In the same letter, Auden commented on my lively account of a party given by Chester in his flat in the Esslingasse in Vienna. Among the broad assortment of guests one individual stood out who with his rasping voice and aggressive, know-all manner had led many of us to take refuge in the kitchen with Chester. Auden answered: 'So! you encountered the one-whose-name-we-never-mention. Why Chester should have been so foolish as to invite him to a party, I cannot imagine. If he is to be seen at all, he must be seen alone.'

Auden liked to amuse and to be amused. It will never be known whether one evening in Vienna he was treating his audience to a bit of traditional stage business. He was lecturing on T. S. Eliot in the hall of the Natural History Museum, and the lecture was very well attended, largely by note-taking students. At some point he told us to imagine a parlour-game: if, like the Trinity, we were made up of three persons, what would they be? Eliot, he said, consisted, firstly, of the American pre-Jackson aristocrat of a kind which died out in 1829. He was a dandy, very carefully dressed in black jacket, striped trousers, and a bowler hat. And he worked two floors underground. Then there was the little boy aged 12, adoring practical jokes such as cushions which fart when you sit on them, and who liked to shock people by saying 'Goethe is awful' and so on. 'Finally there was the Yiddish Momma . . .' At this point a cascade of papers slid off the lectern. Auden disappeared altogether from our sight, scuffled about on the floor, and finally emerged, very slowly to complete the sentence: '. . . who wrote the poems'. By now a very small number of people were wiping the tears from their eyes, while the students,

---

[13] ALS to me, from New York, 3 Feb. 1966.

blank-faced and puzzled, with biros poised, were waiting for all this to stop.[14]

One day at lunch, abruptly (as he said most things), Auden announced: 'Kokoschka wants to paint me.' He explained that Oskar Kokoschka had written and asked him to come to Switzerland. But Auden felt it was too much of an effort, and evidently the painter felt the same way, so that nothing came of it. But the thought satisfied Auden. 'After all', he said as he reached for his wine glass and narrowed his eyes to slits, against the sunlight seeping in from the garden, 'After all, I AM a Kokoschka painting.'

But why? Why was Auden, in his sixties and indeed much earlier, prematurely aged? Some time after Auden's death Chester Kallman gave me his explanation: he put the phenomenon down to benzedrine. According to Chester, Auden had begun taking it in his early years in the States and stopped only when he began to spend his summers in Austria. Chester felt he had used up his body at an accelerated rate; perhaps he needed benzedrine simply because he lived at an accelerated pace, going to so many places, meeting so many people, lecturing and writing continuously.

All the same, Auden utterly disapproved of experimentation with drugs by the young. In lectures and interviews he made that abundantly clear. In February 1968 when he flew over to Vienna to interview a couple after the death of the immortalized Frau Emma, we had lunch at the Opern-Café (this was one of the very few occasions when I made a note afterwards). I told him I was glad he had been telling young people in England that LSD, the fashionable drug of that period, is a dead duck for creative workers. This led to a long account of the experiments with LSD and Mescalin that he himself had carried out in the presence of his doctor. He was perfectly certain that no original line of poetry and no work of art had ever been created under the influence of drugs, and he was convinced that Aldous Huxley did a lot of harm by publishing his experiences with Mescalin, and making people believe it to be an artistic experience. The point is, he said, that young people need to discover who and what they are. And LSD doesn't tell them; it has a purely passive effect in which there is alienation from self. You concentrate on things: a chair, the ceiling, etc.—and people become unimportant. There is a curious feeling when you listen to music: the music

---

[14] Auden was very proud that he had preached in Westminster Abbey, commenting triumphantly: '*Eliot* never did that.'

STELLA MUSULIN 215

becomes intolerable as the sounds lose their interrelation and form.
Basically, what you achieve is a mild degree of schizophrenia. After
the experiment was over, Auden told me that he and the doctor went
round to the local bar. Suddenly through a window he saw a postman
waving at him, and he thought, my God, this is it. Later on the postman said: 'I waved to you, why didn't you answer?'

On the 19th of May 1970 I was mildly horrified to receive a
telegram asking: 'If I sent half hour speech in a few days could you
translate soon into German—Love Wystan'. I did my best, and he
delivered the speech in Neulengbach in the presence of the
Landeshauptmann (governor) of Lower Austria. It consists of the
story of his passion for the limestone landscape of his youth, his
childhood preoccupation with lead-mining, and the principles which
he drew from all this as they applied to artistic fabrication. He had
certainly said or written much of the text before, in *The Dyer's Hand*
and elsewhere, but parts of the speech are less familiar. It is a closely
argued statement and must surely have floated past the ears of most
of his listeners. Indeed, this demanding speech in Neulengbach shows
something else about Auden: he never talked down to people. His
principle was that his audiences would absorb as much as they were
ready for, and some would have understood a great deal.[15]

As the speech reveals, Auden's attitude towards language was in
the exact sense of the word, sacramental. Not surprisingly he held
strong views on modern translations of the Bible—a subject he often
came back to in conversation—and revised liturgies. The new banality
offended his acute sense of the power possessed by words and phrases
which have brought mankind into mystical contact with what he
called the Primary World: darkness, silence, nothing, death. Hence
his suspicion of close textual analysis; he felt it important that—gross
misunderstandings apart—the reader should receive something from a
poem. And he laughed when he told me that some earnest person
wanted to know just what he had meant by a word written thirty
years ago. 'Ridiculous! How should I know?'

As the years passed, Auden became more and more English. The
process annoyed Chester, who would expostulate at any sign of it.
Auden liked to hear the rounded, cool tones of the British country
gentry; he intensely admired Ronald Blythe's *Akenfield*, he loved and
pressed on me the Lucia novels of E. F. Benson; he happily reviewed

[15] See Appendix 1.

The Rise and Fall of the British Nanny; and he was addicted to English whodunnits. One afternoon I dropped in to return a book on my way to Vienna. Auden came pounding down the rickety outside staircase, greeted me with his usual warmth, urged me to come in, to stay. 'No no', I said, 'you're busy and I have to get on.' 'Oh!', he exclaimed, as though he were begging me not to infringe the most basic rule of British hospitality, 'but you *can't* go without having a cup of tea!'[16]

In those days at Kirchstetten Chester still retained his sardonic Jewish wit of the kind known as *Galgenhumor* ('gallows humour') which Auden enjoyed so much; physically he was a wreck. It was difficult to imagine him when the 32-year old Auden, already a poet with an established reputation, first met him. Chester never wanted to earn his living, and all his life he was supported financially by others, particularly by Auden. He often promptly lost what he was given through being robbed or because he gave it away. One winter evening in the Esslingasse in Vienna, a 'friend' of Chester's went off with what cash he could lay his hands on; this, I only realized later, was no isolated occasion but, as it were, a calculated hazard. When, later, Chester took with him to Athens 80,000 sch. in notes (proceeds of the sale of a building plot) and lost it all on the way, the mishap seemed almost a foregone conclusion.

Chester picked up languages with uncommon facility; Wystan's spoken German was execrable but his comprehension unerring. In general, Auden did most of the talking and most of the asking as well; part of his great charm lay in his alert interest in other people's work, and he would draw one out on the odder backwaters of Austrian history. When I took the historian Friedrich Heer out to lunch at Kirchstetten he and Auden were entranced with one another's company and sparks flew all afternoon; Chester was silent. Of that conversational brilliance which old friends have described there was little sign. Once Chester asked me to lunch at a restaurant just off the Kärntnerstrasse. A young man was with him whose background clearly lay somewhere within the crime-belt near the Prater. Soon the youth and I were engrossed in conversation, while Chester, feeling out of it, sulked.

---

[16] That study of his was so bare when I last saw it. It is the 'Cave of Making' which he wished he could have shown to Louis MacNeice, along with the house and garden. In 1989, at the last moment, the crumbling house was restored, and an extension made to the attic workroom to display a small permanent exhibition. (All credit to Peter Müller, without whose determination nothing would have been done.)

Chester's intelligence and wit had not deserted him but they had too little scope, and he was liable, particularly perhaps among Austrians, to be underestimated. He was good-natured, in the course of time even affectionate, hospitable, and amusing. But it cannot have been easy living on a long-term basis with Auden in New York while attempting, however fitfully, to develop his own personality and talents. Putting up with Auden's fads, his insistence on punctuality, and the rigid routine was one thing; to grow up, to mature in the shade of this oversized tree was another. There was not enough light. So he fled, yet without 'Mother' he could not live at all.

In the light of what happened latterly, it is as well to remember Auden's generosity. His biographer, Humphrey Carpenter, mentions the two boys whose further education was financed by Auden. They were the sons of an artist—neighbours of ours for five years. The effect was dramatic; both made rapid careers in industrial management. He also helped with the studies of a student of technology in Vienna. And then there was the brief flurry of activity during the uprising in Czechoslovakia in August and September 1968. We had been discussing the idea of lending the house to two Czechs. In mid-October he wrote from London:

Got back from Oxford yesterday and found your letter waiting.
1) I think I ought to take the couple in, but I must leave it to you to decide whether they are O.K. If they are, all rooms, including my study (which can't be heated) are open to them. 2) How much money will they need to keep going? And how shall I make the arrangements for payment. 3) Will they be able to find work or emigrate before I return in April, when I'm afraid there will not be room for them? 4) I'm worried about how they will get gas cylinders for cooking from Neulengbach, since, presumably, they have no car. I expect someone in the village will help. 5) If and when they come, I must know in advance so that I can write a note to the Burgomeister [sic].[17]

In the end nothing came of it, but the letter is characteristic; the follow-up from New York is even more so. 'Many thanks for your letter. Of course, selfishly, I'm rather relieved. How horrid one is! The U.S. is grim.'[18]

Auden was one of those people who can be generous in big things but stingy over trifles. On the other hand, he would sometimes order things to be sent out from Vienna without a second thought. After his car smash I was rung up by his attorney, and I drove at once to

---

[17] ALS, from London.   [18] ALS, from New York, 6 Nov. 1968.

Kirchstetten. He was dishevelled and cross. 'It's a funny thing', he said, 'the first chap who takes any notice of you when you're carried into hospital is not the doctor but the man from the accounts office asking how you intend to pay for your treatment.' No, he said, he didn't really need anything and Chester would be arriving in a day or two, but he was short of gin—could I have a few bottles sent out from a shop on the Neuer Markt? It turned out that the shop made no deliveries to the country, but, said the voice on the telephone, they made special trips for the Herr Professor. The voice agreed with me that the well-known brand could be bought in the local town, but added that it was not for us to criticize.

The title of the poem 'On Installing an American Kitchen in Lower Austria'[19] may have made readers wonder what was so American about it. When fitted kitchens first came in the Austrians called them 'American', a term now as extinct as 'Russian' tea. The house in Kirchstetten has a tidy line-up consisting of fridge, sink, low cupboards providing a good working surface, a corner cupboard, and a gas stove. Both men were very proud of their kitchen and it became Chester's habitat. But the whole point of a modern kitchen—the labour-saving work area, ample storage space, etc.—was cancelled out by the permanent clutter. It was a matter of principle with Chester to have all ingredients conveniently to hand, but nothing was ever put away, and where his loving eye saw method, the least fussy visitor could only see a shambles.

It seemed clear to me, watching the pair in the kitchen, that they were not so much drinking as eating their way into their graves. I remember my horror one day as I watched the gravy being prepared to accompany a roast duck. Chester took equal parts of rendered down duck fat and heavy cream, added a little seasoning and poured the fluid into the mixer to form a sauce which would have sustained a miner at the coal face for some considerable time. If they could possibly help it, of course, neither Wystan nor Chester ever walked a yard.

But it was not only that which killed Auden. Chester was convinced that a major factor was the matter of the alleged arrears on his income tax. Contrary to what Auden had been assured by his adviser, he had run up, he was informed, enormous debts to the Austrian Fiscus. It was a terrible shock because the demand wiped out his sav-

---

[19] This was the title when the poem appeared in *Homage to Clio* (1960). Auden changed it to 'Grub First, Then Ethics (Brecht)' when he incorporated it into 'Thanksgiving for a Habitat'; see *CP91* 704.

ings. He had thought he could live out his life in peace, but now, he said, he would have to go back on the circuit. I believe that he appealed to the then Chancellor, Bruno Kreisky, and that the sum was reduced. His statement to the taxation authorities, in which Auden patiently explains how poetry comes to be written, must be a unique literary document.[20]

*

Postlude

'Every day for the past year', said Chester, 'I have stood outside his door in the early morning, afraid to go in.'

That remark came later. Now, Auden was dead, the voice issuing from my car radio had just said so. Just a few days ago we had talked about his reading at the Society for Literature on 28 September. I had said that unfortunately I was obliged to drive to Linz and to spend the night there, but he and Chester were welcome to use my Vienna flat. It was maddening and I would just as soon put off my trip. No, said Auden, mustn't do that, one should stick to one's commitments. 'And you won't be missing much' he reassured me, 'you've heard it all before.' We would meet again in a few days' time and then he would tell me all about it. He was not sure about the flat but he would let me know in good time. On 24 September he wrote a note to say that he did not need the flat, he would go to the Hotel Altenburgerhof. The handwriting is ragged.

Now Linz already lay far behind. The car radio went on muttering to itself unheeded until the familiar voice of Friedrich Heer came through, reading one of his book reviews. It was consoling in a world where, suddenly, a signpost was missing. It was impossible not to think of Chester; it was not so much a question of how much he would grieve over the death of Wystan, as how he would survive at all. Leaving the autobahn at St Pölten I drove straight to Kirchstetten; it seemed just possible that he might have arrived in the mean time. But the green shutters were closed and there was no one about apart from the wall-eyed dog, a hideous mongrel belonging to Frau Strobl, which barked at me in an irritating falsetto. He barked from a position close beside me while I wrote a note and stuck it in the chink between the door's shutters, and he was still barking as I shut the garden gate behind me.

---

[20] See Appendix 2.

The answer to my note was a telephone call from Frau Strobl: Herr Kallman said, would I come over to tea the next day, Sunday?

When I arrived, the sitting-room seemed to be filled with people. Chester was sitting on the corner seat facing the door, where Auden always sat. He hurried across the room, hugged me and said 'The whole thing's terrible, you have to help me.' I was introduced to the others. Mrs Thekla Clark and her daughter had come up from Florence; there was Frau Maria Seitz, headmistress of the high school in Kirchstetten whom I already knew from that first tea-party; Herr Enzinger the local mayor; the film scriptwriter Adolf Opel; two young men were sitting on the floor drinking beer.

Chester was barely coherent, but he managed to explain his point of view. He loathed, he said, everything in the way of *pompes funèbres*. He wanted to bury Auden quietly and privately, and if possible on Tuesday. He had already let Wystan's brother Dr John Auden, Stephen Spender, and others know of his intentions and asked them to come immediately, or on Tuesday morning at the latest. But the mayor wanted to lay on a really big show with brass bands and all the trimmings, and this on Saturday, so that the maximum number of people would be able to come. The Ministry of Education and the *Land* government of Lower Austria were to be represented, and—the final straw—the hearse was to drive up to the house. He, Chester, would not allow any of this: 'I can't bear it and I won't have it.'

I looked enquiringly at Mayor Enzinger who drew a deep breath. For a start, he pointed out, the body of the deceased had not yet been released by the authorities, so Tuesday was impossible. Everything takes time, said Herr Enzinger. And how could anyone expect him, the Bürgermeister, to refrain from notifying the cultural departments in Vienna of the death of Herr Professor Auden? Now Frau Seitz offered her opinion, which was that the people of Kirchstetten would not bury a dog in the manner proposed by Herr Kallman.

Chester's attitude was understandable. To him, an American of Jewish origin and a non-believer, the pomp and circumstance of a traditional Austrian funeral were abhorrent. In the case of persons of even local prominence the local brass band is a must, followed where appropriate by groups representing the voluntary fire brigade, the Austrian Federal Railways, the veterans' association, and others besides, while the gamekeepers blow their horns at the graveside and wish the deceased good hunting in the Elysian fields. To Chester, such folksy rituals were as alien as the burial rites of the Incas. (Not

so long ago in Lower Austria, a bachelor—as Auden was assumed to
be—would have been accompanied by a 'bride' dressed in white with
a wreath in her hair.) Perhaps it never struck Chester that Auden
himself might have been entranced at the prospect of a slap-up
funeral—one can almost hear his Olympian laughter—followed by a
hearty meal at his familiar inn. (In the event, Chester got no marks
from the villagers for this finale either, as the meal consisted of
Leberkäs and vegetables, i.e. slices off a loaf of a flabby substance
which is neither liver nor cheese but is distantly related to the
Knackwurst or the Frankfurter sausage.)

The room had become unpleasantly stuffy and Chester would not
be able to stand much more pressure. He had withdrawn his insistence on the Tuesday for the funeral, but a great deal still had to be
settled: the form of service in the church and at the graveside. It was
agreed that Mrs Clark would telephone London, and Chester asked
me to talk everything else over with Frau Seitz and Herr Enzinger.
Thankfully, we all got to our feet, and Chester came across to me:
'I'll do anything you say, just try to hold the others in check. Don't
worry about me, I shall be all right. I'm crammed full of tranquil-
lizers and all I need is a bit of rest.' He embraced me warmly and left
the room.

In Frau Seitz's sitting-room at the opposite end of the village we
got down to essentials. The mayor was worried about the safety of
the deceased poet's property and belongings. 'It's amazing', he said,
'how things can disappear without trace.' He begged me to make sure
that at least the workroom was locked up to protect the manuscripts.
This was done by the notary public, but subsequently Herr
Enzinger's warning was justified; a Cheshire cat-like process of grad-
ual disappearance of half-remembered objects began and continued, if
sporadically, until quite recently.

Herr Enzinger now gave way over Saturday and unnecessary civic
display was struck off the programme. I was able to go back to the
house and tell Chester: funeral on Thursday, brass band as an irre-
ducible token of civic (self)-respect, hearse to back up to the garden
gate. Not one of us, however, thought of asking who was to pay for
the band. In due course, the local council sent a bill to Chester, who
was furious: the brass band had been forced upon him. So enraged
was he that he could not wait to see the last of Kirchstetten. With no
consultation—with, for example, the Austrian Society for Literature—
he sold the house and garden against an annuity.

On the eve of the funeral the party from England kept Chester company in Kirchstetten. Dr John Auden was there, Sir Stephen Spender, David Luke from Christ Church, Sonia Orwell, the Clarks, and Chester's current Greek friend Konstantin, a warmhearted creature exuding tongue-tied sympathy with all around him. Charles Monteith, Chairman of Faber and Faber, arrived next morning.

Partly in the house, partly in the garden, the assembling crowd of mourners stood about waiting. Chester was composed. The coffin, its head-end raised, was in Auden's bedroom. As I went in, his spiritual presence struck me with great force. It was Wystan Auden, out-distancing, now, all his human frailty, remote and unknowable as perhaps he always had been. It might have been of him that Spender wrote: 'I think continually of those who were truly great.'[21] Chester shut the sitting-room door. Surprised and slightly embarrassed we stood and listened to the 'Siegfriedstod'. Then we left the house.

The rich variety among the human contacts of Auden and Kallman was reflected in the long defile now slowly winding its way through the village to the church. English and Austrian cultural institutions were represented. The underworld of Athens had sent one of its own, but so had Vienna. Hugi, or Hügerl,[22] lover and reformed convict, was there too, wearing a tidy suit and accompanied by his wife. From my position about half-way down the procession I watched with interest while a male figure weaved its way with determination and skill row by row towards the front just behind the chief mourners. It was 'he-whose-name-we-never-mention' (or if it was, Chester confirmed, Auden crossed himself). My final encounter with this cloven-footed character came at lunchtime, when he sat opposite me. Weakened by emotion, I forgot my manners. 'My God!' I exclaimed, and he smiled. 'Yes', he said with great satisfaction, 'It's me.'

To British ears quite unremarkable, the ecumenical service was much talked about locally because nothing of the kind had been known before. The Revd Bruce Duncan used the Book of Common Prayer and the reading from the First Letter of St Paul to the Corinthians, chapter 15, verses 20 to 58.

Auden has celebrated Kirchstetten village, the church where he sang so flat and where, in the churchyard, he lies buried, and the house he lived in. He has celebrated the whole quiet, unexciting landscape and

---

[21] 'The Truly Great', *Collected Poems* (London, 1985), 30.
[22] See 'Glad', *CP91* 746–7.

its war-torn past, and even the autobahn which lies between the church and his home, bisecting the invisible line joining one to the other. But he would not want us to take him too literally. 'What appears to be the theme is only the focus, an opportunity to express certain thoughts about Nature, God, History, Mankind, etc which may have been present in the poet's mind for a long time'.[23] In other words:

> To speak is human because human to listen,
> beyond hope, for an Eighth Day,
> when the creatured Image shall become the Likeness:
> Giver-of-Life, translate for me
> till I accomplish my corpse at last.[24]

Reaching for my Authorized Version, for surely no one would have dared to use any other, on second thoughts I also took out the New Testament as translated into German by Martin Luther. After reading the English text through very slowly, and then a second time, I did the same with the Lutheran Bible and lost in thought compared the two, verse by verse.

'How nice to see you,' said Auden, who was sitting on one of the white garden chairs with the red covers, 'it's a bit *einsam* here. And I wanted to write and tell you that the technical word for *buddle* is *Erzwaschtrog*. I hope there is an equivalent German euphemism for 'senior citizen'. Oh and *adit* is *Stollen*, and although I may be wrong, I guess *concentration mill* is *Vereinigungsmühle*.'

'What a mercy you've told me', I heard myself say, relieved. 'I should have to have dug up such frightful words in the British Council Library.'

'There is one glory of the sun', I was saying, 'and another glory of the moon, and another glory of the stars: for one star differeth from another in glory'.

'Ah' he said, 'you've been reading Corinthians 1, chapter 15. I've been looking up the German text. Have you ever compared the Authorized Version with Martin Luther?'

'Funny you should ask that', I said. 'It's one of the things I forgot to talk to you about.'

---

[23] From Auden's statement to the tax authorities, see Appendix 2, p. 232.
[24] 'Prologue at Sixty', *CP91* 831–2.

Appendix 1
Neulengbach Speech

Auden's original English text of the speech he delivered in Stella Musulin's German translation at Neulengbach in May 1970. A few slips of the pen have been corrected; substantive emendations are shown in square brackets. The punctuation is Auden's own. (Typescript in possession of Stella Musulin.)

Sehr Verehrter Herr Landeshauptmann, meine Damen und Herren:

I hope you will pardon me if I speak somewhat personally. I do so, not out of vanity, but because I do not wish to give the impression that I am attempting to lay down absolute laws which are valid for all. I give you my experiences as a poet, in the hope that you will be able to compare them with yours, and form your own judgment about them.

Most of what I know about the writing of poetry, or at least about the kind I am interested in writing, I discovered long before I took any interest in poetry itself.

Between the ages of six and twelve, I spent a great many of my waking hours in the fabrication of a private secondary sacred world, the basic elements of which were a) a limestone landscape mainly derived from the Pennine Moors in the North of England and b) an industry—lead-mining.

It is no doubt psychologically significant that my sacred world was autistic—that is to say, I had no wish to share it with others nor could I have done so. However, though constructed for and inhabited by myself alone, I needed the help of others, my parents in particular, in collecting its basic materials; others had to procure for me the necessary text-books on geology and machinery, maps, catalogues, guide-books and photographs, and, when occasion offered, to take me down real mines, tasks which they performed with unfailing patience and generosity.

From this activity, I learned certain principles which I was later to find applied to all artistic fabrication. First, whatever other elements it may include, the initial impulse to create a secondary world is a feeling of awe aroused by encounters, in the Primary World, with sacred beings or events. This feeling of awe is an imperative, that is to say, one is not free to choose the object or the event that arouses it. Though every work of art is a secondary world, it cannot be constructed *ex nihilo*, but is a selection from and a recombination of the contents of the Primary World. Even the 'purest' poem, in the French Symboliste sense, is made of words which are not the poet's private property, but the communal creation of the linguistic group to whom he belongs, so that their meaning can be looked up in a dictionary.

Secondly, in constructing my private world, I discovered that, though this was a game, or rather precisely *because it was a game*— that is to say, not a necessity like eating or sleeping, but something I was free to do or not as I chose—it could not be played without rules. Absolute freedom is meaningless: freedom can only be realised in a choice between alternatives. A secondary world, be it a poem, or a game of football or bridge, must be as much a world of law as the Primary, the only difference being that in the world of games one is free to decide what its laws shall be. But to all games as to real life, Goethe's lines apply.

> In der Beschränkung zeigt sich erst der Meister,
> Und das Gesetz nur kann uns Freiheit geben.

As regards my particular lead-mining world, I decided, or rather, without conscious decision I instinctively felt, that I must impose two restrictions upon my freedom of fantasy. In choosing what objects were to be included, I was free to select this and reject that, on condition that both were real objects in the Primary World, to choose, for example, between two kinds of water-turbine, which could be found in a text-book on mining machinery or a manufacturer's catalogue: but I was not free to invent one. In deciding how my world was to function, I could choose between two practical possibilities—a mine can be drained either by an adit or a pump—but physical impossibilities and magic means were forbidden. When I say forbidden, I mean that I felt, in some obscure way, that they were morally forbidden. Then there came a day when the moral issue became quite conscious. As I was planning my Platonic Idea of a concentrating-mill, I ran into difficulties. I had to choose between two types of a certain machine for separating the slimes, called a buddle. One type I found more sacred or 'beautiful', but the other type was, I knew from my reading, the more efficient. At this point I realised that it was my moral duty to sacrifice my aesthetic preference to reality or truth.

When, later, I began to write poetry, I found that, for me, at least, the same obligation was binding. That is to say, I cannot accept the doctrine that, in poetry, there is a 'suspension of belief'. A poet must never make a statement simply because it sounds poetically exciting: he must also believe it to be true. This does not mean, of course, that one can only appreciate a poet whose beliefs happen to co-incide with one's own. It does mean, however, that one must be convinced that the poet really believes what he says, however odd the belief may seem to oneself.

Between constructing a private fantasy world for oneself alone and writing poetry, there is, of course, a profound difference. A fantasy world exists only in the head of its creator: a poem is a public verbal object intended to be read and enjoyed by others. To become conscious of others is to become conscious of historical time in various ways. The contents of a poem are necessarily past experiences, and the goal of a poem is necessarily in the future, since it cannot be read until it has been written. Again, to write a poem is to engage in an activity which human beings have practised for centuries. If one asks why human beings make poems or paint pictures or compose music, I can see two possible answers. Firstly all the artistic media are forms of an activity peculiar to human beings, namely, Personal Speech. Many animals have impersonal codes of communications, visual, olfactory, auditory signals, by which they convey to other members of their species vital information about food, territory, sex, the presence of enemies, etc, and in social animals like the bee, such a code may be exceedingly complex. We, too, of course, often use words in the same way, as when I ask a stranger the way to the railroad station. But when we truly speak, we do something quite different. We speak as person to person in order to disclose ourselves to others and share our experiences with them, not because we must, but because we enjoy doing so. This activity is some-times quite erroneously called 'self-expression'. If I write a poem about experiences I have had, I do because I think it should be of interest and value to others: the fact that it has till now only been my experi-ence is accidental. What the poet or any artist has to convey is a per-ception of a reality common to all, but seen from a unique perspective, which it is his duty as well as his pleasure to share with others. To small truths as well as great, St Augustine's words apply.

The truth is neither mine nor his nor another's; but belongs to us all whom Thou callest to partake of it: warning us terribly, not to account it private to ourselves, lest we be deprived of it.

Then the second impulse to artistic fabrication is the desire to transcend our mortality, by making objects which, unlike ourselves, are not subject to natural death, but can remain permanently 'on hand' in the world, long after we and our society have perished.

Every genuine work of art, I believe, exhibits two qualities, Nowness and Permanence. By Nowness I mean the quality which enables an art-historian to date a work, at least, approximately. If, for example, one listens to a composition by Palestrina and one by Mozart, one knows immediately that, quite aside from their artistic merits, Palestrina must have lived earlier than Mozart: he could not possibly have written as he did after Mozart. By Permanence, I mean that the work continues to have relevance and importance long after its creator is dead. In the history of Art, unlike the history of Science, no genuine work of art is made obsolete by a later work. Past science is of interest only to the historian of science, not to what scientists are doing at this moment. Past works of art, on the other hand, are of the utmost importance to the contemporary practitioner. Every artist tries to produce something new, but in the hope that, in time, it will take its proper place in the tradition of his art. And he cannot produce anything significantly original unless he knows well what has already been done, that is to say, he cannot 'rebel' against the past without having a profound reverence for it.

There are periods in history when the arts develop uninterruptedly, each generation building on the achievements of the previous generation. There are other periods when radical breaks seem to be necessary. However, when they are, one will generally find that the 'radical' artist does not disown the past, but finds in works of a much earlier period or in those of [another] culture than his own, the clue as to what he should do now. In my own case, for example, I know how much I owe to Anglo-Saxon and Medieval Poetry.

When I review the contemporary artistic scene, it strikes me how extraordinarily fortunate men like Stravinsky, Picasso, Eliot, etc, that is, those persons we think of as the founders of 'modern' art, were in being born when they were, so that they came to manhood before 1914. Until the First World War, western society was still pretty much what it had been in the nineteenth century. This meant that for these artists, the felt need to create something new arose from an artistic imperative, not a historic imperative. No one asked himself: 'What is the proper kind of music to compose or picture to paint or poem to write in the year 1912?' Secondly, their contemporary audiences were mostly conservative, but honestly so. Those, for instance, who were scandalised by *Le Sacre du Printemps*, may seem to us now to have been old fogies, but their reaction was genuine. They did not say to themselves: 'Times have changed and we must change with them in order not to be left behind.'

Here are a few statements by Stravinsky to which the young, whether artists or critics would do well to listen and ponder over.

In my youth the new music grew out of, and in reaction to, traditions, whereas it appears to be evolving to-day as much from social needs as interior artistic ones . . . The status of new music as a category is another incomparable. It had none at all in my early years, being in fact categorically opposed, and often with real hostility. But the unsuccess of composers of my generation at least kept them from trading on success, and our unsuccess may have been less insidious than the automatic superlatives which nowadays kill the new by absorbing it to death.

* * *

The use of the new hardware naturally appears to the new musician as 'historically imperative'; but music is made out of musical imperatives, and the awareness of historical processes is probably best left to future and different kinds of wage-earners.

* * *

In times, like our own, of rapid social change and political crisis, there is always a danger of confusing the principles governing political action and those governing artistic fabrication. The most important of such confusions are three.

Firstly, one may come to think of artistic fabrication as a form of political action. Every citizen, poets included, has a duty to be politically 'engagé', that is, to play a responsible part in seeing that the society of which he is a member shall function properly and improve. But the poet, qua poet, has only one political function. Since language is his medium, it is his duty, by his own example, to defend his mother-tongue against corruption by demagogues, journalists, the mass-media etc. As Karl Kraus said: 'Die Sprache ist die Mutter, nicht das Magd, des Gedankens', and when language loses its meaning, its place is taken by violence. Of course, the poet may use political and social events as subject-matter for poems—they are as much a part of human experience as love or nature—but he must never imagine that his poems have the power to affect the course of history. The political and social history of Europe would be what it has been if

Dante, Shakespeare, Goethe, Michael Angelo, Titian, Mozart, Beethoven, etc, had never existed.

Where political and social evils are concerned, only two things are effective: political action and straightforward, truthful, detailed journalistic rapportage of the facts. The Arts are powerless.

The second confusion, of which Plato is the most famous example, is to take artistic fabrication as the model for a good society. Such a model, if put into practice, is bound to produce a tyranny. The aim of the artist is to produce an object which is complete and will endure without change. In the 'city' of a poem, there are always the same inhabitants doing exactly the same jobs for ever. A society which was really like a good poem, embodying the aesthetic virtues of order, economy, and subordination of the detail to the whole, would be a nightmare of horror for, given the historical reality of actual men, such a society could only come into being through selective breeding, extermination of the physically and mentally unfit, absolute obedience to its Director, a large slave class kept out of sight in cellars and the strictest censureship of the Arts, forbidding anything to be said which is out of keeping with the official 'line'.

The third confusion, typical of our western 'free' societies at this time, is the opposite of Plato's, namely to take political action as the model or artistic fabrication. Political action is a necessity, that is to say, at the very moment something has to be done, and it is momentary—action at this moment is immediately followed by another action at the next. Artistic fabrication, on the other hand, is voluntary—the alternative to one work of art can be no work of art—and the artistic object is permanent, that is to say, immune to historical change. The attempt to model artistic fabrication on political action can therefore, only reduce it to momentary and arbitrary 'happenings', a conformism with the tyranny of the immediate moment which is far more enslaving and destructive of integrity than any conformism with past tradition.

At this point, a little digression on the subject of 'free' verse, which seems now to be almost universal among young poets. Though excellent examples, the poems of D. H. Lawrence, for example, exist, they are, in my opinion the exception, not the rule. The great virtue of formal metrical rules is that they forbid automatic responses and, by forcing the poet to have second thoughts, free him from the fetters of self. All too often, the result of not having a fixed form to be true to, is a self-indulgence which in the detached reader can only cause boredom. Further, in my experience, contrary to what one might expect, the free-verse poets sound much more like each other than those who write in fixed forms. Whatever freedom may do, it does not, it would seem, make for originality.

What then, can the Arts do for us? In my opinion, they can do two things. They can, as Dr Johnson said, 'enable us a little better to enjoy life or a little better to endure it'. And, because they are objects permanently on hand in the world, they are the chief means by which the living are able to break bread with the dead, and, without a communication with the dead, I do not believe that a fully human civilised life is possible.

Perhaps, too, in our age, the mere making of a work of art is itself a political act. So long as artists exist, making what they please or think they ought to make, even if their works are not terribly good, they remind the Management of something managers need to be reminded of, namely, that the managed are people with faces, not anonymous numbers, that *Homo Laborans* is also *Homo Ludens*.

And now, I hope those of you who know no English will forgive me if I concluded these remarks with a light poem of my own, entitled 'Doggerel by a Senior Citizen'.[1]

[1] See *CP91* 851–2.

Appendix 2
Letter to the Austrian Tax Authorities

Auden's letter to the Austrian tax authorities, composed in mid-July 1972, was translated into German for him by Hilde Spiel, one of his translators. The text printed here is based on Auden's English typescript (now in the Spiel Papers, Österreichisches Literaturarchiv, Österreichische National-bibliothek, Vienna) but incorporates two additional passages (printed here in brackets) that were apparently sent to Spiel later. The original English text of these passages is now lost; the translations from Spiel's German used here are by Stella Musulin.

Statement

Gentlemen,

My stand-point is quite simple. One pays income-tax where one earns money, which in my case, as a writer writing in English, means the United States and England. In Austria I don't earn a groschen; I only spend schillings.

You assert that I have a 'material' interest in Austria, by which you mean, I presume, a 'financial' interest. This could only possibly be true if I had to say to myself: 'I must come to Austria because only in Austria can I work.' But this is not the case. I have lived in many places and a number of countries and have always been able to work, wherever I was.

Of course I have a 'personal' interest in Austria: otherwise I should not come here. I like the landscape and I find the Austrians I meet charming and friendly.

You say, and it is true, that I once received an Austrian literary prize. That was a great honor of which I am very proud. But you cannot seriously believe, gentlemen, that I calculated: 'If I keep coming to Austria, perhaps I shall win a prize.' Before I received it, I had never heard of this prize. It is also clear that I cannot receive it a second time. Again, you say that there is now a street in Kirchstetten named

Audenstrasse. That was a most friendly gesture by the Gemeinde, but I cannot be said to profit financially from it.

You say, and it is true, that I have written some poems with an Austrian background. About this I have three points to make.

1) I have never received a penny in Austria for my poems. A few have been translated into German, but it is the translators who get the money, not me.

2) I don't think you understand how poems are written. What appears to be the theme is only a focus, an opportunity to express certain thoughts about Nature, God, History, Mankind, etc, which may have been present in the poet's mind for a long time. For instance I wrote a poem for the twentieth anniversary of Josef Weinheber's death. But the poem is really about, firstly the love which any good poet, no matter what his nationality, has for his mother-tongue, and, secondly about what happened after the war in those countries which lost it, that is to say, not only Austria, but also Germany and Italy.

   Again, in 1964 I wrote a poem called 'Whitsunday in Kirchstetten', because I happened to be here. But the setting is unimportant. What the poem is really about is the question: 'What, to a Christian, is the significance of Pentecost?' And that is the same in all countries.

3) I dont think you understand the financial situation of a poet. A novelist, if he is successful, may earn a great deal of money from his novels. A poet, even if he is well known, cannot, for poems are only read by a minority. The greater part of my income, for example, comes not from the sale of my volumes of poetry, but book-reviews, translations, etc, activities which have nothing to do with Austria. Talking of translations, reminds me that you say, quite truly, that I have a great interest in German and Austrian literature—let me add music—but I don't have to come to Austria in order to read and listen to it.

[You see from all this that the arguments brought forward by you for subjecting me to payment of income tax are not valid. The most pertinent argument against it is that in the course of one year I always stay under six months in Austria and never spend more than three months here consecutively.]

In conclusion I must say this. If this, to my mind, unjust foolishness goes any further, I shall leave Austria for ever, never to return, which would be very sad for me and perhaps also for the shopkeepers. And, if I have to, I must tell you frankly, Gentlemen, that I am in the position to make a world-scandal.

W. H. Auden

[You ask why I have made over my half of our property in Kirchstetten to Mr. Chester Kallman who is not related to me. Mr. Kallman is my heir. I have no children and for years past he has been my literary collaborator. Jointly, we have written five new opera libretti, *The Rake's Progress*, [*Delia*,] *Elegy for Young Lovers*, *The Bassarids* and *Love's Labour's Lost*. And together we have made new translations of *The Magic Flute*, *Don Giovanni*, *Die Sieben Todsünden*, *Mahagonny* and *Archifanfaro*. I am now 65 years old and must reckon with all eventualities such as a heart attack. As you know better than I, in the event of sudden death great difficulties arise for the heirs of landed property, particularly in a foreign county.]

'For the Time Being': A Relocation of the Poet

ALFRED CORN

COMFORTABLE familiarity with the substance of Auden's biography in the years 1939 to 1942 may actually hinder an imaginative reconstruction of the feelings of a poet, a particularly vulnerable one at that, who had left his country and family behind, abandoned the ideology characteristic of his young adulthood, emigrated to a new world largely unknown to him (losing thereby the support of former associates in Britain), taken up a series of temporary residences in a frenetic metropolis, and witnessed the eruption of a war potentially even more devastating than the one two decades before that had destroyed most of the old European order.

Personal crises—from a psychological standpoint paired—have to be added to this picture of dislocation and anxiety: in the summer of 1941, Auden's mother (the closer of his parents and the dedicatee of 'For the Time Being') died. Death of a loved one is often experienced as abandonment, and roughly a month earlier Chester Kallman had told Auden that the physical side of their relationship had come to an end, and that, moreover, he was involved with another man.[1] Given the importance to Auden of friendship as well as love, we can see another loss for him in Christopher Isherwood's moving to California shortly after the love affair with Kallman began. Auden would have new friends of course, but they wouldn't be able to understand all of his jokes, at a time when humour was more necessary than ever. His temperament thrived on certainties and permanences; the first years of his residence in America offered him practically none, not even the certainties of poetic practice. In discarding radical politics, he also discarded the premiss that art is an effective instrument of social

---

[1] Carpenter quotes him on his reaction to the news: '"I was forced to know," he afterwards wrote of the days that followed his discovery of Chester's unfaithfulness, "what it is like to feel oneself the prey of demonic powers, in both the Greek and the Christian sense, stripped of self-control and self-respect, behaving like a ham actor in a Strindberg play"' (311).

change. The most important of Auden's contemporary poetic models were Hardy, Yeats, and Eliot, and the second died just as Auden came to America, leaving only one other, who had described himself as royalist, classicist, and Anglo-Catholic. The ring of authority in such a statement stood in contrast to the confusion and alienation of a world Eliot himself had earlier termed a 'waste land'. Many others besides Auden saw his example as a spar to cling to in the global tempest about to break.

In 1939 Auden entered his thirty-third year, the Christological associations certainly not lost on him as he adjusted to new circumstances. A dimension of religious mythology needs to be added to the picture we have of the uprooted poet getting to know the streets and subway system of Manhattan, its varieties of speech, its intelligentsia, its nightlife, and returning to a hotel room or small flat, shutting out traffic noises (if only the better to hear the clamour of war across the Atlantic) and beginning to compose the writings that mark his resumption of Christian faith and practice. These include the 'New Year Letter', the sestina sequence 'Kairos and Logos', 'The Dark Years', 'Blessed Event', 'The Council', *The Double Man*, and reviews of theological works by Reinhold Niebuhr published early in 1941. Writing, producing a text with cognitive content, would act as an endorsement to whatever new certainties the poet found to replace former ones and serve as a counterweight to a sense of 'death all too substantial in the thinning air'.[2] Of course the new stance was not altogether new for Auden. At the level of daily experience, attending Sunday services at St Ann's in Brooklyn was like returning to an English childhood, the church his mother loved, and a prayer-book the language of which was engraved in his memory. Christian faith was one remedy for historical despair at a time when other ideologies offered little or no reassurance, but it was also the recovery of affectionate memories that survived the loss of a parent. Chaotic New York, so long as one was Christian there, would be a place where God might

> Instruct us in the civil art
> Of making from the muddled heart
> A desert and a city where
> The thoughts that have to labour there
> May find locality and peace.[3]

---

[2] 'The Dark Years', *CP91* 284.   [3] 'New Year Letter', *CP91* 242.

At the same time, Auden's Christianity could never conform to conventional piety or orthodoxy, even if he hadn't been an intellectual eager to take contemporary science, political theory, and progressive theology into account. His sexual variance was, at least in theory, not condoned by Christianity, but there is no evidence that he saw his new-found faith as an obstacle to continuing a relationship with Kallman. So far we have scant information about the precise doctrinal content of Auden's Christianity, in particular, his views on religion and sexual practice, but the picture emerging from the Carpenter biography is one of salutary neglect, where the contradiction is dismissed with a joke. Auden more than once described himself as a 'sinner', as sincere Christians must, but the degree to which that judgement included negative views of his own active sexuality, as opposed to a general acknowledgement of human failings, has not been established. In any case, Auden cannot have been unaware of the considerable number of Anglican priests living out precisely the same contradiction and perhaps concluded that grace available to the clergy might apply to a layman as well. During the 'Celebration of W. H. Auden' held on the tenth anniversary of his death by the Academy of American Poets, I heard Ursula Niebuhr describe his religious views as being markedly more conservative than her own, and certainly we find no evidence in his writings of professional competence concerning textual analysis of the Bible, the sort that is likely to dismantle literal or orthodox readings of it. He was drawn to Christian philosophy and theology, and to Cranmer's Book of Common Prayer, but not to the 'Higher Criticism' of biblical scholars.

In English poetic tradition since the Enlightenment, poems debating Christian belief or coming to accept it are often associated with evocations of the Nativity or with the modern Christmas holiday. The longest and best known instance is *In Memoriam*, but Browning's 'Christmas-Eve' and Hardy's lyric 'The Oxen' should also be included in the list. The Feast of the Incarnation is appositely seen as the time to confess a new-born faith or a lack (sometimes regretful) thereof. The 'New Year Letter''s 'thoughts that have to labour there' may be considered as going through the labour of birth, in order to find 'locality and peace'. For Auden a poem like 'For the Time Being' could inscribe itself in the tradition of faith reaffirmed just as it could point up an analogy between the Incarnation and the author's relocation in a New World. Certainly the poem is a curious and mostly unprecedented mingling of religious tradition and brash contemporaneity, juxtaposed in what amounts to a stereoscopic view, appropriate enough for Auden's Double Man. The axiomatic modernism of a work like Eliot's *Ash Wednesday* did not mean that it contained unabashed 20th-century *realia* such as chorus-girls and pressed pants, but Auden's poem includes these, along with lines that must still give pause to religious traditionalists, as when his updated St Joseph remarks, 'The bar was gay, the lighting well-designed'; or the faculty of Sensation observes this scene: 'In a wet vacancy among the ash cans | A waiter coupled sadly with a crow.'[4]

'The Temptation of St Joseph' (from which the first quotation is taken) stands out as the section of the poem that admits more of contemporaneity than any other. It is also the section with the keenest dramatic edge, where we witness the working through of a human choice and are led to care about the outcome. By contrast other incidents in Auden's Nativity narrative are rendered more familiarly and are to that degree less suspenseful. What the author has done (as he admitted privately) is to lend some of his own emotions to Joseph: just as Auden was forced to end or continue his relationship with Chester Kallman, Joseph must decide whether or not to abandon a betrothed who will give birth to a child not his own. The biblical account records Joseph's hesitation but conveys nothing like the anxiety painfully registered in the monologue in the 'Temptation''s first part:

> Where are you, Father, where?
> Caught in the jealous trap
> Of an empty house I hear
> As I sit alone in the dark
> Everything, everything,
> The drip of the bathroom tap,
> The creak of the sofa spring,
> The wind of the air-shaft, all
> Making the same remark
> Stupidly, stupidly,
> Over and over again.[5]

Without this depiction of human suffering, the Narrator's injunction to 'choose what is difficult all one's days',[6] would have had much less force. Careful readers of Auden would also hear an echo of the first line of 'September 1, 1939' in 'As I sit alone in the dark',[7] which sug-

---

[4] *CP91* 362, 357.   [5] Ibid. 363.   [6] Ibid. 365.   [7] Ibid. 363.

gests that a purely personal crisis summoned emotions in a pattern resembling the one already outlined in a poem about crisis on an international or even cosmic scale. Auden sees that Joseph's salvation is mandated on his decision not to reject his betrothed. This saintly acceptance is a small paradigm of the Incarnation itself, God giving up the perfection of eternity in favour of a flawed and mortal existence in the world of time. A personal inference for Auden was that accepting Christian faith as the best response to international crisis meant acknowledging his own imperfect nature, and so forgiving an errant mate as well. For Auden 'Chester' might in addition have stood for 'America', epitomizing advantages (freedom from strict social codes) as well as whatever drawbacks (failure to make important distinctions, sexual infidelity) Auden may have perceived in his new country. His decision to write a Christmas poem and in oratorio form (an acknowledgement of Kallman's and Constance Auden's devotion to music) implies that the crisis was at least temporarily resolved and, respective failings notwithstanding, Chester and the American reality embraced. With this in mind, we can see why the Semi-Chorus that concludes 'The Temptation' catalogues, among behaviours in need of redemption, an excessive trust in the myth of romantic love as well as the 'indolent fidelity' of the bourgeoisie, who are 'tempted | To incest not adultery'.[8] Of course the Nativity is not finally a fable of infidelity, and one way to think about Auden's treatment of it is as a negotiation between his loyalties to Kallman and to a recently deceased mother. The poem is dedicated to Auden's mother—faithfully, yet on the occasion of her death.

A much more resounding orchestration of crisis is presented in 'Advent', the first section of 'For the Time Being', where the stagnation and anxiety of the Roman Empire is made to prefigure the crises of the low, dishonest decade, the one Auden wanted to leave behind as he assumed a new faith. When the Semi-Chorus cites the failed example of Hercules, Auden is reminding us that Hercules is one of classical mythology's few examples of a mortal who became a god, the converse of the Incarnation, but, alas, one that did not 'reinvigorate the Empire'. It is interesting that Hercules 'cannot | Even locate his task',[9] a reminder of Auden's own struggle to find a suitable base for his poetic and spiritual opus, the problem now considered solved by coming to New York and accepting Christian Incarnation.

[8] Ibid. 367.   [9] Ibid. 349.

The Empire's realm of darkness and despair Auden renders in verses that, despite or because of considerable technical ingenuity, do not fall comfortably on the ear. Critics have cited Dryden's *Secular Masque* (written in iambic trimeter, with the substitution of one anapest per line) as the metrical model for section I of 'Advent'.[10] That model covers, however, only part of the case. Auden establishes a contrast between the meters of the rhyming Chorus, which is close to Dryden's pattern, and the unrhymed Semi-Chorus, whose lines are irregular trimeter but still maintain a syllable-count of seven syllables per line (so long as contiguous vowels are counted as one syllable). Not all of the Chorus's lines, however, follow the meter of the *Secular Masque*, in fact, not even the first: 'Darkness and snow descend' is iambic trimeter with trochaic, not anapestic, substitution in the first foot. A closer description of the meters in the Chorus is that two consecutive syllables of weak stress appear in every line, usually provided by anapests, but sometimes by the juxtaposition of a trochee and an iamb. These consecutive weak syllables give a sort of skip to the lines, which unanalytic readers, without stopping to account for it, may still register as part of the stanzas' special rhythm. Some few lines fail to conform to the pattern, for example, 'Love is not what she used to be',[11] *two* anapests followed by an iamb, or 'Ebbs from the heavy signet ring',[12] which must be hypermetrical unless one forces it into trimeter by scanning it as a dactyl followed by an anapest and then an iamb; but this does violence to the ear and gives a scansion where four weak stresses fall consecutively, an impossibility in English for all readers except those who accept the theories of Hopkins. Close inspection of the meters throughout this and other sections will show that a dominant pattern is established but not maintained in every line. In section II of 'Advent' the Narrator speaks in lines that can almost always be scanned as accentual meter with five stresses per line; but they also contain (a quantity easier to establish) thirteen syllables per line, so long as contiguous vowels count as one syllable. A line such as 'So that, taking the bad with the good, the pattern composed',[13] even though it may be scanned with five strong stresses, contains fourteen syllables, and 'So impossible after all; to cut our losses',[14] again scannable as a five-stress line, contains only twelve syllables, unless we ignore Auden's usual practice of counting contiguous vowels as one syllable. These variants probably

---

[10] See e.g. Spears, 206.   [11] *CP91* 349.   [12] Ibid. 350.
[13] Ibid. 351.   [14] Ibid.

ought not be discounted as inadvertences or faulty technique. They serve as purely metrical signifiers of the flawed condition of the pre-Christian Empire (and Auden will provide, when they appear in the narrative, the angel Gabriel, Mary, and Joseph with lines of much more dependable regularity). The stanzas of 'Advent''s Chorus, incidentally, are irregular sonnets, with the curious rhyme-scheme of *AbacdAecbefdfA*, where '*A*' stands for the identical rhymes of the refrain. Taking the refrain as a division marker, the sonnet is thereby divided into an opening sestet followed by an octave, a transposed formal feature that may signify the perversity of a world where a mortal like Hercules aspires to become a god, a transformation opposite to the plan of the Incarnation. In any case, the sonnets' envelope structure certainly reflects the circular nature of pre-Christian concepts of time, where a wearying cycle of repetition obviates any prospect of progress or hope.

Auden is on record as intending his Christmas oratorio for musical setting by Britten, but no one with musical understanding could be surprised that Britten, after reading Auden's text, declined the offer. Only a few of the oratorio's lyrics have the simplicity and clarity of texts intended for vocal performance. It also contains stretches of prose much too long for even *recitativo secco*. If Auden meant prose passages to be spoken without musical accompaniment, the ten- or fifteen-minute interruption of musical flow would be disastrous for the work's coherence. It is none the less clear that Auden consulted at least two musical models, the Bach *Weihnachtsoratorium* and Berlioz's *L'Enfance du Christ*. From Bach he adapted the idea of oratorio form applied to the Nativity, with contrasted lyric and narrative passages assigned to soloists and chorus. Also, for 'The Summons', he composed one chorale reminiscent of the several Lutheran examples Bach included, as well as a 'Fugal Chorus', the fugue, of course, being Bach's signature musical form. From Berlioz, Auden takes the idea of beginning the work in a negative mood, 'Advent', a generalized recasting of the opening scene in *L'Enfance du Christ*, where Herod dramatizes his fears of being dethroned. Auden also follows Berlioz's decision to include a *Récitant* or Narrator, not confined as Bach's Evangelist is, to reciting the scriptural account of the Nativity. In 'For the Time Being' the Narrator is a man of all work, having no distinct character or role; nor is he, for whatever reason, assigned the passages Auden describes as 'recitative': Auden nowhere specifies who is meant to sing these passages. The Narrator often strikes us as a mouthpiece for the author, anxious in a thoroughly modern manner, and, as such, the speaker of some of the poem's most interesting passages, for example, the paragraph in section II of 'Advent', beginning, 'But then we were children', where Kierkegaardian dread is figured by a frightening entry into a world of mirror reversals.[15] (The clock and the mirror, by the way, are recurrent motifs in the poem, appearing in its opening lines and serving as negative symbols of Time and Space throughout.)

Perhaps the least successful section of the poem is 'The Meditation of Simeon', written in prose and for the most part attempting to summarize Auden's philosophical or theological perspectives on the Nativity.[16] Jargon terms such as 'the Positive' and 'the Unconditional' and their surrounding passages are of course the sort that professors of philosophy always blue-pencil for vagueness and lack of rigour, nor do regular interruptions of the Chorus manage to break the log-jam of *a priori* argumentation. So close are Simeon's opinions to Auden's that Simeon fails, on the level of drama, to materialize as a character, however touching his piety whenever the monologue turns to contemplation of the Holy Child. Auden must have thought that the reader would need to have Simeon's arguments well in hand before hearing Herod's monologue ('The Massacre of the Innocents'), which comes next in the sequence.

Herod has two advantages over Simeon: the first that he is rendered as a distinct character, the second that his speech is comically memorable. Edward Mendelson has commented that the monologue amounts to an ironic refutation of statements that Auden himself had made (in prose articles published in 1938) justifying liberal governments' use of coercion to preserve order.[17] The satire of Herod vibrates with the mercilessness reserved for early opinions one has come to renounce. Although readers may laugh at the spectacle of liberal complacency and hypocrisy recorded in this speech, they are even so not required by reason solely to consider all of Herod's thinking ridiculous. When Herod makes the objection that replacing justice with pity will have bad results, so that, 'Every crook will argue: "I like committing crimes. God likes forgiving them. Really the world is admirably arranged"',[18] Auden certainly recognized that satire was not enough to annihilate Herod's objection. Otherwise, he would not have opened 'For the Time Being' with an epigraph from Saint Paul,

---

[15] *CP91* 351–2.   [16] Ibid. 385–90.   [17] *Early Auden*, 302.
[18] *CP91* 394.

the passage in Romans where Paul says, 'Shall we continue in sin, that grace may abound? God forbid.' Law and grace are polar concepts paradoxically united in Christian doctrine, and so pivotal a theologian as Martin Luther said things similar to Herod's hypothetical crook. Herod may be comically obtuse, but not all the objections he raises are negligible.

Auden's use of the Nativity story as an effective vehicle for ideas is sometimes successful, as when (in 'The Summons' and 'At the Manger') he allegorizes the Magi and the shepherds, recasting them respectively as modern intellectuals and the uneducated working class. Stereoscopic perspective used throughout the poem prepares us in general for this doubling, but, if we have any doubts about his intentions here, a letter to Auden's father (dated 13 October 1942) should dispel them. He says he was not trying to give a purely historical account of the Christmas story, rather

I was trying to treat it as a religious event wh[ich] eternally recurs every time it is accepted. Thus the historical fact that the shepherds were *shepherds* is religiously accidental—the religious fact is that they were the poor and humble of this world for wh[ich] at this moment the historical expression is the city-proletariat, & so on with all the other figures . . . The Wise Men represent the Scientific Materialist, the Philosophic idealist and the Liberal rationalist positions wh[ich] are recurrent heathen attempts to arrive at absolute intellectual truth . . . It is only in the last two centuries that religion has been 'humanised,' & therefore treated historically as something that happened a long time ago; hence the nursery picture of Jesus in a nightgown and a Parsifal beard.[19]

Auden's premiss accepted, we can then move to a more precise reading of his intentions. A prime feature for him in the story was the resolution of a conflict that had dogged radical movements from the first: the gulf between intelligentsia and workers. In 'At the Manger' we see both allegorized groups present and, through their adoration of the Holy Child, eventually united. In characteristic fashion, Auden uses metrical ingenuity to present the change, where the second section's variable stichomythia between Magi and shepherds yields to the regular stanzas of section III. Here the Magi speak in a series of seven envelope tercets, the exterior pentameter lines always rhyming the long 'e' vowel, the internal pentameter line always in '–ation'. These tercets alternate with the shepherds' quatrains, which

[19] From a transcription of the letter made by Auden's father, now in a private collection.

consist of a heroic couplet followed by another rhyming couplet composed of a tetrameter and a dimeter. The quatrains' harmonious diminuendo is the occasion for thoughts and judgements that make the possibility of accord with a more intellectual class not so unlikely after all.

> When in dreams the beasts and cripples of resentment
> Rampage and revel to our hearts' contentment,
>   Be then the poetry of hate
>   That replaces hate.[20]

The section's last stanza is a Tutti, where Magi and shepherds join forces in lines retaining the consistent pentameters and rhymes of the Magi's tercets and adding a fifth line to the shepherds' couplet quatrains:

> O Living Love replacing phantasy,
> O Joy of life revealed in Love's creation;
> Our mood of longing turns to indication:
> Space is the Whom our loves are needed by,
> Time is our choice of How to love and Why.[21]

The poem's chronic mirror motif is redeemed here in a face at once divine and human, and the clock's endlessly repetitious cycle left behind in a privileged moment where human freedom may choose salvation. The poetic equivalent of redeemed time is perfected, significant meter. Technical means reinforce Auden's beatific vision of solidarity between disparate groups, so that in addition to the 'poetry of hate', there might also be a poetry of love and unity—a vision plausible to Auden at least for the time being.

---

[20] *CP91* 384.   [21] Ibid. 385.

'In Praise of Limestone'

A Symposium

'IN Praise of Limestone' was first published in *Horizon* in July 1948 and then appeared in *Nones* (1951). Auden revised the poem for *W. H. Auden: A Selection by the Author* (1958) and printed the revised version in *Collected Shorter Poems, 1927–1957* (1966) and *Selected Poems* (1968). The revised version appears in both the 1976 and the 1991 editions of Auden's *Collected Poems* edited by Edward Mendelson. In this Symposium most of the contributors refer to the revised text (see *CP91* 540–2); however, Edward Upward refers to the earlier one throughout his essay and Lawrence Lipking refers to it once, as he makes clear in a note.

Edward Upward

It is only in twenty-two out of the ninety-three lines of this poem that Auden refers in any way to limestone, and when he does so his homesickness is never entirely for limestone landscapes but is mainly for the life he intends them to symbolize. Symbols such as the chuckling springs each 'carving | Its own little ravine whose cliffs entertain | The butterfly and the lizard' may convey a real love of limestone for its own sake, but perhaps the more notable thing about them is how aptly they apply to the longed-for life which is described (though with a slight ironic deprecation) in the lines beginning 'What could be more like Mother or a fitter background | For her son . . .' Auden's symbolic lines have not the vividness of those they may recall for us by Hopkins where in his 'Epithalamion' a 'listless stranger', walking through a hillside wood, is 'beckoned' by a noise of shouts below him to descend and to see, without being seen himself, a bevy of boys from the town disporting themselves in a boisterously beautiful river.[1] The stranger then hies to a hidden neighbouring pool into which, after also doffing his clothes, he enthusiastically dives. The present writer is well aware of not doing justice to the marvellous if idiosyncratic language and imagery that is used in the poem (e.g. the 'chancequarrièd, selfquainèd hoar-huskèd rocks . . . the water warbles over into . . .' cf. Auden's chuckling springs). He is also well aware that bringing in Hopkins may seem quite irrelevant to a discussion of Auden's 'In Praise of Limestone'. But it could be claimed that Hopkins uniquely illuminates Auden.

There can be no question that in scope of subject-matter Auden is superior to Hopkins, and he shows a far greater variety of metrical devices. On the other hand, Hopkins is capable of a depth of feeling, as for instance in the sonnet 'Carrion Comfort' and its companion sonnet beginning, 'No worst, there is none', which is not easily to be found in Auden. There are scholarly critics (the present writer cannot claim to be one of them and in this instance he does not agree with them) who would perhaps say that Auden's not showing deep personal (confessional) feeling is one of his greatest merits. But let us return to 'In Praise of Limestone'.

Auden's poem, nevertheless, seems to be very much a personal family poem about his brothers and his Mother and, not least, about

[1] See *The Poems of Gerard Manley Hopkins*, eds. W. H. Gardner and N. H. MacKenzie, 4th edn. (Oxford, 1967; repr. 1970), 197 ff.

himself. He sees the whole family as occupying a middle position between the best and the worst types of human being. The best sought the granite wastes which proclaimed how permanent death is and made even saints-to-be slip away sighing. And 'Intendant Caesars' (i.e. provincial or colonial officials or senior administrators) are put off by the clays and gravels which offer plenty of room for military drilling and a prospect of slaves to construct tombs for them in the grand manner. Auden, no doubt, is using metaphorical language here, but the reader may find that its logical meaning is not clear and becomes no clearer when, at the beginning of the last section of the poem, he addresses his Mother (if it can be assumed that he is addressing her and not someone else or no one at all): 'They were right, my dear, all those voices were right | And still are; this land is not the sweet home that it looks.'

However, before we go on to examine the obscurities in this poem, let us note an interesting difference between his earlier and his later poems. Those of his earlier poems which have no logical meaning are often exciting to us because of their illogicality. He intends them to be illogical. His later poems, on the other hand, are almost always logical, even when his choice of vocabulary is somewhat quirky.

Now to return briefly to the opening twenty lines of the poem. Everything is lucid enough until we reach the

> . . . nude young male who lounges
> Against a rock displaying his dildo, never doubting
> That for all his faults he is loved, whose works are but
> Extensions of his power to charm?

The reader may be puzzled by the word 'whose' until realizing that it is a repetition of the 'whose' in the lines, 'Its own little ravine whose cliffs entertain | The butterfly and the lizard.' And the remaining lines of the first section following the enigmatic 'Extensions of his power to charm' because more lucid when they refer to 'a child's wish | To receive more attention than his brothers, whether | By pleasing or teasing.'

This theme is developed in the first twenty-three lines of the next section which describe the 'band of rivals' (i.e. the three brothers) 'as they climb up and down | Their steep stone gennels in twos and threes, sometimes | Arm in arm, but never, thank God, in step.' The whole of this passage up to 'could happen to the best and the worst of us' shows Auden at the height of his effectiveness as a poet.

It could be wished that the final section of the poem was equally effective. But, in spite of certain lines which considered in isolation are very striking, there seems no logical cohesion in the section as a whole; and the long cryptic passage beginning

> The poet,
> Admired for his earnest habit of calling
> The sun the sun, his mind Puzzle, is made uneasy
> By these solid statues

shows an arrogance which is technically unacceptable. The passage can be explained, but why should the non-scholarly reader—unless he or she is a keen crossword solver—bother to explain it? However there are other lines which are fascinating enough in themselves to be well worth interpreting, even if the interpretation is one that might not have occurred to Auden himself:

> if
> Sins can be forgiven, if bodies rise from the dead,
> These modifications of matter into
> Innocent athletes and gesticulating fountains,
> Made solely for pleasure . . . .

Did he, the opera enthusiast, have Acis in mind, who was slain out of jealousy by Polyphemus and was changed by the gods into a stream (though not a fountain as in Auden's poem) which rises from Mt. Etna? Perhaps this is not such a trivial question as it may at first seem.

Limestone symbolizes not merely the life that Mother wanted Wystan to lead but also, at the end of this poem, his poignant homesickness for the love she always gave him in spite of all his faults and of his refusal to lead such a limited life. This homesickness might be said to bear a resemblance to the feeling he expresses in his pre-World War II lines 'Unhappy poet, you whose only | Real emotion is feeling lonely'.[2] Few of his post-war poems other than 'In Praise of Limestone' show a deep personal feeling that has remained unchanged over so long a period. However a competitiveness in him which has the strength almost of a passion seems to have been longlasting, and though he can be ironical about a 'child's wish to receive more attention than his brothers', nevertheless in this poem the lines

---

[2] These lines appeared in Auden's 1932 poem 'A Communist to Others' when it was printed in *The Twentieth Century* [Promethean Society] (September 1932) and in *New Country* (London, 1933); later they were dropped. See *AS1* 177.

that almost equal in depth of feeling his longing for his mother's love of him are those that express the wish 'Not to lose time, not to get caught, | Not to be left behind, not, please! to resemble | The beasts who repeat themselves.'

I have been asked if I think that 'Epithalamion' was in Auden's mind when he wrote 'In Praise of Limestone'. There seem to be signs that it was, but what is certain is that all of his literary contemporaries who were young in the Thirties were greatly impressed then by Hopkins, though few were rash enough to try to imitate him then or later. It is interesting that Hopkins felt a conflict between his love for his family and his sorrow that 'in Christ' they were 'not near' to him.[3]

I will end these thoughts by quoting from a 'Prose Piece' I wrote after hearing of the death of Auden.

It was because of his younger self that when I . . . first heard of his sudden death in Vienna, I felt the beginnings of a desolation which was to extend day by day until I came to think it might last for the rest of my life.

But the shadow cast by the older poet over the younger, emphasizing the once venial-seeming faults that had prefigured some of the worst he developed later and diminishing the light of those earlier poems where his potential greatness had been clearest, was lessened when he died, and has disappeared this morning. His younger consciousness, hopeful of the world still, has been brought to life in my consciousness now by a scene much like the other which his poem of forty years ago recorded, and that is why I could almost believe he is invisibly here with me looking at this calm cliff-mirroring sea, these ships diverging on their 'urgent voluntary errands', this gull that 'lodges' (how exact an image) 'a moment on its sheer side'.[4]

I have always believed that Auden will be lastingly remembered, but I do not think he is as great a poet as he might have been. I regret that I must end these thoughts by saying that I regard 'In Praise of Limestone' as an uneven poem.

---

[3] See his Sonnet beginning 'To seem the stranger lies my lot, my life' in *Poems*, 101.

[4] 'Prose Piece' is printed as 'The Poet Who Died' in Upward, *The Night Walk and Other Stories* (London, 1987), 49–51. The quotations are from Auden's 1935 poem later titled 'On This Island' (*CP91* 130–1).

Michael Wood

A voice says 'we', then 'I'; imitates other voices; instructs us to 'mark', 'hear', 'examine', 'watch'. The place of the poem is 'here', 'this land', where the speaker seems to be. But it is also a remembered and projected landscape, the object of homesickness and an image of the life to come, a place and a condition we may know only when we miss it or dream of it.

What seems most haunting in this poem is its delicate shifting of registers, from classical to camp to confessional; the play of pronouns and perspectives. It is a remarkable work which is very hard to place: almost major, we might say, pretending to be nothing of the kind. This is Auden the 'minor atlantic Goethe',[1] an appealing but virtually unimaginable figure, the poet as intricate oxymoron. We try dizzily to put the pieces of the phrase together, to picture a small Atlantic, an oceanic modesty, a Goethe who would be minor, a minor poet who would be Goethe.

'In Praise of Limestone' is a poem about difference, and about shifts in the perception of difference. Its very first lines connect the inconstant with consistency, as if in a riddle. The look of the words, their dependence on so many of the same letters of the alphabet, suggest a closeness in qualities that appear to be morally or temperamentally opposed. Perhaps the inconstant are the least inconsistent of persons, faithful above all to their infidelities. There could be worlds of difference in a few letters, of course; but we also imagine large differences where there are only small modulations.

Here as in so many Auden poems we need to listen to the voices carefully, to ask how many there are, what roles we are asked to play (what roles are available to us) in the imagined encounter, and where the work leaves us. I have worked largely through the dreaded heresy of paraphrase because in delicate situations paraphrase is already a long way into interpretation, and I want to make as clear as I can the outlines of a particular reading. I seem, on previous encounters, to have missed many of this poem's undercurrents; missed the precise tone and colour of its ironies but also the way the ironies dissolve.

'We' are at first 'the inconstant ones'—or at least we may choose to be. We can align ourselves with the voice, involve ourselves in its confession, assume it is speaking to us and for us, speaking to its

---

[1] 'The Cave of Making', in 'Thanksgiving for a Habitat', CP91 693.

kind. The grand imperatives are friendly, mock-classical: we recognize the rounded, water-ridden scenery because it is ours, because it is 'like Mother'. We are the loved and charming son, we watch our likes climb the steep but manageable hills and chat in the shade, and we know that extremes are not for us, the realms of volcanoes and deserts and jungles, for instance, those 'monstrous forms and lives | With which we have nothing, we like to hope, in common.' The voice invites us to watch a 'he' and a 'them', but they are us, their separation a mere grammatical convenience. When the voice speaks of 'the best and the worst of us', we imagine the whole set and include ourselves: we know the way their or our mind works.

It is possible, though, to hear the voice as explaining a difference, addressing others, those who are constant, or homesick for other landscapes. The imperatives remain courteous but become less ironic, sustain a distance, offer genuine instructions: we must pay attention to these contours in order to understand these persons. We shall like them better, perhaps, if we see how clear-eyed and unassuming they can be, how frank and amusing about their privileges and weakness. They know each other 'too well to think | There are any important secrets'—unlike us, no doubt, who know neither ourselves nor each other, and are sure that almost all secrets are important. These charming people 'like to hope' they have nothing in common with the monstrous, but the timing of the sentence suggests hesitation, a certain frailty in the hope; and the hoping subject ('we' again, but altered and separated by the presence of 'one of them' in the next line) may also in this case be humanity at large. 'The best and the worst of us' returns to modesty and explanation: 'we' are the charmers, and for them there is no great gap between the best and the worst and the rest.

But now the two readings, inclusive and instructive, begin to coalesce: we are them and us, they are in us, whoever we are, since the best and the worst have left this comfortable country, indeed have 'never stayed here long'—'never' acquiring an odd emphasis in the context of the slightly seedy self-knowledge just displayed. The inconstant ones are first of all inconstant to their old home—that's why they are homesick. The landscape is so familiar because it is lost, and because it remains in the heart as a memory of indulgence. Those who leave have heard voices—three voices, echoing and modifying the three landscapes the charmers are said not to know—calling them to different destinies: sanctity, empire, solitude. The last voice speaks to 'the really reckless' in an 'oceanic whisper', and chills the whole poem. 'There is no love,' it says. 'There are only the various envies, all of them sad.'

By this time an 'I' has appeared, presumably a member of the initial set of 'we', but its appearance is so discreet we hardly notice it: the voice merely says 'I suppose', and nothing much can hang on such a usage. However, there is an I, there always was, and the singular voice now speaks (has perhaps all along been speaking) to a singular, intimate other: 'They were right, my dear.' And a little later: 'I, too, am reproached, for what | And how much you know.' The ones who are right are not the charmers but the voices calling the best and the worst of the charmers away. The limestone landscape, for all its resemblance to Mother (because of its resemblance to Mother?), 'is not the sweet home that it looks,' not a site of composed 'historical calm'. It begins to look more like an amalgam of ruined old England and certain stranded Italian cities, a place where 'marble statues' tease the poet and 'gamins' chase the scientist: 'A backward | And dilapidated province, connected | To the big busy world by a tunnel'. It has a role, though: it questions everything big and busy about the world.

The 'I', following a now well-established pattern, forms a triad with the 'earnest', 'antimythological' poet and the abstruse scientist: neither poet nor scientist, perhaps, neither saint nor ruler nor 'really reckless', but sharing with all of them the fear and the knowledge of death and the urge to resist it with works and gestures: 'Not to lose time, not to get caught, | Not to be left behind.' The 'I' here seems to be the individual Auden and also a representative, civilized, anxious human. 'Our rights', sarcastically proclaimed as an implicit denial of other things we know about ourselves, are those of everyone driven to refuse their weaknesses, to turn from everything watery, dissolving, and chuckling in their lives:

> these
> Are our Common Prayer, whose greatest comfort is music
>   Which can be made anywhere, is invisible,
> And does not smell.

The 'Common Prayer' is particularly telling, a rather desolate Nietzschean joke which makes Anglicanism itself a form of anxiety, and makes us all Anglicans.

There is much to be said for such striving, of course, as the poem makes clear, even amidst its mockery; the advance of death leaves us little else. Music is the model of a death-denying civilization, and 'no doubt we are right' to make it so, if 'we have to look forward to death as a fact.' As the only final fact. But death and striving forget the resurrection, which appears now at least as a possibility, an 'if' to echo the first word of the poem, and a reminder of the speculative nature of this whole performance. If a faultless love were possible, if there were a life to come, limestone and underground streams would be their image, and a brilliant, disreputable-looking theological thought might well turn our moral lives upside down: 'The blessed will not care what angle they are regarded from, | Having nothing to hide.' The voice at this point is unmistakably personal, saying 'Dear' and 'I', freely confessing that it knows nothing of faultless love or the afterlife; it is direct and vulnerable, no longer arch or amusing. We are witnesses, not accomplices or audience, yet the spotlight on the now fully dramatized couple, in the wake of all the poem's moving identities, means that we can hardly fail to recognize the way their concerns are likely to echo in us—all the more forcefully because they are they and we are we, to adapt a phrase from Montaigne.[2]

Imagining (but only imagining) faultlessness, the voice recalls the identification of the inconstant ones in the opening line, along with dozens of other intricate, obsessive evocations of betrayal and uncertainty in Auden; it repeats the frankness of the loved son, the lads who know how to stay away from immoderation. But in so doing, it redeems weakness as the measure of whatever strengths we have. The love we cannot know, the life to come which may resemble not the best or the worst but the easiest regions of the life we have, are our only answer for the dread oceanic whisper. They are not enough, but they are what we have got; like our fears, they are our own. What Auden has found here is not a justification of the lapsed life, or even forgiveness for sins, in spite of his placing forgiveness and the resurrection together in the last section of the poem. He has found a form of fidelity, a home for his homesickness; has understood where the practice of forgiveness might start, even in this life, and why the spoiled and the blessed are different but not as different as all that.

---

[2] 'If you press me to tell why I loved him, I feel that this cannot be expressed, except by answering: Because it was he, because it was I.' See 'Of Friendship', *The Complete Essays*, trans. Donald Frame (Stanford, Calif., 1958; 1965), 139.

Edna Longley

I am one of those who think that Auden's inspiration gradually ran out or ran shallow. The second half of the massive new *Collected Poems* mostly leaves me cold. But in 1948 Auden wrote a defence of shallowness which reconnected his poetry—though too briefly—with its 'underground streams'.

Unlike all those poems of 'slick and easy generalisation'[1] in slick and esoteric metres, 'In Praise of Limestone' makes real demands on technique. For a start, its form has mimetic point: the free elegiac couplets trellised with a leisurely and elaborate syntax; the anapaestic rhythms; the liquid assonances; the sudden alliterative clusters. 'In Praise of Limestone' brings the Auden landscape physically alive again.

Midway between symbol and discursiveness, the poem occupies the site of parable. But this is an unusual parable, a meta-parable, in that its discourse interprets and justifies its symbolism. At one level 'In Praise of Limestone' speaks from behind its own scenes, from the interval between inspiration and embodiment. It takes shape as a meditation upon why it takes the shape it does. The opening and closing sections embody poetry itself (images, sounds, texture, text, subtext) as a geology which is also a physiology. 'In Praise of Limestone' thus seems to come full circle as a poem about poetry: the speaker may begin by suggesting how to read it and end by suggesting how it might come to be written. Yet these processes dissolve into one another. From 'If it form . . . Mark . . . hear' to 'what I hear . . . what I see', from genesis to revelation, from the physicality of Nature to the physicality of poetry, 'In Praise of Limestone' invokes its own becoming in the imaginations of author and reader. By analogy with fractal geometry (particularly marked in limestone), which includes the idea that geological irregularity remains constant over different scales, the conclusion epitomizes the poem: 'what I hear is the murmur | Of underground streams, what I see is a limestone landscape.'

So whatever else 'In Praise of Limestone' may be, I see it as a Helicon poem like Robert Frost's 'Directive'. 'Directive', published in *Steeple Bush* the year before Auden wrote 'In Praise of Limestone', encodes many layers of Frost's life and work. The speaker sends himself and the reader on a space–time journey through an imaginative

---

[1] 'Letter to Lord Byron', *EA* 171.

topography. This journey takes in mountain country, woods, apple-trees, and much Frostian self-quotation *en route* to a 'lofty and original' spring: 'Here are your waters and your watering place. | Drink and be whole again beyond confusion.'[2] Frost's ending too condenses the 'whole' poem, just as the poem condenses his poetry and its stays against confusion.

'In Praise of Limestone' starts out as a guided tour with similarly Jungian undercurrents, though with a less oblique guide. Whereas 'Directive' delays the imperative mood ('if you'll only let a guide direct you | Who only has at heart your getting lost . . .'), Auden introduces it almost at once: 'Mark . . . hear . . . examine'. Yet this is a muted register of Auden's didactic voice ('What could be more like Mother?') and presumably at odds with the cruder rhetorics emanating from the poetry of 'clays and gravels'. Like 'Directive', 'In Praise of Limestone' seems to be both a *summa* of the poet's *paysage moralisé* and a 'secret system' which encodes personal and literary history. I assume that this includes a homosexual narrative and that, in its aspect as 'mad camp' or Auden's erotic muse, limestone takes on the contours of the male body entertaining its lovers and itself. Homosexuality conditions the poem's portrait of the artist from childish show-off, to his youthful camaraderie with a 'band of rivals', to the self-reproachful solitary of the last section. I take the band of rivals to denote and defend Auden's relation to his Thirties contemporaries: 'in twos and threes, at times | Arm in arm, but never, thank God, in step.' Their appearance 'engaged | On the shady side of a square at midday in | Voluble discourse' conjures up many faded photographs. It may be that the various ways in which 'one of them [might go] to the bad' allude to particular instances of literary sell-out: 'to become a pimp | Or deal in fake jewellery or ruin a fine tenor voice'. In contrast, Auden later writes one contemporary, Louis MacNeice, approvingly into the poem (Frost writes Edward Thomas into 'Directive'). A paraphrase of MacNeice's wartime 'Prayer before Birth' implies continuing shared objectives:

> Not to lose time, not to get caught,
>   Not to be left behind, not, please! to resemble
> The beasts who repeat themselves, or a thing like water
>   Or stone whose conduct can be predicted, these
> Are our Common Prayer . . .

---

[2] *The Poetry of Robert Frost*, ed. Edward Connery Lathem (New York, 1969), 379.

Compare MacNeice:

> I am not yet born; O hear me,
> Let not the man who is beast or who thinks he is God
> come near me.

> I am not yet born; O fill me
> With strength against those who freeze my
> humanity, would dragoon me into a lethal automaton,
> would make me a cog in a machine, a thing with
> one face, a thing, and against all those
> who would dissipate my entirety, would
> blow me like thistledown hither and
> thither or hither and thither
> like water held in the
> hands would spill me.

> Let them not make me a stone and let them not spill me.
> Otherwise kill me.[3]

This solidarity may reflect MacNeice's support for Auden when his domicile in America was attacked by Stephen Spender and others.[4]

'In Praise of Limestone' thus incorporates a collective as well as an individual apologia. The following question goes beyond self-interrogation to enquire into the enduring validity of the Thirties enterprise:

> A backward
> And dilapidated province, connected
> To the big busy world by a tunnel, with a certain
> Seedy appeal, is that all it is now?

One of the histories encoded by the poem concerns the argument about poetry and 'worldly duty' which began in the 1930s and is not over yet. This argument has, for instance, assumed new forms in contemporary Northern Irish poetry and in the critical debates which pivot upon it. Thus it seems no coincidence that Paul Muldoon's long poem '7, Middagh Street' (in *Meeting the British*, 1987), a poem which dramatizes the current issues, should exploit Auden's wartime residence in New York—and MacNeice's visit to him there. Auden tilts 'In Praise of Limestone' towards his 1948 positions, as in the initial images of the '*private* pool' (my emphasis) and 'Its own little

[3] *Collected Poems* (London, 1979), 193–4.
[4] See the essay 'Traveller's Return', in *Selected Prose of Louis MacNeice*, ed. Alan Heuser (Oxford, 1991) 83–91.

ravine' or when he emphasizes the equivalence of poetry to sexual play, 'pleasing or teasing'. At this level, the poem undoubtedly has 'a weakness for bad puns':[5] 'a clever line | Or a good lay'. At the same time, entertainment, the pleasure principle, was always central to Auden's Thirties aesthetic. Where 'In Praise of Limestone' parts company with the latter is over making 'action urgent and its nature clear'.[6] Auden rehearses the abdications from literary leadership, from literature as leadership, announced in 'In Memory of W. B. Yeats' and *The Prolific and the Devourer* (an underrated transitional work). 'Immoderate soils' are given the seductive voices of Yogi and Commissar, the 'clays and gravels' echoing the especially insidious temptations to be the latter ('The voice of the Tempter: "Unless you take part in the class struggle, you cannot become a major writer." '[7]). Auden's irony rejects the poet as saint, the poet as 'Intendant Caesar', and perhaps the self-destructive *poète maudit*—different guises of the egotistical sublime. He may even deconstruct 'Spain' in parodying the topographical imperatives of that poem ('Come!') and in stressing the incongruity between limestone and 'a crater whose blazing fury could not be fixed'. 'In Praise of Limestone' acknowledges and welcomes the limitations of an (English?) poetics remote from 'monstrous forms and lives'.

Yet the poem answers the question 'is that all it is now?' with 'Not quite'. And the self-referential denial that 'its peace [is] the historical calm of a site | Where something was settled once and for all' implies that all Thirties passion has not been spent or understood: that Auden's poetry in particular has not entirely dropped out or dated or settled for middle-aged middle gear, that there is life yet in the old dog beneath the skin.

How, then, does 'In Praise of Limestone' reinterpret the Thirties commitment to 'worldly duty'? The opening lines establish a paradox: 'we, the inconstant ones . . . consistently homesick for,' on which subsequent dialectic depends. One set of adjectives, sometimes as applicable to sexual behaviour as to writing or a way of writing, belongs to limestone: inconstant, short, definite, flirtatious, ingenious, local, external, evasive, accidental. Opposing totalizing adjectives are: important, moral, infinite, grand, big, busy, great, remote. As the Prolific and the Devourer, poetry and ideology, meet again,

[5] 'The Truest Poetry Is the Most Feigning' (1953), *CP91* 619.
[6] 'August for the people and their favourite islands' (1935), *EA* 157.
[7] *PD* 19.

limestone's strategic self-deprecation both undermines the opposition and assumes its own moral aspect: 'it disturbs our rights . . . [makes] uneasy . . . rebukes . . . reproaches.' At first this corrective role is confined to subversion and carnivalesque: 'these gamins, | Pursuing the scientist down the tiled colonnade | With such lively offers'. Yet the poem goes on to make more absolute claims for limestone as not only a healthily permissive society (or poetic-homosexual utopia) but the medium of access to: 'a faultless love | Or the life to come.' Lucy McDiarmid notes in *Auden's Apologies for Poetry* that ' "In Praise of Limestone" turns almost literally into a rite as it invokes the Apostles' Creed.'[8]

This raises the question of whether Auden, if not a saint-to-be, subordinates poetry to religion. McDiarmid argues that at this period: 'Every poem becomes an apology, undermining its own significance and alluding to the value it cannot contain.'[9] That explains the deadness of later Auden: humility being possibly good for the soul but usually bad for art. However, I don't think that 'In Praise of Limestone' can be classified as 'a poem of *Sehnsucht*, of longing for what is not itself' or that 'poetry is not-limestone and limestone is not-text'.[10] This Helicon poem which comes full circle seems to satisfy its own homesick urges (in part for the English Auden and English pastoral), to praise and please itself. Surely Auden internalizes limestone, though not with the unconscious subjectivity of the 'antimythological' poet who calls 'The sun the sun, his mind Puzzle'. Accordingly, from another angle he externalizes limestone: so there is nothing outside the limestone text. The point about limestone is its friability and mutability. It draws attention to Nature as artist, underlines the proximity of rock to statue to flesh, and thereby nudges the imagination of *homo faber*:

> From weathered outcrop
> To hill-top temple, from appearing waters to
> Conspicuous fountains, from a wild to a formal vineyard,
> Are ingenious but short steps . . .

Limestone breaks down boundaries between life and art: 'These modifications of matter into | Innocent athletes and gesticulating fountains'. Such easy intercourse was a Thirties tenet. Equally, 'In Praise of Limestone' may celebrate a timeless formalizing and metamorphic principle. However, it also specifically counters criticism of

---

[8] (Princeton, NJ, 1990), 136.　　[9] Ibid. 12.　　[10] Ibid. 137.

Auden's artistic 'inconstancy' whether exemplified by departure from England or ideological shape-changes or textual revisions. 'In Praise of Limestone', unlike 'The Truest Poetry Is the Most Feigning' and the Foreword to the 1966 *Collected Shorter Poems*, does not base the case for the defence on religiose alibis and a doubtful binary split between fiction and truth, history and transcendence, words and meaning. Limestone functions as more than a correlative for humbly chameleon poetry 'never finished, only abandoned'.[11] As Nature, the body, art, the symbol, has the inexhaustible spaciousness of Yeats's 'images that yet | Fresh images beget' in 'Byzantium' (also a workshop poem). And its logic leads the speaker to realize the interdependence of truths and fictions, absolutes and embodiment, artistic and spiritual responsibilities: 'when I try to *imagine* a faultless love | Or the life to come' (my emphasis). What follows is poetry, not theology. At the end of 'In Praise of Limestone' Auden is close to the Dante who 'was simply a poet asking himself how you would describe Heaven'.[12] And as the poem resolves Auden's recurrent muddle about perfection of the life/work, it parallels Yeats's closure in 1939: 'Man can embody truth, but he cannot know it.'[13]

---

[11] Auden often quoted this statement of Paul Valéry; see for instance *ACW* 423.

[12] Ansen, 36.

[13] Letter to Lady Elizabeth Pelham, 4 Jan. 1939 (last letter) in *The Letters of W. B. Yeats*, ed. Allan Wade (London, 1954), 922.

David Bromwich

This poem gives an impression of Auden talking—the ways of its charm are congruent with the ways of its wisdom. It is, in fact, a sort of 'wisdom poem'; as the Immortality Ode is; as *In Memoriam* wants very much to be. Coming when it does in Auden's career, it earns credit for a certain moral authority and worldliness, at the cost of a sharper style which until then he had cherished as if it were something more than a manner. I believe he wrote it in an unusually clear mood about his life and writing (compounded, in about equal parts, of admiration and distrust), but the thoughts have been so worked upon that they feel like general truths. 'In Praise of Limestone', before it begins, has already come to rest in an attitude, a sense of life that is commonplace but not hackneyed. It accepts the data of physical self-love as a sufficient motive for going on with an individual life. But the attitude is only generalized as far as a group of two. In this poem at last, Auden stops justifying himself. That, as he now sees it, is the business rather of ascetic moralities, all the regimes of personal, social, and religious fanaticism which 'In Praise of Limestone' means to reject.

Nevertheless for its stance the poem owes a debt to his earlier work. The fluency, together with the curious dignity of the middle style here, go back to 'In Memory of Sigmund Freud'. Again the one-sided intimacy, by which a sleeping or silent companion is drawn into a guilty life, recalls the same gesture in 'Lullaby' and elsewhere. With Auden, moments like this are oddly free of both cynicism and pathos, as they would not be, for example, in Byron or in Hart Crane. All his celebrated earlier poems had taken as their listener a liberal Everyman. But they took either public and occasional or, if private, exemplary subjects, and this has changed with 'In Praise of Limestone'. The landscape of the poem is open to view, yet safely off the map, secluded; and a main concern of Auden's has become the mutual influence of public and private experience: 'The blessed will not care what angle they are regarded from, | Having nothing to hide.' It is the warnings against enthusiasm that most mark a post-war feeling. We are not to search, and above all *not now*, for any land that is 'the sweet home that it looks,' or to care much for 'the historical calm of a site | Where something was settled once and for all.'

I like the finished éclat with which Auden unloads the important voices at the end of the second section. These are the voices of 'the best and worst'—including the best and worst of himself—of all, in short, who 'sought | Immoderate soils where the beauty was not so external.' They speak with a final authority but are never far from cruelty, or the cruelty of self-hate. 'How evasive is your humor,' says a first voice from the granite wastes, 'how accidental | Your kindest kiss, how permanent is death.' It is the impartial tone of the analyst and accuser, from the commemoration speech in *The Orators* and Herod's judgement of himself in 'For the Time Being'. Then a second voice answers from the clays and gravels:

> 'On our plains there is room for armies to drill; rivers
>   Wait to be tamed and slaves to construct you a tomb
> In the grand manner: soft as the earth is mankind and both
>   Need to be altered.'

One can hear in this a level parody of totalitarian thinking. It spells out everything Stalin could have meant by the phrase, 'engineers of the soul'. At the same time, the assurance is very like that of the poet who once wrote, 'It is time for the destruction of error.'[1]

A third, 'an older colder voice, the oceanic whisper,' now comes in to close off every prospect:

> 'I am the solitude that asks and promises nothing;
>   That is how I shall set you free. There is no love;
> There are only the various envies, all of them sad.'

This sounds like a generic echo of Eliot's dramatic verse, with some added scraps of existentialist homily—just then being translated in magazines like *Horizon* and *Politics*. But one cannot escape the feeling that in these lines once again a self-criticism is involved. They offer an unpleasant pastiche of the moral atmosphere that pervaded Auden's longer poems of the Forties. Those poems had indeed asserted the presence of love. But the assertion there had been merely dogmatic and argumentative. The basis of Auden's love, as of his morality generally, in a single personal attachment or a small group, had dropped out of the picture in an otherwise admirable series of lay sermons. This kind of forgetfulness seems to have happened to him at intervals. 'A Summer Night' was another, similar, reflection on such a lapse, and I think 'In Praise of Limestone' has the same relation to his writing of the Forties that its predecessor does to his writing of the Thirties.

---

[1] '1929', *CP91* 49; originally published with no title, see *EA* 40.

An elementary point is worth recalling, because it is sometimes lost in disputes of taste or belief, concerning the style which the poem invents and the situation which it clarifies. A native pedantry here proves to be compatible with feelings of wonder. It is surprising to be shown this fact; it is not something that can be explained. But the surprise accounts for the number of persons who, without knowing why, remember the whole first sentence of the poem after reading it just once. The style is sinuous, yet aphoristic, winding where the path of observation winds, but always coming to a full stop. The situation belongs simply to a lover speaking—someone who knows that description itself is a kind of persuasion. So the details of the scene have a warming or seductive interest 'for their own sake' which suggests a return to sexual intimacy later on. The whole conduct of the argument is well suited to an experience as sensational and abstract as the pleasure we take in regarding a landscape.

Lawrence Lipking

Faults

On a Caedmon recording of 'In Praise of Limestone', just as Auden reaches the climax of 'a faultless love', his tongue momentarily betrays him. Instead of 'faultless' he starts to say 'faithless', catching himself after 'faithle—'.[1] It is a fascinating slip. At the very instant when the poem tries to imagine a condition of perfect faith, in which sins can be forgiven and bodies rise from the dead, a disobedient reflex gives it the lie. Auden recovers and finishes his reading; the broken word meant nothing after all. Yet faults can reveal the secret life of a poem. The slip of the tongue associates 'In Praise of Limestone' with the mortal, guilty love of 'Lullaby' ('Lay your sleeping head, my love, | Human on my faithless arm'), and hints what has been repressed in the turn from infidelity to blessedness. A faultless love is unimaginable; no human being can live up to it. Hence both poems admit their inconstancy, and speak of faith in order to deepen the pang of its absence. Auden builds his Eden over a fault.

Perhaps there is no other place to build an Eden or a poem. Without some faults, the most inviting site would lose its character. A limestone landscape is endearing, like a weathered face, because of its wrinkles—creases and scars and cracks. In this respect it resembles the post-structuralist version of a poem or of language itself, internally torn, forever dissolving. The best-turned sentence depends on an abyss of unmeaning, the bottomless ground of what can never be said. Nor is the ground beneath our feet more solid. Limestone eternally equivocates. Faithful only to change, it adapts to each curl in the stream or stroke of the hand, and gives itself, like words, to whoever is willing to shape it. That is why Auden loves it. He sees the stone as an emblem of his own kind: pliant, versatile, faulty, made for art.

On the surface, this point of view might seem to contradict the image of poetry, in *The Dyer's Hand*, as a re-creation of Eden, in which every poem 'is an attempt to present an analogy to that paradisal state in which Freedom and Law, System and Order are united in harmony. . . . Every beautiful poem presents an analogy to the

---

[1] 'W. H. Auden Reading', Caedmon TC 1019. Auden reads the early version published in *Nones*.

forgiveness of sins.'[2] Yet Auden knows that paradise is a myth. Poems never do succeed in shaking off the sins of the world, nor does Eden itself represent a static harmony so much as a balance of tensions. Art and truth are always touched by shadows. In 'New Year Letter', when Auden offers the limestone moors carved out by the Eden River as 'my symbol of us all', he deliberately mingles the serenity of the landscape with an underlying sense of guilt.

> There, where the EDEN leisures through
> Its sandstone valley, is my view
> Of green and civil life that dwells
> Below a cliff of savage fells
> From which original address
> Man faulted into consciousness.[3]

Faults connect the natural scene with human nature and all its dubious works. Reservoirs of darkness undermine the placid surface of the Eden, and the seeming paradise of a poem always covers the never-ending crackle of decay.

Indeed, any lover of limestone must become an expert on faults. This science is the key to geology and theology as well as poetics—a link that Auden himself found quite congenial. Such analogies used to be common. In the eighteenth century, John Dennis came very near to Auden's geological and theological poetics: 'The great Design of Arts is to restore the Decays that happen'd to human Nature by the Fall, by restoring Order.'[4] But for Dennis and his contemporaries, the irregular, cloven state of the earth signified anarchy and sin. In the beginning Eden must have been smooth as an eggshell, without protuberances or pits; a perfect God would infallibly have created a perfect world. That perfection, however, could not survive the effects of sin, which had called down the ravaging deluge and fire and brimstone. Hence mountains and valleys, cliffs and chasms, result, like death or rotten poetry, from human faults.[5] A limestone landscape, all caverns and underground murmurs, approximates Dennis's hell. By these standards Auden appears to be a geological deconstructionist, content and at home in hell. He likes eroding vistas and soluble

---

[2] *DH* 71. [3] *CP91* 227.

[4] 'The Grounds of Criticism in Poetry' (1704), *The Critical Works of John Dennis*, ed. E. N. Hooker (Baltimore, 1939), vol. 1, 336.

[5] Dennis's account of the way that human failings had caused terrestrial upheavals was influenced by *The Sacred Theory of the Earth* (1684), Thomas Burnet's famous effort to justify the ways of God to geologists.

Edens; he wants the rough with the smooth. Thus any sharp distinction between the harmonious, orderly world of the poem and the fallen world of ordinary people quickly breaks down. Auden's perfectionism goes no deeper than the skin. Geologically, theologically, poetically, at heart he is a connoisseur of faults.

He dreams, however, always, of faultless love, and often thinks he has found it—for a time. In the Eden of wishful thinking, opposites will reconcile and lovers will be faithful. Whenever he sees an emblem of this paradisal state it brings a shiver of recognition, like déjà vu. That shiver sets the poem in motion. Among Northerners' tributes to the warm and corrupting loveliness of the South (like that *Italian Journey* of which Auden was so fond),[6] 'In Praise of Limestone' stands out by regarding the Mediterranean landscape as oddly familiar, a place just like home. Italy doubles for Yorkshire, to the poet's or geologist's eye. This resemblance, Auden told Elizabeth Mayer, was where he began: 'I hadn't realised till I came how like Italy is to my "Mutterland", the Pennines. Am in fact starting on a poem, "In Praise of Limestone", the theme of which is that that rock creates the only truly human landscape.'[7] A foreign country reminds the poet of Mother; somehow it has the same features, the same open arms. This is uncanny, of course. But it also suggests a marvellous wit in nature itself, a series of rhymes that do not link words but places and times and things.

That sort of wit, akin to déjà vu, informs each aspect of 'In Praise of Limestone'. It begins and ends with the landscape. Auden drew many details, including the butterfly and the lizard, from Anthony Collett, a quintessentially British observer of outcrops and seasons and weather.[8] Yet the poem ingeniously superimposes these descriptions on a sunnier climate, rubbing out the atmosphere and local names that distinguish one place from another. Nothing is left but the sovereign rock and its subjects. The poet pledges allegiance to a

---

[6] J. W. Goethe, *Italian Journey (1786–1788)*, trans. W. H. Auden and Elizabeth Mayer (New York, 1962). Goethe's incorrigible northernness figures in 'Good-Bye to the Mezzogiorno' (1958), *CP91* 642–5, a weary and sceptical companion-piece to 'In Praise of Limestone'.

[7] Carpenter, 357.

[8] Collett's *The Changing Face of England* (1926) often served Auden as a source (see *Early Auden*, 336–8). Auden's commonplace book, *ACW*, includes Collett's loving sketch of 'Landscape: Limestone'; the butterfly and lizard appear on p. 217. Another relevant passage from Collett is quoted on p. 397, where 'the fountains which stream from gashes in live rock' are said to 'restore for us, among our own scenes of flag and fern, the pictured charm of Italian spouting marbles'.

generic terrain and turns away from its rivals, the granite wastes, the clays and gravels, the oceanic deeps. In spite of all temptations to belong to other formations, he remains a limestone man. He has been here before, he has always been here. Whatever the poet's passport and birth-date may say, it is the eternal landscape that makes him human.

A similar identification of one world with another accounts for the style of the poem. Arriving in Italy, Auden discovers not only the scenery of his boyhood but a silver-age Latin voice. Several eras and languages rhyme across time. If a sense of *déjà vu* haunts 'In Praise of Limestone', one reason may be that Horace has already been there.[9] Auden pays homage to the master in the captivating, sinuous, long-drawn rhythms of the verse sentences, apparently so conversational yet always ready to spill over into miniature lyrics ('hear the springs | That spurt out everywhere with a chuckle'). At the same time he walks in the steps of another tourist, the Goethe of *Roman Elegies*, whose elegant German elegiacs had showed that a Northern language could assume the urbanity and flexibility of the best Latin verse.[10] Auden had often doubted that classical meters could sound anything but clumsy when subjected to the stresses of English.[11] Now, with the aid of Horace and Goethe, he spins out elegiacs as easily as if he had been chatting in them all his life.

Yet the full wit of the poem, its unobtrusive intermingling of strata

[9] Two later poems, 'The Horatians' and 'A Thanksgiving', acknowledge Horace as Auden's 'tutor' in the sort of modest, worldly verse that celebrates 'some particular | place and stretch of country' and 'a bountiful landscape' (*CP91* 771–3, 891–2).

[10] David Luke describes the means by which Goethe adapts quantitative elegiacs to modern accentual verse in *Goethe's Roman Elegies* (New York, 1977), where Luke also records his 'gratitude to the late W. H. Auden for his constantly encouraging interest in the present translation' and cites Auden's 'Natural Linguistics' (1969) as a 'model example of the English elegiac metre here attempted' (p. 22). The final lines of 'Good-Bye to the Mezzogiorno'—'though one cannot always | Remember exactly why one has been happy, | There is no forgetting that one was'—allude to the epigraph of the *Roman Elegies*: 'We were happy once; and now | Let my verse remind us how' (Luke's translation). Goethe's notorious blend of gravity and lubricity seems especially pertinent to 'In Praise of Limestone'.

[11] 'Unfortunately, the English language does not fall naturally into hexameters; . . . if the accentual hexameter can be used in English at all, it is better suited to a low, conversational style than to a high, epic one' (*ACW* 375). 'In Praise of Limestone' adjusts to this situation not only through conversational style but through substituting loose syllabic elegiacs (alternating lines of thirteen and eleven syllables—though the first two lines have fourteen and twelve) for more regular accents. Monotony is also avoided by constant variations in stress and the placement of the caesura as well as frequent enjambment.

of time, emerges most artfully in 'Mother'. Years earlier, under the Freudian spell of 'New Year Letter', Auden had associated the limestone underworld of mines and chasms with the famous, terrible Mothers of *Faust*, 'The deep *Urmutterfurcht* that drives | Us into knowledge all our lives'[12] and wells up in fear and guilt. 'In Praise of Limestone' dispels the fear and cuddles up to Mother. Geologically she is Nature, whose rounded slopes and generous fluids suggest an utterly unthreatening sexuality, both nourishing and erotic. Psychologically she is the principle of unconditional love or security, endowing her son with a confidence in his power to charm that will last him a lifetime. In this happy pre-Freudian landscape, all children are male and Father does not exist; limestone breeds no neuroses. Both these maternal figures conform to the secular ideal of Mother Italy, the *madrepatria* who presides over one big family around a brimming table. But Mother is also religious. The pagan goddess of the opening, who loves her limestone people despite their faults, gradually modulates into Mary or mother church, the Madonna who forgives all sins. This is the miracle of limestone. In every age it takes the shape that answers human needs.

Yet faults and sins cannot be wished away. One plausible explanation for the experience of *déjà vu* would trace it to suppressed anxiety. Coming to a strange place for the first time, uncertain about its rules and dangers, we unconsciously civilize it through a mock memory, the reminiscence of some other time and place when we knew what to do. No harm will come to the stranger; he has lived through this before. Most people find the spell of *déjà vu* not frightening but curiously reassuring. Perhaps 'In Praise of Limestone' obeys a similar logic. In an age of anxiety, amid new scenes, demands, and challenges, the poet makes himself at home. Potential pitfalls, when looked at correctly, are nothing but caves of limestone remembered from childhood; the silver-age poets have passed on whatever manners are needed; and Mother will tuck one in. If poems were wishes, this poem would be a wish to feel at home in the world. But of course it is not. 'This land is not the sweet home that it looks', nor is this poem so sweet. Instead, consistently homesick, it imagines a harmony that its own restlessness keeps dissolving and a way of life that runs away even as it is clutched. Auden's didactic tone puts him at a distance from the unselfconscious ease he celebrates. Even the

---

[12] *CP91* 228. Cf. the 'Dark Gallery' scene of *Faust*, 6173–306.

landscape, pictured at first in naturalistic detail, eventually melts into a contemplative ideal or Wordsworthian intimation. Reality offers no comfort. Limestone, as the poet perceives it, represents not an escape from anxiety but a moral reflection upon it.

Hence the voice of the poem is often at odds with itself; whenever it starts to say 'faultless' it slips into 'faithless'. Other voices condemn the meretriciousness of limestone, and 'all those voices were right | And still are.' The poet remains a stranger in this land. Long ago he abandoned his native limestone and now, at times, he seems afraid of it. The 'Common Prayer' of the poem, its moment of rampant anxiety:

> Not to lose time, not to get caught,
> Not to be left behind, not, please! to resemble
> The beasts who repeat themselves, or a thing like water
> Or stone whose conduct can be predicted

marks the poet's self-reproach or punishment for being unable to accept the landscape of pleasure around him. Yet he subscribes to that Common Prayer, theologically and artistically, and his greatest comfort *is* music. Above all he does not want to dissolve. The immortality promised by limestone, unearned and untroubled, is guaranteed by an utter trust in Mother, who will always be there to catch the sinner when he falls. Auden belongs to another church. He takes death as a fact and hopes to win immortality through his own unpredictable efforts. In spite of its homage to two theological mothers, paganism and Catholicism, 'In Praise of Limestone' expresses a Protestant spirit.[13]

This sense of contradiction runs through the poem. Even the sex seems conflicted. On the one hand, this landscape where 'everything can be touched' and is 'made solely for pleasure' sounds too good to be true. It panders to unashamed, promiscuous delights, not only by yielding the right climate for love but by offering its own body—so soft and responsive, so many orifices to explore. On the other hand, there is something seedy about its appeal, something uncomfortable in the racy diction: 'dildo',[14] 'a good lay', 'pimp', 'gamins', and above all

[13] Auden's paraphrase of the *Book of Common Prayer*, applied to himself, suggests the 'spiritual danger' he thinks characteristic of Protestantism, the desire 'not to get caught' in ritual routines or 'the temptation to imagine one is a special person to whom the common rules do not apply' (*FA* 75).

[14] *N* 13. The 'nude young male . . . displaying his dildo' later became a 'flirtatious male . . . in the sunlight'.

'a mad camp'. The poet clearly enjoys his opportunities, but they also remind him how little he knows about faultless love. Insofar as 'In Praise of Limestone' is a love poem, it muses on a situation in which both partners are free to reach for whatever or whoever else comes to hand. One might call this no-fault love. Auden accepts it in theory. In practice, however, he associates himself with a poet unsettled by statues or a scientist pursued by gamins; these sexy myths and advances disturb 'our' fidelity to higher things. A moralist lurks within this libertine. His fondness for comprehensible human vices plays against a sensitivity to what goes bad when everything is permitted. Even in limestone country he harps on categorical imperatives. Auden wants love to last.[15]

A similar contradiction is latent in what might be regarded as the secret political theme of the poem, its absolution of Italy's fall from grace. The peace of this land, in 1948, is not 'the historical calm of a site | Where something was settled once and for all'; unlike the blessed, many Italians have something to hide. Yet the poem implies that limestone people could never have been *Fascisti*. The 'band of rivals' straggle 'Arm in arm, but never, thank God, in step', and their undisciplined ways provoke 'Intendant Caesars' to desert to the clays and gravels. This puts a good face on the goose-step and Mussolini; they never really belonged here. Auden buys into an expedient Italian myth, which divorces the 'worldly duty' of an easy-going and innocent people from the real political world where citizens collaborate with the Great Powers and seek power for themselves. All memories of war and guilt discreetly fade out of mind. Has the poet forgotten his own anti-Fascist commitments? More likely his argument has persuaded him that the children of this landscape deserve forgiveness; even their faults were always all-too-human. This argument has a flaw. It defines ordinary humanity as a virtue and defence against evil, even though the virtue of humanity is exactly what needs to be proved. A less sentimental judge might point to a crack in the bulwark: original sin. The best and worst of us have never rated humanity so high; and we are suspicious of limestone.

Yet Auden will not surrender his faith in the landscape. In fact he

---

[15] The apparent friction between faithless and faultless love might be salved, as Auden himself liked to suggest, by regarding sexual love as a ladder to the divine: 'Agape is the fulfilment and correction of eros, not its contradiction' (*Theology* (Nov. 1950), 412; quoted by Carpenter, 300). Whether or not God sees love that way, however, Auden does not. However much he enjoys 'a mad camp', he does not want it to be the meaning of life; and he retains a lively sense of sin.

wants it to overcome all contradictions. That impulse is the ultimate, creative fault that makes the whole poem possible. Structurally, limestone embodies the principle of the reconciliation of opposites or miraculous non-contradiction. It serves as an emblem of both permanence and change, of immortality and dissolution. This collapsing of contraries into sameness begins with the first sentence, where the aporia implied by an inconstant consistency toward a disintegrating oneness sets the poem in motion. To be homesick for something inherently unstable recalls the literal sense of 'aporia', a blocked passage; we can't go home again, we never could. Inconstant ones like to keep going, and even their longing takes the form of scenery that is as malleable as they are. Thus, eager not to be left behind, they have always already run away from the one place where they say they belong. Auden comes back to a home he has never seen, and views it as an outsider.

A union of contraries also ends the poem. Faultless love and the life to come are identified, in a vision, with the murmur of streams and a limestone landscape. It is as if desire for the everlasting could be satisfied only by images of perpetual change. For Auden, as for Blake, 'Eternity is in love with the productions of time'.[16] The hardest marble consists of nothing but crystallized limestone; the comfort of the resurrection springs from the flux of a Heraclitean river. Once again geology and theology join in poetics. A pious reading of Auden's conclusion might claim that it reproduces the mystery of Christianity itself, the incarnation of divine or faultless love in the mortal and human. But the poem, with all its disclaimers, is far more modest. It does not pretend to fathom the mysteries at its core, let alone to justify them. Nor will it affirm that sins *can* be forgiven, that bodies *do* rise from the dead. Auden assumes a conditional mood and suspends his personal credo from an 'if' clause. If a limestone landscape is the place where contraries come true, it need not follow that such a place exists. Paradise cannot be located on a map. At the end of the poem, surrounded by real limestone, Auden retreats to the imaginary landscape of his desire.

Only a miracle could resolve the contrary tendencies of 'In Praise of Limestone'; and every miracle, by definition, exposes a fault in nature. Yet the faults on which the poem is built do not belie its strength. Indeed, its place among Auden's best and most characteris-

---

[16] *The Marriage of Heaven and Hell*, plate 7.

tic works may well be carved out by the sense of unresolved contradiction that it imparts. Both sides of the poet are given full play: the
system-making perfectionist who identifies with the best and the
worst, and the tolerant humanist who propagandizes for the middle.[17]
The poem itself acknowledges this split. At once assured and vulnerable, most consistent when most inconstant, it shares its uncertainties,
entertains a faith it does not understand, and asks for indulgence.
This frank confession of faults serves to draw us all in. 'We, the
inconstant ones', turn out to be not only Auden and his friends but
anyone faulty, anyone human. Similarly, the 'Dear' addressed at the
end embraces not only one specific lover but also the reader, allowed
to overhear the endearment and take it personally. The moment
seems peculiarly intimate. As we try to imagine a landscape more perfect than experience gives grounds for, we find ourselves in exactly
the place of the poet. He loves us, he wants us, despite our faithless-
ness. Perhaps this too is a fault. But lovers of limestone cannot ask
anything better. What we hear, what we see, is a frailty just like ours.

[17] Auden's temptation by the very extremism and abstraction he warns against is
particularly clear in *EF*.

'Flouting Papa': Randall Jarrell and W. H. Auden

IAN SANSOM

> Almost all of our relationships begin and most of them continue
> as forms of mutual exploitation, a mental or physical barter, to
> be terminated when one or both parties run out of goods.
>
> But if the seed of a genuine disinterested love, which is often
> present, is ever to develop, it is essential that we pretend to our-
> selves and to others that it is stronger and more developed than
> it is, that we are less selfish than we are.
>
> —'Hic et Ille'[1]

IN May 1935 a 21-year-old Randall Jarrell wrote to Robert Penn
Warren about two articles Warren had encouraged him to write for
The Southern Review: 'I have been working since I got home on the
Auden one. I think it's probably the more interesting. I really know
Auden's poetry pretty well. Outside of your introductory essay, he
hasn't been remotely well treated in this country.'[2] The letter is
significant as an early indication of the interests and obsessions that
were to dominate Jarrell's career. Jarrell's pre-eminence as a critic was
based on his articles about Auden, and his notoriety as a reviewer
derived from his attacks on young Auden-influenced poets. His own
poetry too was influenced by Auden, and engaged with Auden's work
by argument and refutation. The development of Jarrell's career is in
fact identical with the history of his responses to Auden's work and
this history is one of complex successions of love and hate, or what
Freud, borrowing the term from Bleuler, called 'ambivalence': 'the
direction towards the same person of contrary—affectionate and hostile—feelings'.[3]

Jarrell did not just know Auden's poetry 'pretty well'—according to
John Berryman he knew Auden's mind, 'better than anyone ought to

---

[1] *DH* 105.   [2] *Randall Jarrell's Letters*, ed. Mary Jarrell (London, 1986), 2–3.
[3] Lecture 26, 'Introductory Lectures on Psycho-Analysis' (1917), *SE*, vol. 16, 428.

be allowed to understand anyone else's',[4] and he clearly relished his intimate and superior knowledge. In a scene from his novel *Pictures from an Institution* Jarrell gleefully wields knowledge of Auden as an instrument of justice. The novel's narrator (a thinly disguised portrait of Jarrell himself) unmasks the pundit Daudier by revealing his plagiarizing of Auden's ideas:

'For instance, what you said about the ideal education being manual labour and Greek. Now, I was interested in that. I'll bet all of us were interested in *that*. I've seen it somewhere else, though. Who said that first?'

Mr. Daudier said that he thought he'd said it first, though he might have read it somewhere else and forgotten; my heart was hardened, and I said: 'I think it's Auden.' Mr. Daudier looked at me like Pyrrho the Sceptic. Gertrude said, 'Yes, that must be right,' and gestured towards me, saying: '*He* knows Auden by heart, practically.'[5]

If in his fiction Jarrell used Auden's work to exercise his judgement, so in his reviewing it became a shibboleth and a bench-mark: in a letter to the poet and critic Louise Bogan in 1941 Jarrell thanked her, in a tone somewhere between congratulation and condescension—'What I've always felt grateful to you for is the way you've treated Auden'; whilst in a review of Robert Lowell's *Lord Weary's Castle* some years later he nailed up his standards in his opening sentence—'no one younger than Auden has written better poetry than the best of Robert Lowell's, it seems to me'.[6]

These examples are evidence of both utilitarian and idolatrous tendencies on Jarrell's part. He is clearly enamoured of Auden and submits to his authority, but he appeals to that authority for his own ends: he is using Auden. This is not to say, however, that he merely exploited Auden. In 1947 he became depressed by the mindless adulation given to Auden's new volume, *The Age of Anxiety*, and railed against the 'delusions of the reviewers', describing the supposed qualities of the book as 'occupational phantasmagoria of people who are reviewing not one bad poem by Auden, but Auden'.[7] In fairness to the deluded reviewers there is no doubt that Jarrell too was occasionally

---

[4] In Robert Lowell, Peter Taylor, Robert Penn Warren, eds., *Randall Jarrell 1914–1965* (New York, 1967), 10.

[5] *Pictures from an Institution* (London, 1954), 255.

[6] Letter to Bogan, *Letters*, 45. Lowell review, *The Nation* (18 Jan. 1947); repr. in *Poetry and the Age* (London, 1955), 187. (The US edn. of this book was published in 1953.)

[7] *The Nation* (18 Oct. 1947); repr. in Jarrell, *Kipling, Auden & Co.* (New York, 1980), 146.

given to reviewing Auden rather than poems by Auden, but he was distinguished from the herd by his candour and long-term commitment to Auden's work—unlike Auden's fair-weather friends he was as forthright in his criticism as he was unstinting in his praise (the only other contemporary critics of Auden of whom the same might perhaps be said would be Geoffrey Grigson and Stephen Spender). His review of *The Age of Anxiety* is rather petulant, childish even, as if he is the boy who has seen through the Emperor's new clothes. Friends and colleagues of Jarrell note that there was always an air of innocent awe and easily disappointed enthusiasm about him—John Crowe Ransom remembered him as an *'enfant terrible'* and Robert Lowell addressed him, famously, as 'Child Randall'.[8] It was precisely this quality which enabled him to perform the role of the true critic, a role Auden defined in 'Making, Knowing and Judging' as a job for a 'fellow apprentice' or a poet's own internal 'Censor':

When he finds fault, his criticisms are intended to help you to improve. He really wants your poem to be better . . . this is the only kind of criticism from which an author can benefit. Those who could do it for him are generally, like himself, too elsewhere, too busy, too married, too selfish.[9]

Jarrell was, in this sense, selfless—his refusal to patronize Auden or treat him like an 'eleemosynary institution' was rooted in a simple, child-like commitment.[10]

Real commitment, what might be called true love, has to be 'nourished', as Jarrell once remarked, 'on difficulties and prohibitions',[11] and there had been plenty of these to feed Jarrell's interest in Auden. The Auden article Jarrell had promised to Warren in 1935 became a labour of love, taking Jarrell six years to complete, during which time he often complained of it as a burden and a struggle; also during this period he was forced to abandon an MA thesis on Auden, on the advice of an unsympathetic tutor.[12] These trials and long exertions led to Jarrell becoming extremely sensitive to (and about) Auden's work and he increasingly regarded Auden as his own private territory,

[8] Ransom, quoted in William H. Pritchard, *Randall Jarrell: A Literary Life* (New York, 1990), 47. Lowell, 'Randall Jarrell: 1914–1965', *Notebook* (London, 1970), 50–1.

[9] *DH* 40–1.

[10] 'Miss Moore is reviewed not as a poet but as an institution—though not yet, like Auden, as an eleemosynary institution . . .', Jarrell, 'Poetry in War and Peace', *Partisan Review* (Winter 1945); repr. in *Kipling, Auden & Co.*, 127.

[11] 'Love and Poetry', *Mademoiselle* (Feb. 1956); repr. in *Kipling, Auden & Co.*, 252.

[12] See letters to Edmund Wilson and Robert Lowell, *Letters*, 49 and 129. For Jarrell's MA thesis, see the editor's note, *Letters*, 11, and Pritchard, *Literary Life*, 53.

as his letter to Louise Bogan implied. From the mid-1930s onwards Jarrell reviewed scores of new volumes of poetry, conscientiously sniffing out and routing Auden imitations. His infamous attack on Frederic Prokosch in *The New Republic* (which prompted a fierce debate in the magazine about the morality of poetry reviewing and helped to earn Jarrell his reputation as a terror of a reviewer)[13] was committed at the shrine of Auden:

Mr. Prokosch's success in the romantic and superficial exploitation of Auden's materials and methods is really incomparable—a triumph unmitigated by the odd intelligence and sensibility that adulterate obstinately even the laxest and most mechanical of Auden's pages . . . Mr. Prokosch has sublimated Auden's worst vices and Auden's easiest virtues into a method; it is the mechanical operation of this method that produces the mass of *Death at Sea*—the poems pour out like sausages, automatic, voluptuous, and essentially indistinguishable.[14]

This is vitriolic stuff—reading it one can understand why Conrad Aiken was driven to describe Jarrell as 'offensive', 'completely irresponsible', and a 'smart-alec'.[15] What is most worrying about the Prokosch review is that Jarrell is not content with sacrificing Prokosch to Auden, but is inexorably drawn towards attacking Auden as well: thus, Auden is set up as a paragon, but he is a paragon of vices—his 'intelligence' and 'sensibility' are 'odd', they 'adulterate' his 'laxest' pages.

Jarrell's long-awaited sublimation of his ambivalent feelings was 'Changes of Attitude and Rhetoric in Auden's Poetry', a 23-page long article finally published in *The Southern Review* in Autumn 1941.[16] The article is a description and analysis of Auden's development from *Poems* to *Another Time*. Jarrell divides the work into two halves—the early (good) part and the late (bad) part—and catalogues Auden's changing repertoire of linguistic and rhetorical effects, relating them to his changing attitudes towards society, death, evil, and human nature. In an article published four years later—'Freud to Paul: The Stages of Auden's Ideology'—Jarrell redistributed Auden's work into three parts, and charted the evolution of his ideas in relation to a

[13] For an account of the controversy, see Pritchard, *Literary Life*, 84–5.

[14] 'Poets: Old, New, and Aging', *The New Republic* (9 Dec. 1940); repr. in *Kipling, Auden & Co.*, 45.

[15] *Selected Letters of Conrad Aiken* (New Haven, Conn., 1978), 287.

[16] Repr. in Jarrell, *The Third Book of Criticism* (London, 1975), 115–50. (The US edn. of *Third Book* was published in 1969.)

different set of 'organizing forces': 'anxiety, guilt, and isolation—fused
or not yet separated in a sort of sexual authoritarian matrix'.[17] The
essays now form part of the foundations of the systematic theology of
the Auden canon, as John Boly has pointed out in a discussion of
'Freud to Paul': 'Jarrell's argument may be the most influential criticism ever written about Auden. Its idea of a three-step development,
from personal, to social, and then back to personal (religious) concerns, has furnished a framework that both Auden's defenders and
detractors have been obliged to accept.'[18] Primarily and more impor-
tantly, however, Jarrell's arguments are a rationalization of his own
disturbed and deeply felt attraction to Auden as writer and thinker.

Together with his reviews, 'Changes' and 'Freud to Paul' constitute
the bulk of Jarrell's published criticism on Auden.[19] The essays are
impressive for their precise and exhaustive listing of particular effects,
their explanatory and explicit tone, their empathetic descriptions of
the workings of the poems, and the extremely subtle manipulation of
psychological and political contexts. But what is truly extraordinary
about them is that they despair of what they have so lovingly and
carefully described—Jarrell ends up mocking Auden's poetic capacities:
'Auden was like someone who keeps showing how well he can hold his
liquor until he becomes a drunkard . . . he is like a man who will
drink canned heat, rubbing alcohol, anything.'[20] In 'Changes' Jarrell
tries to justify his criticism in a pious and half-apologetic conclusion:
'An essay like this may seem an ungrateful return for all the good
poetry Auden has written . . . But analyses, even unkind analyses of
faults, are one way of showing appreciation; and I hope at another
time to try another way.'[21] But when he does try another way in
'Freud to Paul' he is even more unkind and goes beyond censoring
and censoriousness; the essay amounts to what Karl Shapiro called a
'massive attack',[22] ending in a flurry of accusations and a *coup de grâce*
(in which Auden is condemned for his 'moral imbecility' and 'hysterical blindness') that is based on Jarrell's seemingly wilful misreading
and misrepresentation of a remark by Auden in a review of a book of
Grimms' fairy-tales. What Auden wrote was this:

[17] 'Freud to Paul: The Stages of Auden's Ideology', *Partisan Review* (Fall 1945);
repr. in *Third Book*, see 162.
[18] John R. Boly, *Reading Auden* (Ithaca, NY, 1991), 40.
[19] For a complete list of Jarrell's articles on Auden, see Appendix, p.288.
[20] *Third Book*, 137–8.
[21] *Third Book*, 150.
[22] *Randall Jarrell* (Washington, 1967), 8.

So let everyone read these stories till they know them backward and tell them to their children with embellishments—they are not sacred texts—and then, in a few years, the Society for the Scientific Diet, the Association of Positivist Parents, the League for the Promotion of Worthwhile Leisure, the Coöperative Camp for Prudent Progressives and all other bores and scoundrels can go jump in the lake.[23]

Jarrell responds:

Such a sentence shows that its writer has saved his own soul, but has lost the whole world—has forgotten even the nature of that world: for this was written, not in 1913, but within the months that held the mass executions in the German camps, the fire raids, Warsaw and Dresden and Manila; within the months that were preparing the bombs for Hiroshima and Nagasaki; within the last twelve months of the Second World War . . . In the year 1944 these prudent, progressive, scientific, cooperative 'bores and scoundrels' were the enemies with whom Auden found it necessary to struggle. Were *these* your enemies reader? They were not mine.

Auden, according to Jarrell, had let the side down. Jarrell had enlisted in the army in October 1942 and although he never saw active service he immediately embraced war as a subject for his poetry and began to fashion himself as a war poet.[24] Auden was not alone in being criticized by Jarrell for not sharing his perspective on the war—Marianne Moore also came under attack[25]—but the severity of the criticism is unusual: Jarrell's judgement is far in excess of the evidence, and he refuses to take Auden's comments for what they are—journalistic bluster.

   Auden knew exactly what to make of all this: 'Randall Jarrell is really just trying to flout Papa,' he grumbled to Alan Ansen after the publication of 'Freud to Paul'.[26] Another account of his reaction to Jarrell's criticism has him saying to Stephen Spender, 'Jarrell is in love with me.'[27] Auden realized that the war issue had merely provided an excuse for Jarrell, a focus for his confused emotions. Auden's insights draw of course on Freud's theory of the Oedipus

[23] Auden's review, 'In Praise of the Brothers Grimm', appeared in *The New York Times*, 12 Nov. 1944, sect. 7, p. 28. It is quoted with Jarrell's response, in *Third Book*, 186–7.

[24] See Pritchard, *Literary Life*, ch. 4, 'In Service'.

[25] See 'Poetry in War and Peace', *Partisan Review* (Winter 1945); repr. in *Kipling, Auden & Co.*, 128–30.

[26] Ansen, 19.

[27] Quoted in Eileen Simpson, *Poets in their Youth: A Memoir* (New York, 1982), 110.

complex: 'The relation of a boy to his father is, as we say, an "ambivalent" one. In addition to the hate which seeks to get rid of the father as a rival, a measure of tenderness for him is also habitually present. The two attitudes of mind combine to produce identification with the father'.[28] Jarrell's relation to Auden was analogous to the archetypal family relationship here described by Freud; in other words, Auden got it right—Jarrell did regard him as a father-figure and both loved and hated him. According to Pritchard's biography, Jarrell's relationship with his real father was troubled; Jarrell's parents had divorced when he was ten years old, and apart from a year's stay with his paternal grandparents he lived with his mother until he was 24. Pritchard suggests that the young Jarrell had enjoyed a 'warm relationship' with his father, but also points out that 'he figures in his son's poetry only by his absence' and that Jarrell himself believed that the lack of a father-figure had been 'a determinative condition of his childhood'.[29] Jarrell's relationships in later life with various role-models and surrogate father-figures seem to have involved a large degree of transference of his ambivalent feelings about his absent father. Jarrell always tended to idolize and identify with other writers, for example Denis Donoghue claims that 'his reading of favorite poets was so devoted that he seemed to think his response a paltry effort until he had almost made himself over in their image',[30] a notion that finds startling corroboration from Jarrell's wife Mary's account of his disconcerting habit of literally making himself over into his heroes' images:

When he discovered Freud's birthday was the same as his, we stopped calling it his and celebrated Freud's. When some guests mistook our small framed picture of Chekhov for Randall's father, Randall sighed after they had gone . . . 'People, *people*! Is there no limit to what people don't know?' But before we went to bed that night, he took a long look at Chekhov's picture and a long look at himself in the mirror. 'You know what?' he said. 'What?' I said. 'If you blur your eyes . . .' And I said, 'It's so Randall. It's so.' And with that he made up his mind to have a beard.[31]

As well as going to extraordinary lengths to emulate his heroes Jarrell also often turned against those he most admired. Allen Tate was one mentor who fell from grace—he recalled that 'For an inscrutable reason . . . he liked me very much for some years around 1940, but not

[28] Freud, 'Dostoevsky and Parricide' (1927), *SE*, vol. 21, 183.
[29] Pritchard, *Literary Life*, 12 and 14.
[30] Lowell *et al.*, *Randall Jarrell 1914–65*, 60.   [31] Ibid. 278.

much later on'[32]—but it was undoubtedly Auden who for various reasons felt the full force of Jarrell's subcontrary Oedipal urges.

Jarrell did not dislike Auden, in the way, say, that he grew to dislike R. P. Blackmur;[33] in fact he maintained great personal respect and admiration for Auden. They met on at least three separate occasions—at the infamous Gotham Book Mart photo session in 1948; at the Gauss Seminars in Princeton during 1951 (the following year Jarrell gave a number of lectures on Auden—which Auden did not attend—as part of this seminar series); and at a poetry reading in 1958—and Jarrell recalled each meeting with affection: 'he looks like a disenchanted lion' he told his wife Mary in 1951, 'He was awfully nice.'[34] The simultaneous presence of affectionate and hostile feelings in Jarrell's attitude towards Auden is in general typical of the contradictions of his psychological make-up. The hostility towards Auden in his essays and reviews is in particular an indication of his realization that Auden could no longer be looked up to as a literary hero and role-model. Quite simply, Jarrell had come to realize that Auden was changing, that he was growing up and growing old—as is clear even from their titles, his essays on Auden are predicated on the idea of mutability: '*Changes* of Attitude and Rhetoric . . .', 'Freud to Paul: The *Stages* of Auden's Ideology'. (Interestingly, Jarrell's recollections of meeting Auden often involve comment on how old Auden looked and many of his complaints about Auden imply some hint of disquiet about his ageing: Auden was becoming a fuddy-duddy, he told Lowell, a 'sit-by-the-fire-do-my-embroidery' kind of poet.[35]) Jarrell himself was depressed by the prospect of growing old—his mental breakdown coincided with the approach of his fiftieth birthday—and intimations of mortality continually punctuate and puncture his poetry, which yearns for the lost world of childhood, when family relations were straightforward, the time before life became confusing and disappointing—'that calm country | Through which the stream of my life first meandered'.[36]

What made Auden's ageing and changing difficult for Jarrell to accept—indeed what motivated his love and hate for Auden—was that he had so closely modelled his literary self on the example of early

---

[32] Lowell *et al.*, *Randall Jarrell 1914–65*, 232.

[33] Jarrell admired Blackmur's work but regarded him as personally repellent: see Pritchard, *Literary Life*, 204–5.

[34] *Letters*, 287. For details of the Gauss Seminars, see Appendix, p. 288.

[35] *Letters*, 404.

[36] 'Thinking of the Lost World', *The Lost World* (New York, 1965), 67.

Auden. In contrast to his forthright and abundant critical pronounce-
ments on Auden, Jarrell remained conspicuously silent about Auden's
influence on his own creative work and when questioned directly
about Auden's influence impetuously denied it.[37] None the less, and
notwithstanding Bruce Bawer's recent (failed) attempt to disenfran-
chise him of his Auden inheritance, it has been generally believed by
critics that Auden was an important influence on Jarrell's poetry, and
generally agreed that this influence wore off after Jarrell's first volume, *Blood for a Stranger* (1942).[38] Robert Fitzgerald, in his 1948
review of Jarrell's third volume *Losses*, was one of the first to plot this
notional curve of Jarrell's development away from Auden: 'I believe
he is the only poet of his generation who has been able to assimilate,
use and thoroughly emerge from the bedazzlements of Auden's
verse.'[39] But Jarrell never 'thoroughly' emerged from the bedazzlements of Auden's verse—the shimmer of Auden's virtuoso technique
continued to attract and influence him, and he clung on tenaciously to
those aspects of Auden's work which he had first admired.

M. L. Rosenthal rightly detects what he calls 'Auden-static'[40] in
Jarrell and there are Audenesque crackles and pops in every one of
Jarrell's volumes. These imitative noises vary from the level of pho-
netics (echoes of Auden's consonance and rhyme from 'Love by
ambition' in Jarrell's 'Because of me, because of you': 'Love by
ambition | Of definition | Suffers partition' resounds in 'The star's
distention, the detonation | Of the instant and endless colloca-
tion'),[41] to the level of phraseology (the world-weariness of Jarrell's
'To sit on a chair, to eat from a table . . . It's a way' in 'Scherzo' is
borrowed from Auden's 'Certainly our city', which concludes 'It's a
world. It's a way.')[42] And many commentators have remarked on
Jarrell's use of the characteristic scenery and rhetoric of Auden's
Thirties poetry (literal and metaphoric frontiers, the alienation complex of the omniscient stranger), elements which are clearly in evi-

---

[37] See Pritchard, *Literary Life*, 44.

[38] See Bawer, *The Middle Generation* (Hamden, Conn., 1986), ch. 6, 'Jarrell and the
Influence of Auden'. Critics who acknowledge Auden's influence on Jarrell's early
poetry include Suzanne Ferguson in *The Poetry of Randall Jarrell* (Baton Rouge, 1971),
and M. L. Rosenthal, 'Randall Jarrell', in Denis Donoghue, ed., *Seven American Poets
from Macleish to Nemerov* (Minneapolis, 1975).

[39] *The New Republic*, 118.7 (26 Apr. 1948), 33.   [40] *Seven American Poets*, 134.

[41] *EA* 30; *Blood for a Stranger* (New York, 1942), 27.

[42] 'Scherzo' was first published in *Partisan Review* (Winter 1944), but was uncollected until *The Complete Poems* (London, 1971), 438; *EA* 166. (The US edn. of *The
Complete Poems* was published in 1969.)

dence in *Blood for a Stranger* in poems such as 'On the Railway Platform', 'When You and I Were All', 'Song Not There', and in political poems and ballads such as 'For the Madrid Road'. It seems Jarrell did know Auden by heart, practically—certainly, he had read, studied, and inwardly digested so much Auden that the language and ideas had become second nature to him. Hearing of the death of Freud in September 1939, for example, Jarrell wrote to Allen Tate, 'I felt quite funny after Freud died, it was like having a continent disappear.'[43] The choice of metaphor is more than felicitous—in 'Changes' Jarrell discusses at length 'a certain kind of spatial metaphor Auden uses for people', and quotes approvingly metaphors about Freud as a 'climate, weather', about the 'provinces' of Yeats's body, and Edward Lear's becoming a 'land'.[44] This particular kind of metaphor obviously made a big impression on Jarrell—as well as the letter to Tate it appears in several of his poems, including the grue-some 'La Belle au Bois Dormant'.[45] Auden's more unusual rhythmic structures also seem to have persisted and droned on in Jarrell's mind, for they crop up intermittently throughout his work. In 'New Year Letter' Auden has a passage in which 'Woman, passive as in dreams, | Redeems, redeems, redeems, redeems'; Jarrell chimes on the repetition in *Little Friend, Little Friend* in his poem 'Siegfried': 'the old, old dream: *it happens,* | *It happens as it does, it does, it does*—'.[46] (The contrast between Auden's reiterated 'redeems', sug-gesting a cycle of renewal, and Jarrell's 'it does', suggesting the weight of inevitability, opens up the world of difference that lies between Auden's Christianity and Jarrell's fatalism.) Something simi-lar occurs in *The Seven-League Crutches* in 'An English Garden in Austria' at the moment when Jarrell asks, dramatically, 'And how shall we bear it?' and the answer comes wafting over from 'At the Grave of Henry James':

> Then there is silence; a soft floating sigh.
> *Heut' oder morgen kommt der Tag,*
> And how shall we bear it?
> Lightly, lightly.

---

[43] *Letters*, 24.   [44] *Third Book*, 144.
[45] *The Seven-League Crutches* (New York, 1951), 77.
[46] *NYL* 66; *CP91* 236. *Little Friend, Little Friend* (New York, 1945), 21.

Auden had written:

> Lightly, lightly, then, may I dance
> Over the frontier of the obvious . . .[47]

Such snatches from Auden occasionally provide the key to inter-
pretive puzzles in Jarrell. The poem 'Jerome', in *The Woman at the
Washington Zoo* begins teasingly, 'Each day brings its toad, each night
its dragon',[48] and the line has troubled and fascinated readers, as
Jarrell's wife explains: 'This line has prompted a number of people to
ask me, or write me, for its "source". Is it Goethe? Is it Milton? Is it
Shakespeare? Is it Psalms? Is it Greek? Until I was wondering myself,
what *is* its source?'[49] The probable source is a passage in 'New Year
Letter':

> the heart,
> As ZOLA said, must always start
> The day by swallowing its toad
> Of failure and disgust.

(Though Auden got his own source wrong—the toads come from
Chamfort, not Zola—the reference turns up, correctly attributed, in
his *Book of Aphorisms*.)[50]

It is worth pointing out in passing that snatches of Jarrell can also
help explain enigmas in Auden. Auden famously revised 'September
1, 1939', altering the line 'We must love one another or die' to 'We
must love one another and die', and he justified his revision in his
Foreword to Bloomfield's *Bibliography*: 'Rereading a poem of mine,
"1st September, 1939", after it had been published, I came to the line
"We must love one another or die" and said to myself: "That's a
damned lie! We must die anyway." So, in the next edition, I altered it
to "We must love one another and die".'[51] Auden's brisk, no-
nonsense explanation purposefully overlooks the crises in his own life
and in world events that had affected his decision to revise. What he
left more tellingly unremarked is that the change of 'or' to 'and' finds

[47] *The Seven-League Crutches*, 21. Auden, *Collected Shorter Poems 1930–1944*
(London, 1950), 141; he later dropped the lines.
[48] *The Woman at the Washington Zoo* (New York, 1960), 61.
[49] *Jerome: The Biography of a Poem* (New York, 1971), 10.
[50] *NYL* 72; *CP91* 241. The citation in *The Faber Book of Aphorisms* (London,
1965), 18, reads: 'A man must swallow a toad every morning if he wishes to be sure of
finding nothing still more disgusting before the day is over.'
[51] B. C. Bloomfield, *W. H. Auden: A Bibliography* (Charlottesville, Va., 1964), p.
viii.

a prompt in various sources, including Jarrell. Auden's crucial revision appeared in 1955, when 'September 1, 1939' was reprinted in Oscar Williams's *The New Pocket Anthology of American Verse*. A year previously Jarrell had published *Pictures from an Institution*, which had been an instant critical and commercial success.[52] In chapter 4 of the novel, 'Constance and the Rosenbaums', Jarrell wrote:

Flo Whittaker had once gently reproved Dr. Rosenbaum for his attitude toward politics. She had done so by quoting to him, in tones that rather made for righteousness, a line of poetry that she had often seen quoted in this connection: 'We must love one another or die.' Dr. Rosenbaum replied: 'We must love one another *and* die.'[53]

Auden was never too proud to borrow or steal, and he may well have owed something to Dr Rosenbaum's wisdom (equally, he may have owed something to Cyril Connolly, who had first suggested the change some years previously[54]).

In 'Freud to Paul' Jarrell had expressed his preference for the 'Old Auden, the Ur-Auden', with his deterministic view of human development, his 'narrative morality', his identification of the Mother as a figure of authority, and his 'Freudian view of ontogenetic development as an unaccountably faithful recapitulation of phylogenetic development.'[55] The post-Freudian thrust of Auden's later work was perhaps the greatest disappointment to Jarrell, who had adopted with enthusiasm Auden's brand of Freudianism, with its peculiar emphases and elaborations. In *Blood for a Stranger*, for example, he had imagined the traumas of birth in 'A Little Poem', in which a speaker remembers how in the womb 'My brother was a fish', and recalls the moment when 'my gills began to fall', being born, and shouting to his brother ' "O go back!" '[56] The longing for a return to the womb is standard Freudian stuff—in *Civilisation and Its Discontents* (1930) Freud described how 'the dwelling-house was a substitute for the mother's womb, the first lodging, for which in all likelihood man still longs, and in which he was safe and felt at ease.'[57] But the dependent image of the primal organism as a fish seems to be garnered from cryptic references in Auden's 'To ask the hard question is simple' and 'It's no use raising a shout': 'In my veins there is a wish | And a

---

[52] The first edition went through three printings within four months and several chapters had already appeared in periodicals and magazines before book publication.

[53] *Pictures from an Institution*, 173–4.   [54] See *Libretti*, 739.

[55] *Third Book*, 153, 154, 165, 167.   [56] *Blood for a Stranger*, 11–12.

[57] *SE*, vol. 21, 91.

memory of fish'; 'Shall memory restore | The steps and the shore
. . . Shall the fish dive'.[58] Jarrell borrowed from the 'Old Auden' a
range of theories loosely derived from Freud and Groddeck and they
became a mainstay of his work—the malevolent and murderous
mother-figure from *The Ascent of F6* and *The Orators* is a recurrent
feature in Jarrell (it is essential, for example, to 'Mother, said the
Child', 'The Difficult Resolution', and 'The House in the Wood'),[59]
and the exemplary use of fairy-tale elements to objectify psychological
states, a contrivance pioneered by Auden in 'The Quest', became a
dominant mode in Jarrell in poems such as 'The Märchen' and
'Cinderella'.[60]

Jarrell's final encounter and confrontation with Auden came in his
last collection, *The Lost World*, in the poem 'The Old and the New
Masters'. During the final ten to fifteen years of his life Jarrell
became more self-sufficient as a poet and critic, becoming more
confident in his own poetic voice and relying less on his opinions
about Auden to see him through. As early as 1951 he had been genuinely surprised and a little wistful when John Berryman had brought
up the subject of his 1940s essays on Auden: 'Berryman was very
complimentary about my (long past now) Auden pieces.'[61] He did,
however, remain professionally involved with Auden's work, giving
the six lectures on Auden at the Princeton seminars in 1952, and
often reading Auden's poetry on the ever expanding poetry-reading
circuit.[62] Given the long and complex history of Jarrell's involvement
with Auden, it is surprising that it was not until the very end of his
career that he carried over an argument with Auden into verse
(though he had, early on, written an out-and-out parody, 'Auden's
Popular Song Style', published in the Vanderbilt University student
literary magazine *Pursuit* in 1938).[63] Jarrell's apparent reticence in
confronting Auden was perhaps owing to the strong influence Auden
continued to exert over his verse. Ironically, even at this late stage,
when Jarrell most strongly asserts his disagreement and dissatisfaction
with Auden, he still finds himself drawn towards approbation and
accord. 'The Old and the New Masters' begins:

[58] *EA* 43 and 55.

[59] *Little Friend, Little Friend*, 41–3, and 22; *The Lost World*, 53–4.

[60] *Losses*, 41–4; *The Woman at the Washington Zoo*, 4–5.   [61] *Letters*, 278.

[62] In a letter to Karl Shapiro in 1956 Jarrell refers to his habit of reading Auden's
poems on his West Coast poetry-reading tours: *Letters*, 417.

[63] Listed by Stuart Wright in *Randall Jarrell: A Descriptive Bibliography 1929–1983*
(Charlottesville, Va., 1986), 225.

> About suffering, about adoration, the old masters
> Disagree. When someone suffers, no one else eats
> Or walks or opens the window—no one breathes
> As the sufferers watch the sufferer.

This is flouting of the first order—it is a rebuttal of Auden's 'Musée des Beaux Arts':

> About suffering they were never wrong,
> The Old Masters: how well they understood
> Its human position; how it takes place
> While someone else is eating or opening a window or just walking
>   dully along.[64]

Jarrell goes on to provide a long, detailed analysis of two paintings which refute Auden's point about the habitude of suffering. His final stanza, however, swings round, and comes into near complete agreement with the conclusion to Auden's poem:

> After a while the masters show the crucifixion
> In one corner of the canvas: the men come to see
> What is important, see that it is not important.
> The new masters paint a subject as they please,
> And Veronese is prosecuted by the Inquisition
> For the dogs playing at the feet of Christ,
> The earth is a planet among galaxies.
> Later Christ disappears, the dogs disappear: in abstract
> Understanding, without adoration, the last master puts
> Colors on canvas, a picture of the universe
> In which a bright spot somewhere in the corner
> Is the small radioactive planet men called Earth.[65]

Jarrell's lament that men 'come to see | What is important, see that it is not important', and his dismay that the last master paints 'without adoration' sharply refocuses Auden's pitying observation of Brueghel's ploughman to whom 'it was not an important failure' that Icarus falls, and of the indifference of the ship, which 'must have seen | Something amazing' yet sailed on:

> In Brueghel's *Icarus*, for instance: how everything turns away
> Quite leisurely from the disaster; the ploughman may
> Have heard the splash, the forsaken cry,
> But for him it was not an important failure; the sun shone

---

[64] *EA* 237.   [65] *The Lost World*, 63–4.

As it had to on the white legs disappearing into the green
Water; and the expensive delicate ship that must have seen
Something amazing, a boy falling out of the sky,
Had somewhere to get to and sailed calmly on.

Auden's poem implies that it is a moral failure on the part of the ploughman and of the ship not to notice suffering. Jarrell draws out this implication into an indictment. In Auden, Icarus disappears, is ignored; in Jarrell, Christ 'disappears', is painted out of the picture. 'The Old and the New Masters' thus begins as a rebuttal but turns into a rewrite of 'Musée des Beaux Arts'—as Suzanne Ferguson points out: 'Auden's conception of "indifference" in the old masters and Jarrell's of "abstract understanding" in the new finally come to almost the same thing.'[66] The poem demonstrates Jarrell's profound dependence on Auden as a role-model and father-figure who must be resisted but who cannot be denied. Jarrell, in the end, was inexorably and indubitably bound to Auden: 'If you would like to see the most accomplished poet alive doing as he pleases, buy W. H. Auden's *The Shield of Achilles*' he recommended in 1955,

A few of the poems are good, and all of them are brilliant, self-indulgent, marvelously individual . . . *Nones* was a better book, but this one is worth reading; Auden's laundry list would be worth reading—I speak as one who's read it many times, all rhymed and metered. After all—this is the point people rarely make—when Homer nods it's quite a performance.[67]

And this is another point people rarely make—the drama of Jarrell's encounter with Auden was more than a performance and remains exemplary in its absolute, questioning loyalty.

[66] Ferguson, *Poetry of Jarrell*, 197.
[67] 'The Year in Poetry', *Harper's* (Oct. 1955); repr. in *Kipling, Auden & Co.*, 246.

Appendix: Jarrell's Articles on Auden

1940   Review of *Another Time*: 'Poetry in a Dry Season', *Partisan Review* (Mar.–Apr. 1940), repr. in Jarrell, *Kipling, Auden & Co.* (New York, 1980), 33–7.

1941   Review of *The Double Man*: 'New Year Letter', *The Nation* (12 Apr. 1941), repr. in *Kipling, Auden & Co.*, 55–7.

       'Changes of Attitude and Rhetoric in Auden's Poetry', *The Southern Review* (Autumn 1941), repr. in *The Third Book of Criticism* (London, 1975), 115–50.

1945   'Freud to Paul: The Stages of Auden's Ideology', *Partisan Review* (Fall 1945), repr. in *Third Book*, 153–87.

1947   Review of *The Age of Anxiety*, *The Nation* (18 Oct. 1947), repr. in *Kipling, Auden & Co.*, 145–6.

1955   Review of *The Shield of Achilles*: 'Recent Poetry', *The Yale Review* (Summer 1955), repr. in *Kipling, Auden & Co.*, 221–30.

       Review of *The Shield of Achilles*: 'The Year in Poetry', *Harper's* (Oct. 1955), repr. in *Kipling, Auden & Co.*, 242–7.

There also seems to have been much material that was not published: in a letter to Elisabeth Eisler in Jan. 1949 Jarrell claimed, 'Mostly I've been writing prose about Auden, when I've written anything' (*Randall Jarrell's Letters*, ed. Mary Jarrell (London, 1986), 216). Some of this material was undoubtedly incorporated into Jarrell's six two-hour lectures on Auden given at Princeton as the Christian Gauss Seminars in 1952. Jarrell's notes for these seminars survive only in draft form in the Berg Collection—they show that Jarrell had not significantly altered his position as stated in 'Changes' and 'Freud to Paul' (see William H. Pritchard, *Randall Jarrell: A Literary Life* (New York, 1990), 229–31). Jarrell also seems to have intended more than he could achieve: a note to 'Freud to Paul' when it first appeared in *Partisan Review*, reads '(This essay by Randall Jarrell is a section from a longer study of Auden. Another section will appear in *Partisan Review* in the near future.)' This other section never appeared. There is also a poignant prefatory 'Note' to *The Third Book of Criticism*: 'Not long before he died, Randall Jarrell wrote out by hand a list headed "3rd criticism book." He did not live to write two of the essays he listed, "The Best of Auden" and one on *The Three Sisters*' (p. ix).

Published Letters by W. H. Auden:
A Bibliography

EDWARD MENDELSON

THIS is a list of books, periodicals, and sale catalogues that quote or describe letters that Auden did not intend for publication. It replaces the corresponding section in *W. H. Auden: A Bibliography 1924–1969*, 2nd edn. (Charlottesville, Va., 1972), compiled by B. C. Bloomfield and Edward Mendelson. Letters that Auden intended for publication are listed in section **C** of the *Bibliography* and in the supplement to the *Bibliography* printed in the first volume of *Auden Studies*. Letters written as blurbs for book jackets will be listed in a future volume of *Auden Studies*.

This list is limited to publications that quote from Auden's letters or reliably paraphrase or infer their contents. It excludes items that merely reprint letters or parts of letters quoted in earlier publications.

At least two of the items listed below (**H1** and **H46**) may have been intended for publication, but I have preferred to err on the side of inclusiveness. Many items in booksellers' catalogues have inevitably escaped notice, and a complete list would undoubtedly be somewhat longer than this one. I have omitted references to the printed invitations that Auden sent out a few weeks before the parties that he occasionally held on his birthday, 21 February. He had at least seven sets of invitations printed, one for 1955 and one for each year from 1958 through 1963; the invitation for 1963 stated that the party was in joint celebration of Auden's birthday and the publication of Chester Kallman's *Absent and Present*. Copies of one or more of the invitations may be found in the Berg Collection of the New York Public Library, Columbia University Library, Yale University Library, and many other large libraries.

In some instances the notes below supplement or correct the information in the publications cited, especially where booksellers imperfectly deciphered Auden's hand. I have supplied some dates and recipients' names that were omitted or misreported in catalogues and other publications, although I have made no systematic effort to do so. Where I happened to remember the current locations of letters listed in auction catalogues, booksellers' catalogues, and a few other items, I have reported the locations. I have not reported the locations of letters when the work cited specifies their location. A few major collections have changed hands after they had already been mined for quotations. Auden's letters to E. R. Dodds, for example, are now in the Bodleian Library; almost all his letters to Stephen Spender and to James and Tania Stern are now in the Berg Collection.

As in the bibliographical supplements in earlier volumes of *Auden Studies*, I have used a simplified transcription of title-pages and have listed imprints in conventional style (place: publisher, date). As in the normal practice of descriptive bibliography, capitalization of titles has been reduced to the level of prose. The list is arranged by chronological sequence of publication, but undated catalogues follow books published in any one year, followed in turn by periodicals and dated catalogues. A few items that I have seen only in the form of press cuttings are listed without page references.

Many friends and colleagues have contributed to this list. Among those to whom I owe thanks are B. C. Bloomfield, Katherine Bucknell, Richard Davenport-Hines, John Fuller, George Hecksher, Nicholas Jenkins, and John Whitehead.

The compiler will be grateful for additions and corrections, which may be sent to him in care of the Department of English, 602 Philosophy Hall, Columbia University, New York, New York 10027.

H1 School notes. *St. Edmund's School chronicle*, 7. 10 (Mar. 1921), 162.

'From Auden we have heard that he is enjoying [Gresham's School] Holt very much. He says:—"The buildings are excellent and also the teaching. We all have studies. Your first few terms you share with three others, then less, and finally you get a single study. John [Auden] (1915–1917) is in the Science VIth at Marlborough. He has just joined the English Literature Society and enjoys it very much."'

H2 Erika and Klaus Mann. *Escape to life*. Boston: Houghton Mifflin, 1939.

Three sentences from a letter to Erika Mann about his plans to go to Spain, [?late 1936], p. 163. In the German edition based on the original manuscript, *Escape to life: deutsche Kultur im Exil* (München: Spangenberg, 1991), p. 183.

H3 Margaret Church. For this is Orpheus: or, Rilke, Auden and Spender. M.A. diss., Columbia University, 1942.

Letter to Church about German influences, 12 Nov. 1941, p. iii.

H4 Malcolm Cowley. Auden's versification. *Poetry*, 65. 6 (Mar. 1945), 345.

Indirect quotation on verse forms in 'The sea and the mirror'.

H5 Cecil E. Hinkel. A production study and text of the Auden and Isherwood *The ascent of F6* as presented at Catholic University. M.F.A. diss., Catholic University, 1947.

Letter to Hinkel about productions of the play, 17 Feb. 1947, p. 36 in appendix.

H6 Kenneth Lewars. The quest in Auden's poems and plays. M.A. diss., Columbia University, 1947.

Extracts from a letter to Lewars on the quest theme and his conversion, 17 Sept. 1947, pp. 3, 19, 104.

H7 Exhibition shows how a book is born. *New York times*, 9 Dec. 1950, p. 13.

Description of a letter to a printer pointing out that a line from 'Precious five' had been omitted, and of the manuscript with the line missing; from an exhibit at the American Academy of Arts and Letters.

H8 *Poesie di W. H. Auden*, introduzione, versione, e note di Carlo Izzo. Parma: Guanda, 1952.

Brief extracts from letters to Izzo, 10 Dec. 1951 and 9 Apr. 1952, about details in the poems, pp. xxiv, 218–19, 221–6, 228–9.

H9 Daniel G. Hoffman. *Paul Bunyan: last of the frontier demigods*. Philadelphia: University of Pennsylvania Press for Temple University Publications, 1952.

Brief extract from a letter to Hoffman, 17 Jan. 1949, on *Paul Bunyan*, p. 144. Reprinted from Hoffman's dissertation of the same title (M.A., Columbia University, 1949), p. 178.

H10 House of Books, Ltd. First editions . . . [catalogue]. New York, [?1952].

Paraphrase of a letter to Mrs Kuratt about possible changes to new editions of *Poems* and *The orators*, 16 Aug. [1932], p. 3 (now at the State University of New York at Buffalo).

H11 John Lehmann. *The whispering gallery: autobiography I*. London: Longmans Green, 1955.

Extract from a reader's report for *New writing* about the influence of Hopkins, p. 329 (also quoted in **H126**). Reprinted in Lehmann's *In my own time* (Boston: Little, Brown, An Atlantic Monthly Press Book, 1969), pp. 221–2.

H12 W. H. Auden. Tre poesie. *Prospetti*, Firenze, 14 (Spring 1955), 24–5.

Extract in Italian from a letter to one of the translators (E. B. or C. T.) about 'The old man's road', Oct. 1955.

H13 Frank Hollings Bookshop. First editions . . ., catalogue no. 259. London, 1957.

Extract from a letter to Geoffrey Grigson noting two corrections in the 'poem I sent you', 28 Jan. 1934, p. 1.

H14 John Willett. *The theatre of Bertolt Brecht: a study from eight aspects*. London: Methuen, 1959.

Extract from a letter to Willett about Brecht, p. 220.

H15 Una lettera di W. H. Auden. *Studi americani*, 5 (1959), 383.

Letter to Carlo Izzo, 9 Apr. 1952, about *The scarlet letter* as opera.

H16 House of Books, Ltd. First editions . . . [catalogue]. New York, [1959].

Brief extract from a letter to Mr Mais about school books, 4 Dec. 1934, p. 3 (now at HRC).

H17 John Pudney. *Home and away: an autobiographical gambit*. London: Michael Joseph, 1960.

Extracts from letters to Pudney [18 Sept. 1932] with advice on literature, p. 72, and [28 July 1932], about group-life and sexual attitudes, p. 206. Both quotations are reprinted in his *Thank goodness for cake* (London: Michael Joseph, 1978), p. 50.

H18 Igor Stravinsky and Robert Craft. *Memories and commentaries*. Garden City, NY: Doubleday, 1960.

Twelve letters and telegrams to Stravinsky about *The rake's progress* 1947–51, pp. 145–54 (also partly quoted in **H287**). Also in the English edition (London: Faber & Faber, 1960), pp. 155–66. The book was reprinted in *Stravinsky in conversation with Robert Craft* (Harmondsworth: Penguin, 1962). Includes letters not published in **H164**.

H19 Richard J. Beckley. Some aspects of Brecht's dramatic techniques in light of his adaptations of English plays. M.A. diss., University of London, King's College, 1961.

Paraphrase of a letter to Beckley reporting that in *The duchess of Malfi* 'Brecht's part in the adaptation was very slight', 16 Jan. 1960, p. 45.

H20 House of Books, Ltd. First editions . . . [catalogue]. New York, [1961].

Paraphrase of a letter contributing 'The sabbath' to a periodical, 30 July [?1959], p. 3.

H21 Michael Davidson. *The world, the flesh and myself*. London: Arthur Barker, 1962.
Vague account of letters to Davidson, 1923–4, pp. 127–30.

H22 Monroe K. Spears. *The poetry of W. H. Auden: the disenchanted island*. New York: Oxford University Press, 1963.
Extracts from five letters to Spears, 19 Mar. 1962–11 May 1963, about his poems, pp. 20, 157, 246, 271, 340, 341; indirect quotations, pp. 153, 218, 230, 241.

H23 B. C. Bloomfield. *W. H. Auden: a bibliography*. Charlottesville: University Press of Virginia, 1964.
Extract from a letter to T. S. Eliot about Frederic Prokosch's 1933 pamphlet *Poem*, p. 11 (also quoted in **H63**).

H24 *A creative century: selections from the twentieth century collections at the University of Texas, an exhibition held in November 1964 at the Academic Center & Undergraduate Library: The University of Texas*. Austin: Humanities Research Center, The University of Texas, 1964.
Letter to Lee Hollander, 17 Feb. 1947, about Skaldic poetry, pp. 7, 9.

H25 William Channing West. Concepts of reality in the poetic drama of W. B. Yeats, W. H. Auden, and T. S. Eliot. Ph.D. diss., Stanford University, 1964.
Brief extracts from a letter to West about his visits to Berlin, 26 Jan. 1963, pp. 91, 108.

H26 Parke-Bernet Galleries. Sale no. 2254: from the collections of the late Philip Ward, Jr. . . . [catalogue]. New York, 11 Feb. 1964.
Extracts from social notes to Mr Dewar, 21 Mar. 1940, and to Harry Brown, [?1946].

H27 W. H. Auden. *Poezija*. Zagreb: Mladost, 1964 [for 1965].
Extracts from a letter to the translator Tomislav Sabljak about details in the poems, 30 Mar. 1964, pp. 100–1.

H28 Hugh D. Ford. *A poet's war: British poets and the Spanish Civil War*. Philadelphia: University of Pennsylvania Press, 1965.
Brief extract from a letter to Ford about his visit to Spain, 29 Nov. 1962, p. 288.

H29 Frank MacShane. *The life and work of Ford Madox Ford*. London: Routledge & Kegan Paul, 1965.
Brief extract from a letter to Ford, p. 257.

H30 *Opere poetiche di W. H. Auden*, volume primo . . . Milano: Lerici, 1966.

Italian translation of an extract from a letter to the translator Aurora Ciliberti, Sept. 1965, about revisions, p. 9 (also quoted in **H256**).

H31 William J. Bruehl. The Auden/Isherwood plays. Ph.D. diss., University of Pennsylvania, 1966.

Brief extracts from a letter to Bruehl about the composition of the plays, 18 Mar. 1965, pp. 20, 29, 67, 105, 106; indirect quotations, pp. 54, 153, 232.

H32 John M. Muste. *Say that we saw Spain die: literary consequences of the Spanish Civil War.* Seattle: University of Washington Press, 1966.

Brief extract from a letter to Muste, 3 Mar. 1966, p. 56.

H33 Peter Stansky and William Abrahams. *Journey to the frontier: Julian Bell & John Cornford: their lives and the 1930s.* London: Constable, 1966.

Letter to John Cornford about writing, 4 May 1932, pp. 173–4.

H34 *Master poems of the English language*, edited by Oscar Williams. New York: Trident Press, 1966.

Mark Schorer's introduction to 'September 1, 1939' reports the revision from 'or die' to 'and die' that Auden required when Williams asked to reprint the poem in his *The new pocket anthology of American verse* (1955), p. 1025.

H35 Breon Mitchell. W. H. Auden and Christopher Isherwood: the 'German influence'. *Oxford German studies*, 1 (1966), 163–72.

Brief extracts from a letter to Mitchell on the plays, pp. 165–6, 169–70.

H36 D. P. M. Michael. [Letter to the editor.] *Times literary supplement*, 10 Feb. 1966, p. 103.

Letter to Michael, 1958, about 'A shilling life'; partly quoted in another letter to the editor by Michael, 'A shilling life', *Sunday times*, 6 Apr. 1980, p. 12.

H37 [John Plotz.] Interview with W. H. Auden. *Island*, Cambridge, Mass., 2 (Spring 1966), 2–7.

Letter to Plotz about revisions, Jan. 1966, p. 7.

H38 Sotheby & Co. Catalogue of nineteenth century and modern first editions . . . London, 12 July 1966.

Descriptions of a letter to T. S. Eliot with a copy of *Poem* (printed by Frederic Prokosch), 1933 and of a letter to John Hayward accompanying *The dog beneath the skin*, 1935, p. 4; descriptions of postcards and letters to John Hayward, 1938 and 1950, p. 106 (also quoted in **H250**; now in the Berg Collection).

H39 Richard Ellmann. *Eminent domain: Yeats among Wilde, Joyce, Pound, Eliot and Auden.* New York: Oxford University Press, 1967.
Brief extract from a letter to Ellmann about magic, 20 Apr. 1967, p. 111.

H40 Paul C. Richards, Autographs. The Beacon bulletin 14 (catalogue no. 23). Brookline, Mass., [1967].
Brief extract from a letter to Leonard (?) about plans to join the G. P. O. Film Unit, [1935], p. 5.

H41 Carlo Izzo. 'Good-bye to the Mezzogiorno'. *Shenandoah*, 18. 2 (Winter 1967), 80–2.
Extracts from letters to Izzo about Izzo's translations, 22 Aug. 1950 and 8 July 1958.

H42 *Brian Howard, portrait of a failure*, edited by Marie-Jaqueline Lancaster. London: Anthony Blond, 1968.
Brief extract from a letter to Howard about poetry, [?1948], p. 493. A later reminiscence of Howard is quoted on p. ix.

H43 Sotheby & Co. Catalogue of nineteenth century and modern first editions . . . London, 8–9 July 1968.
Extract from a letter to Frederic Prokosch accompanying a gift of a notebook, p. 128 (now at HRC).

H44 Alan Hancox, Fine Books. Catalogue no. 114. Cheltenham, 1969.
Extracts from a letter to Geoffrey Grigson on a contribution to *New verse* and declining to write on Hopkins, 1935, item 10 (also quoted in **H51**; now at HRC); from a postcard to Grigson on his review of *The poet's tongue*, 2 July 1935, item 11 (also quoted in **H62**, **H78**, **H213**, **H276**; now at Wichita State University); and from a letter to Frederick Alderson on the name Wystan, 30 Mar. [1966], item 13 (also quoted in **H52** and printed in full in **H101**; now at Connecticut College).

H45 Howard S. Mott. Catalog 189. Sheffield, Mass., [1969].
Extract from a letter on engineering students and education, 3 June [1948], p. 3 (also quoted in **H53**).

H46 *The Penguin book of socialist verse*, edited with an introduction by Alan Bold. Harmondsworth: Penguin Books, 1970.
Extract from a letter to Bold on 'Spain', p. 60.

H47 *America's 85 greatest living authors present: this is my best in the third quarter of the century*, edited by Whit Burnett. Garden City, NY: Doubleday, 1970.
Undated letter declining to comment on the three poems he selected for this anthology, p. 470.

H48 Margrit Hahnloser-Ingold. *Das englische Theater und Bert Brecht.* Bern: Francke, 1970.

Extracts from a letter to Hahnloser-Ingold about Brecht's influence, 9 Aug. 1965, p. 87 (quoted in full in **H116**).

H49 Robert H. Black. Catalogue 125. Upper Montclair, NJ, [1970].

Quotation from a letter with bibliographical information on *Poems* (1928), 21 May 1947, p. 3 (also quoted in **H50, H129, H137, H166, H201**).

H50 House of Books, Ltd. First editions . . . [catalogue]. New York, [1970].

Paraphrase of a letter with bibliographical information about *Poems* (1928), 21 May 1947 (also quoted in **H49, H129, H137, H166, H201**), and a brief extract from a letter to Faber & Faber on his *Collected shorter poems 1927–1957*, 1966, p. 3.

H51 Kenneth W. Rendell, Inc. Autograph letters . . . , catalogue 48. Somerville, Mass., [1970].

Extract from a letter to Geoffrey Grigson on a contribution to *New verse* and declining to write on Hopkins, 1935, p. 3 (also quoted in **H44**; now at HRC).

H52 Paul C. Richards, Autographs. Catalogue no. 47. Brookline, Mass., [1970].

Extract from a letter to Frederick Alderson on the name Wystan, 30 Mar. [1966], p. 6 (also quoted in **H44** and printed in full in **H101**; now at Connecticut College).

H53 Paul C. Richards, Autographs. Catalogue no. 58. Brookline, Mass., [1970].

Extract from a letter on engineering students and education, 3 June [1948], p. 10 (also quoted in **H45**).

H54 Charles Hamilton. Auction number 46 . . . [catalogue]. New York, 10 Dec. 1970.

Extracts from letters to Gerald Sanders with information for use in Sanders's anthology *Chief modern poets of England and America*, 1940–1, p. 18 (the first of these also quoted in **H113** and now at Pennsylvania State University).

H55 *Cyril Connolly's one hundred modern books from England, France and America 1880–1950.* Catalogue by Mary Hirth . . . an exhibition: March–December 1971. Austin: The Humanities Research Center, The University of Texas at Austin, 1971.

Facsimile and text of first page of a letter on poetry to an unidentified recipient, 8 Nov. 1937, p. 85 (now at HRC; also quoted in **H288**).

H56 Alexis Levitin. A study in revision: W. H. Auden's A voyage and Sonnets from China. Ph.D. diss., Columbia University, 1971.

Quotations from a letter to Levitin, 8 Sept. 1971, on 'Sonnets from China', pp. 3, 38, 48, 140, and 151, and indirect quotation from a letter of 29 Sept. 1971 on the manuscript of 'City without walls', p. 21.

H27 Joel Roache. *Richard Eberhart: the progress of an American poet.* New York: Oxford University Press, 1971.

Extracts from a letter to Eberhart about Auden's stay at St Mark's School, [11 July 1939], pp. 105–6. First quoted in Roache's dissertation: Richard Eberhart: a poet in America 1904–1961. Ph.D. diss., University of Pennsylvania, 1967, p. 129.

H58 Radcliffe Squires. *Allen Tate: A Literary Biography.* New York: Pegasus, 1971.

Indirect quotation from a letter to Tate on one of Tate's poems, 19 Aug. [?1954], p. 207.

H59 Edd D. Wheeler. W. H. Auden and his American experience. Ph.D. diss., Emory University, 1971.

Extracts from a letter [to Richard Eberhart], 17 Apr. [1956], p. 143, and from a letter to Wheeler on his experience of America, 19 June 1970, pp. 3, 173.

H60 Kenneth W. Rendell, Inc. Autograph letters . . . , catalogue 55. Somerville, Mass., [1971].

Extract from a postcard to Eric Capan, apparently about a production of a play, 27 Nov. 1936, p. 5 (also quoted in **H114**).

H61 Paul C. Richards, Autographs. Autographs . . . , catalogue 65. Brookline, Mass., [1971].

Extract from a letter to James Butt on Auden's translations of Yugoslav children's poetry, 20 Jan. 1968, p. 13.

H62 Paul C. Richards, Autographs. Autographs . . . , catalogue 66. Brookline, Mass., [1971].

Extract from a postcard to Geoffrey Grigson on Grigson's review of *The poet's tongue*, 2 July 1935, p. 24 (also quoted in **H44**, **H78**, **H213**, **H276**; now at Wichita State University).

H63 B. C. Bloomfield and Edward Mendelson. *W. H. Auden: a bibliography, 1924–1969*, 2nd edn. Charlottesville: University Press of Virginia, 1972.

Extracts from letters to T. S. Eliot on the printing of Frederic Prokosch's edition of *Poem* (1933), p. 13 (also quoted in **H23**); to Bennett Cerf on *The ascent of F6*, 6 Oct. 1936, p. 23; to Cerf asking that the American edition

of *Look, stranger!* be titled *On this island*, [Oct. 1936], pp. 26–7; to Nancy
Cunard on *Spain*, [?July 1936], p. 29; to Cerf on *On the frontier*, 11 Sept.
1937, p. 35; to Bloomfield on *Epithalamion*, p. 40; indirect quotation from
a letter to Random House on *For the time being*, 18 Sept. 1944, p. 51; indirect quotation from a letter to Random House proposing the book that
became *Collected poetry*, 8 Jan. 1942, p. 58; and quotations from other letters about the same book, 20 Sept. 1944–23 Jan. 1945, p. 59. (Letters to
Cerf and Random House are now at Columbia University; letter to
Bloomfield is at Edinburgh University.)

H64 Nevill Coghill. Thanks before going, for Wystan. *For W. H.
Auden, February 21, 1972*, edited by Peter H. Salus and Paul B.
Taylor (New York: Random House, 1972), pp. 33–4.

Extract from a letter to Coghill on scholars and private letters, 31 Dec.
1970, p. 34. (This letter is not among Coghill's letters to Auden in the
Berg Collection or at Edinburgh University.)

H65 Dean Edward Dowling. A concordance to the poetry of W. H.
Auden. Ph.D. diss., Columbia University, 1972.

Reports of letters to Dowling listing the works to be included in the concordance, Nov. 1971 and Mar. 1972, p. ii.

H66 Richard Meran Barsam. *Nonfiction film: a critical history*. New
York: E. P. Dutton, 1973.

Indirect quotation of a letter to Barsam confirming a reading in 'Night
mail', 17 Mar. 1972, p. 60.

H67 Joanna Richardson. *Enid Starkie*. London: John Murray, 1973.

Letters to Starkie about the election for Professor of Poetry at Oxford, 5
Aug. 1955–30 Apr. 1956, pp. 196–9.

H68 I[an] Y[oung]. W. H. Auden: 1907–1973. *Body politic*, Toronto,
10 (1973), 19.

Extract from a letter to Young about the sexuality of the intended audience of his poetry, 13 June 1972. Quoted in Claude J. Summers, '"And
the earth can still astonish": W. H. Auden and the landscape of eros',
Windless orchard, 32 (Summer–Fall 1978), 27–36 (letter on p. 28).

H69 Michael Newman. In praise of East Fifth. *New York times*, 27
Jan. 1973, p. 29.

Extract from a letter to Newman with complaints about life at Oxford (7
Dec. 1972; now in the Berg Collection). Publication of this letter caused
comment. Auden's responses to questions about it in telephone interviews
were reported in: 'Oxford "hell" says Auden', *Daily telegraph*, 30 Jan.
1973, p. 17; and Mel Juffe, 'Auden glares at limelight', *New York post*, 31
Jan. 1973, p. 3. The letter and comments were variously quoted again in

'Notes on people', *New York Times*, 31 Jan. 1973, p. 47; 'Sayings of the week', *Observer*, 4 Feb. 1973, p. 9; 'Newsmakers', *Newsweek*, 81. 7 (12 Feb. 1973), 44; and 'People', *Time*, 101. 7 (13 Feb. 1973), p. 9.

H70 Golo Mann. . . . und unabhängig zum Erstaunen: Erinnerungen an dem Dichter W. H. Auden. *Süddeutsche Zeitung*, 6–7 Oct. 1973, pp. 111–12.

Extract from a letter about Germany, 1965. Translated as 'W. H. Auden, a memoir', *Encounter*, 42. 1 (Jan. 1974), 7–11; reprinted as 'A memoir' in *W. H. Auden, a tribute*, edited by Stephen Spender (London: Weidenfeld & Nicolson, 1975), pp. 98–103.

H71 J. B. Widdowson. Auden's memory. *Daily telegraph*, 16 Oct. 1973.

The headmaster of the Larchfield School, Helensburgh, reports that 'some 36 years after he left, I approached him in connection with the develop- ment campaign then in progress here. He replied, saying how vividly he remembered the school and the town, enclosed a most handsome contribu- tion to the fund, and added a postscript expressing the hope that assistant masters were better fed now than in his day.'

H72 I. D. Edrich. Letters, manuscripts . . . [catalogue 'Narrator']. London, [1973].

Extract from a letter declining to read for the Poetry Society, 1935, p. 22 (also quoted in **H96**).

H73 Kenneth W. Rendell. Autograph letters . . . , catalogue 89. Newton, Mass., [1973].

Extracts from seven letters to Vernon Watkins, apparently about recom- mendations for the Poetry Book Society, 30 Nov. 1956–9 Dec. 1957, p. 5.

H74 Edward Mendelson. Auden in New York: 1939–1941. *Adam*, 379–384 (1973–4), 27–33.

Extract from a letter on America to Margaret Gardiner, 19 Nov. 1939, pp. 31–2 (now in the Berg Collection).

H75 The Auden connection. *Evening standard*, 30 Aug. 1973.

Auden's reply to an invitation from the Derby Library Committee to open a branch library: he had not got 'the faintest idea what to say on such occasions'; 'perhaps you can give me some suggestions?'

H76 William Meredith [and] Monroe K. Spears. W. H. Auden [letter to the editor]. *Times literary supplement*, 9 Nov. 1973, p. 1372.

Extract from a letter to Edward Mendelson asking him to publish after Auden's death a request that his friends destroy his letters when finished with them, 9 May 1972. The same letter to the editor also appears in: *New York times*, 16 Dec. 1973, section 7 (book review), p. 26; and *New York review of books*, 20. 21–2 (24 Jan. 1974), 53. Comments by Stephen

Spender, Geoffrey Grigson, and Charles Monteith appear in 'The Times diary: Auden's wish: burn all my letters', *Times*, 8 Nov. 1973, p. 20. See also letters by: Charles Monteith and William Chapman, *Times literary supplement*, 16 Nov. 1973, p. 1401; Peter Dunn, ibid., 23 Nov. 1973, pp. 1448–9; Christina Colvin, ibid., 30 Nov. 1973, p. 1477; Hugh Brogan, ibid., 7 Dec. 1973, p. 1508; and further comment in 'Auden and a delicate conundrum', *Evening standard*, 9 Nov. 1971, p. 20.

H77 *Preferences: 51 American poets choose poems from their own work and from the past*, commentary on the choices and an introduction by Richard Howard. New York: Viking, 1974.

Extracts from a letter to Howard on Campion, p. 17.

H78 Sotheby and Co. Catalogue of nineteenth century and modern autograph letters . . . London, 4 Dec. 1973.

Extracts from an undated note to Mr Moody declining to send a photograph, and from a postcard to Geoffrey Grigson, 2 July 1935, p. 9 (postcard to Grigson also quoted in **H44**, **H62**, **H213**, **H276**; now at Wichita State University).

H79 Bell, Book & Radmall. Catalogue no. 1. London, [1974].

Extract from a letter to Hedwig Petzold sending a typescript of 'Mountains', [9 July 1954], p. 47 (also quoted in **H83**). This letter is not part of the collection of Auden's letters to Petzold in the Berg Collection.

H80 House of Books, Ltd. First editions . . . [catalogue]. New York, [1974].

Extracts from three letters to Donald Bell about poets and poetry, 1965, p. 5.

H81 George S. MacManus Co. Catalogue 222. Philadelphia, [1974].

Extract from a letter in response to a request for an autograph, 25 Mar. 1972, p. 6.

H82 Redcliffe Concerts of British Music. Programme, Queen Elizabeth Hall, London, 2 February 1974. Supplementary programme notes.

This mimeographed leaflet, with a note by John Gardner to *The entertainment of the senses*, includes an extract from a letter to Gardner, 17 Sept. 1973, and indirect quotation from a further letter, 26 Sept. 1973 (both also quoted in **H287**).

H83 Sotheby & Co. Catalogue of nineteenth century & modern first editions . . . London, 15–16 July 1974.

Extracts from letters to Hedwig Petzold and Christa Esders, 1949–67, p. 48 (now in the Berg Collection). The catalogue also quotes a letter to Petzold sending a typescript of 'Mountains', [9 July 1954], p. 47 (also quoted in **H79**; not located in any library collection).

H84 A. S. T. Fisher. Auden's juvenilia. *Notes and queries*, n.s. 21. 4 (Oct. 1974), 370–3.

Extracts from a letter authorizing Fisher to print some early poems, Nov. 1972 (letter now in Christ Church, Oxford), p. 370.

H85 Sotheby & Co. Catalogue of nineteenth century & modern first editions . . . London, 16–17 Dec. 1974.

Extracts from letters to Arnold Snodgrass, 1932–7, to Mrs Snodgrass, to Alan and Iris Sinkinson, *ca.* 1932–6 (all now in the Berg Collection), to Rachel Peck, 10 Feb. 1972, and descriptions of letters to Mr Clark and Harley J. Usill, pp. 53–5.

H86 John Auden. A brother's viewpoint. *W. H. Auden, a tribute*, edited by Stephen Spender. London: Weidenfeld & Nicolson, 1975, pp. 25–30.

Extracts from letters; this essay was also printed in *Sunday times*, 16 Mar. 1975, magazine, pp. 20–1, 23–4.

H87 Michael Yates. Iceland 1936. *W. H. Auden, a tribute*, edited by Stephen Spender. London: Weidenfeld & Nicolson, 1975, pp. 59–68.

Extracts from a letter to Yates, 1936, p. 59.

H88 Cyril Connolly. Some memories. *W. H. Auden, a tribute*, edited by Stephen Spender. London: Weidenfeld & Nicolson, 1975, pp. 68–73.

Extracts from letters to Connolly. Also printed as 'Remembering Auden', *Encounter*, 44. 3 (Mar. 1975), 90–3.

H89 Basil Boothby. An unofficial visitor. *W. H. Auden, a tribute*, edited by Stephen Spender. London: Weidenfeld & Nicolson, 1975, pp. 93–7.

Report of a thank-you letter after a visit to Iceland, July 1964, p. 97.

H90 Ursula Niebuhr. Memories of the 1940s. *W. H. Auden, a tribute*, edited by Stephen Spender. London: Weidenfeld & Nicolson, 1975, pp. 104–18.

Extracts from letters to Reinhold and Ursula Niebuhr (partly quoted in **H272**; now at the Library of Congress).

H91 James Stern. The indispensable presence. *W. H. Auden, a tribute*, edited by Stephen Spender. London: Weidenfeld & Nicolson, 1975, pp. 123–7.

Extracts from letters to James and Tania Stern (now in the Berg Collection).

H92 Robert Craft. The poet and the rake. *W. H. Auden, a tribute*, edited by Stephen Spender. London: Weidenfeld & Nicolson, 1975, pp. 149–55.

Letter to Craft on *The rake's progress*, 16 Feb. 1951 (also quoted in **H127**), p. 153. Also printed in *New York review of books*, 21. 20 (12 Dec. 1974), 30–4.

H93 Oliver Sacks. Dear Mr A. . . . *W. H. Auden, a tribute*, edited by Stephen Spender. London: Weidenfeld & Nicolson, 1975, pp. 187–95.

Extract from a letter to Sacks, 1973, p. 194.

H94 Virginia Spencer Carr. *The lonely hunter: a biography of Carson McCullers*. Garden City, NY: Doubleday, 1975.

Extract from a letter to Carr about Auden's house on Middagh Street, 21 Sept. 1971, p. 124.

H95 Robert A. Wilson. *Auden's library*. New York: Phoenix Book Shop, 1975.

Facsimile of a postcard with an invitation to Wilson, 1964, p. [iv]; text, p. 1.

H96 I. D. Edrich. Modern first editions [catalogue 'Quay']. London, [1975].

Extract from a letter declining to read for the Poetry Society, 1935, p. 2 (also quoted in **H72**).

H97 William Meredith. One of the high ones: some recollections of W. H. Auden. *Harvard advocate*, 108. 2–3 ([1975]), 10–12.

Extract of a letter to Meredith reporting that Meredith's poems had not arrived. Reprinted as 'Recollections of W. H. Auden', *Connecticut College Library bulletin*, 2 (Fall 1975), 1–5; and in Joseph the Provider, Books, The Carter Burden collection of the works of W. H. Auden [sale catalogue] (Santa Barbara, 1989), not paged (see **H247**).

H98 Northern Book Auctions. Catalogue 4/1975. Hull, 1975.

Extensive extracts from letters to W. L. McElwee, 1927–9 and 1962 (now in the British Library), with other catalogue entries noting revisions in copies of *Oxford poetry 1926* and *1927*, pp. 4–5.

H99 Kenneth W. Rendell. Catalogue 102. Newton, Mass., [1975].

Extract from a letter to Rosamund Harcourt-Smith about America, 21 Apr. 1940, p. 5.

H100 Evelyn A. Flory. Auden and Eiseley: the development of a poem. *Concerning poetry*, 8. 1 (Spring 1975), 67–73.

Extract from a letter to Alice Walrath about 'The aliens', 2 May 1973, p. 70.

H101 Robley J. Evans. An Auden manuscript in Palmer Library. *Connecticut College Library bulletin*, 2 (Fall 1975), 6–7.

Facsimile and text of a letter to Frederick Alderson about the name Wystan, 30 Mar. 1966 (also quoted in **H44** and **H52**).

H102 V. S. Yanovsky. W. H. Auden. *Antaeus*, 19 (Autumn 1975), 107–35.

Extracts from letters, 1969–73 (now at Columbia University).

H103 Christopher Isherwood. *Christopher and his kind, 1929–1939*. New York: Farrar, Straus & Giroux, 1976.

Extracts from letters, *passim*.

H104 *Modern literary manuscripts from King's College, Cambridge: an exhibition in memory of A. N. L. Munby*. Cambridge: Fitzwilliam Museum, 1976.

Extract from a letter to John Hayward about Auden's sixtieth birthday poem for T. S. Eliot, 6 May 1948, item 2 (now at King's College, Cambridge).

H105 Alice Prochaska. Young writers of the thirties. London: National Portrait Gallery, 1976.

Exhibition catalogue, with extract from a letter to Edward Upward, 6 Oct. 1930, p. 9.

H106 Susan Edmiston and Linda D. Cirino. *Literary New York: a history and guide*. Boston: Houghton Mifflin, 1976.

Extract from a letter on his Brooklyn house, 20 Apr. 1970, p. 350.

H107 William B. Wahl. *Poetic drama interviews: Robert Speaight, E. Martin Browne & W. H. Auden*. Salzburg: Institut für englische Sprache und Literatur, Universität Salzburg, 1976. (Salzburg Studies in English Literature, Poetic Drama & Poetic Theory, 24.)

Inaccurate transcripts of three letters to Wahl setting up an interview, July–Aug. 1973, pp. 96, 97–8, 105.

H108 Janet Adam Smith. Mr Eliot's proposal: the making of *The Faber book of modern verse*. *Times literary supplement*, 18 June 1976, pp. 726–8.

Extract from a postcard about the anthology to Michael Roberts, 5 Apr. 1935, and from a letter about his failure to get a job at Bryanston, 22 Apr. 1935 (both now in the Berg Collection). Reprinted in *Michael Roberts' The Faber book of modern verse: a reissue of the original edition with an account of its making by Janet Adam Smith* (London: Faber & Faber, 1982), p. xxv.

H109 Bernard Crick looks at the 'Young writers of the thirties' exhibition currently showing at the National Portrait Gallery. *New review*, 3. 28 (July 1976), 57–61.

Extract from a letter to E. R. Dodds about Spain, 8 Dec. 1936, p. 59.

H110 Margaret Gardiner. Auden: a memoir. *New review*, 3. 28 (July 1976), 9–19.

Extracts from letters, some cited from memory (surviving letters now in the Berg Collection). Reprinted in her *A scatter of memories* (London: Free Association Books, 1988), 135–61.

H111 Sotheby's. Catalogue of modern literary manuscripts . . . London, 23 July 1976.

Extracts from a letter to Dilys Powell [misread by the cataloguer as Pavell] about her review of *The ascent of F6*, 1936, p. 6 (now in the Berg Collection); from two letters to Charles Osborne, [?1963], p. 7 (now in the Berg Collection); and from three letters to Camille Honig regretting his inability to receive a visit, 1971, p. 7 (now in the Berg Collection).

H112 W. H. Auden. Letter to Delmore Schwartz. *Antaeus*, 23 (Autumn 1976), 193–7.

Full text of a letter on Schwartz's poetry, 26 Aug. 1942, with introductory note by James Atlas. Extracts appear in Atlas's *Delmore Schwartz* (New York: Farrar, Straus & Giroux, 1977), pp. 217–20; the book also includes an extract from a letter to James Laughlin, p. 129.

H113 House of Books, Ltd. First editions . . . [catalogue]. New York, [1976].

Indirect quotation of a note turning down an invitation, p. 2; extract from a letter inviting the recipient to Kirchstetten, 6 June [no year], p. 4; extracts from a letter to Gerald Sanders with information for use in Sanders's anthology of modern poetry, 1940–1, p. 5 (also quoted in **H54**; now at Pennsylvania State University).

H114 Bernard Quaritch Ltd. [Catalogue] 960. London, 1976.

Extract from a letter transmitting 'The more loving one', 10 Sept. 1957, and a postcard to Eric Capan, 27 Nov. 1936 (also quoted in **H60**), p. 4.

H115 W. H. Auden. *The English Auden: poems, essays and dramatic writings 1927–1939*, edited by Edward Mendelson. London: Faber & Faber, 1977.

Extracts from letters to Christopher Isherwood and others, pp. xiii–xxiii.

H116 *Bertolt Brecht in Britain*, compiled and edited by Nicholas Jacobs and Prudence Ohlsen, to accompany an exhibition at the National Theatre, London . . . London: Irat Services, TQ Publications, 1977.

Letter to Margrit Hahnloser-Ingold about Brecht's influence, 9 Aug. 1965, p. 67, facsimile on p.68 (also quoted in **H48**).

H117 Humphrey Carpenter. *Tolkien: a biography*. London: Allen & Unwin, 1977.

Extract from a letter to Tolkien in praise of Tolkien's lecturing, p. 133.

H118 E. R. Dodds. *Missing persons: an autobiography*. Oxford: Clarendon Press, 1977.

Extracts and paraphrases of letters to Dodds, 1932–40, pp. 119–23. Partly based on 'Background to a poet: memories of Birmingham, 1924–36', *Shenandoah*, 18. 2 (Winter 1967), 6–11.

H119 Marjorie Perloff. *Frank O'Hara: poet among painters*. New York: George Braziller, 1977.

Extract from a letter to O'Hara on O'Hara's poems, 3 June 1955, p. 62 (also quoted in **H153** and **H289**).

H120 Charles Hamilton Galleries. Auction number 104. New York, 7 Apr. 1977.

Extract from a letter to Mr Woods on editing magazines, 15 July [?1956], p. 11 (now in the Berg Collection).

H121 Sotheby & Co. Catalogue of nineteenth century & modern first editions . . . London, 28[–9] July 1977.

Extracts from a letter to John Davenport on help for a German writer, ?Sept. 1938, p. 112 (now at Pennsylvania State University).

H122 John Mizner. An Auden letter about *The orators*. *Colby Library quarterly*, 13. 4 (Dec. 1977), 275–7.

Letter to Harry Bamford Parkes, 6 Dec. 1932. Cf. correction by Edward Mendelson, ibid., 14. 2 (June 1978), 103.

H123 Dorothy Commins. *What is an editor? Saxe Commins at work*. Chicago: University of Chicago Press, 1978.

Extracts from letters to Commins, Auden's editor at Random House, 1944–7, pp. 138–42; and facsimile of a letter to Dorothy Commins, 8 Oct. 1958, p. 231.

H124 E. M. Forster. *Commonplace book: facsimile edition*, edited by P. N. Furbank. London: Scolar, 1978.

Extract from a cable to Forster on his eightieth birthday, 11 Jan. 1959; transcribed in the typeset edition: E. M. Forster, *Commonplace book*, edited by Philip Gordon (London: Scolar, 1985), p. 208. Quoted in Furbank's *E. M. Forster: a life: volume two, Polycrates' ring (1914–1970)* (London: Secker & Warburg, 1978), p. 305.

H125 *Der Georg-Büchner-Preis 1951–1978: eine Ausstellung des Deutschen Literaturarchivs Marbach und der Deutschen Akademie für Sprache* *und Dichtung Darmstadt.* Marbach am Neckar: Deutsche Schillergesellschaft, 1978.

Full text of a letter to Golo Mann, 2 Oct. 1965, pp. 231–2.

H126 John Lehmann. *Thrown to the Woolfs.* London: Weidenfeld & Nicolson, 1978.

Extracts from a reader's report about the influence of Hopkins, telegram to Lehmann, p. 75 (reprinted from **H11**), and from a telegram on contractual problems with *New Year letter*, p. 77.

H127 Vera Stravinsky and Robert Craft. *Stravinsky in pictures and documents.* New York: Simon & Schuster, 1978.

Extracts from a letter to Stravinsky on *The rake's progress*, 20 Nov. 1947, p. 398; and letters to Craft, 1949, p. 650, 16 Feb. 1951 (also quoted in **H92**), p. 407, 10 Feb. 1959, p. 650 (many also quoted in **H287**). This last letter is paraphrased by Paul Griffiths in *Igor Stravinsky, The rake's progress* (Cambridge: Cambridge University Press, 1982), p. 14, with an error corrected in Stephen Walsh, *The music of Stravinsky* (London: Routledge, 1988), p. 288.

H128 Peter Sutcliffe. *The Oxford University Press: an informal history.* Oxford: Clarendon Press, 1978.

Extracts from a letter about the *Oxford book of light verse*, p. 244.

H129 Heritage Book Shop, Inc. Heritage miscellany, number one [catalogue]. Los Angeles, [?1978].

Description of a letter with bibliographical information on *Poems* (1928), 21 May 1947, p. 1 (also quoted in **H49, H50, H137, H166, H201**).

H130 Katie Louchheim. The truth is not the proper thing to tell. *Washington post*, 5 Nov. 1978, magazine, pp. 20–1, 23–4.

Extract from a thank-you letter, Oct. 1939, p. 21.

H131 Lucy S. McDiarmid. W. H. Auden's 'In the year of my youth . . .' *Review of English studies*, n.s. 39. 115 (Aug. 1978), 267–312.

Extract from a letter to Naomi Mitchison about the poem, 18 Oct. 1932, p. 267.

H132 Edward Mendelson. Oxford light verse [letter to the editor]. *Times literary supplement*, 14 July 1978, p. 798.

Extract from a letter [to Edward Kallman, 1 June 1939] on changes in the second printing of *The Oxford book of light verse*.

H133 Anne Chisholm. *Nancy Cunard.* New York: Alfred A. Knopf, 1979.

Extracts from letters to Cunard on *Spain* and *Authors take sides on the Spanish war*, 1937, pp. 239–41.

H134 Brian Finney. *Christopher Isherwood: a critical biography*. London: Faber & Faber, 1979.

Paraphrase of a letter to T. S. Eliot about the authorship of *The dog beneath the skin*, [?Feb. 1935], p. 108; extract from a letter to Stephen Spender about Erika Mann, [?June 1935], p. 120; paraphrase of a letter to J. M. Keynes about *On the frontier*, 9 Oct. 1937, p. 136; extract from a letter to Spender about the same play, [?July 1938], p. 139; paraphrase of and extract from a letter to Spender about *The dog beneath the skin*, June 1935, pp. 158 and 160; extract from a letter to Spender about Isherwood, 13 Mar. 1941, p. 182. An appendix includes a poem to Isherwood written on 3 Sept. 1937 in a copy of D. H. Lawrence's *Birds, beasts and flowers* (1931), pp. 287–9.

H135 Naomi Mitchison. *You may well ask: a memoir 1920–1940*. London: Victor Gollancz, 1979.

Extracts from letters to Mitchison in the chapter on Auden, 'The bright star', pp. 117–26 (now in the Berg Collection); Mitchison's text is unreliable.

H136 Charles Osborne. *W. H. Auden: the life of a poet*. London: Eyre Methuen, 1979.

Extracts from letters, *passim*.

H137 Joseph the Provider. Modern literature: supplementary list M. [catalogue]. Santa Barbara, [1979].

Extracts from a letter about rights to 'Night mail', 3 Oct. 1943, item 42 (also quoted in **H166**); a letter about bibliographical information on *Poems* (1928), 21 May 1947, item 45 (also quoted in **H49**, **H50**, **H129**, **H166**, **H201**); from a letter agreeing to translate poems by Yevtushenko and a letter reporting his inability to do so, 20 Mar. and 16 June 1969, item 51.

H138 David Roberts. W. H. Auden's mountain. *Horizon*, 22. 5 (May 1979), 56–61.

Extracts from three letters to Roberts, 1968–9.

H139 Swann Galleries, Inc. Rare books . . . , sale number 1141. New York, 10 May 1979.

Extracts from letters to Rhoda Jaffe, 1946–51, item 15. The catalogue of Swann Galleries sale 1140, 3 May 1979, item 3, briefly quotes Auden's inscriptions on photographs given to Rhoda Jaffe. (Letters and photographs now in the Berg Collection.)

H140 *The Penguin book of Spanish Civil War verse*, edited by Valentine Cunningham. Harmondsworth: Penguin, 1980.

Extracts from two letters to E. R. Dodds, Dec. 1936, p. 67.

H141 Sean Day-Lewis. *C. Day-Lewis, an English literary life.* London: Weidenfeld & Nicolson, 1980.

Extracts from letters to Day-Lewis, pp. 52, 54, 55, 252, and a verse-letter, Mar. 1929, pp. 309–11.

H142 Anne Morrow Lindbergh. *War within and without: diaries and letters of Anne Morrow Lindbergh 1939–1944.* New York: Harcourt Brace Jovanovich, 1980.

Extract from a letter to Lindbergh about her *The wave of the future*, Oct. 1940, p. 149.

H143 Rosalee Jackson Sprout. Marianne Moore: the poet as translator. Ph.D. diss., Tufts, 1980.

Extract from a letter to Moore on her translation of La Fontaine, 24 Feb. 1945, p. 18; extract from a letter to Moore's editor, Walter Pistole, Feb. 1945, p. 80.

H144 Bell, Book & Radmall Ltd. Catalogue 25. London, [1980].

Extract from a letter to Professor Feiling (?) on Auden's election as Professor of Poetry at Oxford, 16 Mar. 1956, p. 1. Probably the same letter as that quoted in **H180**.

H145 Richard Hoggart. Auden's life-music. *Listener*, 103. 2652 (6 Mar. 1980), 314–15.

Review of Charles Osborne's *W. H. Auden*, with extracts from a letter to Hoggart, Jan. 1958 (also quoted in **H279**).

H146 Charles Osborne. Wystan Auden: untangling the facts from the gossip. *Times higher educational supplement*, 14 Mar. 1980, p. 9.

Letter to Osborne about arrangements for a poetry festival, [?June 1973].

H147 Sotheby Parke Bernet & Co. The collection of autograph letters . . . [catalogue]. London, 2–4 June 1980.

Description of a postcard to Edward Upward, 30 Dec. 1930 [misdated in the catalogue 30 Feb. 1930] (also quoted or described in **H182** and **H226**); extract from a letter to Mr Taylor on English rhymes, 20 July [1971] (closing of the letter in facsimile), p. 299.

H148 *The letters of J. R. R. Tolkien*, selected and edited by Humphrey Carpenter. London: George Allen & Unwin, 1981.

Brief extracts and description of letters to Tolkien, 1955–65, pp. 211, 355, 359, 378.

H149 Humphrey Carpenter. *W. H. Auden: a biography*. London: George Allen & Unwin, 1981.

Extensive extracts and full texts of letters, *passim*.

H150 Edward Mendelson. *Early Auden*. New York: Viking, 1981.
Extensive extracts and full texts of letters, *passim*.

H151 Edward Mendelson. W. H. Auden 1907–1973. *American writers: a collection of literary biographies*, edited by A. Walton Litz, supplement II, part 1 (New York: Charles Scribner's Sons, 1981), pp. 1–28.
Extract from a letter to George A. Auden on *For the time being*, p. 17 (also quoted in **H258**).

H152 Donald Mitchell. *Britten and Auden in the thirties: the year 1936*. London: Faber & Faber, 1981.
Letter to Britten on his personality and music, 31 Jan. 1942, pp. 161–2; frequently quoted or reprinted in later books about Britten.

H153 Marjorie Perloff. *The poetics of indeterminacy: Rimbaud to Cage*. Princeton: Princeton University Press, 1981.
Letter to Frank O'Hara on O'Hara's poems, 3 June 1955, pp. 249–50 (also quoted in **H119** and **H289**).

H154 House of Books. First editions . . . [catalogue]. New York, [?1981].
Extract from a postcard to Geoffrey Grigson listing his publications, 27 May 1937, p. 3 (now at Columbia University); and from a letter with an anecdote about a lady's confusion of 'Christian and his soldiers' for 'Tristan and Isolde', 6 June 1967, pp. 4–5.

H155 Robert Medley. The Group Theatre 1932–39: Rupert Doone and Wystan Auden. *London magazine*, n.s. 20. 10 (Jan. 1981), 47–60.
Reports of letters to Medley and Rupert Doone (also reported in **H176**).

H156 W. H. Auden: Ode to the George Washington Hotel. *New York times*, 8 Mar. 1981, section 7 (book review), p. 11.
The headnote by Edward Mendelson includes an extract from a letter to Benjamin Britten recommending the hotel, 8 June 1939.

H157 Marshall McLuhan / W. H. Auden: duel or duet?, edited by Robert O'Driscoll. *Canadian forum*, 61. 709 (May 1981), 5–17, 17.
O'Driscoll's opening comments include extracts from Auden's letters to him, 1970, p. 5.

H158 *Passing through: letters and documents written in Philadelphia by famous visitors*, compiled and described by Clive E. Driver. Philadelphia: The Rosenbach Museum & Library, 1982.
Letter to Marianne Moore, 24 Feb. 1945, pp. 123–4.

H159 Ian Hamilton. *Robert Lowell: a biography*. New York: Random House. 1982.

Extract from a letter to Charles Monteith on Lowell, 20 Dec. 1965, p. 345.

H160 Maurice Isserman. *Which side were you on?: the American Communist Party during the Second World War*. Middletown, Conn.: Wesleyan University Press, 1982.

Extract from a letter to the League of American Writers, 8 Nov. 1939 (misread by Isserman as 11 Aug. 1939), p. 38.

H161 William McGuire. *Poetry's catbird seat: the Consultantship in Poetry in the English Language at the Library of Congress 1937–1987*. Washington: Library of Congress, 1988.

Infers from Archibald MacLeish's reply the content of Auden's letter asking for help in obtaining American citizenship, Oct. 1939, p. 52. Also inferred in: Scott Donaldson, in collaboration with R. H. Winnick, *Archibald MacLeish: an American life* (Boston: Houghton Mifflin, 1992), p. 326.

H162 Robyn Marsack. *The cave of making: the poetry of Louis MacNeice*. Oxford: Clarendon Press, 1982.

Extract from a letter to MacNeice, 21 Jan. 1945, p. 82. The same extract appears in Marsack's D.Phil. thesis of the same title, Oxford, 1979, p. 139.

H163 Martin Seymour-Smith. *Robert Graves: his life and work*. London: Hutchinson, 1982.

Letter to Graves on his election to the Oxford professorship of poetry, 1961, p. 508 (also quoted in **H191**).

H164 [Igor] Stravinsky. *Selected correspondence*, volume 1, edited with commentaries by Robert Craft. New York: Alfred A. Knopf, 1982.

Letters to Stravinsky, 1947–65, pp. 299–324 (also partly quoted in **H18**, **H127**, **H287**; now at the Paul Sacher Foundation, Basel). Does not include all the letters printed in **H18**. Excerpted in 'The progress of *The rake*', *Observer*, 20 June 1982, pp. 25–6.

H165 Elisabeth Young-Bruehl. *Hannah Arendt: for love of the world*. New Haven: Yale University Press, 1982.

Infers the content of a letter to Arendt on *The human condition*, Feb. 1960, pp. 371–2.

H166 Joseph the Provider. Literature: modern first editions, catalogue 16. Santa Barbara, [?1982].

Extract from a letter about rights to 'Night mail', 3 Oct. 1943 (also quoted in **H137**); and from a letter with bibliographical information about *Poems* (1928), 21 May 1947 (this letter also quoted in **H49**, **H50**, **H129**, **H137**, **H201**), p. [5].

H167 Hamish Riley-Smith. The papers of Sir Roy Harrod [catalogue]. Swanton Abbot, [1982].

Extracts from two letters to Harrod about a cheque and about a translation project by Harrod, undated and 1960 (now at Chiba University of Commerce, Japan), p. 73.

H168 David Schulson Autographs. [Catalogue] 10. New York, [1982].

Extract from a letter to Richard Heron Ward offering a poem for an anthology, 1935, p. 3 (also quoted in **H204** and **H293**). This letter precedes the 30 Aug. 1935 letter to Ward quoted in **H183**, **H203**, and **H248**.

H169 Sotheby Parke Bernet Inc. Fine books and manuscripts . . . [catalogue]. New York, 6 Apr. 1982.

Extract from a postcard to Mrs Harry Wechsler describing a manuscript she had purchased, 30 Apr. 1940, item 3 (now in the Berg Collection).

H170 Roger Berthoud. The artist as writer, teacher, enthusiast. *Times*, 12 June 1982, p. 12.

Quotes (from memory) a letter to Lawrence Gowing (the 'artist' of the title), sent from Iceland probably in the summer of 1936; quoted again in Gowing's obituary, *Times*, 7 Feb. 1991, p. 12. A further remembered quotation from this letter appears in Bruce Laughton, *The Euston Road School, a study in objective painting* (Aldershot: Scolar, 1986), p. 176.

H171 Swann Galleries, Inc. 19th & 20th century American & English literature . . . , sale number 1263 [catalogue]. New York, 24 June 1982.

Extracts from two postcards to Theodore Spencer, 16 July 1943 and 30 Jan. 1946, p. [3] (also described in **H184**).

H172 Peter Jolliffe. Catalogue no. 25. London, Oct. 1982.

Extract from a correspondence card [to Mrs Heckstall Smith] on teaching and his departure for film work, 1935, p. 1 (now at Wichita State University).

H173 Sotheby Parke Bernet & Co. English literature . . . [catalogue]. London, 15 Dec. 1982, p. 71.

Extracts from a letter to John Layard, June 1939, pp. 226–7 (now at the University of California, San Diego).

H174 Glen Cavaliero. *Charles Williams, poet of theology*. London: Macmillan, 1983.

Extract from a letter to Williams about Williams's poetry, probably 1944, p. 171.

H175 Ekbert Faas. *Young Robert Duncan*. Santa Barbara: Black Sparrow, 1983.

Extract from a letter asking Duncan not to publish an essay on Auden's homosexuality, Jan. 1946, p. 195; quoted from a transcript of the letter by Duncan. (Original now at the State University of New York at Buffalo.)

H176 Robert Medley. *Drawn from the life: a memoir.* London: Faber & Faber, 1983.

Reports of letters to Medley and Rupert Doone, *passim* (partly reprinted from **H155**).

H177 Charles H. Miller. *Auden: an American friendship.* New York: Charles Scribner's Sons, 1983.

Extracts from letters to Caroline Newton and to Miller, pp. 67, 83–4, 158.

H178 David Pryce-Jones. *Cyril Connolly: journal and memoir.* London: Collins, 1983.

Extract from a letter to Connolly, 15 Nov. 1938, p. 272.

H179 Gotham Book Mart & Gallery. Quick list 78 addenda [catalogue]. New York, [?1983].

Extract from a letter [to John Lehmann], 1940, about plans for *The double man*, p. 1 (also quoted in Gotham Book Mart's Quick list 79 [?1983], p. 1, **H202**, and **H262**; now at Wichita State University).

H180 House of Books, Ltd. Modern first editions . . . [catalogue]. New York, [1983].

Extracts from a letter to Professor F— that refers to the 'Governing Body', p. 2. Probably the same letter as that quoted in **H144**.

H181 Joseph the Provider. Literature: modern first editions, catalogue 17. Santa Barbara, [?1983].

Extract from a letter submitting *An Elizabethan song book* to its publisher Jason Epstein [*ca.* 1954], item 22 (also quoted in **H201** and **H266**; now at Edinburgh University).

H182 Paul Rassam. First editions & presentation copies [catalogue]. London, [?1983].

Extract from a postcard to Edward Upward, 30 Dec. 1930 [misdated in the catalogue 30 Feb. 1930], item 23 (also described or quoted in **H146** and **H226**); extract from a letter to Herbert Murrill on a performance of *The dance of death*, item 24 (also quoted in **H197** and **H215**).

H183 David Schulson Autographs. [Catalogue] 14. New York, [1983].

Extracts from a letter to Richard Heron Ward about this earlier offer of a poem for anthology, 30 Aug. 1935 (also quoted in **H203** and **H248**); and a letter of recommendation to the director of the B'nai B'rith Hillel Foundation, 14 May 1942, p. 3. The letter to Ward follows the letter quoted in **H168** and **H204**.

H184 Phoenix Book Shop. Catalogue 182. New York, Summer 1983.

Descriptions of two postcards to Theodore Spencer, 16 July 1943 and 30 Jan. 1946, p. 22 (also quoted in **H171**).

H185 Robin Waterfield Ltd. Catalogue 46. Oxford, [1983].

Extracts from two letters to David Wright submitting the poem 'Thanksgiving for a habitat' to the periodical *X*, 30 Aug. and 11 Sept. 1962, p. 2 (also quoted in **H188**; now at Wichita State University).

H186 Robin Waterfield Ltd. Supplementary list no. 13. Oxford, [1983].

Extract from a letter to Cyril Lakin, editor of *The daily telegraph*, apparently about Auden's first review for the paper, [?Nov. 1936], p. 1 (also quoted in **H281**; now at Edinburgh University).

H187 Christie, Manson & Woods, Ltd. Valuable autograph letters . . . [catalogue]. London, 20 July 1983.

Extract from a letter to James Michie on a book by Michie and the poem 'Thanksgiving for a habitat', 28 Feb. 1966, p. 37 (also quoted in **H205**, **H224**, **H241**; now at Edinburgh University).

H188 Sotheby Parke Bernet & Co. English literature . . . [catalogue]. London, 21–22 July 1983.

Description of two letters to David Wright submitting 'Thanksgiving for a habitat' to the periodical *X*, 30 Aug. and 11 Sept. 1962, p. 122 (also quoted in **H185**; now at Wichita State University).

H189 Michael Black. The long pursuit. *The Leavises: recollections and impressions*, edited by Denys Thompson. Cambridge: Cambridge University Press, 1984, pp. 86–102.

Extracts from letters to Black first refusing, then agreeing to allow his contributions to *Scrutiny* to be reprinted, p. 88.

H190 Dorothy J. Farnan. *Auden in love*. New York: Simon & Schuster, 1984.

Extensive extracts from letters to Chester Kallman and others, *passim*.

H191 Robert Graves. *Between moon and moon: selected letters of Robert Graves 1946–1972*, edited, with a commentary and notes, by Paul O'Prey. London: Hutchinson, 1984.

Briefly paraphrases a letter to Graves after Graves's election as Professor of Poetry at Oxford, 1961, p. 304 (also quoted in **H163**).

H192 *Before the romantics*, an anthology of the enlightenment, chosen by Geoffrey Grigson. Edinburgh: Salamander, 1984.

Description of a letter to Grigson on the 1946 edition of the anthology, p. [vii].

H193 Erika Mann. *Briefe und Antworten*, herausgegeben von Anna Zanco Prestel, Band I, 1922–1950. München: Spangenberg, 1984.

German translation of a letter to Mann, late May 1939, pp. 130–1.

H194 Michael J. Sidnell. *Dances of death: the Group Theatre of London in the thirties*. London: Faber & Faber, 1984.

Extracts from letters to Robert Medley and Rupert Doone, *passim*.

H195 Neil Tierney. *William Walton: his life and music*. London: Robert Hale, 1984.

Extract from a letter to Stewart Craggs reporting incorrectly that Auden and Walton had no correspondence about *The twelve*, 8 Dec. 1972, p. 150. (see **H260**.)

H196 John Willett. *Brecht in context: comparative approaches*. London: Methuen, 1984.

The chapter 'The case of Auden' has extracts from letters to James and Tania Stern, Theodore Spencer, and Willett, 1944–71, *passim*, pp. 59–72. The chapter also appears as a separate essay in *Transformations in modern European drama*, edited by Ian Donaldson (London: Macmillan, 1983), pp. 162–76.

H197 Paul Rassam. Catalogue 14. London, [?1984].

Extract from a letter to Herbert Murrill on a performance of *The dance of death* (also quoted in **H182** and **H215**), p. 6.

H198 David Schulson Autographs. [Catalogue] 18. New York, [1984].

Extract from a letter to Robert Nye offering a work for publication in *The Scotsman*, 12 Aug. 1970, p. 3. (The work was 'Talking to dogs', which the newspaper rejected because it contained the word 'prick'; Nye returned the poem to Auden.)

H199 R. A. Gekoski. Modern first editions, catalogue 5. Leamington Spa, Autumn 1984.

Extract from a letter to John Betjeman, 20 Mar. [1946] (also quoted in **H200** and **H227**; now in the Berg Collection), p. 2.

H200 Peter Jolliffe. Catalogue no. 29. London, [1984].

Extracts from a letter to John Betjeman, 20 Mar. [?1946] (also quoted in **H199** and **H227**; now in the Berg Collection), p. 2.

H201 Joseph the Provider. Literature: modern first editions, catalogue 18. Santa Barbara, [?1984].

Extract from a letter with bibliographical information about *Poems* (1928), 21 May 1947 (also quoted in **H49**, **H50**, **H129**, **H137**, **H166**); and from a letter submitting *An Elizabethan song book* to its publisher Jason Epstein [*ca.* 1954] (also quoted in **H181** and **H266**; now at Edinburgh University), p. [2].

H202 Joseph the Provider. Modern first editions: literature, catalogue 26. Santa Barbara, [1984].

Extract from a letter [to John Lehmann] describing and announcing the title for *The double man* (also quoted in **H179** and **H262**; now at Wichita State University), item 8.

H203 David Schulson Autographs. [Catalogue] 26. New York, [1984].

Extract from a letter to Richard Heron Ward about his earlier offer of a poem for an anthology, 30 Aug. 1935 (also quoted in **H183** and **H248**), p. 3.

H204 Swann Galleries, Inc. Autographs & manuscripts . . . sale number 1327 [catalogue]. New York, 8 Mar. 1984.

Extract from a letter to Richard Heron Ward offering a poem for an anthology, 1935, item 32 (also quoted in **H168** and **H293**).

H205 Phillips, Son & Neale. Books . . . sale no. 25,009 [catalogue]. London, 7 June 1984.

Extract from a letter to James Michie on a book by Michie and 'Thanksgiving for a habitat', 28 Feb. 1966, p. 49 (also quoted in **H187**, **H205**, **H241**, **H224**; now at Edinburgh University).

H206 Sotheby's. English literature . . . [catalogue]. London, 16–17 July 1984.

Extract from a letter to Miss Boyd on poetry for children, 1937, item 120. Items 121–3 include extracts from versions of 'Johnny', 'James Honeyman', and the then unpublished poem 'My love is like a red red rose', which Auden sent with his letter.

H207 Robert Craft. Lives of the poets. *New York review of books*, 31. 14 (27 Sept. 1984), 7–8, 10.

Extract from a letter to Vera Stravinsky, 25 Mar. 1972. Reprinted as 'Wystan in and out of love' in his *Small Craft advisories* (London: Thames & Hudson, 1989), pp. 63–70.

H208 Eric Bentley. *The Brecht memoir*. New York: PAJ Publications, 1985.

Extracts from letters to Bentley about Brecht, 1948–59, pp. 42–4. In the revised British edition (Manchester: Carcanet, 1989), pp. 48–9.

H209 Elizabeth Frank. *Louise Bogan: a portrait*. New York: Alfred A. Knopf, 1985.

Extract from a letter to Bogan, 17 Nov. 1941, p. 297; indirect quotations from other letters, pp. 296–7.

H210 *The complete letters of Sigmund Freud to Wilhelm Fliess, 1887–1904*, translated and edited by Jeffrey Moussaieff Masson. Cambridge, Mass.: Harvard University Press, 1985.

Extract from a letter to Ernest Jones on Jones's biography of Freud, 4 Nov. 1953, p. 22.

H211 Walter Hussey. *Patron of art: the revival of a great tradition among modern artists.* London: Weidenfeld & Nicolson, 1985.
Letters to Hussey on *Litany and anthem for S. Matthew's day*, 30 Jan. and 1 July 1946, p. 83.

H212 *Dearest Bubushkin: the correspondence of Vera and Igor Stravinsky, 1921–1954, with excerpts from Vera Stravinsky's diaries, 1922–1971*, edited by Robert Craft. London: Thames and Hudson, 1985.
Extracts from letters to Craft, 21 Aug. and 9 Sept. 1951, p. 151.

H213 Joseph the Provider. Modern first editions, literature, catalogue 28. Santa Barbara, [1985].
Extract from a letter to 'Harold', *ca.* 1938, reporting that he had recommended him for Shrewsbury School, item 19; postcard to Geoffrey Grigson on his review of *The poet's tongue*, 2 July 1935, item 22 (also quoted in **H44**, **H62**, **H78**, **H276**; now at Wichita State University).

H214 David Schulson Autographs. [Catalogue] 28. New York, [1985].
Extract from a letter to William Cole about the text of *A certain world*, 6 Jan. 1967, p. 2 (now at Wichita State University).

H215 Any Amount of Books. Catalogue no. 7. London, June 1985.
Letter to Herbert Murrill on a performance of *The dance of death*, p. [5] (also quoted in **H182** and **H197**).

H216 Wendell Stacy Johnson. Auden in order: a memoir and commentary. *Confrontation* (Long Island University), 29 (Winter 1985), 70–9.
Extracts from a letter to Johnson about the difficulties of writing, 1953, p. 79.

H217 Harold Norse. Begging to differ: amateur recreation. *Advocate*, 419 (30 Apr. 1985), Advocate review of books, Spring 1985, p. 15.
Brief extract from a letter to Norse (now at the Lilly Library, Indiana University).

H218 Alexander Bloom. *Prodigal sons: the New York intellectuals & their world.* New York: Oxford University Press, 1986.
Letter to F. W. Dupee sending an article for *Partisan review* (probably 'The Public v. the late Mr William Butler Yeats'), 18 Mar. 1939, p. 82.

H219 Katherine Bucknell. W. H. Auden: the growth of a poet's mind (1922–1933). Ph.D. diss., Columbia University, 1986.
Extensive quotations from letters to friends and family, *passim.*

H220 Charles Osborne. *Giving it away: the memoirs of an uncivil servant.* London: Secker & Warburg, 1986.
Letter to Osborne on a festival reception, p. 139.

H221 Christiane Puffer. W. H. Auden's and Christopher Isherwood's *On the frontier*, Stephen Spender's *Trial of a judge*, and Rex Warner's *The professor*: the Auden group and literature as sociopolitical commitment. Diss., Wien, 1986.
Extract from a letter to J. M. Keynes on *On the frontier*, 9 Oct. 1937, p. 109.

H222 Kenneth Karmiole, Bookseller, Inc. A miscellany of fine books [catalogue]. Santa Monica, [1986].
Extract from a letter to M. F. K. Fisher, 18 Aug. 1963, item 14 (also quoted in **H247**).

H223 David Schulson Autographs. [Catalogue] 35. New York, [1986].
Extracts from letters to Charles Turner on 'The ballad of Barnaby', 5 Dec. 1968 and 6 June 1969, p. 3 (also quoted in **H232**).

H224 Robin Waterfield Ltd. Catalogue 66. Oxford, 1986.
Extract from a letter to James Michie on a book by Michie and 'Thanksgiving for a habitat', 28 Feb. 1966, item 433 (also quoted in **H187**, **H205**, **H224**, **H241**; now at Edinburgh University).

H225 Christie, Manson & Woods Ltd. Valuable autograph letters . . . [catalogue]. London, 29 May 1986.
Extensive extracts from a letter [to Christopher Isherwood, ?July 1927], p. 68.

H226 *Slightly soiled* [periodical-style catalogue of the bookseller Paul Rassam]. London, June 1986.
Description and partial facsimile of a postcard to Edward Upward, 30 Dec. 1930 [misdated in the catalogue 30 Feb. 1930], p. 14 (also described in **H146** and **H226**).

H227 Sotheby's. English literature and history [catalogue]. London, 10–11 July 1986.
Extract from a letter to John Betjeman, 20 Mar. [1946], item 157 (also quoted in **H199** and **H200**; now in the Berg Collection).

H228 Nicolas Barker. *The butterfly books: an enquiry into the nature of certain twentieth century pamphlets.* London: Bertram Rota, 1987.
Describes a letter from Auden to Frederic Prokosch suggesting the possibility of privately printing a sequence of sonnets, 1934 (now in the Berg Collection).

H229 *The lost notebooks of Loren Eiseley*, edited and with a reminiscence by Kenneth Heuer. Boston: Little, Brown, 1987.

Extracts from letters to Eiseley, 21 Mar. 1973, p. 165, [May 1972], pp. 222–3, and 23 Nov. 1972, p. 224. The May 1972 letter includes an early text of 'Unpredictable but providential'. These extracts are quoted again in various studies of Eiseley.

H230 Kathleen Tynan. *The life of Kenneth Tynan*. London: Weidenfeld & Nicolson, 1987.

Extract from a letter to Kenneth Tynan refusing to write pornography for an anthology, 26 June [?1970], p. 295. In the American edition (New York: William Morrow, 1987), on p. 384. Also quoted in **H304**.

H231 Glenn Horowitz, Bookseller. Catalogue 14. New York, [1987].

Extract from a letter [to Cheryl Layton] on poetry, 1971, p. 2.

H232 David Schulson Autographs. [Catalogue] 43. New York, [1987].

Extracts from letters to Charles Turner on 'The ballad of Barnaby', 5 Dec. 1968 and 6 June 1969, p. 4 (also quoted in **H223**).

H233 Nicholas Jenkins. Mrs Busy Bee's lecture. *Times literary supplement*, 3 July 1987, p. 717.

Extract from a letter to Mrs A. E. Dodds about a place for Isherwood to stay in Oxford, 1937.

H234 Sotheby's. English literature and history [catalogue]. London, 23–24 July 1987.

Extracts from letters to Anne Bristow, 1930–2, with reproductions of two inscribed photographs of Auden, pp. 84–5. Also quotes the opening line of a musical manuscript with text in Auden's hand but probably not composed by him ('Here we come a piping in springtime, in springtime, in springtime . . .').

H235 W. H. Auden. *Il mare e lo specchio: commentario a 'La tempesta' di Shakespeare*, a cura di Aurora Ciliberti. Milano: Studio Editoriale, 1988.

Italian translation of a letter to Ciliberti on the style of 'Caliban to the audience', Mar. 1965, p. [113].

H236 W. H. Auden and Christopher Isherwood. *Plays and other dramatic writings by W. H. Auden 1927–1938*, edited by Edward Mendelson. Princeton: Princeton University Press, 1988.

Extracts from letters, *passim*.

H237 Kenneth S. Brecher. *Too sad to sing: a memoir with postcards*. San Diego: Harcourt Brace Jovanovich, 1988.

Postcard to Robin Holloway on Holloway's suggestion that Auden write a libretto based on Nathaniel West's *Miss Lonelyhearts*, p. 58: 'Dear Holloway: Too sad to sing. Yours, W. H. Auden.'

H238 *The grand obsession: an anthology of opera*, edited by Rupert Christiansen. London: Collins, 1988.

Transcript of a list of recordings that Auden sent to Christopher Wilson, President of the St Edmund Hall Music Society at Oxford in 1973 in response to an invitation to present and discuss his favourite recordings at an evening meeting of the Society, p. 87. The programme was performed in his memory after his death.

H239 Valentine Cunningham. *British writers of the thirties*. Oxford: Oxford University Press, 1988.

Extracts from letters to Stephen Spender, 1941, p. 35 (also quoted in **H254**), and from letters to Naomi Mitchison, 1930 and 1932, p. 146, 1932, p. 146, 1932, p. 174, and Nov. 1936, p. 247.

H240 Alan Levy. Auden as interviewee. *W. H. Auden 1907–1973: Ergebnisse eines Symposions . . .* Redaktion: Michael O'Sullivan. Wien: Niederösterreich-Gesellschaft für Kunst und Kultur, 1988.

Extracts from letters arranginging an interview, 1971, pp. 126–7.

H241 James Fergusson Books & Manuscripts. Footnotes, catalogue one. London, 1988.

Extracts from letters to Nevill Coghill, 13 May 1952, 31 Jan. 1956, and 10 Feb. 1956, items 15–16 (now at Edinburgh University); and a letter to James Michie on a book by Michie and 'Thanksgiving for a habitat', 28 Feb. 1966, item 19 (also quoted in **H187**, **H205**, **H224**; now at Edinburgh University). All these letters are quoted again in Fergusson's unnumbered catalogue *More of the Obelus*, London, 1992, items 115–16 and 118.

H242 Eleni Ponirakis. Wandervogel. *W. H. Auden Society newsletter*, 1 (Apr. 1988), 4.

Extract from a letter to William McElwee, Spring 1927.

H243 Christie, Manson & Woods Ltd. Valuable autograph letters . . . [catalogue]. London, 22 June 1988.

Extracts from letters to Adolf Opel, 1959–72 (also quoted in **H270**; now in the Berg Collection), and extracts from a letter to Mr Gonin on suicide, 27 May 1965, p. 41.

H244 Donald L. Miller. *Lewis Mumford: a life*. New York: Weidenfeld & Nicolson, 1989.

Quotes a letter to Mumford praising his books, 1938, p. 302. Although the book reports that all Mumford's papers were to go to the University of Pennsylvania Library, the library cannot locate this letter.

H245 Harold Norse. *Memoirs of a bastard angel*. New York: William Morrow, 1989.

Extracts from letters to Norse, *passim* (also quoted in **H297**).

H246 Bauman Rare Books. A catalogue of rare books . . . catalogue 'red'. Philadelphia, [1989].

Extract from a gossipy letter to Delmore Schwartz, 8 Feb. 1943, p. 37.

H247 Joseph the Provider, Books. The Carter Burden collection of the works of W. H. Auden [sale catalogue]. Santa Barbara, 1989.

Extract from a letter to M. F. K. Fisher, 18 Aug. 1963, item 182 (also quoted in **H222**).

H248 David Schulson Autographs. [Catalogue] 45. New York, [1989].

Extract from a letter to Richard Heron Ward about his earlier offer of a poem for an anthology, 30 Aug. 1935, p. 3 (also quoted in **H183** and **H203**).

H249 Katherine Bucknell. Freelance [weekly column]. *Times literary supplement*, 19–25 May 1989, p. 544.

Brief extracts from two letters to Christopher Isherwood.

H250 Sotheby's. English literature and history . . . [catalogue]. London, 20 July 1989.

Extracts from postcards and letters to John Hayward, 1938 and 1950, p. 83 (also described in **H38**; now in the Berg Collection). A signed photograph of Auden is reproduced on p. 82.

H251 J. A. Stargardt. Autographen . . . [catalogue]. Marburg, 4 Oct. 1989. [Not seen.]

Extract from a letter to Eric Bentley, agreeing to the inclusion of 'our versions of Mahagonny and Die sieben Todsunde[n] in your collection', item 10.

H252 Sotheby's. English literature and history . . . [catalogue]. London, 14 Dec. 1989.

Extract from a gossipy postcard to T. S. Eliot, [?1955], p. 62.

H253 Auden's 'Writing' essay, edited by Katherine Bucknell. Editor's introduction. *W. H. Auden: 'The map of all my youth': early works, friends and influences*. Auden Studies 1. Edited by Katherine Bucknell and Nicholas Jenkins. Oxford: Clarendon Press, 1990, pp. 17–34.

Extracts from letters to Naomi Mitchison, 10 Oct. 1932, p. 30, and to Stephen Spender, [?June 1933], p. 32.

H254 Eleven letters from Auden to Stephen Spender. Edited by Nicholas Jenkins. *W. H. Auden: 'The map of all my youth': early* *works, friends and influences.* Auden Studies 1. Edited by Katherine Bucknell and Nicholas Jenkins. Oxford: Clarendon Press, 1990, pp. 54–93.

Partly quoted in **H239**.

H255 A change of heart: six letters from Auden to Professor and Mrs E. R. Dodds written at the beginning of World War II. Edited by Kathleen Bell. *W. H. Auden: 'The map of all my youth': early works, friends and influences.* Auden Studies 1. Edited by Katherine Bucknell and Nicholas Jenkins. Oxford: Clarendon Press, 1990, pp. 95–115.

Letters, 1939–40 and extracts from two letters, Dec. 1936 and 11 July 1939.

H256 John Fuller. 'The hero': Auden and Flaubert. *W. H. Auden: 'The map of all my youth': early works, friends and influences.* Auden Studies 1. Edited by Katherine Bucknell and Nicholas Jenkins. Oxford: Clarendon Press, 1990, pp. 135–46.

Extracts from letters to John B. Auden, 1927, p. 135, and to Aurora Ciliberti, Sept. 1965, p. 145 (also quoted in **H30**).

H257 Philip Hoare. *Serious pleasures, the life of Stephen Tennant.* London: Hamish Hamilton, 1990.

Extract from a letter to Tennant about Tennant's work, 20 Nov. [?1972], p. 349.

H258 Lucy McDiarmid. *Auden's apologies for poetry.* Princeton: Princeton University Press, 1990.

Extracts from a postcard to John Auden, 1940, p. 71, and from a letter to George Augustus Auden on *For the time being*, p. 95 (also quoted in **H151**).

H259 Charles Molesworth. *Marianne Moore: a literary life.* New York: Atheneum, 1990.

Paraphrase of thank-you letter after a dinner, 1939, p. 360.

H260 Sir William Walton. *Christopher Columbus—suite; Songs after Edith Sitwell; Anon in love; A song for the Lord Mayor's table; The twelve.* CHAN 8824 [compact disc recording]. Colchester: Chandos Records, 1990.

The booklet that accompanies the recording includes programme notes to 'The twelve' by Christopher Palmer, with an extract from a letter to Walton, Dec. 1964: 'Here at last is a draft of that bloody anthem. I've never felt so at sea before. How is one to be contemporary without being South Banky?', p. 8. The first sentence is reprinted by Bayan Northcott in

'Auden's music', *Musical times*, 134. 1800 (Feb. 1993), 68–72, quotation on p. 71.

H261 Katherine Bucknell. The guilty vocation. *Times literary supplement*, 3–9 Aug. 1990, p. 819.

Extract from a letter to Stephen Spender, Mar. 1941.

H262 Nicholas Jenkins. Auden's *The double man*. *Notes and queries*, n.s. 235. 4 (Dec. 1990), 441–2.

Extract from a letter [to John Lehmann] describing and announcing the title for *The double man* (also quoted in **H179** and **H202**; now at Wichita State University).

H263 Nicholas Jenkins. 'All types that can intrigue the writer's fancy.' *W. H. Auden Society newsletter*, 6 (Dec. 1990), 1–2.

Extract from a letter to Bennett Cerf on the typography of *For the time being*, 13 June 1944 (at Columbia University).

H264 Stephen Crook. Auden on the record. *W. H. Auden Society newsletter*, 6 (Dec. 1990), 4–5.

Extract from a letter to Nevill Coghill on revisions for *Collected shorter poems 1927–1957*, 1965.

H265 John Fuller. Grand definitive statements. *W. H. Auden Society newsletter*, 6 (Dec. 1990), 10–11.

Brief extract from a letter to Theodore Spencer, [1944], about the style of 'Caliban to the audience'.

H266 Michael Silverman. Manuscripts: catalogue two. London, 1990.

Extract from a letter submitting *An Elizabethan song book* to its publisher Jason Epstein [*ca.* 1954], p. 26 (also quoted in **H201**; now at Edinburgh University).

H267 Bloomsbury Book Auctions. Catalogue of printed books . . . London, 22 Feb. 1990.

Extract from a letter to Frederic Prokosch praising Prokosch's *The Asiatics*, 30 Dec. 1935, p. 24 (also quoted in **H284**).

H268 J. A. Stargardt. Autographen . . . [catalogue]. Marburg, 27–28 June 1990. [Not seen.]

Extract from a letter to an unnamed recipient, agreeing that the purpose of writing is 'to enable readers a little better to enjoy life . . .', item 10.

H269 R. A. Gekoski. The Allen D. McGuire collection of books from Cyril Connolly's *The modern movement* . . . [catalogue]. London, Summer 1990.

Postcard to John Betjeman, 16 Nov. 1937, p. 37.

H270 Christie, Manson & Woods Ltd. Medieval and illuminated manuscripts . . . London, 28 Nov. 1990, item 254.

Extracts from letters to Adolf Opel, 1959–72, p. 145 (also quoted in **H243**; now in the Berg Collection).

H271 Editor-in-chief: Donald Mitchell. *Letters from a life: the selected letters and diaries of Benjamin Britten 1913–1976*, volume one, 1923–1939 [*and* volume two, 1939–1945], edited by Donald Mitchell, assistant editor Philip Reed . . . [London:] Faber & Faber, [1991].

Full and partial texts of letters to Britten, 1935–43, vol. 1, pp. 392, 487, 546, 548, 573, 590–1; vol. 2, pp. 658–9, 689, 1015–17, 1039, 1040, 1092, 1093, 1095; also, Auden's draft of a 1940 letter to the Japanese Vice-Consul in New York, written to be signed by Britten, vol. 2, pp. 889–90.

H272 *Remembering Reinhold Niebuhr*, letters of Reinhold and Ursula M. Niebuhr, edited by Ursula M. Niebuhr. New York: HarperSanFrancisco, [1991].

Full and partial texts of letters to Reinhold or Ursula Niebuhr, pp. 280–95 (partly also quoted in **H90**).

H273 Clifton Snider. *The stuff that dreams are made on: a Jungian interpretation of literature*. Wilmette, Il.: Chiron Publications, 1991.

Brief letter in response to Snider's praise, 12 Apr. 1972, pp. 146–7.

H274 Michael Silverman. Manuscripts: catalogue five. London, 1991.

Extract from a letter to Alan Rook on Rook's poetry, 13 Jan. 1939 (now at Edinburgh University), p. 19.

H275 Gerard A. J. Stodolski, Inc. Autograph letters, manuscripts, documents; catalogue one. Manchester, NH, [1991].

Extract from a letter declining an invitation from a Mr Jones, 6 Sept. 1972, p. 1.

H276 Swann Galleries, Inc. Modern literature . . . sale number 1551 [catalogue]. New York, 7 Feb. 1991.

Extract from a postcard to Geoffrey Grigson about Grigson's review of *The poet's tongue*, 2 July 1935, item 6 (also quoted in **H44**, **H62**, **H78**, **H213**; now at Wichita State University).

H277 The New York Public Library. News release: behind the printed page. 8 May 1991.

News release on the opening of an exhibit, 'New in the Berg Collection: 1986–1990'. Extract from a letter to Monroe K. Spears, 11 May 1963, p. 2.

H278 Humphrey Carpenter. *Benjamin Britten: a biography*. London: Faber & Faber, 1992.

Extract from letters to Britten, *passim*, and to Mrs A. E. Dodds, 1940, p. 134.

H279 Richard Hoggart. *An imagined life (life and times, volume III: 1959–91)*. London: Chatto & Windus, 1992.

Brief extract from a letter to Hoggart about Hoggart's work, Jan. 1958, p. 100 (also quoted in **H145**).

H280 Cynthia Zarin. Profiles: Jaz. *New Yorker*, 68. 5 (23 Mar. 1992), 41–64.

Extract from a letter to James Laughlin recommending Ronald Firbank, 24 July 1947, p. 54.

H281 I. D. Edrich. Young writers of the thirties [catalogue]. London, [1992].

Extract from a letter to Cyril Lakin, editor of *The daily telegraph*, apparently about Auden's first review for the paper, [?Nov. 1936], item 1 (also quoted in **H186**; now at Edinburgh University).

H282 Michael Silverman. Manuscripts: catalogue six. London, 1992.

Extracts from two letters to Jack Matthews, declining invitations to give readings, 24 July 1957 and 20 Mar. 1967, p. 19 (now at Edinburgh University).

H283 R. A. Gekoski. Catalogue 16. London, Spring 1992.

Extracts from a letter to Ted Hughes about plans for a poetry festival, 10 June 1967, p. 1 (now at Edinburgh University).

H284 Phillips, Son & Neale. Autograph letters . . . [catalogue]. London, 11 June 1992. [Not seen.]

Extract from a letter to Frederic Prokosch, 30 Dec. 1935, item 184 (also quoted in **H267**).

H285 Paul C. Richards, Autographs. [Unidentified catalogue.] Brookline, Mass., [late 1992]. [Known only from a tearsheet.]

Extract from a letter to Mr Halpern on world peace, 18 July 1971, item 192.

H286 Swann Galleries. Modern literature . . . Sale number 1607 [catalogue]. New York, 5 Nov. 1992.

Extract from a postcard to Lloyd Frankenberg thanking him for sending a copy of his review [of *The double man*] 'particularly as it was such a generous one', 15 May 1941, item 6.

H287 W. H. Auden and Chester Kallman. *Libretti and other dramatic writings by W. H. Auden 1939–1973*, edited by Edward Mendelson. Princeton: Princeton University Press, 1993.

Extracts from letters to Benjamin Britten, Igor Stravinsky, Hans Werner Henze, Nicolas Nabokov, and others, *passim* (some reprinted from **H18**, **H127**, **H164**).

H288 Ashok Bery. Problems of language and identity in the early work of W. H. Auden (1927–1941). Ph.D. diss., Birkbeck College, London, 1993.
Extracts from letters to William McElwee about sex, 1927, p. 103; to an unidentified recipient, 8 Nov. 1937, pp. 167–8 (also quoted in **H55**); to E. R. Dodds on *A certain world*, 5 Sept. 1968, p. 304.

H289 Brad Gooch. *City poet: the life and times of Frank O'Hara*. New York: Alfred A. Knopf, 1993.
Extract from a letter to O'Hara on O'Hara's poems, 3 June 1955, p. 260 (also quoted in **H119** and **H153**).

H290 James V. Hatch. *Sorrow is the only faithful one: the life of Owen Dodson*. Urbana: University of Illinois Press, 1993.
Extracts from letters and recommendations, 1941–53, pp. 103, 115, 116, 186, 187, 314.

H291 John Whitehead. *Literary essays and reviews*. Munslow, Shropshire: Hearthstone, 1993.
Extract from a letter to Whitehead on Whitehead's transcript of an early notebook, p. xi.

H292 Stephen Sandy. 'Writing as a career': an early W. H. Auden lecture in the States. *W. H. Auden Society newsletter*, 10–11 (Sept. 1993), 3–8.
Letters and telegrams to Henry Simon and Dorothy Hendricks, arranging a lecture at Bennington College, 1939 (now at Bennington).

H293 The Scriptorium. Catalogue no. nine. Beverly Hills, [1993].
Facsimile and misquoted extract from a letter to Richard Heron Ward offering a poem for an anthology, 1935, p. 3 (also quoted in **H168** and **H204**). This letter precedes the 30 Aug. 1935 letter to Ward quoted in **H183**, **H203**, **H248**.

H294 Michael Silverman. Manuscripts: catalogue nine. London, 1993.
Extract from a letter to Miss Medinz on the Hölderlin translations in *A certain world*, 20 Aug. 1969, p. 3 (now at Edinburgh University).

H295 Swann Galleries. Autographs . . . sale 1633 [catalogue]. New York, 14 Sept. 1993.
Extract from a letter to Brother Rigney about the Doctrine of the Incarnation, 4 Aug. [195?], item 26 (now in the Berg Collection).

H296 W. H. Auden. *Juvenilia: poems 1922–1928*, edited by Katherine Bucknell. London: Faber & Faber, 1994.

Extracts from letters to Christopher Isherwood, Stephen Spender, Elizabeth Mayer, James Stern, A. S. T. Fisher, John Auden, and others, *passim*.

H297 Harold Norse. Harold Norse 1916– . *Contemporary authors autobiography series*, Joyce Nakamura, editor, vol. 18. Detroit: Gale Research, 1994, pp. 275–92.

Extracts from letters to Norse, 1939–41, pp. 280–1 (also quoted in **H245**).

H298 Nicholas Jenkins. W. H. Auden. *The Oxford companion to twentieth-century poetry in English*, edited by Ian Hamilton. Oxford: Oxford University Press, 1994, pp. 21–5.

Brief extract from a letter to Theodore Spencer about 'The sea and the mirror', 26 Feb. 1944, p. 23.

H299 Amy Gamerman. Rhyme and reason: editing the poet of the century. *Wall Street journal*, 20 Jan. 1994, p. A12.

Paraphrased extracts from letters to Edward Mendelson.

H300 Chapel Hill Rare Books. Catalogue 85. Chapel Hill, Feb. 1994.

Mentions a postcard to Frances M. Mayer [reporting his summer address], 20 June 1940, item 8.

H301 Swann Galleries. Autographs . . . sale 1653 [catalogue]. New York, 17 Mar. 1994.

Extract from a letter to 'Jimmy' [?Schuyler] about financial arrangements for Bill [?Aalto], 2 July 1949, item 10.

H302 Robert McCrum. A life in the margins. *New Yorker*, 70. 8 (11 Apr. 1994), 46–55.

Two words ('Dear Greene') from a letter to Graham Greene, [7 Apr. 1934], p. 47.

H303 Alan Jacobs. Auden at the opera. *American scholar*, 63. 2 (Spring 1994), 287–95.

Extract from a letter to Monroe K. Spears praising his book on Auden, 1963, p. 287.

H304 Laurence Marks. To Ken, dear or detested. *Observer*, 29 May 1994, p. 27.

Extract from a letter to Kenneth Tynan on pornography; also quoted in **H230**.

ADDENDUM TO *AUDEN STUDIES 2*

After *Auden Studies 2* was published, further information about Robert Russell, the Downs School pupil who was the addressee of the Auden poem beginning 'When a little older, Robert' and printed on page 41 of that volume, emerged. Robert Henry Russell, born in March 1924, was the second son of (Sir) Gordon Russell, the furniture designer. He was apparently a moody, artistic child, especially devoted to the Downs's Art Master Maurice Feild.

NOTES ON CONTRIBUTORS

G. W. BOWERSOCK is Professor of Ancient History at the Institute for Advanced Study in Princeton and previously taught at Harvard University. He is the author of many books on the history of the Roman and early Byzantine Empire, most recently *Hellenism in Late Antiquity* (1990), *Fiction as History—Nero to Julian* (1994), *Studies on the Eastern Roman Empire* (1994), and *Martyrdom and Rome* (1995).

DAVID BROMWICH is Professor of English at Yale University, and the author of *Hazlitt: The Mind of a Critic* (1983), *A Choice of Inheritance* (1989), and *Politics by Other Means* (1992).

KATHERINE BUCKNELL was a Charlotte Newcombe Fellow and a Mrs Giles Whiting Fellow at Columbia University and a Junior Research Fellow at Worcester College, Oxford. She edited *Juvenilia: Poems 1922–1928* by W. H. Auden (1994).

ALFRED CORN is the author of six volumes of poetry, the most recent titled *Autobiographies* (1992). He has also published a collection of critical writings, *The Metamorphoses of Metaphor* (1987).

NICHOLAS JENKINS, a Harkness Fellow from 1986 to 1988, is the editor of *The Table Talk of W. H. Auden* (1990) and *By With To & From: A Lincoln Kirstein Reader* (1991). He is completing a D.Phil. on Auden.

LAWRENCE LIPKING is Chester D. Tripp Professor of Humanities at Northwestern University, where he teaches English and Comparative Literature. His books include *The Life of the Poet* (1981), winner of the 1982 Christian Gauss Award, and *Abandoned Women and Poetic Tradition* (1988).

EDNA LONGLEY is a Professor of English at Queen's University, Belfast. Her most recent publication is *The Living Stream: Literature and Revisionism in Ireland* (1994).

EDWARD MENDELSON, who teaches English and Comparative Literature at Columbia University, is Auden's literary executor. His edition of the Auden–Kallman libretti, the second volume in *The Complete Works of W. H. Auden*, was published in 1993.

STELLA MUSULIN is a freelance journalist and broadcaster in English and German. She has published two books in England, *Austria—People and Landscape* (1971), to which Auden wrote the introduction, and *Vienna in the Age of Metternich* (1975). She lives in Austria.

IAN SANSOM is an adult literacy tutor and teaches English at the West London Institute for Higher Education. He is working on a D.Phil. thesis about Auden's influence on other writers, and he reviews poetry and fiction for a variety of British newspapers and journals.

EDWARD UPWARD, born in 1903, was a schoolmaster from 1931 until 1961. His first prose works appeared in the 1930s, including *Journey to the Border* (1938). In the 1960s, he began publishing a semi-autobiographical trilogy whose parts eventually appeared together as *The Spiral Ascent* (1977). His newest work is collected in *The Night Walk and Other Stories* (1987) and *An Unmentionable Man* (1994).

MICHAEL WOOD is Professor of English at Princeton University, and the author of books on Stendhal, García Márquez, Nabokov, and American movies. He is working on a biography of Proust.

INDEX

Acton, Harold 36–7
Adler, Alfred 141
Agee, James 90
Aiken, Conrad 276
Aldington, Richard 79–81
Ambler, Eric; *A Coffin for Demetrios* 88
America 6, 30, 43, 171, 235, 237, 239, 299, 302
The American Scholar 10–11, 13
Anderson, Hedli 43, 97
Ann Arbor, Michigan 68; *see also* University of Michigan
Andersen, Hans 25, 200; *The Ice Maiden* 156, 160, 197, 200–2; *The Snow Queen* 19, 156–60, 184, 197, 200–1
Ansen, Alan 52, 173, 278
Apuleius 129
Arendt, Hannah 56, 310
Aristotle 126–8
Auden, Constance B. (mother) 45, 83, 165, 168, 170–1, 175, 183, 185, 190, 224, 235–6, 239, 246, 248
Auden, George A. (father) 45, 83, 100, 103, 142, 151, 165, 170–1, 175, 183, 190, 224, 243, 309, 321
Auden, Harold Allden (Uncle Harry) 162–3, 185–6
Auden, John B. (brother) 67, 83, 103, 140–1, 148, 165, 185, 220, 222, 246, 290, 301, 321, 326
Auden, W. H.: on art and the artist 16, 146–8, 150–1, 155, 178, 227–30; his Christianity 2–3, 61, 112, 232, 236–7, 282, 291; attitude to Christmas 63, 92, 106–7, 163, 185, 210, 243; crisis with Kallman 51, 92, 146, 163; on democracy 23, 29; Didymus (pseudonym) 2; health 214, 218; heterosexual relationships 56, 61, 202; on homosexuality 87–8, 99, 100; on imagination 187–9, 190; income tax 218–19; attitude to Jews 46, 97, 143, 174, 213; on marriage 20, 28, 51, 56–7, 80, 88, 105, 183; his metre 240–1, 243–4, 266; mines and mining 148–9, 151–5, 170–2, 187–93, 224–5; on passion 16–17, 22–4, 26–8; on psycho-analysis 2, 140, 145, 151, 155, 181, 191; on psychiatrists and psychologists 9, 141–4; on psychoanalysis and poetry 179–81; his rhyme scheme 241, 244; on symbols 150, 186, 189, 194; on vocation 17, 19, 20, 23–4, 26, 28, 147, 170, 190; on writing poetry 154, 190, 194–5, 224–30, 232

WORKS
About the House 56; 'Address on Henry James' 16; *The Age of Anxiety* 18, 48, 51, 57, 81, 87, 113, 158–9, 274–5, 288; 'The Aliens' 302; 'Allendale' 170; 'Amor Loci' 84, 151, 154, 193; *Another Time* 276, 288; *The Ascent of F6* 160, 173, 201, 285, 291, 297, 304; 'As It Seemed to Us' 187, 189; 'A Summer Night' 64, 261; *Archifanfaro* 233; 'Atlantis' 57; 'At the Grave of Henry James' 52, 282–3; 'Archaeology' 118–19; 'August for the people and their favourite islands' 257; 'Augustus to Augustine' 6, 111–12; 'The Ballad of Barnaby' 317–18; *The Bassarids* 233; 'Blessed Event' 236; 'The Cave of Making' 48, 216, 250; 'The Cave of Nakedness' 57; 'Certainly our city . . .' 281; *A Certain World* 149, 152, 164, 168–9, 173–4, 184, 187, 190, 195–8, 205, 265–6, 316, 325; 'Christmas Eve' 157; 'Christmas 1940' 18, 28; Christmas 1941 letter-poem to Kallman 20, 25, 46, 58; 'City Without Walls' 297; *Collected Poems* 254; *Collected Poetry* 2, 298; *Collected Shorter Poems* 259, 296, 322; 'A Communist to Others' 2–3, 248; 'The Council' 236; 'C. P. Cavafy' 113, 115; *The Dance of Death* 312, 314, 316; *The Dark Valley* 169–70, 173; 'The Dark Years' 236; *Delia* 233; *The Dog Beneath the Skin* 294, 307; 'Doggerel by a Senior Citizen' 230; *Don Giovanni* 233; *The Double Man* 18, 20, 28, 236, 288, 312, 315, 322, 324; *The Duchess of Malfi* 292; *The Dyer's Hand* 215, 263; 'The earth turns over and our side feels the cold' 170; *Elegy for Young Lovers* 37, 159–60, 233; *The Enchafèd Flood* 17, 18, 271; *The Entertainment of the Senses* 300; 'Epistle to a Godson' 91; *Epithalamion* 298; 'Eros and Agape' 16; 'Eulogy' 47; 'The Fall of Rome' 112, 114, 136; *Forewords and Afterwords* 207; 'For the Time Being' 20, 47, 51, 53–4, 77, 80, 83, 209, 235, 237–44, 261, 298, 309, 321–2; 'The Freud-Fliess Letters' 144; 'Frost' 157; *Gedichte–Poems* 209; 'Genius and Apostle' 18; 'Get there